SCHOLASTIC

100 MATHS FRAMEWORK LESSONS

TERMS AND CONDITIONS

IMPORTANT - PERMITTED USE AND WARNINGS - READ CAREFULLY BEFORE USING

Licence

Save for these purposes, or as expressly authorised in the accompanying materials, the software may not be copied, reproduced, used, sold, licensed, transferred, exchanged, hired, or exported in whole or in part or in any manner or form without the prior written consent of Scholastic Ltd. Any such unauthorised use or activities are prohibited and may give rise to civil liabilities and criminal prosecutions.

The material contained on this CD-ROM may only be used in the context for which it was intended in *100 Maths Framework Lessons*, and is for use only in the school which has purchased the book and CD-ROM, or by the teacher who has purchased the book and CD-ROM. Permission to download images is given for purchasers only and not for users from any lending service. Any further use of the material contravenes Scholastic Ltd's copyright and that of other rights' holders.

This CD-ROM has been tested for viruses at all stages of its production. However, we recommend that you run virus-checking software on your computer systems at all times. Scholastic Ltd cannot accept any responsibility for any loss, disruption or damage to your data or your computer system that may occur as a result of using either the CD-ROM or the data held on it.

YEAR 4

Scottish Primary 5

Minimum specification:

- PC or Mac with a CD-ROM drive and 512 Mb RAM (recommended)
- Windows 98SE or above/Mac OSX.1 or above
- Recommended minimum processor speed: 1 GHz

For all technical support queries, please phone Scholastic Customer Services on 0845 603 9091.

Ann Montague-Smith and
Claire Tuthill

CREDITS

Authors
Ann Montague-Smith and Claire Tuthill

Series Consultant
Ann Montague-Smith

Development Editor
Niamh O'Carroll

Editors
Frances Ridley and Helen Kelly

Assistant Editors
Dodi Beardshaw, Jennifer Regan and Margaret Eaton

Series Designers
Micky Pledge and Joy Monkhouse

Designers
Melissa Leeke, Micky Pledge, Geraldine Reidy and Yen Fu

Illustrations
Andy Keylock and Adrian Barclay (Beehive Illustration)

CD-ROM development
CD-ROM developed in association with Vivid Interactive

Published by Scholastic Ltd
Villiers House
Clarendon Avenue
Leamington Spa
Warwickshire CV32 5PR

www.scholastic.co.uk

Designed using Adobe InDesign.

Printed by Bell and Bain Ltd, Glasgow

3456789 7890123456

British Library Cataloguing-in-Publication Data
A catalogue record for this book is available from the British Library.

ISBN 978-0439-94549-3

ACKNOWLEDGEMENTS

Extracts from the *National Numeracy Strategy* (1999) and the Primary National Strategy's *Primary Framework for Mathematics* (2006) www.standards.dfes.gov.uk/primaryframework and the Interactive Teaching Programs originally developed for the National Numeracy Strategy © Crown copyright. Reproduced under the terms of the Click Use Licence.

Every effort has been made to trace copyright holders for the works reproduced in this book, and the publishers apologise for any inadvertent omissions.

Contents

100 Maths Framework Lessons

About the series

100 Maths Framework Lessons is designed to support you with the implementation of the renewed *Primary Framework for Mathematics*. Each title in the series provides clear teaching and appropriate learning challenges for all children within the structure of the renewed Framework. By using the titles in this series, a teacher or school can be sure that they are following the structure and, crucially, embedding the principles and practice identified by the Framework.

About the renewed Framework

The renewed *Primary Framework for Mathematics* has reduced the number of objectives from the original 1999 Framework. Mathematics is divided into seven strands:

- Using and applying mathematics
- Counting and understanding number
- Knowing and using number facts
- Calculating
- Understanding shape
- Measuring
- Handling data.

The focus for teaching is using and applying mathematics, and these objectives are seen as central to success for the children's learning. While the number of objectives is reduced, the teaching programme retains the range of learning contained in the 1999 Framework. There are, though, significant changes in both the structure and content of the objectives in the new Framework and this series of books is designed to help teachers to manage these changes of emphasis in their teaching.

About this book

This book is set out in the five blocks that form the renewed *Primary Framework for Mathematics*. Each block consists of three units. Each unit within a block contains:

- a guide to the objective focus for each lesson within the unit
- links with the objectives from the 1999 objectives
- the 'speaking and listening' objective for the unit
- a list of key aspects of learning, such as problem solving, communication, etc.
- the vocabulary relevant to a group of lessons.

Within each unit the 'using and applying' objectives are clearly stated. They are incorporated within the individual lessons through the teaching and learning approach taken. Sometimes they may be the only focus for a lesson.

Lessons

Each lesson contains:

- A guide to the type of teaching and learning within the lesson, such as Review, Teach, Practise or Apply.
- A starter activity, with a guide to its type, such as Rehearse, Reason, Recall, Read, Refine, Refine and rehearse, or Revisit.
- A main activity, which concentrates on the teaching of the objective(s) for this lesson.
- Group, paired or individual work, which may include the use of an activity sheet from the CD-ROM.
- Clear differentiation, to help you to decide how to help the less confident learners in your group, or how to extend the learning for the more confident. This may also include reference to the differentiated activity sheets found on the CD-ROM.
- Review of the lesson, with guidance for asking questions to assess the children's understanding.

You can choose individual lessons as part of your planning, or whole units as you require.

What's on the CD-ROM?

Each CD-ROM contains a range of printable sheets as follows:

- **Core activity sheets** with answers, where appropriate, that can be toggled by clicking on the 'show' or 'hide' buttons at the bottom of the screen.
- **Differentiated activity sheets** for more or less confident learners where appropriate.
- Blank core activity sheets or **templates** to allow you to make your own differentiated sheets by printing and annotating.
- **General resource sheets** (such as number grids) designed to support a number of lessons.
- **Editable curriculum grids** (in Word format) to enable you to integrate the lessons into your planning.

In addition, the CD-ROM contains:

- **Interactive whiteboard resources** – a set of supporting resources to be used with the whole class on any interactive whiteboard or on a PC for small group work. These include number grids, money, clocks and so on.
- **Interactive Teaching Programs** – specific ITPs, originally developed for the National Numeracy Strategy, have been included on each CD-ROM.
- **Whiteboard tools** – a set of tools including a 'Pen', 'Highlighter' and 'Eraser', have been included to help you to annotate activity sheets for whole-class lessons. These tools will work on any interactive whiteboard.
- **Diagrams** – copies of all the diagrams included on the lesson pages.

How to use the CD-ROM

System requirements

Minimum specification:

- PC or Mac with a CD-ROM drive and 512 Mb RAM (recommended)
- Windows 98SE or above/Mac OSX.1 or above
- Recommended minimum processor speed: 1 GHz

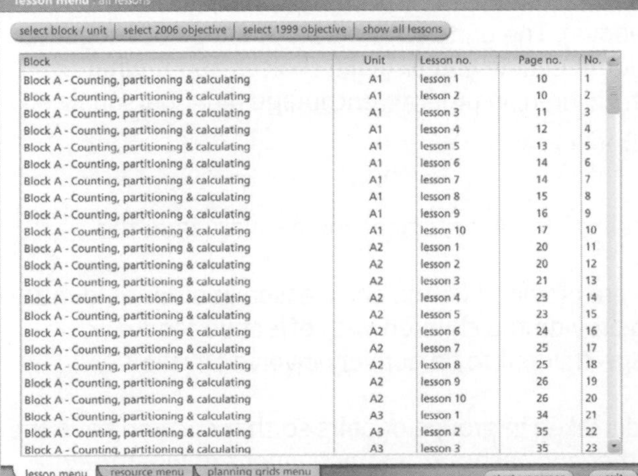

Block	Unit	Lesson no.	Page no.	No.
Block A - Counting, partitioning & calculating	A1	lesson 1	10	1
Block A - Counting, partitioning & calculating	A1	lesson 2	10	2
Block A - Counting, partitioning & calculating	A1	lesson 3	11	3
Block A - Counting, partitioning & calculating	A1	lesson 4	12	4
Block A - Counting, partitioning & calculating	A1	lesson 5	13	5
Block A - Counting, partitioning & calculating	A1	lesson 6	14	6
Block A - Counting, partitioning & calculating	A1	lesson 7	14	7
Block A - Counting, partitioning & calculating	A1	lesson 8	15	8
Block A - Counting, partitioning & calculating	A1	lesson 9	16	9
Block A - Counting, partitioning & calculating	A1	lesson 10	17	10
Block A - Counting, partitioning & calculating	A2	lesson 1	20	11
Block A - Counting, partitioning & calculating	A2	lesson 2	20	12
Block A - Counting, partitioning & calculating	A2	lesson 3	21	13
Block A - Counting, partitioning & calculating	A2	lesson 4	23	14
Block A - Counting, partitioning & calculating	A2	lesson 5	23	15
Block A - Counting, partitioning & calculating	A2	lesson 6	24	16
Block A - Counting, partitioning & calculating	A2	lesson 7	25	17
Block A - Counting, partitioning & calculating	A2	lesson 8	25	18
Block A - Counting, partitioning & calculating	A2	lesson 9	26	19
Block A - Counting, partitioning & calculating	A2	lesson 10	26	20
Block A - Counting, partitioning & calculating	A3	lesson 1	34	21
Block A - Counting, partitioning & calculating	A3	lesson 2	35	22
Block A - Counting, partitioning & calculating	A3	lesson 3	35	23

Getting started

The *100 Maths Framework Lessons* CD-ROM should auto run when you insert the CD-ROM into your CD drive. If it does not, use **My Computer** to browse the contents of the CD-ROM and click on the '100 Maths Framework Lessons' icon.

From the start-up screen there are four options: click on **Credits & acknowledgements** to view a list of acknowledgements. You should also view the **Terms and conditions** of use and register the product to receive product updates and special offers. Finally, you can access extensive **How to use this CD-ROM** support notes and (if you agree to the 'Terms and conditions') click on **Start** to move to the main menu.

Each CD-ROM allows you to search for resources by block, unit or lesson. You can also search by Framework objective (both 2006 and 1999 versions) or by resource type (for example, activity sheet, interactive resource or ITP).

Planning

The renewed Framework planning guidance sets out the learning objectives in blocks, and then subdivides these into units. The blocks are entitled:

- **Block A:** Counting, partitioning and calculating
- **Block B:** Securing number facts, understanding shape
- **Block C:** Handling data and measures
- **Block D:** Calculating, measuring and understanding shape
- **Block E:** Securing number facts, relationships and calculating.

Within each block there are three progressive units, which set out the learning objectives for a two- or three-week teaching period. Because of the interrelated nature of learning in mathematics, some of the same learning objectives appear in different blocks so that the children have the opportunity to practise and apply their mathematics.

	Block A: Counting, partitioning and calculating (6 weeks)	**Block B:** Securing number facts, understanding shape (9 weeks)	**Block C:** Handling data and measures (6 weeks)	**Block D:** Calculating, measuring and understanding shape (6 weeks)	**Block E:** Securing number facts, relationships and calculating (9 weeks)
Autumn	Unit A1	Unit B1	Unit C1	Unit D1	Unit E1
Spring	Unit A2	Unit B2	Unit C2	Unit D2	Unit E2
Summer	Unit A3	Unit B3	Unit C3	Unit D3	Unit E3

It is recommended that planning for the year takes the blocks and units in the following order:
However, the book has been structured in block order (Block A1, A2, A3 and so on), so that teachers can plan progression across units more effectively, and plan other configurations of lessons where required. You can use the different menus on the CD-ROM to find suitable teaching and learning material to match your planning needs.

In each unit in this book, the 1999 Framework objectives are listed, so that it is possible to use materials from previous planning alongside these lessons. The CD-ROM has a facility that allows for filtering by 2006 and 1999 learning objectives in order to find suitable lessons.

The blocks and units, taught in the order above, make a comprehensive teaching package which will effectively cover the teaching and learning for this year group.

Differentiation

Each lesson contains three levels of differentiation in order to meet the wide variety of needs within a group of children. There are differentiated activity sheets for many lessons that can be accessed on the CD-ROM (see 'What's on the CD-ROM', above). The units within a block are placed together in this book. This is in order to enable you to make choices about what to teach, when and to which children, in order to encourage more personalised learning.

Assessment

Within this book the guidelines for 'Assessment for learning' from the Framework are followed:

- Assessment questions are provided within each lesson in order to identify children's learning and to provide the children with effective feedback.
- The questions encourage children to be actively involved in their own learning.
- Many activities are undertaken in groups or pairs so that children have the opportunity to plan together and assess the effectiveness of what they have undertaken.
- The assessment outcomes give the teacher the opportunity to adjust teaching to take account of the results of assessment.
- The crucial importance of assessment is recognised, and the profound influence it has on the motivation and self-esteem of children, both of which are essential for learning.
- The assessment questions offer children the opportunity to understand what they know, use and understand and also to understand how to improve.

Counting, partitioning and calculating

Key aspects of learning
- Problem solving
- Evaluation
- Communication
- Motivation

Expected prior learning

Check that children can already:

- identify the calculation needed to solve a word problem
- explain and record their methods and solutions to problems and calculations
- read, write, partition and order whole numbers to 1000
- use £.p notation
- understand and use the < and > signs
- round two- or three-digit numbers to the nearest 10 or 100
- recall addition and subtraction facts for each number to 20
- add or subtract mentally combinations of one- and two-digit numbers
- derive number pairs that total 100
- use informal written methods to add and subtract two- and three-digit numbers
- estimate sums and differences of two- or three-digit numbers
- recall multiplication and division facts for the 2, 3, 4, 5, 6 and 10 times-tables
- multiply one- and two-digit numbers by 10 and 100
- use informal written methods to multiply and divide two-digit numbers
- round remainders up or down, depending on the context.

Objectives overview

The text in this diagram identifies the focus of mathematics learning within the block.

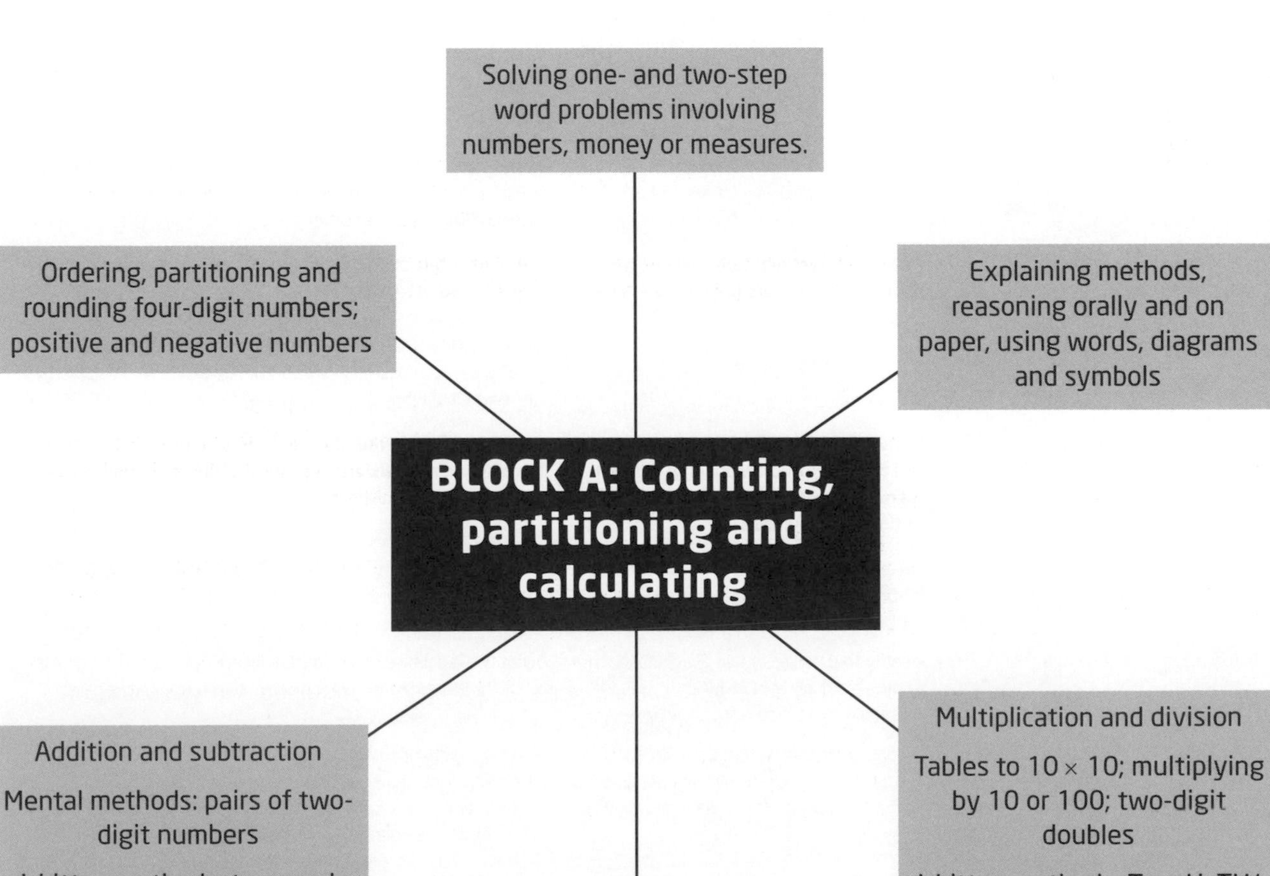

Unit 1 2 weeks

Counting, partitioning and calculating

Speaking and listening objectives

- Use and reflect on some ground rules for dialogue (eg making structured, extended contributions, speaking audibly, making meaning explicit and listening actively).

Introduction

The lessons in this unit include coverage of the strands of Counting and understanding number, Knowing and using number facts, Calculating, and Using and applying mathematics. Children are introduced to the calculator, which is used for checking their calculations. They use the symbols <, > and = in the context of negative numbers. They use estimating, rounding and inverses in order to check calculations. They begin to learn and use the 7, 8 and 9 times-table facts, making use of what they already know from the 2 to 6 times-tables. They are encouraged to use diagrams where this will help them to either calculate or to display the answers to problems and to explain to others how they solved problems.

Lesson	Strands	Starter	Main teaching activities
1. Review and teach	Counting	Partition, round and order four-digit whole numbers; use positive and negative numbers in context and position them on a number line; state inequalities using the symbols < and > (eg $-3 > -5$, $-1 < +1$).	Partition, round and order four-digit whole numbers; use positive and negative numbers in context and position them on a number line; state inequalities using the symbols < and > (eg $-3 > -5$, $-1 < +1$).
2. Teach and practise	Counting	Multiply and divide numbers to 1000 by 10 and then 100 (whole-number answers), understanding the effect; relate to scaling up or down.	As for Lesson 1
3. Teach and apply	Counting	Partition, round and order four-digit whole numbers; use positive and negative numbers in context and position them on a number line; state inequalities using the symbols < and > (eg $-3 > -5$, $-1 < +1$).	As for Lesson 1
4. Teach and practise	Knowledge	Use knowledge of addition and subtraction facts and place value to derive sums and differences of pairs of multiples of 10, 100 or 1000.	• Use knowledge of addition and subtraction facts and place value to derive sums and differences of pairs of multiples of 10, 100 or 1000. • Use knowledge of rounding, number operations and inverses to estimate and check calculations.
5. Practise and apply	Calculate	**Add or subtract mentally pairs of two-digit whole numbers (eg $47 + 58$, $91 - 35$).**	• **Add or subtract mentally pairs of two-digit whole numbers (eg $47 + 58$, $91 - 35$).** • Use a calculator to carry out one-step and two-step calculations involving all four operations; recognise negative numbers in the display, correct mistaken entries and interpret the display correctly in the context of money.
6. Review and practise	Knowledge	**Derive and recall multiplication facts up to 10×10, the corresponding division facts and multiples of numbers to 10 up to the tenth multiple.**	**Derive and recall multiplication facts up to 10×10, the corresponding division facts and multiples of numbers to 10 up to the tenth multiple.**
7. Teach and practise	Calculate	Recognise and continue number sequences formed by counting on or back in steps of constant size.	Multiply and divide numbers to 1000 by 10 and then 100 (whole-number answers), understanding the effect; relate to scaling up or down.
8. Teach and apply	Knowledge	Identify the doubles of two-digit numbers; use to calculate doubles of multiples of 10 and 100 and derive the corresponding halves.	Identify the doubles of two-digit numbers; use to calculate doubles of multiples of 10 and 100 and derive the corresponding halves.
9. Teach and apply	Use/apply Calculate	Multiply and divide numbers to 1000 by 10 and then 100 (whole-number answers), understanding the effect; relate to scaling up or down.	• Report solutions to puzzles and problems, giving explanations and reasoning orally and in writing, using diagrams and symbols. • Use a calculator to carry out one-step and two-step calculations involving all four operations; recognise negative numbers in the display, correct mistaken entries and interpret the display correctly in the context of money.
10. Apply and evaluate	Use/apply	As for Lesson 9	Report solutions to puzzles and problems, giving explanations and reasoning orally and in writing, using diagrams and symbols.

Using and applying mathematics

- Report solutions to puzzles and problems, giving explanations and reasoning orally and in writing, using diagrams and symbols.

Lessons 1-5

Preparation

Lesson 2: 'Place value chart' and 'Rolling the dice' enlarged to A3 or copied onto OHT.

You will need

Photocopiable pages
'A bigger place?' (page 17), 'Rolling the dice' (page 18) and 'Negative numbers' (page 19).
CD resources
Core, support, extension and template versions of 'Partition party', 'Rolling the dice' and 'Negative numbers'; core, support and extension versions of 'Sums and differences of multiples of 10'; core version of 'Add and difference'. General resource sheets: 'Numeral cards' and 'Place value chart'.
Equipment
OHP/whiteboard calculator; dice for each pair; interactive whiteboard; sticky notes.

Learning objectives

Starter

- Partition, round and order four-digit whole numbers; use positive and negative numbers in context and position them on a number line; state inequalities using the symbols < and > (eg -3 > -5, -1 < +1).
- Use knowledge of addition and subtraction facts and place value to derive sums and differences of pairs of multiples of 10, 100 or 1000.
- Add or subtract mentally pairs of two-digit whole numbers (eg 47 + 58, 91 - 35).
- Multiply and divide numbers to 1000 by 10 and then 100 (whole-number answers), understanding the effect; relate to scaling up or down.

Main teaching activities

2006

- Partition, round and order four-digit whole numbers; use positive and negative numbers in context and position them on a number line; state inequalities using the symbols < and > (eg -3 > -5, -1 < +1).
- Use knowledge of addition and subtraction facts and place value to derive sums and differences of pairs of multiples of 10, 100 or 1000.
- Add or subtract mentally pairs of two-digit whole numbers (eg 47 + 58, 91 - 35).
- Use a calculator to carry out one-step and two-step calculations involving all four operations; recognise negative numbers in the display, correct mistaken entries and interpret the display correctly in the context of money.
- Use knowledge of rounding, number operations and inverses to estimate and check calculations.

1999

- Recognise negative numbers in context (eg on a number line, on a temperature scale).
- Use symbols correctly, including less than (<), greater than (>), equals (=).
- Derive quickly all pairs of multiples of 50 with a total of 1000 (eg 850 + 150).
- Add three two-digit multiples of 10, such as 40 + 70 + 50.
- Use known number facts and place value to add or subtract mentally.
- Use known number facts and place value for mental addition and subtraction (eg 470 + 380, 810 - 380).
- Use known number facts and place value to add or subtract mentally, including any pair of two-digit whole numbers.
- Develop calculator skills and use a calculator effectively.

Vocabulary

problem, solution, calculate, calculation, equation, operation, answer, method, explain, predict, reason, reasoning, pattern, relationship, rule, place value, partition, thousands, digit, four-digit number, positive, negative, above/ below zero, compare, order, greater than (>), less than (<), equal to (=), add, subtract, multiply, divide, calculator, display, key, enter, clear, constant, degrees Celsius (°C)

Lesson 1 (Review and teach)

Starter

Rehearse: Give the children copies of activity sheet 'A bigger place'. Explain that you will draw three numeral cards at random from a set of 0–10 numeral cards, and after each card is drawn the children should write that digit in either the H, T or U section of the first box on their worksheets. Their aim is to make the highest possible three-digit number. Repeat this several times.

Main teaching activities

Whole class: Using the OHP or whiteboard calculator, ask a child to enter a number up to 1000. Ask the rest of the class to read out the number. Point to each of the digits and ask its value. Partition the number on the OHP or whiteboard: for example, '346 = 300 + 40 + 6'. Now introduce the thousands place. Write 1352 on the board with the word 'thousand' and ask the children to say the value of each digit. Repeat this for numbers up to 5000. When the children are confident with numbers up to 9999, introduce the ten thousands place and write the number 10,000 on the board.

Independent work: Give the children copies of activity sheet 'Partition party'. Explain that they have to partition the remaining nine numbers in a similar way to the example given.

Review

Tell the children that you are thinking of a four-digit number, and the sum of the digits (ignoring their place value) is 22. *What possible number could it be?* (4639, for example.) Allow the children to work in pairs for about five minutes to find as many different answers as they can. Ask each pair to write one of their numbers on the board. Then ask the class questions such as: *Which is the smallest number? Which is the largest number? Which number is closest to 1200?*

Assess which children can read the numbers without hesitation. Those who struggle will need further experience of reading and partitioning three- and then four-digit numbers.

Differentiation

Less confident learners: Use the support version of 'Partition party', which has smaller numbers to partition.

More confident learners: Use the extension version of the activity sheet, which has larger numbers to partition.

Lesson 2 (Teach and practise)

Starter

Rehearse: Write '27' onto the enlarged 'Place value chart'. Ask the children: *What is the value of the 7?* (7 units.) *What is the value of the 2?* (2 tens.) *What would 27 multiplied by 10 be?* (270.) Write '270' on the chart, emphasising the movement as you move each of the digits to the next column, and repeat the questions: *What is the value of the 7? What is the value of the 2?*

Write in the chart progressively larger numbers, up to 10,000, continually referring to the headings at the top of each column. Check that the children realise that a digit written in the thousands column has a value ten times larger than the same digit written in the hundreds column, and so on.

Main teaching activities

Whole class: Display the 'Rolling the dice' activity sheet, and roll a dice to generate two digits, for example 2 and 6. Then ask for a volunteer to make both two-digit numbers (26 and 62). Record the two numbers on the sheet. Ask: *Which is the larger number? How do you know? What is the difference between the numbers?* Introduce 'greater than' and 'less than' and, if the two digits are the same, 'equal to' (26 < 62 and 62 > 26). Make the > and < into crocodiles: the crocodile always eats the larger fish!

Now repeat for three rolls of the dice. Ask: *How many three-digit numbers can be made?* Write an example of numbers, in order, on the board, for example, '123, 132, 213, 231, 312, 321'. Repeat this for four rolls of the dice to make four-digit numbers. Draw a 1000–10,000 number line on the board. Choose two of the four-digit numbers and invite a child to position these numbers, in order, onto the line (using sticky notes). Ask: *What numbers could fit between these two? How do you know that?* Repeat for another pair of numbers.

Paired work: Provide copies of the 'Rolling the dice' sheet and dice. The core version requires the children to use four rolls of the dice to generate four-digit numbers and then to write their numbers in words.

Whole class: On the board, draw a number line from 1000 to 10,000. Ask pairs of children to write their largest four-digit numbers on sticky notes and place them on the number line. Discuss.

For each number, use appropriate vocabulary: *Is it nearer to 1000 or 10,000? Which number would be halfway between 1000 and 10,000? Is your number closer to 1000, 5000 or 10,000? Is your number greater than or less than 5000?*

Differentiation

Less confident learners: Use the support version of the activity sheet, which focuses on rolling three-digit numbers.

More confident learners: Provide copies of the extension version, on which children roll five-digit numbers.

Review

Invite children to pick two sticky notes from the board and describe a relationship using a number sentence, for example: '2134 is less than 2341' or '1000 is ten times smaller than 10,000'. Write these on the board, using < or > signs. Ask: *How do you know which is the bigger number? Which digit/digits tell us? What is the value of the digit? A three-digit number has rounded to the nearest ten to 260. What could that number have been?*

Lesson 3 (Teach and apply)

Starter

Revisit: Call out a number, for example, 9412. Ask the children to write the number, in digits, on their whiteboards. Then ask: *What is the value of the 2? The 9?* Repeat with several examples.

Main teaching activities

Whole class: Ask: *Where would you see negative numbers?* Discuss examples such as bank accounts, temperature, floors in a building (lifts that go below ground level), divers descending to the bottom of the sea, and so on. Show the children a thermometer and explain that the thermometer tells the temperature in degrees Celsius (°C). Record some temperatures around the school, eg near central heating, in a fridge, etc. Compare climates and discuss the different times of the year or parts of the world where temperatures will be below zero.

In the classroom, draw a vertical number line on the board. Mark and label the positions +5, 0 and -5, then ask individual children to add the missing numbers on sticky notes. When the line is completed ask the whole class to count back and forward from -5 to 5, then place the sticky notes randomly around the board. Pick -2 and -4 and ask: *Which is the smaller number? Which would be the lower temperature?* Invite two children to pick two sticky notes and use them to make a number sentence with < or >, for example -4 < -2.

Independent work: Give each child a copy of the 'Negative numbers' sheet to complete.

Differentiation

Less confident learners: Provide the support version of 'Negative numbers', with extra support and an additional number line activity.

More confident learners: Provide the extension version of the activity sheet, with a wider range of numbers (-20 to 20). Children are asked to write some number sentences using negative numbers.

Review

Attach the sticky notes to the board. Ask the children to close their eyes and then remove a number. Ask: *Which number is missing?* Remove three or four numbers in the same way, then ask: *Can you put these numbers in order of size? Which is the largest number? Which is the smallest number?* Repeat, and to extend this ask: *Can you give me four numbers that are less than 4? Less than 2? Less than -1?... I measured the temperature in the morning and the evening. By evening the temperature had dropped by 6 degrees. What could the morning and evening temperatures have been? How did you work that out? Tell me two temperatures that lie between 5 degrees and -6 degrees. Which temperature is warmer? Explain how you can tell.*

Lesson 4 (Teach and practise)

Starter

Recall: Explain that you will say a multiple of 10. Ask the children to say together the complement to make 100. So, if you say 70 they say 30. Keep the pace of this sharp. Then repeat, this time for complements to make 1000. So if you say 400, they say 600.

Main teaching activities

Whole class: Write on the board 40 + 70 and ask: *How can we work this out?* Discuss how this gives the same answer as 70 + 40. Draw an empty number line on the board and demonstrate counting up.

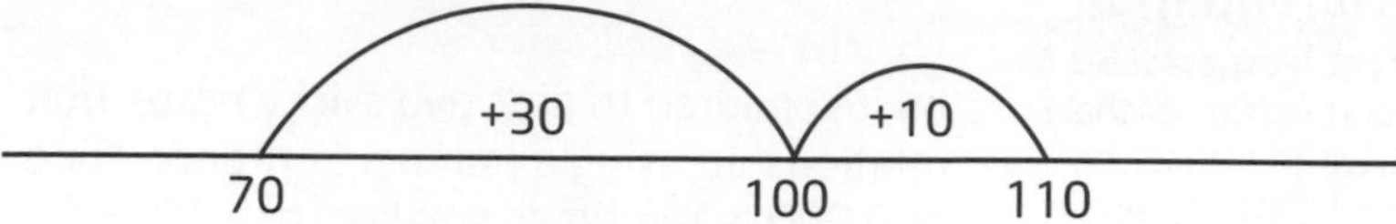

Discuss how this could be checked by subtraction, or by repeating the addition in a different order. Repeat this for other examples of addition of multiples of 10 which cross the hundreds barrier. Repeat this for subtraction, such as 80 - 50, using an empty number line to model the subtraction.

Paired work: Ask the children to draw their own empty number line and work out 600 + 500. Give them about two minutes to try this for themselves.

Whole class: Draw an empty number line and model the addition: 600 + 400 + 100 = 1100. Repeat for another example, such as 900 + 600, and then for a subtraction such as 900 - 500.

Extend this with addition and subtraction of thousands in the same way, such as 6000 + 2000 and 9000 - 3000.

Independent work: Provide each child with a copy of 'Sums and differences of multiples of 10'. Ask them to decide how they will calculate each question, draw a diagram if necessary, then to write a check calculation, such as addition in a different order, or using inverse operations.

Differentiation

Less confident learners: Provide the support version of the activity sheet, which uses addition and subtraction to 1000 only.

More confident learners: Challenge the children to use the core version of the sheet and to work mentally to answer all the questions.

Review

Write on the board 90 - 40 and ask: *What is the answer? How did you calculate this? How can you check it?* Repeat for other examples, such as 40 + 70; 600 + 700; 700 - 300; 4000 + 3000; 8000 - 2000. Discuss the different ways in which answers can be checked, including altering the order of addition or using an inverse operation.

Lesson 5 (Teach and apply)

Starter

Rehearse: Explain that you will say a two-digit number. Ask the children to work out the complement to make 100. For example, if you say 35 they say 65, and so on. Give some thinking time, if necessary, for the majority of the children to find the answer. Begin with complements which have 5 as the digit, then extend to other digits as the children become more confident.

Main teaching activities

Whole class: Display an OHP or interactive whiteboard calculator. Write 48 + 36 and ask: *What is your estimate of the answer? How did you decide on your estimate?* Now ask: *How can we calculate this mentally?* Input 48 + and ask: *What should we do next?* Write the suggestion on the board (for example, + 2) and input the suggestion. Now ask: *What do we do next?* The children will probably suggest + 30 + 4. Input this and press =. Write 48 + 36 = 48 + 2 + 30 + 4 = 50 + 30 + 4 = 84. Repeat this for other calculations, such as 48 + 67, where this crosses the hundreds barrier, and for subtractions such as 94 - 36, which will cross the tens barrier.

Differentiation

Less confident learners: Decide whether to work together as a group and to discuss each addition and difference sentence. The children will benefit from using a diagram, such as an empty number line, to help them to work mentally.

More confident learners: Ask the children to write a check calculation for each number sentence.

Paired work: Provide each pair with two sets of 0–10 numeral cards. Ask the children to shuffle the cards together and to take turns to make two two-digit numbers by choosing four cards. They add the two numbers and find their difference. They record their answers on the activity sheet 'Add and difference' and use their calculators to check their answers.

Review

Write 48 on the board and ask: *What do I need to add to this number to make 83? How did you work that out? Is there a different way to do it? How can you check that your answer is correct?* Repeat this for other calculations such as what to add to 54 to make 87; what to subtract from 94 to leave 45, and so on.

Lessons 6-10

Preparation

Lesson 6: For the interactive version, set the 'Multiplication square' interactive resource so that just the facts for the two- to six-times tables are available. Reveal the multipliers, but not the facts within the table. Or, if necessary, copy the 'Blank multiplication square' resource sheet onto OHT.

You will need

CD resources

Core, support, extension and template versions of 'Ten times Bingo questions' and 'Length word problems'; core version of 'Ten times Bingo instructions'. General resource sheets: 'Blank multiplication square'; 'Numeral cards'; 'Place value chart'; '100 square'. Interactive resources: 'Multiplication square' and 'Number sentence builder'.

Equipment

Calculators; whiteboard/OHP calculator; interactive whiteboard; dice.

Learning objectives

Starter

- Recognise and continue number sequences formed by counting on or back in steps of constant size.
- Derive and recall multiplication facts up to 10 × 10, the corresponding division facts and multiples of numbers to 10 up to the tenth multiple.
- Multiply and divide numbers to 1000 by 10 and then 100 (whole number answers), understanding the effect; relate to scaling up or down.
- Identify the doubles of two-digit numbers; use to calculate doubles of multiples of 10 and 100 and derive the corresponding halves.

Main teaching activities

2006

- Report solutions to puzzles and problems, giving explanations and reasoning orally and in writing, using diagrams and symbols.
- Derive and recall multiplication facts up to 10 × 10, the corresponding division facts and multiples of numbers to 10 up to the tenth multiple.
- Multiply and divide numbers to 1000 by 10 and then 100 (whole-number answers), understanding the effect; relate to scaling up or down.
- Identify the doubles of two-digit numbers; use to calculate doubles of multiples of 10 and 100 and derive the corresponding halves.
- Use a calculator to carry out one-step and two-step calculations involving all four operations; recognise negative numbers in the display, correct mistaken entries and interpret the display correctly in the context of money.

1999

- Multiply or divide any integer up to 1000 by 10 (whole-number answers), and understand the effect; begin to multiply by 100.
- Know by heart all multiplication facts up to 10 × 10; derive quickly corresponding division facts.
- Recognise multiples of 6, 7, 8, 9, up to the 10th multiple.
- Recognise multiples of 2, 3, 4, 5 and 10, up to the tenth multiple.
- Derive quickly doubles of all whole numbers to 50, multiples of 10 to 500 and multiples of 100 to 5000, and the corresponding halves.
- Develop calculator skills and use a calculator effectively.
- Explain methods and reasoning about numbers orally and in writing.

Vocabulary

problem, solution, calculate, calculation, equation, operation, answer, method, explain, predict, reason, reasoning, pattern, relationship, rule, add, subtract, multiply, divide, sum, total

Lesson 6 (Review and practise)

Starter

Recall: Display the 'Multiplication square' interactive resource. (Alternatively use the 'Blank multiplication square' resource sheet as an OHT.)

Ask a multiplication question, such as 5 × 4. As the children respond, explain that you will reveal the relevant fact for them to check if they were correct. (If you are using the OHT, write the answers in.) Ask questions from the two-, three-, four-, five- and six-times tables.

Main teaching activities

Whole class: Ask the children to count in fours from 0 to 80 and back again. Now ask them to count in eights from 0 to 80. Do this more slowly to allow for thinking time. Explain that these are the numbers that fit in the answers to the eight-times table. Write the eight-times table on the board, with the children providing the answers as you go.

Repeat the activity, this time counting in sevens from 0 to 70 and writing up the seven-times table on the board for the children to give the answers.

Count in threes from 0 to 90. Now count in nines from 0 to 90. Discuss how the nine-times table can be found from the three-times table. Write up the nine-times table, with the children giving the answers.

Paired work: Ask the children to work in pairs, working firstly with the eight-times table. They take turns to take a 1–10 numeral card and to say the relevant multiplication table fact. For a 5, they would say 5 multiplied by 8 is 40. Their partner checks that they agree. They repeat this for the seven-, then the nine-times tables.

Differentiation

Less confident learners: Decide whether to work as a group and to count up, in, say, eights, to find any facts that the children cannot generate for themselves.
More confident learners: Challenge the children to go beyond the tenth fact to find the eleventh to fifteenth facts.

Review

Reveal the complete multiplication square using the interactive resource (or display the completed 'Blank multiplication square' on the OHP). Show the children where the seven-, eight- and nine-times tables facts can be found, both down the table and across. Discuss how these facts tend to be practised the least so that the children need to really learn these facts so that these are secure. Point out that they will already know some of the facts. Ask: *What is 8 multiplied by 3? So what is 3 multiplied by 8?* Show where both facts are in the chart. Now cover the answers on the chart and ask multiplication facts for the seven-, eight- and nine-times tables which the children should be able to derive from their other tables, such as 8 × 6 for 6 × 8. Then extend this to the new table facts. Write on the board 56 ÷ 8 and ask: *What is the answer? How can you work this out?* Repeat for other division facts and their corresponding multiplication facts.

Lesson 7 (Teach and practise)

Starter

Recall: Start from 10 and together count on in tens up to at least 200, then from 200 count back in tens. Next, start at 55 and count on in tens up to about 255, and then back again. Repeat with other starting points, such as 27, 66, 174, 821. Repeat the activity counting on and back in hundreds from two-digit and three-digit starting points – for example, 71, 126, 333.

Main teaching activities

Whole class: Provide each child with a whiteboard and pen. Explain to them that when you call out a single-digit number they should write the answer to that number multiplied by 10 and then show you. Repeat for several single-digit numbers and then move on to two-digit numbers. Ask: *How did you get the answer? What are you doing to multiply by 10?* Be sure that the children realise that the digit zero is being placed at the end of the number, and why this happens.

Now ask: *Give me the number that is ten times larger than...* (27, 270, for example). *Now give me the number that is ten times smaller than...* (500,

50, for example). Check responses. Extend this to multiplying by 100 in the same way. Now ask the children to repeat this for dividing by 10 and then 100. For example, ask: *What is 600 divided by 10? What is 600 divided by 100? What is 60 divided by 10? Can you explain why 60 ÷ 10 gives the same answer as 600 ÷ 100?*
Group work: Split the class into groups of four or five, by ability. Explain to the children that they will be playing 'Bingo'. In each group, one child should be the caller and should be given the set of 'Ten times Bingo instructions' and questions to read. Tell the children to call out if they get a line or a full house. Provide each child with a copy of the activity sheet 'Ten times Bingo questions' or prepare bingo cards with different sets of numbers.

Differentiation

Less confident learners: Provide children with the support version of 'Ten times Bingo questions', which uses a smaller grid and asks for multiples of 10.
More confident learners: Provide children with the extension version of 'Ten times Bingo questions', which challenges the children to search for multiples of 10, 100 and 1000.

Review

Write up 27 and 270 on the board. Ask: *What is the relationship between these numbers?*

Display the 'Place value chart' and ask various children to write in three- and four-digit numbers, including multiples of 10 and 100.

Write up the number 27 and ask a child to write up the answer to 27 multiplied by 10. Then ask: *What would happen if we divided 270 by 10?* Repeat with another two-digit number.

Now ask: *What would happen if we divided 3000 by 100? Can you work out what 3100 divided by 10 would be? How did you work this out?*

Lesson 8 (Teach and apply)

Starter

Recall: Explain that you will say an even number between 2 and 100. Ask the children to call out the half of this number quietly. Again, keep the pace sharp.

Main teaching activities

Whole class: Use the 'Number sentence builder' interactive resource to display the following: '16 × 4 = □' and ask: *Who can tell me a way of working this out that uses doubling?* Show them the following method: 16 × 2 + 16 × 2 = 32 + 32 = 64. (Alternatively, display the calculations on the board or OHP.)

Explain that it is possible to work out unknown multiplication facts from those that you know, such as using doubling and halving methods. Display '13 × 20 = *a*'. Ask the children to think how they could work this out using doubles. Invite a child to write their response: 13 × 10 + 13 × 10 = 130 + 130 = 260. Repeat this for some more examples.

Now ask: *How could you work out multiplication by 8?* Agree that it can be done by multiplying by 2, then doubling and doubling again. Ask the children to calculate 15 × 8 by this method. Discuss how, in order to multiply by 5, it can be useful to multiply by 10 and then halve the result. Ask: *How could we multiply by 20?* Children will probably suggest multiplying by 10, then doubling that result.

Display the number 37. Ask the children to work out the double mentally. Ask: *How did you do this?* Discuss the methods chosen, such as double 40 minus 3 minus 3. Show the OHP/whiteboard calculator. Now ask: *What is double 370? And double 3700?* Invite the children to explain why, if you can work out double 37, the other answers can be derived from this, and how to do that. Now ask: *What is half of 56? How did you work that out?* (Maybe half of 50 then half of 6.) *So what is half of 560? Half of 5600?* Again invite the children to explain how you can use what you know to calculate the other halves.
Group work: Ask the children to work in pairs with the '100 square'. One child must choose a number on the square, double it, then multiply it by 10, then 100, and write their results on a sheet of paper. The other child then writes the halves of these numbers. The children should then swap roles.

Differentiation

Less confident learners: Decide whether to limit the children to doubling the numbers 1 to 50.
More confident learners: Challenge the children to also try this activity with numbers greater than 100 (numbers could be generated using dice or numeral cards).

Review

Invite children from each group to give an example for the others to try. Invite the child to explain how they carried out the calculation on the board. Ask: *How did you work that out? Who used a different method?* Then ask: *What is half of 68? And half of 680? And half of 6800? How did you work that out?*

Lesson 9 (Teach and apply)

Starter

Rehearse: Enter a number less than 100 into the OHP/whiteboard calculator and tell the children that you are going to multiply the number by 10. The children have to write what they think is the answer on their whiteboards. When you have entered × 10 and pressed =, ask how many children had the correct answer. Ask them what happened to the original number. Repeat this for other two-digit numbers.

Main teaching activities

Whole class: Explain that for the next two lessons the children will be engaged in solving word problems about measurements. Say: *In the school sports day, two children did the standing long jump. Ali jumped 76 centimetres and he was 120 centimetres tall. Daisy jumped 88 centimetres but she was only 110 centimetres tall. Who jumped further? How much further?*

Then ask the children to discuss the following questions: *What is the important information in the problem? What is the information that doesn't help you solve the problem? What is the answer to the problem? How did you work it out?* Invite a child to write a number sentence on the board to show the answer to the problem. Talk about how sometimes in word problems there can be information that is not useful in solving the problem.
Group work: Ask the children to work in pairs to answer the problems on the activity sheet 'Length word problems'. Explain that they should not expect to finish all of these problems in one session. Provide calculators for the children to check their answers.

Differentiation

Less confident learners: Use the support version of the activity sheet, which uses smaller numbers and just centimetres.
More confident learners: Use the extension version, which uses larger numbers and requires more conversions of units.

Review

Review the first problem from the core version of the activity sheet. Then question the children. For example: *What was the hardest problem? Why? What was the easiest problem? Why? What methods of calculation did you use? Who used a different method? Tell me one of your calculations. How did you use your calculator to check the answer? Did you try a different calculation? What could you have tried?*

Lesson 10 (Apply and evaluate)

Starter

Rehearse: Repeat the Starter from Lesson 9, this time extending the numbers to be multiplied to beyond 100.

Main teaching activities

Whole class: Invite the children to provide suggestions for word problems for number sentences such as 56 + 37, 198 + 47, 93 – 48... Let them continue to work in groups on the activity sheet 'Length word problems'.

Review

Review Question 6 from each version of the activity sheet 'Length word problems', inviting the children to suggest possible word problems for the number sentences given. Ask: *Which number operations would you need to use to solve these word problems? Suppose the problem had these numbers. Would that change the way that you would solve the problem? What diagram would you draw to help you to solve the problem?*

Name ______________________________ Date ____________________

A bigger place?

As your teacher calls out a number name, write it in one of the three boxes.

Try to make the largest number you can each time.

1.			
2.			
3.			
4.			
5.			
6.			
7.			
8.			
9.			
10.			

Name ______________________ Date ______________

Rolling the dice

Roll the dice four times and record your numbers in the boxes below.

Numbers

With these four numbers I can make ☐ numbers.

Words

Write your numbers in order, smallest first.

Now place one of your numbers in each box to make these statements correct.

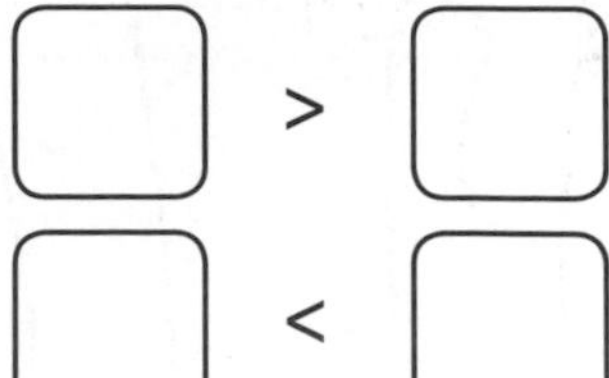

Name ______________________ Date ______________

Negative numbers

Write the correct temperatures in the boxes below.

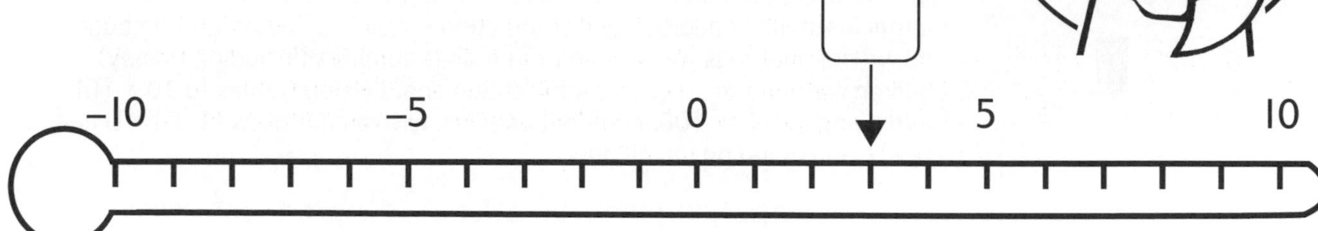

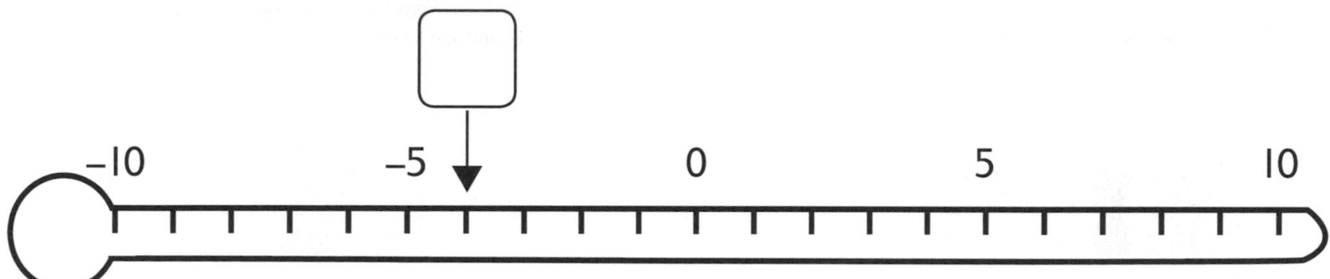

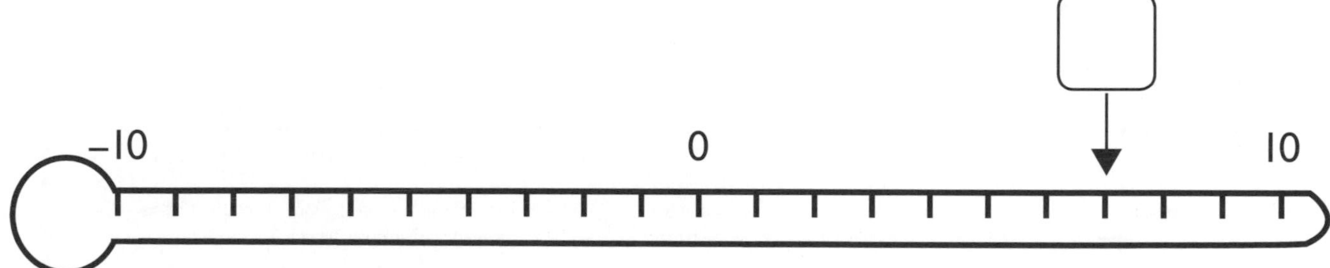

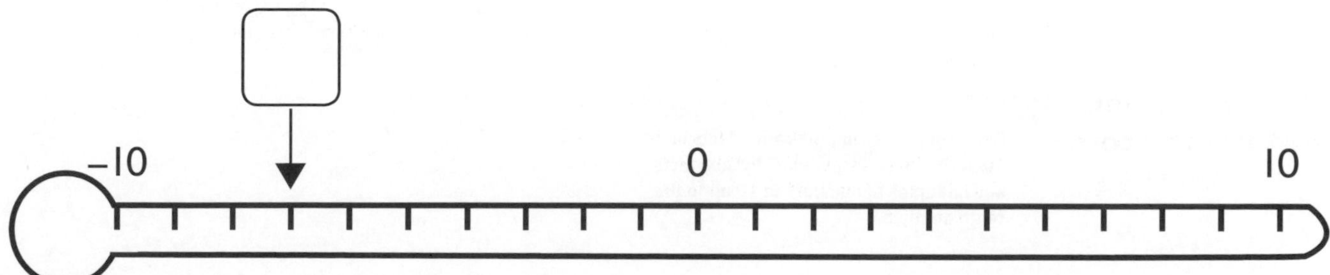

Unit 2 2 weeks

Counting, partitioning and calculating

Speaking and listening objective

- Respond appropriately to others in the light of alternative viewpoints.

Introduction

In this unit children have ten lessons which cover the strands of Counting and understanding number, Knowing and using number facts and Calculating. They explain their methods and reasoning orally and on paper, using words, diagrams and symbols. Children continue to order, partition and round four-digit numbers and positive and negative numbers. They use mental methods of addition and subtraction for pairs of two-digit numbers and written methods for two- and three-digit numbers (including money). Children continue to practise multiplication and division (tables to 10 × 10), multiplying by 10 or 100, two-digit doubles, written methods for TU × U and TU ÷ U, and rounding remainders.

Using and applying mathematics

- Report solutions to puzzles and problems, giving explanations and reasoning orally and in writing, using diagrams and symbols.

Lesson	Strands	Starter	Main teaching activities
1. Teach	Counting	Use decimal notation for tenths and hundredths and partition decimals; relate the notation to money and measurement; position one-place and two-place decimals on a number line.	Use decimal notation for tenths and hundredths and partition decimals; relate the notation to money and measurement; position one-place and two-place decimals on a number line.
2. Practise	Counting	As for Lesson 1	As for Lesson 1
3. Review	Calculate Use/apply	• Use knowledge of addition and subtraction facts and place value to derive sums and differences of pairs of multiples of 10, 100 or 1000 (revision of Block A, Unit1). • Use knowledge of rounding, number operations and inverses to estimate and check calculations.	• **Add or subtract mentally pairs of two-digit whole numbers (eg 47 + 58, 91 - 35).** • Report solutions to puzzles and problems, giving explanations and reasoning orally and in writing, using diagrams and symbols.
4. Apply	Calculate Use/apply	As for Lesson 3	• As for Lesson 3 • Refine and use efficient written methods to add and subtract two-digit and three-digit whole numbers and £.p.
5. Teach	Calculate	Use knowledge of rounding, number operations and inverses to estimate and check calculations.	Refine and use efficient written methods to add and subtract two-digit and three-digit whole numbers and £.p.
6. Practise	Calculate	As for Lesson 5	As for Lesson 5
7. Review and teach	Calculate	Multiply and divide numbers to 1000 by 10 and then 100 (whole number answers), understanding the effect; relate to scaling up or down.	Multiply and divide numbers to 1000 by 10 and then 100 (whole number answers), understanding the effect; relate to scaling up or down.
8. Practise	Calculate	**Derive and recall multiplication facts up to 10 × 10, the corresponding division facts and multiples of numbers to 10 up to the tenth multiple.**	As for Lesson 7
9. Teach	Calculate	As for Lesson 8	**Develop and use written methods to record, support and explain multiplication and division of two-digit numbers by a one-digit number, including division with remainders (eg 15 × 9, 98 ÷ 6).**
10. Review	Calculate	As for Lesson 8	As for Lesson 9

Lessons 1-2

You will need

Photocopiable pages
'Dotty decimals' (page 31).

CD resources
Support, extension and template versions of 'Dotty decimals'.

Equipment
£1 coin and a mixed bag of coins so that the £1 can be split into change to share; rulers; calculators.

Learning objectives

Starter

- Use decimal notation for tenths and hundredths and partition decimals; relate the notation to money and measurement; position one-place and two-place decimals on a number line.

Main teaching activities

2006

- Use decimal notation for tenths and hundredths and partition decimals; relate the notation to money and measurement; position one-place and two-place decimals on a number line.

1999

- Understand decimal notation and place value for tenths and hundredths, and use it in context, eg order amounts of money; convert a sum of money such as £13.25 to pence, or a length such as 125cm to metres; round a sum of money to the nearest pound.
- Order a set of numbers or measurements with one or two decimal places.

Vocabulary

place value, partition, thousands, digit, four-digit number, decimal point, decimal place, tenths, hundredths, compare, order, greater than (>), less than (<), equal to (=), round, estimate, approximately, pound (£), pence (p), pattern, relationship, rule, sequence

Lesson 1 (Teach)

Starter

Rehearse: Display a number line from 0 to 1 and mark in 0.5 together. Now explain that you will write a decimal on the board (not on the number line) and if they think that the decimal is greater than 0.5, then they must stand and if it is less than 0.5 they must sit. Pick examples and encourage individuals to explain their understanding to the class using diagrams, symbols or orally whilst placing the numbers on the number line. Repeat using 0.25 and 0.75 as starting points.

Fraction	Decimal
$\frac{1}{10}$	0.1
$\frac{2}{10}$	0.2
$\frac{3}{10}$	
$\frac{4}{10}$	
$\frac{5}{10}$	
$\frac{6}{10}$	
$\frac{7}{10}$	
$\frac{8}{10}$	
$\frac{9}{10}$	
$\frac{10}{10}$	

Main teaching activities

Whole class: Take a £1 coin and say: *I would like to share this among ten of you. How could I do it? How much should I give each person?* (Exchange for smaller coins and give each person 10 pence.) *So how many 10p in £1? What is 10 pence as a fraction of £1?* ($^1/_{10}$) *How would you write 10 pence in pounds?* (£0.10) *So in decimals, one tenth is 0.1.* ('zero point one'). Write 0.1 on the board. Ask: *How could I write 2 divided by 10?* Explain that £2 /10 = 20 pence which is £0.20 so is 0.2 of a pound ('zero point two'), that 20p is two-tenths of £1. Discuss the fact that with money it is important to include the zero, for example £0.30, but it is not necessary in decimal notation: you can just write 0.3. Write $^2/_{10}$ = 0.2 on the board and draw up a table (as shown left). Illustrate how decimals can be calculated using a calculator by showing 2 divided by 10 = 0.2. Complete the table with the children, recognising and highlighting equivalences such as $^2/_{10} = {}^1/_5$, $^4/_{10} = {}^2/_5$, $^5/_{10} = {}^1/_2$, $^6/_{10} = {}^3/_5$ and $^8/_{10} = {}^4/_5$.

Unit 2 2 weeks

Draw a number line on the board with 0 at one end and 1 at the other. Prompt the children to complete the number line in tenths using decimal notation. When it has been completed, count with the class from 0 to 1 in fractions ($^1/_{10}$, $^2/_{10}$...), then in decimals (0.1, 0.2...). Emphasise that the point separates the whole number from the tenths (NB: Watch in particular for any child saying 'zero point ten' for one whole). Ask: *What happens when we count past 1?*

Discuss suggestions and write on the board $^{10}/_{10} + ^1/_{10} = ^{11}/_{10}$. Establish that the count continues to $^{12}/_{10}$, $^{13}/_{10}$, and so on. Ask: *What is this the same as?* Continue the count on the board, recording values on the number line... 1.1, 1.2, 1.3, etc. Compare the two fraction forms and ask questions about them, for example: *What is $^{15}/_{10}$ in decimals?* Record these in your table to $^{20}/_{10}$ or 2.0.

Independent work: Ask each child to draw three lines 10cm long. They should use a ruler to partition each line into tenths. Tell them to mark the first line so that it runs from 0 to 1, the second from 1 to 2 and the third from 2 to 3. They should mark the tenths in decimal and improper fraction notation. These can be checked using calculators if appropriate.

Differentiation

Less confident learners: Work with the groups focusing on 0 to 1. Highlight the position of the decimal point and how this separates the whole number from the tenths.

More confident learners: Challenge the children to write their own start and finish number - perhaps using two-digit whole numbers.

Review

Write on the board: 23.4. Ask: *What is the value of the 2? The 3? The 4?* Discuss and put the headings T, U and t above the number. For example:

T	U	.	t
2	3	.	4

Write some numbers underneath the headings and challenge individual children to read the numbers, emphasising the decimal point. For each number ask a child: *What is the value representing... ?* Repeat for other numbers including some three-digit numbers such as 127.9.

Lesson 2 (Practise)

Starter

Rehearse and refine: Repeat the Starter for Lesson 1 but add in more two-place decimals - for example, 0.12 and 0.55.

Main teaching activities

Whole class: Ask: *How do we write one penny in pounds?* (£0.01) Repeat the activity for Lesson 1, dividing £1 by 100 and write $^1/_{100}$ = 0.01 ('zero point zero one'), $^2/_{100}$ = 0.02, and so on. Ask: *What would seven hundredths be as a decimal? What would ten hundredths be? Is this the same as one tenth?* Write some amounts on the board such as £3.24. Ask: *What is the 3 worth? What is the 2 worth? What is the 4 worth?* Emphasise that the 3 is three whole pounds and that the other digits represent parts of £1.

Repeat the above for measures such as 4.50kg and 4.05kg. Ask: *Which is the heavier? Why?*

Independent work: Give each child a copy of the 'Dotty decimals' sheet and let them practise ordering whole number and decimal amounts. Discuss ways of converting from pounds to pence and metres to centimetres.

Differentiation

Less confident learners: Use the support version of 'Dotty decimals', which includes mainly whole numbers and tenths.

More confident learners: Use the extension version of the sheet, which includes two-digit and three-digit whole numbers to order as well as a final challenge to make up a question for a partner. Remind the children that they will need to know how to order the numbers before setting the challenge.

Review

Write on the board: £2.69, £2.79, £2.89. Ask: *What would be the next number in this sequence? What is the rule?* Establish that you are adding one tenth each time and discuss the leap to £3.09, £3.19. Now ask: *Starting with £2.69 again, what would happen if I added one hundredth?... two hundredths?*

Lessons 3-6

Preparation

Lesson 3: Copy the '100 square' onto OHT or enlarge to A3 for display.

You will need

CD resources

Core, support, extension and template versions of 'Subtraction'; 'The Grid Game instructions', 'The Grid Game board' and 'The Grid Game score sheet'. General resource sheets: '100 square' and 'Numeral cards'. Interactive resources: 'Number sentence builder'. ITP 'Number grid'.

Equipment

Interactive whiteboard; number fans; calculators.

Learning objectives

Starter

- Use knowledge of addition and subtraction facts and place value to derive sums and differences of pairs of multiples of 10, 100 or 1000 (revision of Block A, Unit 1).
- Use knowledge of rounding, number operations and inverses to estimate and check calculations.

Main teaching activities

2006

- Add or subtract mentally pairs of two-digit whole numbers (eg 47 + 58, 91 - 35).
- Report solutions to puzzles and problems, giving explanations and reasoning orally and in writing, using diagrams and symbols.
- Refine and use efficient written methods to add and subtract two-digit and three-digit whole numbers and £.p.

1999

- Use known number facts and place value to add or subtract mentally, including any pair of two-digit whole numbers.
- Develop and refine written methods for: column addition and subtraction of two whole numbers less than 1000, and addition of more than two such numbers; money calculations (eg £7.85 ± £3.49).
- Check results of calculations.

Vocabulary

problem, solution, calculate, calculation, equation, operation, answer, method, explain, predict, reason, reasoning, pattern, relationship, place value, partition, thousands, digit, four-digit number, add, subtract

Lesson 3 (Review)

Starter

Revisit: Display the numbers 17, 3 and 20 on an interactive whiteboard, and ask the children to write on their whiteboards two addition sentences using the three numbers (17 + 3 = 20, 3 + 17 = 20). Show these using the 'Number sentence builder' interactive resource. Check responses and then ask: *Now can you write two subtraction sentences using the three numbers?* (20 - 17 = 3 and 20 - 3 = 17). Explain to the children that you will call out an addition sentence and would like them to write down a corresponding subtraction sentence. For example, call out: 3 + 12 = 15, and they can respond '15 - 12 = 3' or '15 - 3 = 12'. You may have to write the three numbers on the board to support the less confident children. Repeat this with several examples, highlighting the two different possible subtraction sentences. Discuss the use of these rules in checking calculations.

Main teaching activities

Whole class: Explain that this is the first of two lessons on adding and subtracting mentally. In this lesson the children will be looking at patterns within addition and subtraction sentences that can help to add and subtract. Display the ITP 'Number grid' on the interactive whiteboard (or use the '100 square' general resource sheet). Highlight 53 and ask: *What would I add to make 100?* Repeat with other examples such as 57, 76 and 82, each time illustrating how a 100 square can be used.

Paired work: One child writes a two-digit number on their whiteboard and then writes down the corresponding total to 100. The other child uses the '100 square' to do the same thing. Check and discuss calculations in pairs.

Whole class: Pick two children at random. Write 34p on one whiteboard and 67p on the other and compare their amounts in pence. Say, for example: *Tom has 34p and Yas has 67p. How much more does Yas have?* Discuss their answers and then ask: *How much would they have altogether?* Discuss, and write these two questions on the board.
Paired work: Back in pairs, ask children to repeat this activity by each writing an amount of money on their whiteboard. Encourage them to discuss calculations in answer to the two questions.

Differentiation
Less confident learners: Give these children guidance for suitable two-digit numbers so that they can count on or use the 100 square.
More confident learners: Suggest larger numbers with three or four digits, such as 278 or 1134.

Review
Write on the board: 45m - 39m = □. Ask the children: *How could you work this out?* Discuss individual ideas. Take a vote on who may count on, as the numbers have a near difference. Say: *Give me an example of a subtraction question where you could count on to find the difference. Give me an example of a calculation where you would not use this method. What might you do?*

Lesson 4 (Apply)

Starter
Revisit: Repeat the Starter from Lesson 3 but start with 23, 46 and 69. Ask the children to write the two possible addition sentences and the two possible subtraction sentences on their whiteboards. Then ask some quick-fire question such as: *What would 23p plus 46p be? What is the difference between 96kg and 46kg? How much more would I add to £2.30 to make £6.90?*

Main teaching activities
Whole class: Recap the main points from Lesson 3. Refer back to pairing numbers to make addition easier, counting on to find the difference and using the 100 square to aid calculations (using either the ITP 'Number grid' or the '100 square' general resource sheet).
Paired work: Explain that the children are going to play a game in pairs. Discuss how playing a game sometimes requires you to respond appropriately to other people's viewpoints. Using the activity sheets 'The Grid Game instructions', 'The Grid Game score sheet' and 'The Grid Game board', the children take turns to pick two numbers from the number grid that they think that they can add together. They must pick at least one three-digit number. The other player can use a calculator to check their response. If the number sentence is correct they get a point and cross the two numbers off the grid; if they get an incorrect answer they do not get a point and it is the other player's turn. The winner is the person who has more points when all the numbers are crossed off the grid. Use the score sheet to keep a tally. Remind the children to use the method that they have been practising for the last few lessons and that it will get more difficult as the game progresses because they cannot pick their numbers so freely. Take a more difficult example, such as 444 + 87. Illustrate the expansion method for this calculation and discuss it.

```
   444      = 400 +  40 +  4
+   87      = 000 +  80 +  7
              400 + 120 + 11 = 531
```

Differentiation
Less confident learners: Children could play in mixed-ability pairs.
More confident learners: Challenge these children to alter the numbers to make them all three digits.

Review
Discuss efficient methods for winning the game. Ask:
- *Were you always right?*
- *When did you get the answer wrong?*
- *What did you need to do to get the correct answer?*
- *Did you and your partner solve problems in the same way?*
- *Which do you think was the best way? Why?*

Illustrate a few more written expansion method examples.

Lesson 5 (Teach)

Starter

Rehearse: Rehearse rounding two- and three-digit numbers to the nearest 10 and 100 by calling out numbers and encouraging the children to show you the rounded number on their number fans.

Main teaching activities

Whole class: Write on the board: 369 + 76 = □ and 785 - 76 = □. Ask: *How can we use rounding to help us estimate these answers?* (369 + 76 will be less than 500 as 400 + 100 = 500 and 785 - 76 will be close to 800 - 100). Ask: *How can we work these out more accurately?* Explain that with bigger numbers the children may need a method of recording their work. Rewrite the addition calculations in vertical format and the subtraction using the number line and demonstrate the steps to calculate the answers.

```
  369        = 300 +  60 +  9
+  76        = 000 +  70 +  6
               300 + 130 + 15 = 445
```

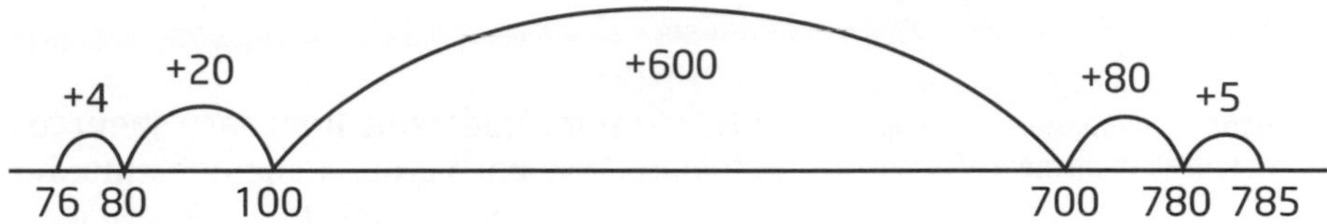

Repeat this for another example, such as 623 + 187. Ask the children to remind you of the steps needed to find the sum. Now provide an example for the children to try in pairs, such as 521 + 178. Invite children from each ability group to explain each step. Repeat for subtraction, using for example 234 - 179 as a whole group and 346 - 267 in pairs.

Paired work: Provide each pair with a set of 0–10 digit cards and some squared paper to assist in keeping numbers vertically aligned. Ask them to take turns to shuffle the numeral cards, then take the top five cards and make a three-digit and a two-digit number. They write an addition and then a subtraction sentence with these numbers, and solve it using the expanded method for addition and the number line method for subtraction.

Differentiation

Less confident learners: Ask the children to work together as a group to make subtraction sentences to solve. Invite each child to help in solving a number sentence. When the children are confident, ask them to work in pairs to solve one for themselves.

More confident learners: If the children are confident with this method, encourage them to think about how subtraction can be calculated vertically.

Review

Invite a pair of children from each group to write one of their number sentences on the board for the others to solve. Ask the children who wrote up the problem to solve it for the class, and to explain each step. Listen to the language that they use and check that they understand that this method involves counting up to find the difference. Ask questions such as: *Why do you do that? Who can explain this?*

Lesson 6 (Practise)

Starter

Refine and rehearse: Call out calculations and encourage the children to write an estimate for their answer by using rounding up or down on their whiteboards. For example, 599 + 88, 78 + 121, 311 + 199, 222 + 888, then 599 - 88, 121 - 88, 311 - 199, 888 - 222.

Main teaching activities

Whole class: Work out 311 - 199. Review subtraction by counting on a number line from Lesson 5 and develop this to show vertical recording.
Independent work: Provide the activity sheet 'Subtraction' for the children to use individually.

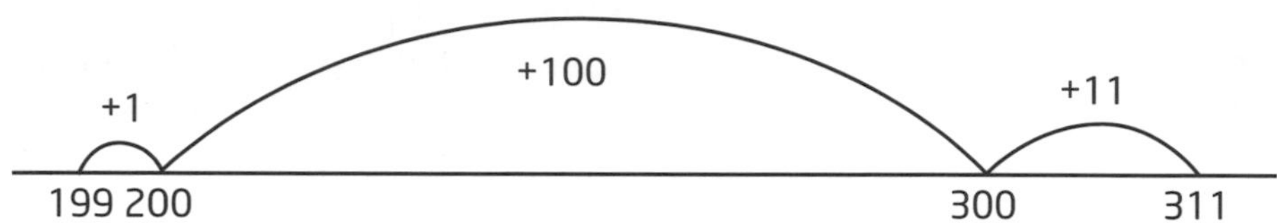

Differentiation

Less confident learners: Use the support version of the activity sheet, with subtraction of two-digit numbers. The children can use either the counting-on method or the empty number line method.
More confident learners: Use the extension version of the activity sheet. It includes questions that ask for the differences between two three-digit numbers, then two four-digit numbers. Children with a firm understanding of the expansion method can move towards refining their recordings to make them more efficient.

Review

Choose some questions from each sheet to review with the children. Invite children from each group to demonstrate how they solved the problem, writing on the board. Ask: *How did you work it out?*

Lessons 7-10

Preparation

Lesson 8: Copy 'Place value chart' onto OHT or enlarge to A3 for display.
Lesson 10: Copy 'Blank number lines' onto OHT or enlarge to A3 for display.

You will need

CD resources
Core, support, extension and template versions of 'Moving digits' and 'Grid method multiplication'; core version of 'Bigger or smaller'. General resource sheets: 'Place value chart' for display; 'Place value grids 1-1000' for support; 'Blank number lines' for display.
Equipment
Number fans; squared paper.

Learning objectives

Starter

- Multiply and divide numbers to 1000 by 10 and then 100 (whole-number answers), understanding the effect; relate to scaling up or down.
- Derive and recall multiplication facts up to 10 × 10, the corresponding division facts and multiples of numbers to 10 up to the tenth multiple.

Main teaching activities

2006

- Multiply and divide numbers to 1000 by 10 and then 100 (whole-number answers), understanding the effect; relate to scaling up or down.
- Develop and use written methods to record, support and explain multiplication and division of two-digit numbers by a one-digit number, including division with remainders (eg 15 × 9, 98 ÷ 6).

1999

- Multiply or divide any integer up to 1000 by 10 (whole-number answers), and understand the effect; begin to multiply by 100.
- Develop and refine written methods for TU X U, TU ÷ U.
- Find remainders after division; divide a whole number of pounds by 2, 4, 5 or 10 to give £.p; round up or down after division, depending on context.

Vocabulary

problem, solution, calculate, calculation, equation, operation, answer, method, explain, predict, reason, reasoning, pattern, relationship, multiply, divide, product, quotient, remainder

Lesson 7 (Review and teach)

Starter

Recall and rehearse: Ask a child to use a number fan to show a two-digit number. Copy that number, for example 23, onto the class demonstration number fan, then say aloud the result of multiplying that number by 10 (230) and alter your number fan to show it. Compare to the question: *How many 10 pence pieces would there be in £2.30?* Repeat with a couple of examples and ask: *What am I doing to the numbers? What am I doing to my number fan?* Swap roles by showing a two-digit number and asking the children to multiply it by 10. Extend to multiplying selected three-digit integers by 10 (eg 124, 210, and so on).

Main teaching activities

Whole class: Briefly remind the children about previous work on multiplication and division by 10. Revise division by 10, using the Starter activity but reversing the operation. Ask a child to show you a multiple of 10 on their number fan, then show them the result of dividing this number by 10. Repeat and ask: *What have I done to divide by 10?* Continue giving examples until the whole class is confident.

Write '1' on the board and ask: *What is 1 multiplied by 10?* (10) Ask: *What is 10 multiplied by 10?* (100)

Introduce 10,000, 100,000 and 1,000,000 by continuing the pattern of shifting the digit one place to the left and putting a zero at the end. Discuss the name of each number as it arises.

Group work: Ideally, take the class outside for this activity. Alternatively, move the furniture back against the walls. Put the children into groups of four and give each child a whiteboard. Give each group a single-digit number and ask one child to write that number on her/his whiteboard. Ask all the other children to write 0 on their whiteboards. Explain to the class that you will call out a series of questions involving multiplying by 10 and dividing by 10 and that each group needs to work together as a team to display the answers by combining their whiteboards. Start with the example shown:

- Start with 5.
- Multiply by 10. (50)
- Multiply by 10. (500)
- Multiply by 10. (5000)
- Divide by 10. (500)
- Divide by 10. (50)
- Divide by 10. (5)

Now mix up the multiplication and division instructions, praising teams that work well to display the correct answers. You could introduce a competitive element by eliminating the slowest team each time. Next, include a 'multiply by 100' question and ask: *What is happening now? How many zeros are we putting at the end? How many digits are now involved?* Establish that the numbers move two places to the left and that the zeros (called place holders) fill the spaces.

Continue with mixed questions involving multiplication by 10 and 100 and division by 10.

Independent work: Back in the class, give each child a copy of 'Moving digits' to complete. Remind the children that no matter what the starting number, they must always follow the pattern, eg 110 ×100 = 11,000; 12 × 100 = 1200.

Differentiation

Less confident learners: Provide the support version of 'Moving digits', which focuses upon multiplying integers up to 1000 by 10. Work with individuals on the movement of the digits.

More confident learners: Provide the extension version of 'Moving digits', which includes examples above 1000.

Review

Discuss the answers to the problems and the strategies to solve them. Write on the board 234 × 11 = □ and ask: *How could you find an approximate answer to this question?* (234 × 10 = 2340.) *Will the answer be a four-digit number?* (Yes.) *What did you do to multiply by 10? How could you find the exact answer?* (Add on 234, 234 × 11 = 2574.)

Repeat with approximations for 348 × 12 (approximate by working out

348 × 10, exact answer 4176) and 56 × 111 (approximate by working out 56 × 100, exact answer 6216).

Lesson 8 (Practise)

Starter

Recall: Call out different multiplication questions, up to 10 × 10. Ask the children to respond on their whiteboards or number fans. For example, 8 × 7, 6 × 7, 8 × 9. Keep up a good pace. Be sure that the children recognise that calculations such as 6 × 7 and 7 × 6 will give the same answer. Write to one side any calculations that seemed to cause hesitation for use in the Review.

Main teaching activities

Whole class: Remind the children that when a whole number is multiplied by 10 the digits move one place to the left, so 35 × 10 = 350. Similarly, when a whole number ending in 0 is divided by 10 the digits move one place to the right, so 350 ÷ 10 = 35. Use the 'Place value chart' on OHT to demonstrate this pattern and extend to other examples.

Next, ask: *What number is 100 times bigger than 10?* (1000.) *What number is 100 times smaller than 1000?* (10.) Remind the children that this time the digits move two places to the left or right to correspond with the number of zeros. So 35 × 100 = 3500 and 3500 ÷ 100 = 35. Point out that multiplying by 100 is the same as multiplying by 10 and then by 10 again.

Complete the activity sheet 'Bigger or smaller?' together to reinforce the pattern. Finally, give the children quick-fire questions multiplying and dividing by 10 and 100. The children can respond individually or as a whole class using number fans.

Independent work: Give each child a copy of the activity sheet 'Bigger or smaller?' to complete on her/his own. If time is available, ask the children to write some number sentences using ×10, ×100, ÷10 or ÷100.

Differentiation

Less confident learners: Provide copies of the 'Place value grids 1-1000' or structured equipment to support children with this activity, as a visual point of reference to spot patterns. The children might also benefit from completing 'Bigger or smaller?' with adult support.

More confident learners: Set a time limit (eg ten minutes) to complete this activity. If time is available, ask the children to multiply the first set of numbers by 1000.

Review

Using a calculation from the Starter as a starting point (for example, 8 × 9), ask: *What is the answer to 80 × 9? ... 8 × 90? ... 80 × 90? ... 800 × 9? ... 900 × 8? What would 81 divided by 9 be? How about 810 divided by 9? ... 810 divided by 90?*

Lesson 9 (Teach)

Starter

Recall and refine: Play Multiplication bingo. Provide the children with squared paper and ask them to draw a 3 × 3 grid on it. Explain that you will be calling out multiplication questions from the two-, three- or six-times tables. Ask them to fill each square of the grid with an answer number. Start to pose questions from the two- or three-times tables. If the answer to a question is on a child's sheet, tell them to cross it out. The first child to complete their card shouts 'Times table bingo'. Keep the pace of this sharp.

Ask questions at the end of the game, such as:

- *Which numbers did you choose?*
- *Why did you choose those?*
- *What about numbers that are in both the two- and the three-times tables, such as 6, 12 ...?*

Main teaching activities

Whole class: Show the children how to do multiplication by the grid method. Write on the board '26 × 3 = □'. Ask the children what they think the rough (approximate) answer would be, and how they worked that out (25 × 3). Write the following grid on the board:

×	20	6
3		

and then fill in the gaps. Write underneath: '60 + 18 = 78'.

Demonstrate another example, such as 34 × 4. Now provide an example, such as 27 × 5, for the children to try for themselves, working in pairs. Review this together, with a confident child writing out the grid method on the board.

Independent work: Give the children the activity sheet 'Grid method multiplication'. Ask them to write down their approximations and then use the grid method to find the answers.

Differentiation

Less confident learners: Provide the support version of the activity sheet, which involves multiplying teens numbers by single-digit numbers.

More confident learners: Provide the extension version, which asks the children to use the grid method for HTU × U. If a child has a firm grasp of this first step grid method, they may wish to move on to the next step.

Review

Review some of the examples from each of the three levels of the activity sheet, rewrite a few examples using the next step (see above).

Lesson 10 (Review)

Starter

Recall: Repeat the Starter from Lesson 9, but this time for multiplication facts from the two-, four- and eight-times tables.

Main teaching activities

Whole class: Use the enlarged version of 'Blank number lines' and write up '65 ÷ 5 = □'. The range should be 0-65. Invite the children to suggest an approximate answer, and to explain how they worked this out. Ask: *What multiplication facts do you know with these numbers?* Agree that 10 × 5 is 50 and 3 × 5 is 15, 50 + 15 = 65, so 65 ÷ 5 = 13. Illustrate this on a blank number line, marked in jumps of 5 from 65 back to 0:

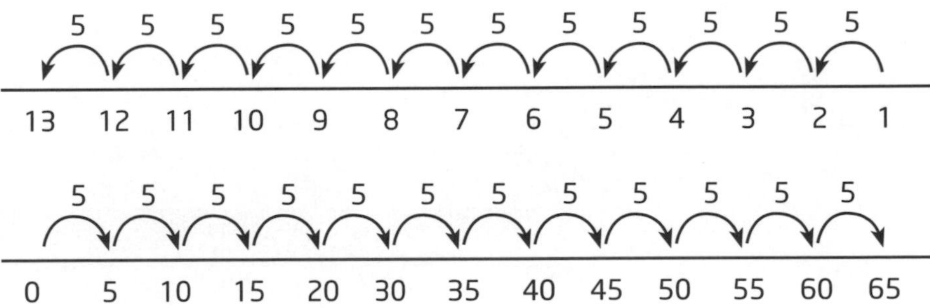

Discuss the fact that each time there is a jump back along the number line, 5 is subtracted, and that this happens 13 times (ie ten times and three times). Illustrate this vertically as:

```
   65
 - 50     (5 × 10)
   15
 - 15     (5 × 3)
   0                  Answer is 13.
```

Now ask the children, working in pairs, to try 56 ÷ 4. Review this example with the class to check that they understand how to use this method. Explain to the children how ten groups of 4, then four groups of 4 have been subtracted. Provide another example of this for the children to try in pairs: 48 ÷ 3. Ask them to write an approximate answer first. When the children have worked through this, invite a pair to write their solution on the board. Remind the children that it can be useful to subtract in multiples of 10, where possible.

Now provide an example where there is a remainder, such as 45 ÷ 4. Again, ask the children to work through this example in pairs, beginning with an approximate answer. Review this on the board as shown below:

$$\begin{array}{rl} & 45 \\ - & \underline{40} \quad (10 \times 40) \\ & 5 \\ - & \underline{4} \quad (1 \times 4) \\ & 1 \end{array}$$

45 ÷ 4 = 11 (r1)

Differentiation

Less confident learners: Decide whether to work as a larger group and to work through some more examples together. Try 30 ÷ 5; 24 ÷ 3; 42 ÷ 3; 56 ÷ 4; 37 ÷ 3.

More confident learners: Challenge the children to write three more division questions, each of which has an answer that includes 'remainder 2'.

Group work: Ask the children to work in pairs and to write and answer five division questions of their own. Remind them to try an approximation first. Give them about ten minutes to work on these, then ask them to join with another pair and to try each other's questions.

Review

Invite children from each group to give examples of division questions for the others to try. Ask your more confident group to provide an example with an answer that includes remainder 2. Ask: *How did you work these out? Was your answer close to your approximation? How did you approximate the answer?* Ask: *What other diagrams could you draw to help you?*

Name ____________________ Date ____________________

Dotty decimals

Put the numbers or amounts in order of size, starting with the smallest.

1. 6.2 5.7 5.2 4.5 7.6 6.7

2. 58p £58 £0.05 £0.85 £0.08 £5.80

3. 1.3m 1.03m 3.1m 31cm 13 cm

4. 200g 2kg 2.4kg 1kg 240grams

5. 19p £9.90 99p £0.90 £0.09

6. 13m 120cm 1200cm 1.25m 0.15m

7. 2.25 3.52 1.34 3.05 3.54 2.55

8. 3.05kg 3.54kg 554g 3.45kg 400g

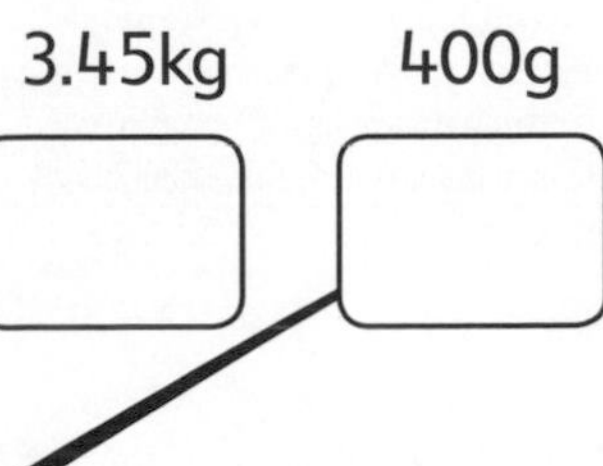

Unit 3 2 weeks

Counting, partitioning and calculating

Speaking and listening objective

- Identify the main points of a speaker; compare their arguments and how they are presented.

Introduction

In this unit children have ten lessons which include the strands of Counting and understanding number, Knowing and using number facts, Calculating and Using and applying mathematics. Children solve one- and two-step word problems involving numbers, money or measures. They explain their methods and reasoning, orally and on paper, using words, diagrams and symbols. Children continue to order, partition and round positive and negative four-digit numbers. They use mental addition and subtraction methods for pairs of two-digit numbers and written methods for two- and three-digit numbers (including money). Children also practise multiplication and division, including tables to 10 × 10, multiplying by 10 or 100, two-digit doubles, written methods for TU × U, TU ÷ U and rounding remainders.

Lesson	Strands	Starter	Main teaching activities
1. Review	Calculate	**Add or subtract mentally pairs of two-digit whole numbers (eg 47 + 58, 91 - 35).**	Refine and use efficient written methods to add and subtract two-digit and three-digit whole numbers and £.p.
2. Review, teach and practise	Calculate	As for Lesson 1	As for Lesson 1
3. Apply	Use/apply Calculate	Use decimal notation for tenths and hundredths and partition decimals; relate the notation to money and measurement; position one-place and two-place decimals on a number line .	• Solve one-step and two-step problems involving numbers, money or measures, including time; choose and carry out appropriate calculations, using calculator methods where appropriate. • Refine and use efficient written methods to add and subtract two-digit and three-digit whole numbers and £.p.
4. Review and teach	Calculate Knowledge	Solve one-step and two-step problems involving numbers, money or measures, including time; choose and carry out appropriate calculations, using calculator methods where appropriate.	• Solve one-step and two-step problems involving numbers, money or measures, including time; choose and carry out appropriate calculations, using calculator methods where appropriate. • Refine and use efficient written methods to add and subtract two-digit and three-digit whole numbers and £.p. • Use knowledge of rounding, number operations and inverses to estimate and check calculations.
5. Teach and practise	Calculate	Use decimal notation for tenths and hundredths and partition decimals; relate the notation to money and measurement; position one-place and two-place decimals on a number line .	Use a calculator to carry out one-step and two-step calculations involving all four operations; recognise negative numbers in the display, correct mistaken entries and interpret the display correctly in the context of money.
6. Teach and practise	Calculate	**Derive and recall multiplication facts up to 10 × 10, the corresponding division facts and multiples of numbers to 10 up to the tenth multiple.**	As for Lesson 5
7. Review	Calculate Knowledge	**Add or subtract mentally pairs of two-digit whole numbers (eg 47 + 58, 91 - 35).**	• **Add or subtract mentally pairs of two-digit whole numbers (eg 47 + 58, 91 - 35).** • Use knowledge of rounding, number operations and inverses to estimate and check calculations.
8. Review and practise	Counting	**Derive and recall multiplication facts up to 10 × 10, the corresponding division facts and multiples of numbers to 10 up to the tenth multiple.**	• Partition, round and order four-digit whole numbers; use positive and negative numbers in context and position them on a number line; state inequalities using the symbols < and > (eg -3 > -5, -1 < +1). • Use decimal notation for tenths and hundredths and partition decimals; relate the notation to money and measurement; position one-place and two-place decimals on a number line .
9. Practise and apply	Counting	Partition, round and order four-digit whole numbers; use positive and negative numbers in context and position them on a number line; state inequalities using the symbols < and > (eg -3 > -5, -1 < +1).	As for Lesson 8
10. Review, practise and apply	Calculate	As for Lesson 9	**Develop and use written methods to record, support and explain multiplication and division of two-digit numbers by a one-digit number, including division with remainders.**

Using and applying mathematics

- Solve one-step and two-step problems involving numbers, money or measures, including time; choose and carry out appropriate calculations, using calculator methods where appropriate.

Lessons 1-6

Preparation

Lesson 6: Buy a net of lemons or limes and the same number of lemons or limes sold separately. Copy the receipt for display on the OHP/interactive whiteboard.

You will need

Photocopiable pages
'Subtraction pairs' (page 42), 'Number differences questions' (page 43) and 'Totally different shopping' (page 44).

CD resources
Support, extension and template versions of 'Subtraction pairs', 'Number differences questions', 'Totally different shopping' and 'Party planning'; core version of 'Carry on calculator cards'. Interactive resource: 'Number sentence builder'.

Equipment
Number fans; squared paper; a net bag of lemons or limes, the same number of lemons or limes bought individually, and the receipt; calculators; an OHP/interactive whiteboard calculator (with a constant function).

Learning objectives

Starter

- Solve one-step and two-step problems involving numbers, money or measures, including time; choose and carry out appropriate calculations, using calculator methods where appropriate.
- Use decimal notation for tenths and hundredths and partition decimals; relate the notation to money and measurement; position one-place and two-place decimals on a number line .
- Add or subtract mentally pairs of two-digit whole numbers (eg 47 + 58, 91 - 35).
- Derive and recall multiplication facts up to 10 × 10, the corresponding division facts and multiples of numbers to 10 up to the tenth multiple.

Main teaching activities

2006

- Solve one-step and two-step problems involving numbers, money or measures, including time; choose and carry out appropriate calculations, using calculator methods where appropriate.
- Refine and use efficient written methods to add and subtract two-digit and three-digit whole numbers and £.p.
- Use a calculator to carry out one-step and two-step calculations involving all four operations; recognise negative numbers in the display, correct mistaken entries and interpret the display correctly in the context of money.
- Use knowledge of rounding, number operations and inverses to estimate and check calculations.

1999

- Use all four operations to solve word problems involving numbers in 'real' life, money and measures (including time), using one or more steps, including converting pounds to pence and metres to centimetres and vice versa.
- Choose and use appropriate number operations and appropriate ways of calculating (mental, mental with jottings, pencil and paper) to solve problems.
- Round up or down after division, depending on context.
- Check results of calculations.
- Choose appropriate ways of calculating: calculator.
- Develop and refine written methods for: column addition and subtraction of two whole numbers less than 1000, and addition of more than two such numbers; money calculations (eg £7.85 ± £3.49).
- Develop calculator skills and use a calculator effectively.

Vocabulary

problem, solution, calculate, calculation, equation, operation, answer, method, explain, predict, reason, reasoning, pattern, relationship, rule, sequence, place value, partition, thousands, digit, four-digit number, decimal point, decimal place, tenths, hundredths, positive, negative, above/below zero, compare, equal to (=), round, estimate, approximately, add, subtract, multiply, divide, sum, total, difference, plus, minus, product, quotient, remainder, calculator, display, key, enter, clear, constant

Lesson 1 (Review)

Starter

Revisit: Call out pairs of two-digit whole numbers for the children to add, for example 47 + 58, 91 + 35. Invite the children to show you their answers on a whiteboard or number fan. Ask questions such as: *How did you work out the sum? Did you approximate your answer first? Did anyone work this out in a different way?*

Main teaching activities

Whole class: Write on the board '79 - 57 = □' and ask: *How would you work this out? What is the answer?* ((79 - 60) + 3 = 22, or 70 - 50 = 20 and 9 - 7 = 2 so 20 + 2 = 22). Now write on the board '679 - 57 = *a*' and ask the children to work out the answer in any way that they choose, recording their methods on their whiteboards. Discuss various methods and compare solutions. Look at the different methods and jottings.

Use the board to demonstrate methods of recording that could help. For example:

Answer: 679 - 57 = 622 (43 + 500 + 79 = 622)

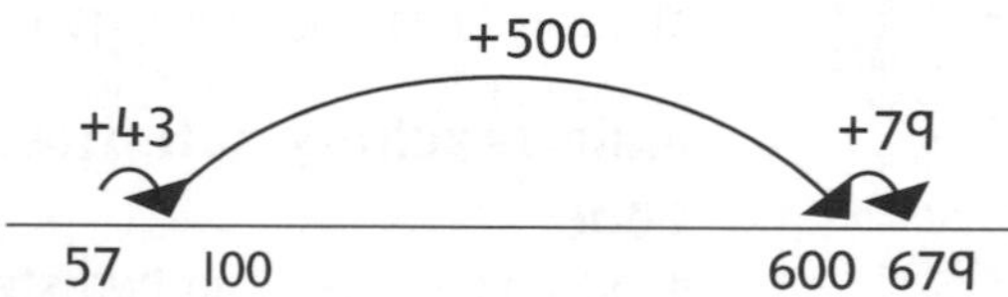

Remind the children of this strategy, learned previously, of counting up from the lower number to the higher number. Invite children to the board to model similar examples such as 688 - 246, 725 - 153, and so on. Ask the children if they have any difficulties with this method (for example difficulty in adding the numbers together). Remind children of the written calculations in columns they have used previously ('counting up', which involves the same process as the number line method and 'compensation' subtracting too much and then adding back). Demonstrate the two methods using the same subtraction, for example 627 - 159. Stress the need to align numbers in columns.

Compensation

```
   627
 - 159
   427   (627 - 200)
 +  41   (since 100 - 59 = 41)
   468
```

Counting on

```
   627
 - 159
     1  (Counting on to make 160)
    40  (Counting on from 160 to make 200)
   400  (Counting on from 200 to make 600)
    20  (Counting on from 600 to make 620)
     7  (Counting on from 620 to make 627)
   468
```

Independent work: Give each child a copy of the 'Subtraction pairs' sheet in which they are given two sets of numbers - one between 500 and 1000 and the other between 100 and 250. Ask the children to select one number from each set, and then use them for a subtraction. Ask them to practise one of the written methods shown above. Allow enough time for the children to complete three examples. If necessary, give the children squared paper to help them line up the numbers in columns.

Differentiation

Less confident learners: Work with these children and help them with explanations of the two methods. If necessary, give the children the support version of 'Subtraction pairs', which includes three-digit numbers in one set and two-digit numbers in the other.

More confident learners: Challenge these children to complete the sheet in the time allowed and to provide alternative methods where possible. If necessary, give them the extension version of the sheet, which includes higher numbers, including one four-digit number.

Review

Write on the board '567 - 99 = □' and ask: *Do you need to write anything down to help you answer this?* Help the children to decide that they do not, as (567 - 100) + 1 = 468. Stress that they need to look carefully at the numbers in a question before they decide to use a column method. Repeat with 567 - 186, 567 - 239, 567 - 312 and 567 - 448. Agree that you might need to use a written column method to help you answer some of these questions. Go through the questions on the 'Subtraction pairs' sheet and one or two of the examples above, as time allows. Emphasise the need to write the units, tens and hundreds aligned in the appropriate columns.

Ask: *How can you check? Can you find an approximate answer?* Say that there will be more about this column (decomposition) method in the next lesson.

Lesson 2 (Review, teach and practise)

Starter

Revisit: Repeat the Starter from Lesson 1, this time asking subtraction calculations.

Main teaching activities

Whole class: Explain that in this lesson the children will be looking again at a written subtraction method that is even easier than the ones in the previous lesson as it will cut down the amount of working out required. Write on the board: 376 - 187. Demonstrate using decomposition.

```
  376  =    300  +  70  +  6
- 187  =  - 100  +  80  +  7
```

We can exchange one 10 from the 70, leaving 60 and add it to the 6 to make it 16:

```
       =    300  +  60  +  16
       =  - 100  +  80  +   7
```

Next, we can exchange one 100 from the 300, leaving 200, and add it to the 60 to make 160.

```
       =    200  +  160  +  16
       =  - 100  +   80  +   7
```

This can also be written as the following:

```
  ²3̸ ¹⁶7̸ ¹6
-  1  8  7
   1  8  9
```

When we subtract each column the answer is 189.

Give another example (eg 543 - 256) and ask one child to write it vertically and another child to work through it on the board with help from the rest of the class. Remind them about putting the digits in the correct place and that we start from the right and work to the left.

Paired work: After completing this task, give each pair at least one copy of the 'Number differences questions'. Go through one example if necessary. The children should work together to discuss the method, lay out each question on the grid and answer it. The pairs could take it in turns to check each answer using a calculator.

Differentiation

Less confident learners: Provide the support version of 'Number differences questions' on which multiples of 10 are subtracted from the larger number in the first few examples. A written example is included to support the children.

More confident learners: Provide the extension version of the sheet, with additional questions, including a four-digit by three-digit example.

Review

Review the subtraction vocabulary used in each question, the children's answers and the methods used. Review the decomposition method and discuss children's other ideas for answering the questions. Write the subtraction shown here on the board.

```
  2 ¹3̸ ¹4
-    6  9
  2  7  5
```

Ask: *What is the problem with this subtraction? What have I done wrong? How can you tell that the answer is wrong?* (The answer in the units column is correct but in the tens column the '1' has not been taken from the 3 (it should be 12 not 13) and the same with the hundreds column (should be 100 not 200).)

Stress that the subtraction could be checked, as (234 - 100) + 31 or (234 - 70) + 1.

Lesson 3 (Apply)

Starter

Revisit: Remind the class that money, written in pounds, is tenths and hundredths. For example, £4.85 is 8 tenths and 5 hundredths or 8 ten pence pieces and 5 one pence pieces. Call out different amounts of money. Start with £6.73 and ask: *What does the 7 represent? What does the 3 represent?* Ask the children to respond on their whiteboards or number fans.

Main teaching activities

Whole class: Discuss the column addition and subtraction methods you have been working on recently. Explain that the same methods could be applied to working out answers to money problems. Model the use of the decomposition method for money problems. For example: *Mr Shah wants to buy a plant costing £4.85. He takes £7.27 to the shop. How much would he have left if he buys the plant?*

Discuss other methods you might use to solve this, such as the compensation method – adjusting from the pence to the pounds (727 pence - 485 pence) before using decimal notation. Explain that you will be giving the children some shopping problems to solve. Discuss vocabulary such as 'more/less expensive' and finding the difference in costs.

Independent work: Distribute the 'Totally different shopping' sheet, which shows objects for sale in a shop and sets some addition and subtraction questions about them. Talk about the items on the sheet and work through the first two questions as a class, reminding the children to align the decimal points, as well as the numbers, in columns. Give the children a supply of squared paper to support them with this task.

Differentiation

Less confident learners: Provide the support version of 'Totally different shopping', which has slightly lower prices.

More confident learners: Provide the extension version of the sheet, which includes a challenge for these children to spend £12.00, deciding what to buy and how much change they would receive.

Review

Discuss the answers from the activity sheet, each time asking how the child worked out the answer and which method was used. Provide children with a calculator or display an OHP/whiteboard calculator and ask: *How could we check these on a calculator?* Ask: *Which two objects from the shop would cost the most to buy? How much would they cost? Which two objects could you buy if you only had £5? £6? £7? Which two items have the greatest difference in price? What is the difference between the prices?*

Lesson 4 (Review and teach)

Starter

Reason: Explain to the children that you will write a number sentence on the board and you would like them to write down, on their whiteboards, the sign that would make the sentence correct. You may wish to use the 'Number sentence builder' interactive resource for this. Start with '23 □ 49 = 72' (+) and then ask: *How can you tell that the sign is add? What would be a good way to work out the sum 23 + 49?* Discuss methods and then repeat with '34 □ 2 = 17' (÷), '23 □ 2 = 46' (×), '36 □ 19 = 17' (-). Each time, discuss appropriate methods for working out the answer. End with '123 □ 76 = 47' (-) and revise the vertical 'carrying' method.

Main teaching activities

Whole class: Explain that in this lesson the children will again be looking at shopping problems. On this occasion they need to use multiplication and division to answer some of the questions they will be asked. Ask: *Think about shopping at the supermarket. Who can think of a question for which you would need to use multiplication or division?* Show the class the lemons or limes, establishing that there is the same number in the net as there are separate fruits. Read out the prices of the lemons or limes from the receipt and compare the price for the net with the price for the same number of individual fruits. Discuss how much one lemon or lime from the net cost and which was the cheaper buy. Ask the children to suggest other shopping examples such as multiple packs of crisps, biscuits, cans of drink or multipacks in general.

Independent work: Give each child a copy of 'Party planning', on which they are asked a number of shopping questions involving addition, subtraction, multiplication and division with one or more steps. Remind them that although they have been practising written methods of addition and subtraction, they might find it quicker to work out some of these questions mentally. They might also check the results of their calculations by using a written method of calculation or other checking strategies such as knowledge of sums and differences of odd and even numbers. Remind them of work done on this in the previous unit and lessons. Encourage the children to estimate their calculation by rounding before they begin. They can also use rounding as one method to check their calculations.

Review

Discuss the answers to the questions on the activity sheet, each time asking how the child worked out the answer and which method they used. Again, provide the children with a calculator or display a calculator on the OHP/ whiteboard and ask: *How could we check these on a calculator? How did you know whether to add, subtract, multiply or divide? What clues did you look for in the problem?*

Ask: *Which two objects from the shop would cost the most to buy? How much would they cost? How many chocolate bars could you buy for £1? How many apples? How many packets of biscuits could you buy for £5? How many cakes?* Illustrate logical workings on the board to help the children answer such questions. Include examples from the differentiated activity sheets. Finally, discuss the methods the children used to check their answers.

Differentiation

Less confident learners: Use the support version of 'Party planning', which uses lower prices.

More confident learners: Use the extension version of the activity sheet, which uses higher prices and has an extra challenge.

Lesson 5 (Teach and practise)

Starter

Revisit: Repeat the Starter from Lesson 3, this time using lengths in metres. For example: *In 1.23m, what does the 2 represent? What does the 3 represent?*

Main teaching activities

Whole class: Display an OHP/whiteboard calculator. Call out different amounts of money (for example, £1.20) and ask volunteers to enter it on the calculator. Discuss the use of, for example, 1.2 for £1.20, 0.4 for 40 pence, 0.03 for 3 pence and link this back to the work on tenths and hundredths.

Now provide the children with individual calculators and a card from a shuffled set of 'Carry on calculator cards'. Explain to them that all these cards follow on from each other. Start with the first child, who works out the calculation on the calculator and then clearly reads out the answer and the next instruction. After some of the calculations ask: *What did you type onto the calculator? Show me on your calculator.* Demonstrate, using the display calculator. Once you have been through one loop slowly, redistribute the cards and repeat, this time faster and with fewer interruptions.

Review

Ask: *Which of the calculations would have been easier to do in your head? Which were made easier on the calculator?* Take two 'Carry on calculator cards' and ask: *What is the difference between these two values? What is the sum of these two values? How would I share this with two people? What would you press? What about if I wanted to multiply it by 10?*

Lesson 6 (Teach and practise)

Starter

Revisit and refine: Ask multiplication facts relating to money – for example 5p × 5, 6p × 7, 3p × 2. Ask the children to respond using whiteboards.

Main teaching activities

Whole class: Explain to the children that you will start a sequence and you would like them to join in when they see what is happening. Start with *£1.34, £1.54, £1.74, £1.94...* Ask: *How could you describe the sequence?* (Counting in steps of 20p from £1.34). Display a calculator, type in 1.34 and demonstrate the constant function on the calculator (for example, pressing 1.34 + + 0.2, the calculator adds on 0.2 every time the = sign is pressed.) Repeat, starting with £1.10, this time subtracting 20p. Illustrate this with the calculator and discuss what happens as the number goes negative.

Paired work: Encourage the children to come up with their own sequence using a calculator. They need to say the first few values in the series to their partner, illustrating it on their calculator if appropriate and then their partner will describe what is happening in the sequence. They then swap roles.

Differentiation

Less confident learners: These children should, if possible, work in a group with an adult to direct and help with the calculator if appropriate.

More confident learners: These children should be encouraged to use more complex sequences using negative numbers.

Review

Ask the children to share some of their sequences with the class and, if appropriate, demonstrate some of them on the display calculator. Ask: *What would the next number be? How would I write that amount on my calculator? What operation would I use? How do you know that?*

Lessons 7-10

You will need

CD resources

'Division examples' and 'Decimal number line'; core and support versions of 'Decimal bingo'; core, support, extension and template versions of 'Division dilemmas'.

General resource sheet: 'Blank number lines'.

Interactive resource: 'Number sentence builder'.

Equipment

Whiteboards; interactive whiteboard or OHP.

Learning objectives

Starter

- Partition, round and order four-digit whole numbers; use positive and negative numbers in context and position them on a number line; state inequalities using the symbols < and > (eg -3 > -5, -1 < +1).
- Add or subtract mentally pairs of two-digit whole numbers (eg 47 + 58, 91 - 35).
- Derive and recall multiplication facts up to 10 × 10, the corresponding division facts and multiples of numbers to 10 up to the tenth multiple.

Main teaching activities

2006

- Partition, round and order four-digit whole numbers; use positive and negative numbers in context and position them on a number line; state inequalities using the symbols < and > (eg -3 > -5, -1 < +1).
- Use decimal notation for tenths and hundredths and partition decimals; relate the notation to money and measurement; position one-place and two-place decimals on a number line .
- Add or subtract mentally pairs of two-digit whole numbers (eg 47 + 58, 91 - 35).
- Develop and use written methods to record, support and explain multiplication and division of two-digit numbers by a one-digit number, including division with remainders (eg 15 × 9, 98 ÷ 6).
- Use knowledge of rounding, number operations and inverses to estimate and check calculations.

1999

- Recognise negative numbers in context (eg on a number line, on a temperature scale).
- Use symbols correctly, including less than (<), greater than (>) and equals (=).

- Use known number facts and place value to add or subtract mentally, including any pair of two-digit whole numbers.
- Check results of calculations.
- Understand decimal notation and place value for tenths and hundredths, and use it in context, eg order amounts of money; convert a sum of money such as £13.25 to pence, or a length such as125 cm to metres; round a sum of money to the nearest pound.
- Order a set of numbers or measurements with one or two decimal places.
- Develop and refine written methods for TU × U, TU ÷ U.
- Find remainders after division; divide a whole number of pounds by 2, 4, 5 or 10 to give £.p; round up or down after division, depending on context.

Vocabulary

problem, solution, calculate, calculation, equation, operation, answer, method, explain, predict, reason, reasoning, pattern, relationship, rule, sequence, place value, partition, thousands, digit, four-digit number, decimal point, decimal place, tenths, hundredths, positive, negative, above/below zero, compare, order, greater than (>), less than (<), equal to (=), round, estimate, approximately, add, subtract, multiply, divide, sum, total, difference, plus, minus, product, quotient, remainder, pound (£), pence (p), units of measurement and their abbreviations, degrees Celsius (°C)

Lesson 7 (Review)

Starter

Revisit: Call out various two-digit numbers and ask the children to show you what they would have to add to make 100. Start with 51, 55 and 57.

Main teaching activities

Whole class: Talk through the different strategies that you can use for adding and subtracting numbers mentally, such as rounding up/down (31 + 79, will be like 30 + 80), using knowledge of odd and even numbers (the answer to 34 + 32 will be even), subtracting multiples of ten and then compensating (45 - 11, will be like 45 - 10 + 1). Ask: *Can you think of any other examples?* Discuss. Display the equation, □ + 34 = □7 using the 'Number sentence builder' interactive resource.
Paired work: Challenge the pairs to come up with as many solutions to the equation as they can in a fixed amount of time (say, five minutes).
Whole class: Discuss ideas and write a list of possible solutions using the interactive resource.
Paired work: Repeat, this time solving the equation □ - 36 = □8.

Differentiation

Less confident learners: Talk through a few examples of equations that work with this group before leaving them to find the remainder.
More confident learners: This group could extend the problem by thinking of other solutions to □ + 45 = □6 or □ - 36 = □8.

Review

Discuss solutions to the subtraction equation, allowing each pair to contribute ideas and solutions. Ask: *How did you solve that? What knowledge did you use to help?* Investigate together: *The difference between two two-digit numbers is 13, what could the numbers be?*

Lesson 8 (Review and practise)

Starter

Reason: Write on the board □ × □ = 36 and give the children two minutes to write down possible pairs of missing numbers. Discuss and repeat using □ × □ = 56.

Main teaching activities

Whole class: Display the 'Blank number line', split into 20 (from -5 to +5 but with enough room to show halves). Ask individuals to come up and fill in random numbers from -5 to +5, including halves such as -4.5. Now ask individuals to come and estimate where other decimals would go on the line, for example 4.75, 2.3, -0.1. Take numbers from the number line and state some inequalities such as 3.4 < 3.6 or 0.5 > -1.2. Discuss the use of drawing teeth onto the 'greater than' or 'less than' signs to show that the 'crocodile' always eats the larger number. Write up □ < 1 and ask: *What numbers could make this statement correct?* Repeat with □ > 1.

Paired work: Write □ + □ < 34 and ask pairs of children to investigate which numbers could go into the boxes to make the statement correct (for example, 10 + 22). Repeat with 24 > □ - □ (for example, 52 - 30).

Differentiation

Less confident learners: These children could investigate □ + □ < 10, and 20 > □ - □.

More confident learners: These children could investigate □ + □ < 134, and 124 > □ - □.

Review

Discuss ideas and solutions and then ask each child to write a statement using a positive number, a negative number and a 'greater than' symbol on their whiteboards (for example, 54 - 20 > 32). Go around the class and ask the children to read out their statements, discussing each one.

Lesson 9 (Practise and apply)

Starter

Reason: Write this list of numbers on the board: -2, 3, -4, 7, -5, 5, -3, 8, -1, 0, 1, 9. Ask questions such as: *Which is the smallest number? Largest number? Which numbers are less than -4? 0? 2? Which numbers are greater than 4.5? Make a statement using two of the numbers and a 'less than' sign.* Finally, order them on the board together.

Main teaching activities

Whole class: Display the number line from the 'Decimal number line' sheet. If possible show this in a different orientation from Lesson 8 (vertical or horizontal). Go through a couple of examples of pointing to a space on the number line (such as 3.4 or 3.04) and asking: *What number would fit here?*

Independent work: Give each child a copy of a 'Decimal bingo' grid. Explain that you will point to numbers between 3 and 4 on the number line. If you point to a number that is shown on the sheet then they must cross it off. They must call out when they have a line or a full house. Call out numbers with one decimal place first, progress to twentieths and then some other two-decimal-place numbers.

Differentiation

Less confident learners: Use the grid from the support version of 'Decimal bingo', which gives the values in ascending order.

More confident learners: Ask more confident children to make their own bingo grid, using decimals between 2 and 3.

Review

Use the numbers on the bingo board and put them on the number line. Ask individual children to help you and to explain their positioning to the rest of the class. Ask: *What does the 3 represent? What does the 4 represent? Can you make a statement using two of the decimals and a 'greater than' sign?*

Lesson 10 (Review, practise and apply)

Starter

Rehearse: Call out various statements about positive and negative numbers and ask the children to stand up if they agree with the statement and sit down if they do not. Start with -3 > 4, 4 > -3, -3 > -2, -2 > 0, and so on.

Main teaching activities

Whole class: Remind the children that a remainder is what is left over after dividing and that remainders are always written as whole numbers. Work through some of the questions on the activity sheet 'Division examples'. Invite the children to write estimates for each answer on the board and ask them to explain the methods used (any reasonable mental method will do, such as halving and halving again).

When you have probed the children's mental methods and agreed the answer to each example, explain that in many practical situations it is necessary to round down or up to get a sensible answer. Read some questions out from the 'Division dilemmas' activity sheet. Discuss rounding up or rounding down for a sensible answer to each one. Ask: *Why should we round down/round up?*

Differentiation

Less confident learners: The 'Division dilemmas' activity could be tackled in mixed-ability pairs. However, a support version has been provided, which includes division facts from the two-, three-, four-, five- and ten-times tables only. The final challenge has also been left out.

More confident learners: Give pairs the extension version of the sheet, which uses more complex examples, including context-based questions involving money and measures.

Agree that rounding down is appropriate when you need to know the number of completed groups and rounding up is appropriate when you need to know the number of all groups, including the final incomplete group.

Paired work: Ask the children to work together to solve the problems on the 'Division dilemmas' sheet. They should estimate their answers first, then discuss methods to solve each problem and decide whether to round up or round down. Finally, they are challenged to write down their own division problems – one that requires rounding up and one that requires rounding down.

Review

Check through the questions. Ask the children to discuss their estimates and methods of working out each answer. Ask: *Which questions did you need to round up/down? Why?* Finish by asking each pair to read one of their own division dilemmas. Review the reasons for rounding up or down again if necessary.

Name ____________________ Date ____________________

Subtraction pairs

Choose one number from each set, and then use them for a subtraction.

Use one of the column methods that your teacher showed you.

Set 1

562	672	634
643	746	823

Set 2

159	215	137
236	161	248

Name ____________________ Date ____________________

Number differences questions

Work out each subtraction with your partner using the column method you have been shown.
Use the grid to help you.

1. 256 – 187 =
2. 363 – 145 =
3. What is the difference between 633 and 274?
4. Decrease 384 by 178.
5. How many less than 482 is 284?

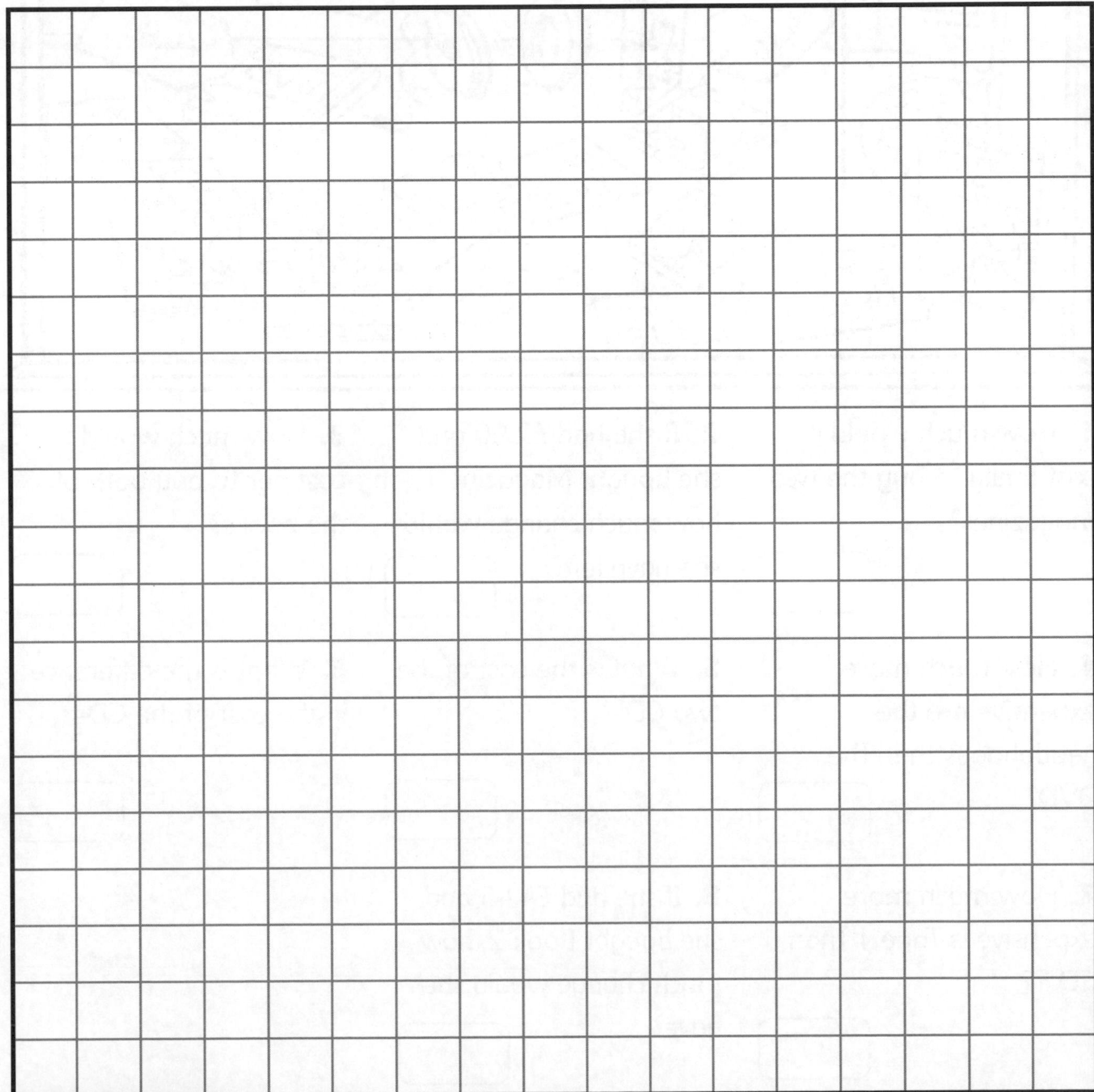

Name ______________________ Date ______________________

Totally different shopping

Emily has been saving up her pocket money and has decided to go shopping. Help her work out how she could spend her money. Set out the questions below on squared paper and work out the answers.

1. How much would it cost Emily to buy the two magazines?

2. If she had £2.90 and she bought Magazine 1, how much change would she have left?

3. How much would it cost her to buy both of the books?

4. How much more expensive are the headphones than the DVD?

5. What is the cost of the two CDs?

6. What is the difference in the cost of the CDs?

7. How much more expensive is Tape 1 than CD 1?

8. If she had £4.45 and she bought Book 2, how much change would she have?

Securing number facts, understanding shape

Key aspects of learning
- Reasoning
- Creative thinking
- Managing feeling
- Social skills

Expected prior learning

Check that children can already:

- recall addition and subtraction facts for each number to 20
- recall multiplication and division facts for the 2, 3, 4, 5, 6 and 10 times-tables
- say a subtraction fact that is the inverse of an addition fact, and a multiplication fact that is the inverse of a division fact, and vice versa
- identify the calculation needed to solve a one-step problem
- name common 2D and 3D shapes, and recognise a 3D shape from a 2D drawing of it
- draw a line of symmetry in a 2D shape
- choose their own criterion for sorting a set of shapes.

Objectives overview

The text in this diagram identifies the focus of mathematics learning within the block.

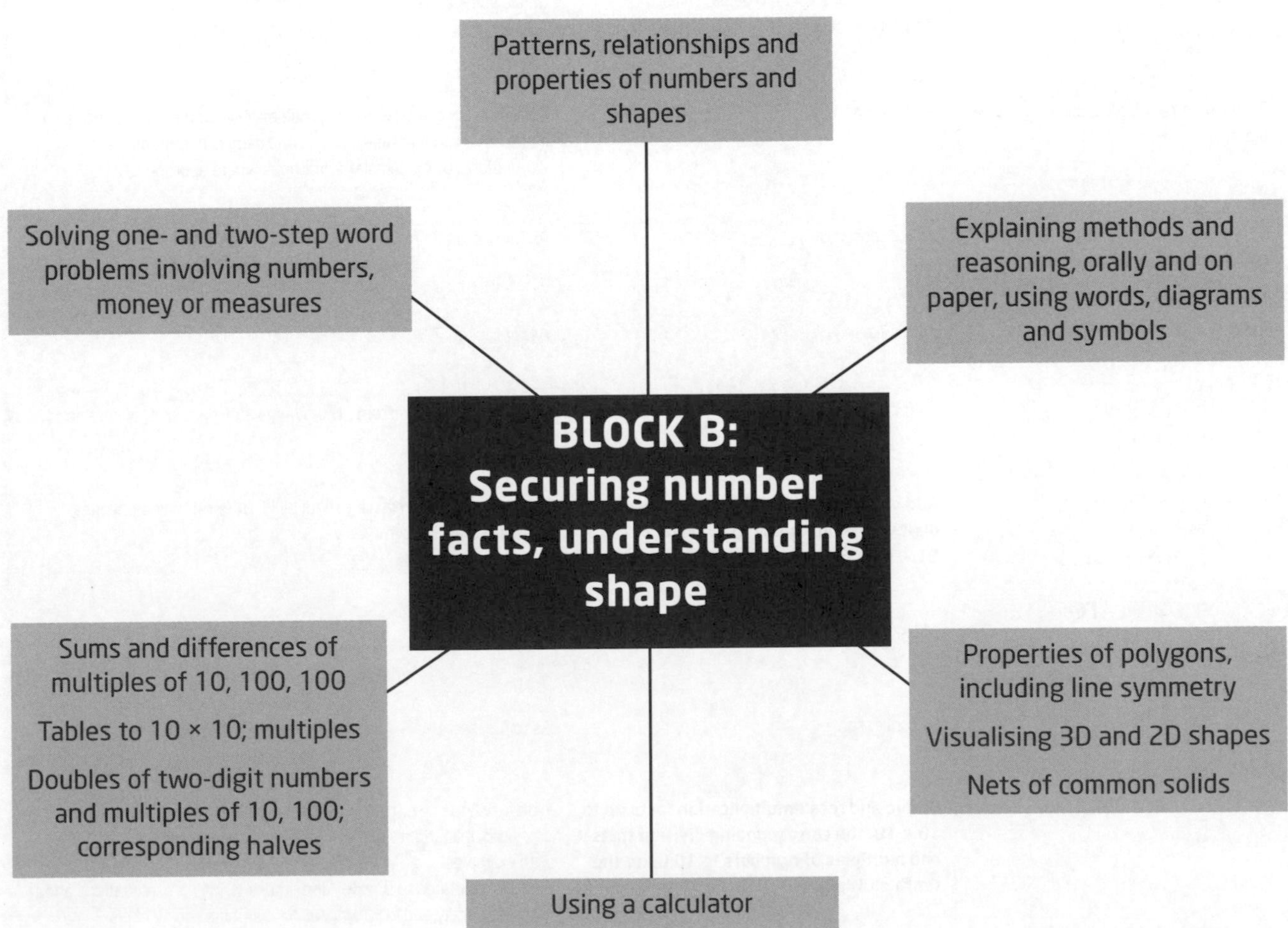

Unit 1 3 weeks

Securing number facts, understanding shape

Lesson	Strands	Starter	Main teaching activities
1. Teach and practise	Knowledge	Use knowledge of rounding, number operations and inverses to estimate and check calculations.	Use knowledge of rounding, number operations and inverses to estimate and check calculations.
2. Teach and practise	Knowledge	**Derive and recall multiplication facts up to 10 × 10, the corresponding division facts and multiples of numbers to 10 up to the tenth multiple.**	**Derive and recall multiplication facts up to 10 × 10, the corresponding division facts and multiples of numbers to 10 up to the tenth multiple.**
3. Teach and practise	Use/apply	Recognise and continue number sequences formed by counting on or back in steps of constant size. (Revision of Block A.)	Identify and use patterns, relationships and properties of numbers or shapes; investigate a statement involving numbers and test it with examples.
4. Teach and practise	Use/apply	As for Lesson 3	As for Lesson 3
5. Review	Use/apply	As for Lesson 3	As for Lesson 3
6. Teach and practise	Knowledge	Use knowledge of addition and subtraction facts and place value to derive sums and differences of pairs of multiples of 10, 100 or 1000.	Use knowledge of addition and subtraction facts and place value to derive sums and differences of pairs of multiples of 10, 100 or 1000.
7. Teach and practise	Use/apply	As for Lesson 6	Solve one-step and two-step problems involving numbers, money or measures, including time; choose and carry out appropriate calculations, using calculator methods where appropriate.
8. Teach and apply	Use/apply	As for Lesson 6	As for Lesson 7
9. Apply and review	Use/apply	As for Lesson 6	As for Lesson 7
10. Teach and apply	Shape	As for Lesson 6	Visualise 3D objects from 2D drawings and make nets of common solids.
11. Teach and practise	Shape	**Add or subtract mentally pairs of two-digit whole numbers (eg 47 + 58, 91 - 35).** (Revision of Block A.)	Draw polygons and classify them by identifying their properties, including their line symmetry.
12. Teach and apply	Shape	As for Lesson 11	As for Lesson 11
13. Review and apply	Shape	As for Lesson 11	As for Lesson 11
14. Review	Use/apply	**Derive and recall multiplication facts up to 10 × 10, the corresponding division facts and multiples of numbers to 10 up to the tenth multiple.**	• Identify and use patterns, relationships and properties of numbers or shapes; investigate a statement involving numbers and test it with examples. • Report solutions to puzzles and problems, giving explanations and reasoning orally and in writing, using diagrams and symbols.
15. Teach, apply and review	Use/apply	As for Lesson 14	As for Lesson 14

Speaking and listening objective

- Identify the main points of each speaker; compare their arguments and how they are presented.

Introduction

In this three-week unit the children estimate and check calculations, continue to recall all multiplication facts to 10 × 10, investigate number patterns and relations, develop their skills in addition and subtraction, and solve word problems. They develop their understanding of the properties of polygons, visualise 3D shapes and draw their nets, and investigate the properties of shapes. Children work in pairs for much of this work, so that they have further opportunities to develop their arguments and to practise ways of presenting them.

Using and applying mathematics

- Solve one-step and two-step problems involving numbers, money or measures, including time; choose and carry out appropriate calculations, using calculator methods where appropriate.
- Identify and use patterns, relationships and properties of numbers or shapes; investigate a statement involving numbers and test it with examples.
- Report solutions to puzzles and problems, giving explanations and reasoning orally and in writing, using diagrams and symbols.

Lessons 1-5

Preparation

Lesson 2: Using the 'Multiplication squares' interactive resource, hide the multipliers in the top row and left-hand column and hide the facts for the seven- to ten-times tables in the last four columns. For main teaching activities, keep the multipliers hidden, and cover all the facts for the two- to six-times tables. If necessary, copy 'Multiplication grid' onto OHT for display.

You will need

Photocopiable pages
'Checking answers' (page 58), 'Multiples' (page 59), 'Counting patterns' (page 60) and 'Odd and even numbers' (page 61).
CD resources
'Multiplication grid'; extension version of 'Checking answers'; core, support and extension versions of 'Multiples', and 'Odd and even numbers'; support, extension and template versions of 'Counting patterns'. General resource sheet: 'Numeral cards'. Interactive resource: 'Multiplication square'.
Equipment
OHP/interactive whiteboard calculator; calculators.

Learning objectives

Starter

- Use knowledge of rounding, number operations and inverses to estimate and check calculations.
- Derive and recall multiplication facts up to 10 × 10, the corresponding division facts and multiples of numbers to 10 up to the tenth multiple.
- Recognise and continue number sequences formed by counting on or back in steps of constant size. (Revision of Block A.)

Main teaching activities

2006

- Use knowledge of rounding, number operations and inverses to estimate and check calculations.
- Derive and recall multiplication facts up to 10 × 10, the corresponding division facts and multiples of numbers to 10 up to the tenth multiple.
- Identify and use patterns, relationships and properties of numbers or shapes; investigate a statement involving numbers and test it with examples.

1999

- Derive quickly all pairs of multiples of 50 with a total of 1000 (eg 850 + 150).
- Add three two-digit multiples of 10, such as 40 + 70 + 50.
- Use known number facts and place value to add or subtract mentally.
- Use known number facts and place value for mental addition and subtraction (eg 470 + 380, 810 - 380).
- Know by heart all multiplication facts up to 10 x 10; derive quickly corresponding division facts.
- Recognise multiples of 6, 7, 8, 9, up to the tenth multiple.
- Recognise multiples of 2, 3, 4, 5 and 10, up to the tenth multiple.
- Solve mathematical problems or puzzles, recognise and explain patterns and relationships, generalise and predict. Suggest extensions by asking 'What if...?'
- Recognise and extend number sequences.
- Make and investigate a general statement about familiar number or shapes by finding examples that satisfy it.

Vocabulary

problem, solution, calculator, calculate, calculation, equation, operation, inverse, answer, method, explain, predict, reason, reasoning, pattern, relationship, rule, sequence, sort, classify, property, add, subtract, multiply, divide, total, difference, plus, minus, product, quotient, remainder, double, halve, factor, multiple, divisor, round

Lesson 1 (Teach and practise)

Starter

Review: Explain that you will say a number and the children must to round it to the nearest 10. Say, for example, *56, 41, 193, 204, 397* ... Invite the children to explain how they made their decisions for the rounding.

Main teaching activities

Whole class: Write on the board 39 + 38 and the numbers 10, 50, 80, 100, 130 and ask: *Which number is about the same as the right answer to the addition? How did you work this out?* Discuss how 39 + 38 is approximately 40 + 40 and that 80 is a good estimate for the answer. Repeat this for other examples, such as 47 + 49, 52 + 47...

Write up 78 + 84 and ask the children to give an estimate of the answer. Ask: *How did you work this out?* One way is: 80 + 80 = 160, rounding the units digit to the nearest 10. Repeat for other examples, such as 96 + 47 and 38 + 91... Ask: *How can we check our answers?* Agree that for addition it can be checked by adding in a different order, or by subtraction. Choose one of the examples on the board and ask the children to do a check calculation.

Paired work: Provide each pair with two sets of 0–10 numeral cards. Ask the children to take turns to take four cards and to make two two-digit numbers from these. They both write down the two numbers as an addition, then write an estimate of the answer using rounding, then write the correct answer. They must also write a check calculation. They record this on the 'Checking answers' activity sheet.

Differentiation

Less confident learners: Decide whether to provide smaller two-digit numbers for the children to work with, such as 34, 29, 17 and so on.

More confident learners: Provide the extension version of the activity sheet, in which children have to find the difference between the two numbers, as well as adding them. Challenge the children to make a three-digit and a two-digit number and to carry out the same procedure with these.

Review

Invite pairs of children from each ability group to present to the rest of the class one of their pairs of numbers. Challenge the children to quickly write an estimate, an answer and a check calculation. Discuss these and ask questions such as: *Did you write this estimate? How did you work it out? Who used a different check calculation?*

Now write on the board: 64 + 22. Ask the children to decide which of these numbers is about the same as the right answer: 50, 80, 90, 120. Ask: *How did you work this out? How did you round these numbers? What is the correct answer?*

Lesson 2 (Teach and practise)

Starter

Recall: Explain that you would like the children to practise their table facts for the two- to six-times tables. Use the 'Multiplication square' interactive resource and reveal the multiplication facts for the 2 to 6 times-tables, with the multipliers covered. (Alternatively, use the activity sheet 'Multiplication grid' as an OHT.) Point to a fact and ask: *What multiplication is this? Now give me a division fact which uses this number.* For example, point to 28 and the fact could be 7 × 4 = 28 and the division 28 ÷ 4 = 7. Repeat for other facts.

Main teaching activities

Whole class: Continuing with the 'Multiplication square', reveal the table facts for the seven- to ten-times tables. Point to 45 and ask: *What table facts can you tell me?* Write these on the board as the children identify them: 5 × 9 = 45; 9 × 5 = 45; 45 ÷ 5 = 9; 45 ÷ 9 = 5. Repeat for other facts. Discuss how if you know one fact then the others can be found.

Ask: *How can you tell if a number is a multiple of 5?* Agree that it will have a 5 or 0 in the digits. Write on the board the numbers 2, 5, 8, 3. Invite the children to use each digit once to make a two-digit number plus two-digit total which is a multiple of 5: 52 + 38 = 90; 58 + 32 = 90. Repeat using 1, 6, 4, 9. Ask: *How did you work this out?* (Make sure the units digits add up to a number ending in 0 or 5, such as 14 + 96, or 64 + 91.)

Paired work: Provide copies of the activity sheet 'Multiples'. Ask the children to complete the sheet individually, then to discuss their answers with a partner and check each other's work.

Differentiation

Less confident learners: There is a support version of the sheet, which covers tables two to six.

More confident learners: There is an extension version of the sheet, which covers all the multiplication tables up to ten.

Review

Discuss how the children found their answers. Praise those who 'knew' the answers. Some children may 'say' the relevant table in order to find the fact. Praise this, as it is a good beginning strategy; however, encourage these children to learn the facts so that they can develop good recall. Ask: *If someone has forgotten the eight-times table, what tips would you give to help them to work this out?*

Lesson 3 (Teach and practise)

Starter

Recall: Split the class into four groups. Give the children a start number such as 345. Each group takes a turn to count up in tens from that number. The groups keep going until you say *Back*, when the children should start counting back in tens. Keep the pace of this sharp, and change from group to group for continuing the count to keep everyone on their toes!

Main teaching activities

Whole class: Use the OHP or whiteboard calculator to add on in twos. (Usually, 2 + + = will generate the required pattern.) Ask the children to shout out what the next number will be before you press the equals key. Ask questions such as:

- *How did you work out what the next number would be?*
- *If we keep going, will 409 come up on the calculator? Why?* (No. It's an odd number and this is an even number pattern.)

Repeat this for counting back (inputting 2 - - =), and again for other generated patterns such as counting in fives, starting on 3, 4... Then repeat for larger increments, such as counting in 20s, then 25s. Ask questions such as:

- *Are we going to get to zero? What will happen then?*
- *Will we get to -78? How do you know that?*

Group work: The children work in pairs with one calculator between each pair. They take turns to think of a number in which they want to count, and input it to the calculator. One child has to predict the next number and the other has to check with the calculator. They can record their sequence of numbers on a sheet of paper. They then choose a different number and repeat the process.

Differentiation

Less confident learners: Suggest to the children that they begin with one-digit numbers.

More confident learners: Challenge the children to produce more complex and challenging sequences.

Review

Invite children from each ability group to say the beginning of one of their sequences of numbers. Ask the other children to say what the counting on number was. Keep the pace of this sharp. Ask:

- *How did you work out the counting on number?*
- *What if we started the sequence on...? What would the next number be?*

Lesson 4 (Teach and practise)

Starter

Recall: Repeat the Starter from Lesson 3, this time extending the counting to include counting on and back in hundreds.

Main teaching activities

Provide further opportunities for extending counting patterns, such as counting in 20s, 30s, and so on. On the board, write '36, 45, 54, 63' and ask: *What is the pattern? How did you work it out?* Repeat this for other examples, where the increase or decrease is a one-digit number.

Provide copies of the activity sheet 'Counting patterns' and ask the children to complete these individually. There are differentiated versions of this sheet for more confident and less confident children.

Review

Write questions from each of the sheets in turn on the board for all the children to think about the answers. Ensure that children from your less confident group have an opportunity to respond about their work.

Lesson 5 (Review)

Starter

Recall: Split the class into four groups and give them a start number such as 275. Each group takes a turn to count up and back in thousands.

Main teaching activities

Whole class: Explain to the children that today's lesson is about odd and even numbers. Ask: *What is an odd number? What is an even number? How can you tell whether any number is odd or even?* (Even numbers can be halved or divided by two to give a whole number.) Encourage the children to explain that any odd number has 1, 3, 5, 7 or 9 in its units, and any even number has 0, 2, 4, 6 or 8 in its units. Write a three-digit even number on the board, such as '246', and ask questions such as:

- *Is this number odd or even?*
- *Who can tell me a three-digit odd number?*

Repeat this for other numbers.

Group work: Give the children copies of the activity sheet 'Odd and even numbers'. There is a practical sorting activity of three-digit numbers into odd and even, and a challenge to complete.

Differentiation

Less confident learners: Decide whether to use the support version of the activity sheet, which has two-digit numbers to sort.

More confident learners: Decide whether to use the extension version of the activity sheet, which has four-digit numbers to sort.

Review

Write 'Odd' and 'Even' in two boxes on the board and invite children from each group to write an appropriate number in each box. Ask them to explain why their number is odd or even. Review the three questions at the end of the activity sheets. Invite children to explain their thinking and to read out the sentences they wrote. Ask the children questions such as:

- *How do you know if a number is odd or even?*
- *What happens when we add two even numbers? Why is that?*

Lessons 6-10

You will need
CD resources
Core, support and extension versions of 'Equations'; core, support, extension and template versions of 'Number equations'; core version of '1 to 20'. Interactive resource: 'Number sentence builder'.
Equipment
OHP/interactive whiteboard calculator; calculators; 2cm squared paper; rulers; scissors.

Learning objectives

Starter
- Use knowledge of addition and subtraction facts and place value to derive sums and differences of pairs of multiples of 10, 100 or 1000.

Main teaching activities
2006
- Use knowledge of addition and subtraction facts and place value to derive sums and differences of pairs of multiples of 10, 100 or 1000.
- Solve one-step and two-step problems involving numbers, money or measures, including time; choose and carry out appropriate calculations, using calculator methods where appropriate.
- Visualise 3D objects from 2D drawings and make nets of common solids.

1999
- Derive quickly all pairs of multiples of 50 with a total of 1000 (eg 850 + 150).
- Add three two-digit multiples of 10, such as 40 + 70 + 50.
- Use known number facts and place value to add or subtract mentally.
- Use known number facts and place value for mental addition and subtraction (eg 470 + 380, 810 - 380).
- Use all four operations to solve word problems involving numbers in 'real life', money and measures (including time), using one or more steps, including converting pounds to pence and metres to centimetres and vice versa.
- Choose and use appropriate number operations and appropriate ways of calculating (mental, mental with jottings, pencil and paper) to solve problems.
- Round up or down after division, depending on the context.
- Choose appropriate ways of calculating: calculator.

Vocabulary
problem, solution, calculator, calculate, calculation, equation, operation, inverse, answer, method, explain, predict, reason, reasoning, pattern, relationship, rule, sequence, sort, classify, property, add, subtract, multiply, divide, total, difference, plus, minus, product, quotient, remainder, double, halve, factor, multiple, divisor, round

Lesson 6 (Teach and practise)

Starter
Recall: Explain that you will say a number between 0 and 20. Ask the children to write the complement to 20 onto their whiteboards. When you say *Show me* the children hold up their boards. Keep the pace sharp.

Main teaching activities
Whole class: Display the 'Number sentence builder' interactive resource. Explain that you will make equations. Put up 2 + 8 = and agree the answer is 10. Now put up 20 + 80 = directly underneath the previous number sentence and ask for the answer. Repeat for 200 + 800 and 2000 + 8000. Ask: *What do you notice about these equations?* Agree that the numbers in each equation are a multiple of 10 more than in the previous equation and that by knowing 2 + 8 the other answers can be derived. Repeat this for subtraction, such as 8 - 5 = 3; 80 - 50 = 30, and so on.

Now ask: *What could the two missing numbers be in this equation?* Display: ○ - □ = 4. Agree that the best way to help you to find a range of answers is to order them: 14 - 10 = 4; 13 - 9 = 4... Repeat for ○ + □ = 17. Write up 16 - 9 and ask: *What other pairs of numbers have a difference of 7?*
Paired work: Provide the activity sheet 'Equations'. Ask the children to order

BLOCK B
Securing number facts, understanding shape

their answers to help them to check that they have not missed any solutions.

Review

Ask the children to find one of their answers from their sheet. Say: *Think of another way to do this equation. Do you get the same answer? Is there another way to work it out? Which is the best way to do this? Why do you think that?* Now ask pairs of children to compare how they calculated with another pair. Ask: *Did you use the same method? Which method was better? Why do you think that?*

Differentiation

Less confident learners: Provide the support version of 'Equations', which asks for fewer answers.

More confident learners: Provide the extension version of the activity sheet, which includes far more options for answers.

Lesson 7 (Teach and practise)

Starter

Recall: Explain that you will input a two-digit number into the OHP/ interactive whiteboard calculator. Ask the children to decide what number must be added to the number on the calculator to make a total of 100. Ask the children to put up their hands to give an answer, and then input their number. Check by showing the total. Keep the pace of this sharp. Use numbers such as 20, 35, 49, 21, 37.

Main teaching activities

Whole class: Explain that the focus of this unit of work is on solving problems. Using the 'Number sentence builder' interactive resource, input '18 □ 22 = 40' and ask: *What operation is this number sentence?* Check that the children understand that the symbol □ in the number sentence, or 'equation', stands for an operation. Ask: *How did you work out that it is an add number sentence?* Repeat this for other operations: subtraction (such as 71 □ 28 = 43), multiplication (such as 70 □ 6 = 420) and division (such as 32 □ 2 = 16).

Group work: Give out copies of the activity sheet 'Number equations' and ask the children to work individually to find which operation signs are needed. There is space on the sheet for the children to invent their own missing symbol questions to give to a partner.

Review

Invite children from each group to set one of their own number sentences for the others to try. Keep the pace of this sharp. Ask questions such as:

- *How did you decide which operation it was?*
- *Who worked this out another way?*

Some children may by now be able to look at an equation and, without working it out, recognise which operation is needed by the size of the numbers. Praise those who can do this.

Differentiation

Less confident learners: Decide whether to use the support version of the activity sheet, which uses simpler number equations.

More confident learners: Decide whether to use the extension version of the activity sheet, which uses harder number equations.

Lesson 8 (Teach and apply)

Starter

Recall: Explain that you have subtracted a two-digit number from 100 and have the answer. The children are to work out what number was subtracted. They can respond by writing a subtraction sentence on their whiteboards and holding these up when you say *Show me*. Keep the pace sharp. Say numbers such as 63, 57, 12.

Main teaching activities

Whole class: Write a number sentence on the board, for example: '81 □ 6 = 486'. Ask: *What is the missing sign? How do you know that?* Ask the children to check with an equivalent calculation to be sure that they have the correct sign. For example: 81 × 6 = 480 + 6 = 486.

Group work: Ask the children to work in pairs using the activity sheet '1 to 20'. This asks them to find a way to make all the numbers from 1 to 20 using the numbers 1, 2, 3 and 4 and the operations +, –, × or ÷ (or a combination of these). The children should write equivalent calculations to check their answers each time. Provide calculators and make it clear that the children should work mentally before trying out their equation with the calculator. Where a negative answer occurs on the calculator, discuss how this has occurred.

Differentiation

Less confident learners: Decide whether to ask these children to work as a group. Work together to solve this problem.
More confident learners: Challenge these children to find different ways of making each number.

Review

Invite children from each group to give examples of how 1, 2, 3... 20 can be made. Write these on the board. Ask questions such as: *What strategies did you use? How did you decide which operation/s to use? What equivalent calculation did you use to check?*

Lesson 9 (Apply and review)

Starter

Recall: Use a combination of questions from the starters for Lessons 8 and 9, asking the children to record their answers on their whiteboards. Keep the pace sharp.

Main teaching activities

Whole class: Write '80 × 4 = 320' on the board, and ask: *What number story might this represent?* Invite the children to suggest possible number stories. Repeat this for 81 ÷ 3 = 27.
Group work: Ask the children to work in pairs. On the board, write three each of addition, subtraction, multiplication and division questions for the children to solve. Remind them to approximate first, then to find the answer. Ask them to invent a number story for each question.

Differentiation

Less confident learners: Decide whether to work with these children in a larger group to help them solve the problems.
More confident learners: Ask these children to come up with some entertaining number stories!

Review

Review how the children solved the questions and ask for examples of a number story from some of the pairs. Ask: *How did you approximate the answer first? How did you find the answer? What checking strategies did you use? What are the important things to remember when solving a word problem?*

Lesson 10 (Teach and apply)

Starter

Recall: Repeat the Starter from Lesson 6. Keep the pace sharp so that children are using fast recall.

Main teaching activities

Whole class: Explain that in this lesson the children will be exploring the nets of regular shapes. Provide each child with some squared paper and hold up a cube. Ask the children to describe the properties of a cube and write the list on the board. For example: each face is square shaped; there are six faces...
Paired work: Explain that cubes can be made from a 2D drawing which is cut out and folded up. This is called a net. Encourage the children to work in pairs and to draw a shape that will fold up to make a cube. Suggest that they use one square on the paper to represent one face. Give the children a few minutes to do this and ask them to cut out and fold up their net.
Whole class: Compare the results. On the board draw the range of nets which will make cubes, as the children demonstrate from their nets.
Paired work: Ask the children to work in pairs to draw, then cut out and make up all the nets they can find to make an open cube.

Review

Collate the nets that the children found by drawing these on the board. Now draw a T shape like this:

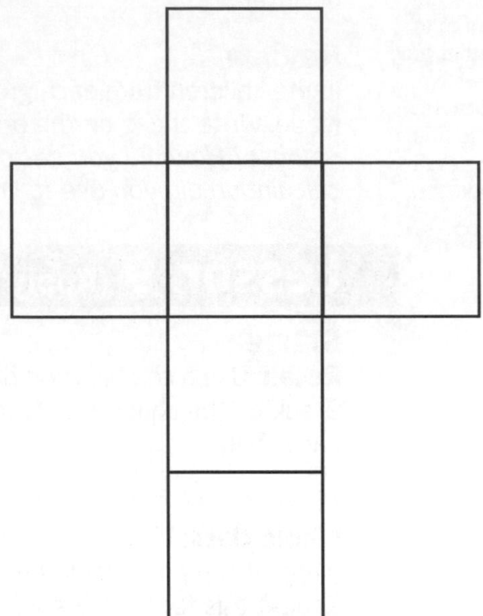

Ask the children to explain how they would turn this into a cube. Ask: *Where would you fold it? If this square was at the bottom of the cube, which square would be at the top?* Ask them to count how many sides there are (ie six squares).

Now say: *I am thinking of a 3D shape. It has a square base. It has four faces which are triangles. What is the name of this shape?* Sketch the shape. Sketch its net.

Differentiation

Less confident learners: Decide whether to work as a group and compare the nets drawn and folded each time.
More confident learners: Challenge the children to draw their nets on plain paper, measuring carefully each time to ensure that the sides of the cube are regular and equal.

Lessons 11-15

Preparation

Lesson 12: If necessary, copy the '2D shapes - polygons' resource sheet onto OHT.

You will need

CD resources

General resource sheets: '2D shapes - polygons' and 'Carroll diagrams'.

Learning objectives

Starter

- Add or subtract mentally pairs of two-digit whole numbers (eg 47 + 58, 91 - 35). (Revision of Block A.)
- Derive and recall multiplication facts up to 10 × 10, the corresponding division facts and multiples of numbers to 10 up to the tenth multiple.

Main teaching activities

2006

- Identify and use patterns, relationships and properties of numbers or shapes; investigate a statement involving numbers and test it with examples.
- Report solutions to puzzles and problems, giving explanations and reasoning orally and in writing, using diagrams and symbols.
- Draw polygons and classify them by identifying their properties, including their line symmetry.

1999

- Classify polygons, using criteria such as number of right angles, whether or not they are regular, symmetry properties.
- Make shapes, eg construct polygons by paper folding or using pinboard, and discuss properties such as lines of symmetry.
- Solve mathematical problems or puzzles, recognise and explain patterns and relationships, generalise and predict. Suggest extensions by asking 'What if...?'
- Recognise and extend number sequences.

- Make and investigate a general statement about familiar numbers or shapes by finding examples that satisfy it.

Vocabulary

problem, solution, explain, predict, reason, reasoning, pattern, relationship, rule, sequence, sort, classify, property, 3D, three-dimensional, 2D, two-dimensional, net, construct, regular, irregular, concave, convex, symmetrical, line of symmetry, vertex, vertices, face, edge, polygon, equilateral triangle, isosceles, triangle, quadrilateral, rectangle, square, oblong, hexagon, heptagon, octagon

Lesson 11 (Teach and practise)

Starter

Recall: Ask the children quick-fire questions such as: 23 + 46 (69); 62 + 13 (75); 56 + 12 (68); 45 + 21 (66); 12 + 32 (44); 89 - 71 (18); 57 - 23 (34); 38 - 17 (21); 67 - 43 (24); 87 - 56 (31). The children can respond with their whiteboards. Ask: *How did you work that out? Who used a different strategy?* Refer back to the ideas explored previously.

Main teaching activities

Whole class: On the board, draw a regular shape with seven sides and write 'heptagon' alongside it. Explain to the children that any seven-sided 2D shape is called a heptagon. Invite the children to use their whiteboards and draw a heptagon. When you say *Show me*, they should hold up their boards for you to see.

Now write the words 'polygon' and 'oblong' on the board and explain that a polygon is any closed and flat shape with three or more sides, and an oblong is another name that is sometimes used for a rectangle. Ask the children to draw any polygon on their boards, and to write its mathematical name underneath it, then hold up their boards when you say *Show me* again. Now say: *I will describe a shape. If that shape is on your board, hold it up.* Take into account the shapes that the children have drawn and describe some of them. For example: *Hold up your board if you have drawn a shape with more than four sides; a shape that has four right angles...*

Group work: Ask the children to work in groups of four. They take turns to give instructions to the others in their group for a shape for them to draw on their whiteboard. Encourage the children to say more than the name of the shape, instead describing the properties of the shape.

Differentiation

Less confident learners: Work with this group. Begin by giving descriptions for the children to draw. As they become more confident, the children can take turns to describe a shape.

More confident learners: When the children have tried this activity a few times in their groups, suggest that they write some descriptions for the others to try during the Review.

Review

Invite some of the more confident children to read out their descriptions for the others to draw. The children can hold up their boards to show you their responses. Ask questions such as:

- *What shape do you think was described?*
- *What other shapes could fit that description?*

Lesson 12 (Teach and apply)

Starter

Recall: Repeat the Starter from Lesson 11. Encourage the children to compare their mental methods in groups of four, so that they hear various ways of calculating mentally.

Main teaching activities

Whole class: Display the '2D shapes - polygons' general resource sheet, and ask the children to look carefully and name each of the shapes. Now discuss the fact that some of the shapes are regular (that is, all of their sides are the same length) and some are irregular. Invite the children to decide which of the shapes on the OHT are regular and which are irregular. Now point to the equilateral triangle, name it and explain that all the sides are equal and all the angles are the same size. Then point to the isosceles triangle and ask the children to decide what is special about this triangle. (Two sides the same length, and the two angles formed by those sides and the base are the same.) Ask: *How can you tell if a shape has a line of symmetry?*

Tell the children that they are going to sort the shapes according to certain criteria. Ask them to suggest some criteria to you and then write them on the board (number of sides; number of angles; regular/irregular; number of lines of symmetry; number of right angles). Ensure the criteria are mathematical and based on properties of shape. Spend some time with the class defining what we mean by each criterion.

	triangles	quadrilaterals
regular		
irregular		

Now draw a Carroll diagram on the board. Explain to the children that they can use a diagram like this to sort their shapes.

Group work: Explain that the activity for this lesson and the next is to sort all the shapes on '2D shapes – polygons' by any criteria they like from the list on the board. After each sort they draw the shapes on their copies of the resource sheet 'Carroll diagrams' and label the diagrams appropriately.

Differentiation

Less confident learners: Adapt the activity by suggesting that the children begin with the criteria of 'triangles' and 'not triangles'; 'regular' and 'irregular'. When the children are confident with this, suggest that they use their own criteria.

More confident learners: Encourage the more confident children to cover as many different sorting criteria as possible in the time available.

Review

Ask the children to explain their shape sorts. Ensure that they are using correct mathematical vocabulary for the names of the shapes and their properties, including line symmetry. Ask questions such as:

- *How many sides has a pentagon? ... hexagon? ... heptagon?*
- *What is a quadrilateral?*
- *Tell me some regular polygons.*
- *Is an isosceles triangle a regular or an irregular polygon? Why is that?*
- *Which shapes have line symmetry? How can you tell?*

Lesson 13 (Review and apply)

Starter

Repeat the Starter from Lesson 11, this time encouraging the children to explain to their partner how they find the answer. This will give the children ideas about other strategies that they might use.

Main teaching activities

Review the names and properties of the shapes from activity sheet '2D shapes – polygons', then ask the children to continue with the sorting activity from Lesson 12. Towards the end of the work time, prepare to talk about favourite sorts of polygons.

Review

Ask children from each group to describe their favourite sort. Then invite the children to describe shapes by asking questions such as: *What is a polygon? What is a vertex?* (A corner.) *Tell me a polygon with three vertices... four vertices.*

Lesson 14 (Review)

Starter

Recall: Ask the children to write the answers to some table fact questions on their whiteboards, and to show you. Ask, for example: *What is 3 × 5; 10 × 4; 35 ÷ 5; 8 × 2; 90 ÷ 10?* Include some word problems such as: *If I share 36 sweets among nine children, how many will they have each?*

Main teaching activities

Whole class: Explain to the children that you will describe a shape. Ask them to shut their eyes, listen carefully to the description and then, when they know what the shape is, put their hands up. Say, for example: *I am thinking of a flat shape. It has seven sides.* (A heptagon.) Or: *I am thinking of a shape with four sides. The sides are not all the same length. The angles are not all right angles. There is no line symmetry.* (An irregular quadrilateral.) Repeat this for other shapes.
Paired work: Ask the children to take turns to make a statement about a shape for their partner to draw.

Differentiation

Less confident learners: Suggest to the children that they begin with easier shapes to describe, such as squares, rectangles or triangles.
More confident learners: Encourage the children to think of more complex shapes and to describe these.

Review

Invite a child from each group, in turn, to describe a shape for the others to draw. Ask questions:

- *What shape is it?*
- *What sentence told you which shape it was?*

Now draw a concave quadrilateral (such as an arrowhead) on the board. Invite the children to take turns to describe this shape. Then ask: *Who can say a sentence that will describe all quadrilaterals?*

Lesson 15 (Teach, apply and review)

Starter

Repeat the Starter from Lesson 14, asking different table fact questions.

Main teaching activities

Whole class: Describe a quadrilateral by saying: *It has four sides, but none of the sides are the same length. What could this shape be?* Encourage the children to draw what they think the shape is and to name it.
Group work: Ask the children to work in pairs and to think of some statements they could make about a 2D shape. You may want to put the children into groups for this, with particular shapes from resource sheet '2D shapes – polygons' assigned to each group.

Review

Invite the children to take turns to read out their descriptions. The other children draw and write the name of the shape they think is being described on their whiteboards. They hold up their whiteboards for checking. Ask: *Was that a good description of a...? Why was that? How could we make the description even better?*

Name ____________________ Date ____________________

Checking answers

You will need two sets of 0–9 cards and a calculator.

Shuffle the cards and take turns to choose four cards each. Make 2 two-digit numbers from your cards and write them down.

Write an addition using the numbers.
Then write an estimate of the answer.
Work out and write down the correct answer and then write a check calculation.

Addition	Estimate	Answer	Check calculation

Now compare your results with your partner.
Discuss how you carried out your calculations.

Name ______________________ Date ______________________

Multiples

Here are some multiples from the six to nine multiplication tables.
For each multiple write two multiplication sentences and two division sentences.

Multiple	Multiplication sentences	Division sentences
30		
54		
72		
63		
48		
56		
42		
35		
90		
40		

Challenge
What is special about this multiple from the six times–table?

36

Write some number sentences to show what is special. ______________________

Name ______________________ Date ______________

Counting patterns

Write in the missing numbers, then write the rule underneath.

1. | 15 | 21 | | | | 45 |

____

2. | | | | 11 | 7 | 3 |

____

3. | | 75 | 78 | 81 | | |

____

4. | 91 | 87 | | | | 71 |

____

Write some counting patterns of your own. Write the rule underneath.

5. | | | | | | |

The rule is ______________________

6. | | | | | | |

The rule is ______________________

7. | | | | | | |

The rule is ______________________

8. | | | | | | |

The rule is ______________________

On the back of this sheet:

9. Write a pattern for the rule 'Start on 13 and increase by 5 each time'.

10. Write a pattern for the rule 'Start on 84 and decrease by 6 each time'.

Name ______________________ Date ______________________

Odd and even numbers

Work with a partner.

You will need a set of 0–9 numeral cards. Take turns to choose three cards and make a three-digit number. Ask your partner to say whether the number is odd or even. Write the number into the odd or even box. Do this 20 times.

Odd	
______	______
______	______
______	______
______	______
______	______
______	______
______	______
______	______
______	______
______	______

Even	
______	______
______	______
______	______
______	______
______	______
______	______
______	______
______	______
______	______
______	______

If you add two odd numbers the answer is always even.
Is this true or false?

Explain your thinking to each other and write your answer here.

Unit 2 3 weeks

Securing number facts, understanding shape

Lesson	Strands	Starter	Main teaching activities
1. Review and teach	Use/apply	**Derive and recall multiplication facts up to 10 × 10, the corresponding division facts and multiples of numbers to 10 up to the tenth multiple.**	• Identify and use patterns, relationships and properties of numbers or shapes; investigate a statement involving numbers and test it with examples. • Report solutions to puzzles and problems, giving explanations and reasoning orally and in writing, using diagrams and symbols.
2. Review	Use/apply	Identify and use patterns, relationships and properties of numbers or shapes; investigate a statement involving numbers and test it with examples.	As for Lesson 1
3. Review	Use/apply	As for Lesson 1	As for Lesson 1
4. Practise	Use/apply	Identify the doubles of two-digit numbers; use to calculate doubles of multiples of 10 and 100 and derive the corresponding halves.	As for Lesson 1
5. Teach, practise and apply	Use/apply	As for Lesson 4	As for Lesson 1
6. Review and apply	Knowledge	Use knowledge of rounding, number operations and inverses to estimate and check calculations.	Use knowledge of rounding, number operations and inverses to estimate and check calculations.
7. Review, practise and apply	Knowledge Use/apply	As for Lesson 6	• Use knowledge of rounding, number operations and inverses to estimate and check calculations. • Report solutions to puzzles and problems, giving explanations and reasoning orally and in writing, using diagrams and symbols.
8. Teach	Knowledge	**Derive and recall multiplication facts up to 10 × 10, the corresponding division facts and multiples of numbers to 10 up to the tenth multiple.**	• Identify the doubles of two-digit numbers; use these to calculate doubles of multiples of 10 and 100 and derive the corresponding halves. **• Derive and recall multiplication facts up to 10 × 10, the corresponding division facts and multiples of numbers to 10 up to the tenth multiple.**
9. Review and teach	Knowledge	As for Lesson 8	As for Lesson 8
10. Review and teach	Knowledge	Identify the doubles of two-digit numbers; use these to calculate doubles of multiples of 10 and 100 and derive the corresponding halves.	As for Lesson 8
11. Teach, practise and apply	Shape	Draw polygons and classify them by identifying their properties, including their line symmetry.	Draw polygons and classify them by identifying their properties, including their line symmetry.
12. Teach	Shape	As for Lesson 11	As for Lesson 11
13. Review, teach, practise and apply	Shape	As for Lesson 11	As for Lesson 11
14. Teach	Shape	As for Lesson 11	Visualise 3D objects from 2D drawings and make nets of common solids.
15. Teach, apply and review	Shape	As for Lesson 11	As for Lesson 14

Introduction

In this three-week unit the children find patterns, relationships and properties of numbers and shapes, explaining methods and reasoning, orally and on paper, using words, diagrams and symbols. They explore using a calculator and continue to find sums and differences of multiples of 10, 100 and 1000, using tables to 10 × 10. They investigate doubles of two-digit numbers and multiples of 10 and 100, and their corresponding halves. Children develop their knowledge of properties of polygons, including line symmetry, visualising 3D and 2D shapes, and finding nets of common solids.

Using and applying mathematics

- Identify and use patterns, relationships and properties of numbers or shapes; investigate a statement involving numbers and test it with examples.
- Report solutions to puzzles and problems, giving explanations and reasoning orally and in writing, using diagrams and symbols.

Speaking and listening objective

- Investigate how talk varies with age, familiarity and purpose.

Lessons 1-5

Preparation

Lesson 4: Copy '3 × 3 grids' onto OHT for display.

You will need

Photocopiable pages
'Number rules' (page 75).
CD resources
Support, extension and template versions of 'Number rules' and 'Investigating statements'; core version of '3 × 3 grids'; support version of 'Pencil squares'.
Interactive resource: 'Number sentence builder'.
Equipment
Interactive whiteboard; straws, coloured pencils or headless matches, enough for 12 per child; Blu-Tack; strips of coloured paper.

Learning objectives

Starter

- Derive and recall multiplication facts up to 10 × 10, the corresponding division facts and multiples of numbers to 10 up to the tenth multiple.
- Identify and use patterns, relationships and properties of numbers or shapes; investigate a statement involving numbers and test it with examples.
- Identify the doubles of two-digit numbers; use to calculate doubles of multiples of 10 and 100 and derive the corresponding halves.

Main teaching activities

2006

- Identify and use patterns, relationships and properties of numbers or shapes; investigate a statement involving numbers and test it with examples.
- Report solutions to puzzles and problems, giving explanations and reasoning orally and in writing, using diagrams and symbols.

1999

- Solve mathematical problems or puzzles, recognise and explain patterns and relationships, generalise and predict. Suggest extensions by asking 'What if...?'
- Recognise and extend number sequences.
- Make and investigate a general statement about familiar numbers that satisfy it.
- Explain methods and reasoning about numbers orally and in writing.

Vocabulary

explain, predict, reason, reasoning, pattern, relationship, rule, sequence, sort, classify, property, square, consecutive, multiple, add, subtract, multiply, divide, sum, total, difference, plus, minus, product, quotient

Lesson 1 (Review and teach)

Starter

Recall: Call out numbers from the six-, seven-, eight- and nine-times tables. If the number is in the six-times table, the children should put their hands on their heads. If it is in the seven-times table, they put up one hand. If it is in the eight-times table, they put their hands in the air and if it is in the nine-times table they hold their hands up in front of them. Call out several numbers. This can be played as a game of elimination, with the last person with the correct answer standing to one side.

Main teaching activities

Whole class: Use the 'Number sentence builder' interactive resource. (Alternatively write the digits 1, 2, 3 and 4 and the four operations symbols +, –, × and ÷ on the board.) Tell the children that it is possible to make 6 by using each of the digits 1, 2, 3 and 4 once, and any operation. Show the example 6 = (4 + 3) - (2 - 1). Ask if the children can think of other ways to do this. Prompt for different methods, for example 6 = (21 + 3) ÷ 4. Explain that the calculations in the brackets are always done first.

Paired work: In pairs, challenge the children to use the digits 1, 2, 3, 4 and 5 and any of the four operations to make each number from 21 to 30. For example:

21 = (5 × 4) + 1; 22 = (5 × 4) + 2; 23 = (5 × 4) + 3; 24 = (5 × 4) + 3 + 1;
25 = 5 × (4 + 1); 26 = 5 × (4 + 1) + (3 - 2); 27 = 3 × (5 + 2);
28 = (4 + 3) × (5 - 1); 29 = (5 × (3 x 2)) - 1; 30 = 5 × 3 × 2.

Differentiation

Less confident learners: If necessary, provide adult support to model some of the number statements and to consolidate understanding of the use of the brackets.

More confident learners: Challenge the children to go further (eg to 50). Ask: *How far can you go? Can you make all multiples of 10 to 100?*

Review

Ask: *Were there any numbers that you could not make?* Prompt for difficult numbers and ask children to explain how they made them. Also, identify how each pair tackled the problem. Did they work systematically? Did they break each number down? Ask: *Did anyone notice any patterns?* For example, if you combined an addition statement with a subtraction statement you could leave a number unchanged, so 23 = 23 + 1 - 1, or 27 = 22 + 5 + 1 + 6 - 3 - 4 or 26 = (24 + 3) - (2 - 1).

Lesson 2 (Review)

Starter

Rehearse and refine: Start at 20 and count up in units, asking the children to join in when they spot the pattern. Stop when all of them have joined in. Now repeat, starting at 10 and count back in units, and continuing past zero to -10. Start at 50 and count up in tens, then back down in tens, continuing to -50. Repeat, starting at 50 and counting in jumps of 5 up to 100 and then back past zero to -20. Then start at 20, counting in jumps of 2, up to 40 and back. Each time ask: *Can you describe what I am doing in this sequence? What happens when we get to zero?*

Main teaching activities

Whole class: Explain that you will be looking at number sequences. Ask: *What are number sequences? Can anyone give me an example of a number sequence? What would its rule be? What would the next number in the sequence be?*

Write '20' on the board, saying that this is the starting number in a sequence. Now draw a number line and write the rule: 'add 3'. Ask: *What will the second, third, fourth number in the sequence be? Will 22 be in the sequence?* Write each term clearly on the board showing an arrow marked + 3 after each term. Change the rule to 'add 25', then 'subtract 5', 'add 2', 'double' and finally 'multiply by 2, then add 1'.

Independent work: Give the children the activity sheet 'Number rules', which has various sequences for the children to generate, given a starting number and a rule each time. The children are asked to decide which sequences will contain the number 40. Then the sheet lists five sequences for which the children need to describe the rule.

Differentiation

Less confident learners: Provide each child with the support version of 'Number rules', focusing on multiples of 2, 5 and 10.

More confident learners: Provide each child with the extension version of the activity sheet, which includes negative numbers and steps of up to 25.

Review

Ask: *What general statements can you make about the number 40?* (Multiples of 2, 4, 5 and 10 all make 40; or 40 has factors of 2, 4, 5 and 10.) Ask: *How did you work these out? Did you write anything down to help you?* Ask each child to offer a number sequence and then make a general statement about it.

Lesson 3 (Review)

Starter

Recall and refine: Write a set of three-digit numbers on the board, for example 247, 369, 411, 385, 564. Ask the children to round each number to the nearest 10. Next, write 260 and ask the children to hold up their whiteboards when they have a number that when rounded to the nearest 10 would give the number on the board. Write the statement: *There are nine numbers that would round to make 260.* Ask the children to decide whether this is true or false, then write their answer on their boards. Discuss.

Main teaching activities

Whole class: Explain that today the children are going to be investigating odd and even numbers. Ask: *Who can give me an example of an odd number? An even number? Who can tell me the rule for the even numbers, starting from 0? What is being added each time?* Repeat with odd numbers. Ask: *Can anyone think of any other statements or rules about odd and even numbers?* Write down the children's suggestions on the board and ask for any examples to satisfy each statement.

Independent work: Give the children the activity sheet 'Investigating statements', which has some general statements about odd and even numbers. Ask them to investigate the statements by working out some examples. The children will need to decide whether each statement is true or false. Go through the first example with the class. Write on the board: *Every even number ends in 0, 2, 4, 6 or 8.* Try several different examples and establish that this rule is correct.

Review

Write on the board 'odd', 'odd', 'even', 'even'. Point to two of the words and say: *Add.* Children who think that the answer will be even stand up and children who think that the answer will be odd touch the floor. Repeat, using different combinations of 'odd' and 'even'. Give an example each time, such as 34 + 22 = 56. Ask: *How can we tell that 56 is even?* (It ends in a 0, 2, 4, 6 or 8.) Write the results of the investigation on the board. O + O = E (the odd 'ones' pair up each time so the answer is always even; for example, 7 + 7 = 14).

E + E = E
E + O = O
O + E = O

Differentiation

Less confident learners: Provide the support version of the activity sheet, with easier statements to investigate.

More confident learners: Provide the extension version of the activity sheet, which includes questions in which the children will need to find the difference between odd and even numbers.

Lesson 4 (Practise)

Starter

Recall: Write a number on the board. Ask the children to write its double on their whiteboards and hold them up. For example, show 50 (100), 40 (80). Repeat, with the children writing on their whiteboards the number that is half of the one on the board.

Main teaching activities

Whole class: Draw a 3 × 3 grid on the board or display the '3 × 3 grids' sheet using an OHP or an interactive whiteboard. Write in the numbers 1-9 as shown:

1	2	3
4	5	6
7	8	9

Point out that these are consecutive numbers and discuss how they have been arranged on the grid.

Challenge the pupils to make some statements about the numbers on the grid. Write down and agree any statements that they make – for example,

All the corner numbers are odd. The middle row, the middle column and both diagonals equal 15. Establish whether all the children agree with this statement.

Paired work: Give each pair of children a copy of the '3 × 3 grids' activity sheet. Write on the board: *When nine consecutive numbers are arranged on a 3 × 3 grid, the middle row, middle column and both diagonals will have the same total.* Ask each pair to investigate this statement using the '3 × 3 grids' sheet. If time is available, suggest another statement, for example: *The sum of three odd numbers is odd.* Ask the children to test this statement using the 3 × 3 grid.

Differentiation

Less confident learners: Focus children on the first of these two statements and limit the range of consecutive numbers they use to investigate the statement.
More confident learners: Give the children an additional challenge: *Arrange the numbers 1-9 in the grid so that each side of the square totals 12.* The answer is:

1	9	2
8	7	6
3	5	4

Review

Ask the class: *Is the statement I made about consecutive numbers true or false? Why?* (Ask the children for examples that match.) Discuss children's understanding of the properties of consecutive numbers. Ask individual children to add two, then three consecutive numbers together. For example, 1 + 2 + 3 = 6; 4 + 5 + 6 = 15. *Is there a pattern in the totals? Can you describe it?* (Multiples of 3.)

Lesson 5 (Teach, practise and apply)

Starter

Rehearse: Say the following numbers in a sequence: 1, 10, 100, 1000, 10,000. Ask the children to join in when they can. Ask: *What is the rule?* (Multiply by 10.) Repeat with 2, 20, 200, 2000, 20,000, then with 5, 50, 500, 5000, 50,000.

Now work backwards, with 40,000, 4000, 400, 40, 4 and then 60,000, 6000, 600, 60 and 6. Ask: *What is the rule?* (Divide by 10.)

Main teaching activities

Paired work: Give each pair a pile of coloured pencils of equal length, headless matchsticks or straws. Ask the children to use four of these rods to make a square.

Now ask: *How many squares do you have?* (1) *How many sticks have you used?* (4) *How could you record these results?* Ask the children to draw a table to show their results:

Number of squares	Number of sticks used

Encourage each pair to take three more sticks and use them to make two squares. Ask them to write the information in their tables. Repeat for three, four and five squares. Now set the challenge:

- *How many sticks are you adding each time?* (3)
- *How many sticks would you need to make 10 squares?* (31) *20 squares?* (61) *30 squares?* (91)...

Ask: *How many more sticks will you need to make 11 squares from that first square?* Point out that you add on 30 (3 × 10). You can illustrate this activity well on an interactive whiteboard.

Differentiation

Less confident learners: Let these children record their results on activity sheet 'Pencil squares', which has a grid to help them identify what is happening.
More confident learners: Ask these children to try to describe, in words, the relationship between the number of sticks and the number of squares. They should find that: the number of sticks = the number of squares multiplied by 3, then add 1. For example, (12 × 3) + 1 = 36 + 1 = 37 or (100 × 3) + 1 = 300 + 1 = 301. Ask: *Can you use your statement to find out how many sticks you would need to make 100 squares?*

Review

Use an interactive whiteboard. Draw a red vertical line, then add three blue lines of the same length to make a square. Ask: *How many squares do I have? How many lines have I used altogether? How many blue? How many red?* Now add on another three blue lines and repeat. Repeat for three squares. Ask: *How many lines do I add on each time? If I have nine blue lines for three squares, can anyone spot a pattern?* (3 × 3 = 9.) *Then how many other lines do I have?* (One red line.) *Can you describe the relationship between the number of squares and the number of lines?* (Number of squares × 3 + 1.) (Alternatively, complete the same sequence using strips of coloured paper, sticking them to the board with Blu-Tack.)

Lessons 6–7

You will need

CD resources

Core, support, extension and template versions of 'Word problems'; core version of 'Exhausting equations'.

Equipment

Calculators; OHP/interactive whiteboard calculator; Cuisenaire rods for support.

Learning objectives

Starter

- Use knowledge of rounding, number operations and inverses to estimate and check calculations.

Main teaching activities

2006

- Use knowledge of rounding, number operations and inverses to estimate and check calculations.
- Report solutions to puzzles and problems, giving explanations and reasoning orally and in writing, using diagrams and symbols.

1999

- Check results of calculations.
- Explain methods and reasoning about numbers orally and in writing.

Vocabulary

problem, solution, calculator, calculate, calculation, equation, operation, inverse, answer, method, explain, add, subtract, multiply, divide, sum, total, difference, plus, minus, product, quotient, remainder, double, halve, factor, multiple, divisor, round

Lesson 6 (Review and apply)

Starter

Revisit and refine: On the board write 50, 25, 2, 5, 10,100, 4 and 20. Ask: *What is 50 ÷ 10?* Establish the answer is 5 and check by multiplying 5 by 10. Establish that the digits move one place to the right. Emphasise the inverse relationship here between multiplication and division and how this can be used as a checking strategy. Ask: *Can you see any other links between the numbers that I have written on the board?* Discuss with reference to the inverse relationships, for example 25 × 4 = 100 and 100 ÷ 4 = 25 or 100 ÷ 25 = 4.

Ask each child to pick three numbers and write down as many calculations as they can using those three numbers. Repeat and compare written equations.

Main teaching activities

Whole class: Review the multiplication and division methods and approximation and checking strategies introduced in this unit using examples such as:

66 ÷ 6 = □
37 × 4 = □

and so on.

Write a word problem on the board such as the following: *88 counters are shared between 8 children. How many counters does each child get?* Ask questions such as: *Which words tell us what type of calculation to do?* (Shared.) *What other information does this problem give us?* Highlight the numbers and key words in the problem. Ask the children to write the calculation on the board (88 ÷ 8 = □). Again, ask all of the children to approximate the answer, then use the 'chunking' method to solve it. Discuss answers and any alternative methods.

Paired work: Provide each pair with a copy of 'Word problems'. Explain that some of the questions include more than one step and that the children should discuss with their partners which operations are required (+, –, × or ÷) before solving each problem.

Differentiation

Less confident learners: Provide the support version of the activity sheet, which has a mixture of single-step and multi-step operations.
More confident learners: Provide the extension version of the sheet, which has more complex multi-step problems.

Review

Show 'Word problems' on the OHP or whiteboard. Work through the problems together, covering up each line, then revealing it. Ask: *What could you write to help you answer this question?* Then work backwards, asking: *What is the opposite of add 1? What is the inverse? What is the opposite of × 2? What is the inverse?* Say: *Therefore the number Henry thought of was 61.* Emphasise the use of inverses as a checking strategy. Repeat the use of inverses with another example.

Lesson 7 (Review, practise and apply)

Starter

Recall: Explain to the children that you will call out a multiplication fact and you would like them to write the associated division fact on their whiteboards. For example, for 7 × 6 = 42, the children can derive 42 ÷ 7 = 6 or 42 ÷ 6 = 7.

Main teaching activities

Whole class: Use the 'Number sentence builder' interactive resource to display □ ÷ 7 = 6. Ask: *Which number goes in this box?* Discuss how inverses could help with this calculation. Give out calculators and ask: *How could this calculator help you?* Discuss that you need to know what to press to work out that 6 × 7 = 42 and so 42 would go in the box.

Repeat with □ × 7 = 84. Use calculators to work out 84 ÷ 7 = 12. Then try □ + 717 = 884, again using a calculator to work out 884 - 717 = 167. Ask: *What else can we do to check our answer here?* Discuss rounding to get an estimate.

Paired work: Using the sheet 'Exhausting equations', the children are asked to discuss the equation and the calculation required to solve it. They record the calculation in the box provided and work out the answer on their calculator. They also make a note of any way that they could check their answer. For the written questions, you may wish to talk through the first example (11) with the class.

Differentiation

Less confident learners: Pair appropriately and give guidance with the worded problems. Cuisenaire rods may help illustrate the missing numbers.
More confident learners: Encourage these children to convert the word problems into equations before working out the answers, then to go back and see if they can make up word problems for the first 12 equations.

Review

Discuss the outcomes from the 'Exhausting equations' sheet, picking different pairs to explain how they were able to calculate each question. Pay particular attention to finding ways in which the children could have checked and estimated their answers.

Discuss the statements: *If I add two numbers I can use subtraction to check whether my answer is correct. If I divide one number by another two numbers I can use multiplication to check whether my answer is correct.*

Lessons 8-10

Preparation

Lesson 10: If necessary, copy '80 square' onto OHT for display.

You will need

CD resources
'80 square'; support version of 'Ending in 8'; core, support and extension versions of 'Doubles and halves'.
Equipment
Coloured pencils; number fans; calculators if appropriate.

Learning objectives

Starter

- Derive and recall multiplication facts up to 10 × 10, the corresponding division facts and multiples of numbers to 10 up to the tenth multiple.
- Identify the doubles of two-digit numbers; use these to calculate doubles of multiples of 10 and 100 and derive the corresponding halves.

Main teaching activities

2006

- Derive and recall multiplication facts up to 10 × 10, the corresponding division facts and multiples of numbers to 10 up to the tenth multiple.
- Identify the doubles of two-digit numbers; use these to calculate doubles of multiples of 10 and 100 and derive the corresponding halves.

1999
- Derive quickly doubles of all whole numbers to 50, multiples of 10 to 500 and multiples of 100 to 5000, and the corresponding halves.
- Know by heart all multiplication facts up to 10 × 10; derive quickly corresponding division facts.
- Recognise multiples of 6, 7, 8, 9, up to the tenth multiple.
- Recognise multiples of 2, 3, 4, 5 and 10, up to the tenth multiple.

Vocabulary
multiples, problem, solution, calculate, calculation, equation, operation, answer, method, explain, predict, reason, reasoning, pattern, relationship, multiply, divide, product, quotient, remainder

Lesson 8 (Teach)

Starter
Refine and revisit: Start by calling out some two-digit numbers and asking the children to show you double the number on their number fan or whiteboard; start with 23. After a few examples, say: *Double 12 is 24. Write down another number fact that you can work out because you know this.* Discuss the responses. For example: half 24 is 12, double 120 would be 240, half 240 would be 120.

Main teaching activities
Whole class: Explain to the children that in today's lesson they will be investigating doubles and the eight-times table.

On the activity sheet '80 square', ask the children to shade in all the numbers in the two-times table in one colour, then put a circle around the numbers in the four-times table in another colour and finally mark the column showing the eight-times table. Discuss the patterns that you see and doubling, for example, from 6 to 12 to 24 to 48 to find 6 × 8 = 48. Next, together complete the doubling, doubling and doubling again chart. Keep this for Lesson 9. Ask: *How could you describe all the numbers in the 2nd column? 3rd column? 4th column?* (Multiples of 2, 4 and 8.) Ask: *Can you describe the relationship between the columns of numbers?* (For example multiples of 4 are double multiples of 2, and multiples of 8 are double multiples of 4.)

Independent work: Children answer the questions at the bottom of the '80 square' sheet. Keep these sheets for reference in Lesson 9.

Differentiation
Less confident learners: These children should have extra help whilst completing their sheet as it will be used as a reference for questions in this lesson and further lessons.
More confident learners: These children should be encouraged to use good mathematical language and vocabulary to answer questions about the relationships between the different columns of numbers.

Review
Look at the following question: *Can you write down five numbers that are multiples of 2, multiples of 4 and also multiples of 8?* Discuss.

Write down 2 × 8 = 16 and ask: *Using doubling, what other calculations can this help us with?* 4 × 8 = 32, 8 × 8 = 64. Repeat using 2 × 9 = 18. (4 × 9 = 36; 8 × 9 = 72.)

Lesson 9 (Review and teach)

Starter
Recall: Call out an equation from the four-times table and then ask a corresponding question from the eight-times table that requires doubling. For example: *3 × 4 = 12, what does 3 × 8 equal? 4 × 4 = 16, what does 4 × 8 equal? 5 × 4 = 20, what does 5 × 8 equal?* Children can respond on their whiteboards or number fans.

Main teaching activities
Whole class: Recap on the main teaching points from Lesson 8. Look at the '80 square' sheet together. Explain that in today's lesson the children will be investigating the statement: *All numbers that end in 8 are multiples of 4.* Write this on the board.

Group/paired work: In groups or pairs, encourage the children to come up with ideas about this statement. They may be guided through it by looking at the '80 square' sheet and observing that the last digit of multiples of 4 is 0, 2, 4, 6 or 8. (There are no odd numbers.)

Encourage the children to write a list of all the numbers ending in 8. They can then test if these are multiples of 4 by halving and halving again or using a calculator.

Differentiation

Less confident learners: Provide these children with the sheet 'Ending in 8'. This will guide them through the activity.
More confident learners: Encourage these children to think of multiples that have 8 as the unit but are not multiples of 4, such as 18 (6 × 3).

Review

Discuss findings, making sure that all groups have an opportunity to contribute. Decide that the statement is false. Come up with some statements that are true as a group.

Lesson 10 (Review and teach)

Starter

Recall: Call out two-digit numbers and ask the children to show you half the number on their whiteboards. Start with multiples of 10 and then move on to numbers in the twenties, forties, sixties and eighties.

Main teaching activities

Whole class: Write 8 + 8 on the board and ask: *What is another way that I could write this?* (8 × 2.) Repeat with 8 + 8 + 8 and 8 + 8 + 8 + 8, and so on.

Now ask some other multiplication questions and ask the children to write a corresponding addition question on their whiteboards. Start with 6 × 4. (Can be 6 + 6 + 6 + 6 or 4 + 4 + 4 + 4 + 4 + 4.) Discuss responses. Now ask: *If we know that 6 × 4 = 24, how can we find out 12 × 4?* Discuss doubling 24. Point out the link between doubling 24 because 12 is double 6. Repeat with 3 × 9 = 27. Discuss how you might double 27 by finding double 20 and then double 7. Illustrate the mental jottings that you may use for this.

```
      27
 20  +    7
         × 2
 40  +  14    =  54
```

Independent work: Distribute the 'Doubles and halves' activity sheet and ask the children to complete the doubling questions, writing down any calculations that they require.
Whole class: Now ask: *If we know that 8 × 3 = 24, how can we find out 4 × 3?* Discuss halving 24, point out the link between halving 24 because 8 is double 4. Repeat with 8 × 8 = 64. Discuss how you might halve 64 by finding half of 60 and then half of 4. Illustrate the mental jottings that you may use for this.

```
      64
 60  +    4
         ÷ 2
 30  +    2    = 32.
```

Differentiation

Less confident learners: Use the support version of the 'Doubles and halves' sheet, which involves doubling and halving numbers that require less carrying.
More confident learners: Use the extension version of the activity sheet, which involves doubling and halving numbers that require carrying in both the tens and the units. When halving, two of the questions involve remainders.

Independent work: Ask the children to complete the halving questions on the activity sheet, writing down any calculations that they require.

Review

Discuss examples from the 'Doubles and halves' activity sheet, in particular halving 128 by halving 120 and halving 8. Show a completed 'doubling, doubling and doubling again' chart (from the activity sheet '80 square') on the OHP or interactive whiteboard and ask double and halves questions that relate to the eight-times table. For example: *What is half of 64? What is double 18? What is half of 240ml? What is double 56kg?* Illustrate patterns in the grid.

Lessons 11-15

Preparation

Lesson 11: If necessary, copy the 'Tons of triangles' sheet onto OHT.
Lesson 12: Cut out the shapes from the 'Regular symmetry' sheet.
Lesson 14: Copy some isometric paper onto OHT.

You will need

CD resources
'Tons of triangles'; 'Regular symmetry', 'Colourful cubes' and 'Open cube'.
Equipment
Interactive whiteboard; geo-rods or equivalent (or interactive whiteboard geometric drawing software); interlocking cubes; scissors; coloured pencils; a collection of 3D shapes; rulers; set squares.

Learning objectives

Starter

- Draw polygons and classify them by identifying their properties, including their line symmetry.

Main teaching activities

2006

- Draw polygons and classify them by identifying their properties, including their line symmetry.
- Visualise 3D objects from 2D drawings and make nets of common solids.

1999

- Classify polygons using criteria such as number of right angles, whether or not they are regular, symmetry properties.
- Make shapes eg construct polygons by paper folding or using pinboard, and discuss properties such as lines of symmetry.
- Visualise 3D shapes from 2D drawing and identify simple nets of solid shapes.

Vocabulary

3D, three-dimensional, 2D, two-dimensional, net, construct, regular, irregular, concave, convex, symmetrical, line of symmetry, vertex, vertices, face, edge, polygon, equilateral triangle, isosceles triangle, quadrilateral, rectangle, square, oblong, hexagon, heptagon, octagon

Lesson 11 (Teach, practise and apply)

Starter

Revisit: Show 'Tons of triangles' on the OHP or interactive whiteboard and ask: *Which of these triangles are equilateral?* The children can record the numbers of the triangles on their whiteboards. Discuss the properties of an equilateral triangle (all sides and all angles are equal). Repeat with isosceles (two sides and two angles are equal) and right-angled triangles (has a 90° angle).

Main teaching activities

Whole class: Use some geo-rods to make a square. Say: *This is a four-sided regular shape. Can you show me a three-sided regular shape?* Ask an individual to show you an equilateral triangle from the board. Now use the geo-rods (or an alternative whiteboard drawing tool) to illustrate a regular pentagon, hexagon, and so on.

Now ask: *What would an irregular three-sided shape look like?* (An isosceles or scalene triangle.) Ask the children to draw an irregular four-sided shape on their whiteboards. Discuss the children's responses and name the shapes.

Build up a bank of quadrilaterals on the board, including a rectangle, parallelogram, rhombus, kite, arrowhead and trapezium (see diagrams overleaf).

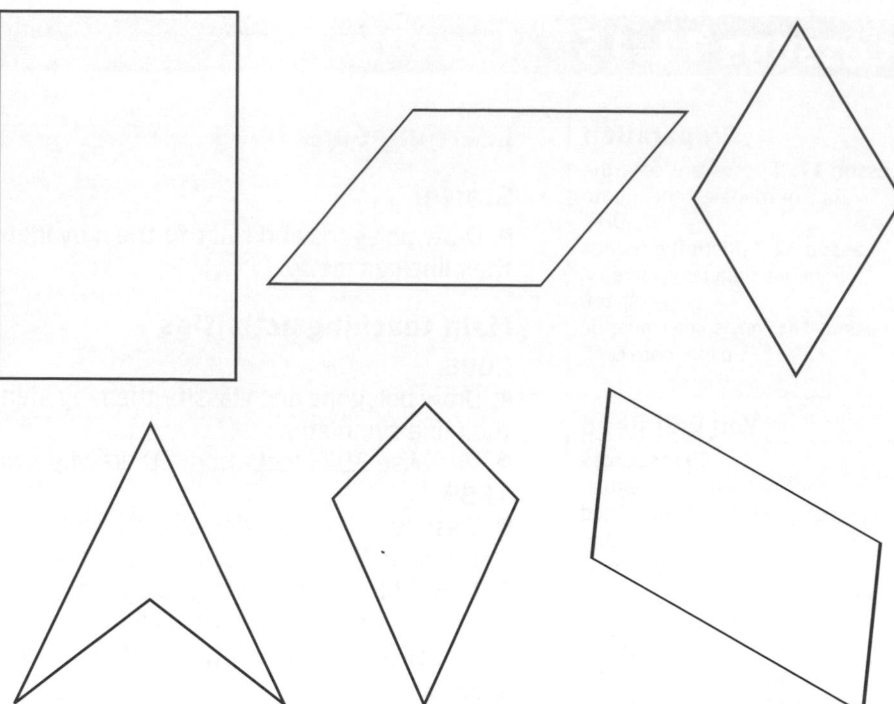

Using geo-rods (or the interactive whiteboard drawing tool), illustrate how one quadrilateral can transform into the next.

Now explain that you will be investigating lines of symmetry. Together, mark lines of symmetry on the triangles, discussing the method.

Paired work: Using the 2D shapes cut from the sheet 'Regular symmetry', ask the pairs to draw on the shapes all the lines of symmetry that they can find. Demonstrate how folding may help with this activity.

Differentiation

Less confident learners: These children may need more guidance and if possible should have adult input. A mirror may also aid them.

More confident learners: These children could investigate finding further shapes with no, one, two or three lines of symmetry.

Review

Collectively, encourage the children to look at the shapes and sort them into those that have no lines of symmetry, one line of symmetry, two lines, and so on. Discuss the shapes' names and properties. Save the shapes for use in Lesson 12.

Lesson 12 (Teach)

Starter

Revisit and refine: Continuing from Lesson 11, ask the children to label their shapes regular/irregular. Discuss properties as appropriate.

Main teaching activities

Whole class: Explain that in today's lesson the children will be using their shapes to investigate some statements in their pairs. Write the following statement on the board: *The number of sides of a polygon is equal to the number of lines of symmetry.*

Paired work: Encourage the children to work with their shapes to answer the statement 'true' or 'false'. When the pairs have decided that the statement is false, ask: *How can you amend the statement to make it true?* (By stating that regular polygons have the same number of sides as lines of symmetry.)

Differentiation

Less confident learners: These children may need more guidance and if possible should have adult input. A mirror may also aid them. Encourage writing the number of sides and the number of lines of symmetry on each shape and then comparing the statement to these results.

More confident learners: These children could investigate further by finding regular polygons with more sides that further illustrate the statement.

Review

Using the interactive whiteboard or OHP, collectively try to draw hexagons with no lines of symmetry, one line, two line, three lines... up to a regular hexagon with six lines. The children can use the whiteboard to help with their workings.

Lesson 13 (Review, teach, practise and apply)

Starter

Revisit and refine: Explain that you are thinking of a 2D shape. Ask the children to ask you a series of questions about the shape. Encourage them to ask about number of sides, lines of symmetry and whether it is regular/ irregular. Explain that you will only answer yes/no. Gradually they should build up an image in their mind about the shape and attempt to name it. Start with a regular pentagon.

Main teaching activities

Whole class: Discuss the types of questions that help to paint a picture of a shape in your mind. Develop this by thinking about the least number of questions that you need to ask to identify a shape. Explain that in today's lesson the children will be working in pairs and trying to discover what 2D shape their partner is thinking about. Introduce some new vocabulary that may help: concave/convex.

Paired work: Using the shapes from Lessons 11 and 12, one child picks a shape (keeping it from their partner) and then their partner asks questions about their shape. Remind them that they can only answer yes/no. Repeat and swap roles. If appropriate, start to pick shapes that do not appear on the sheet 'Regular symmetry'.

Review

Discuss good questions and vocabulary used. Build up a list on the board. Ask: *Who was able to guess in the least number of questions? Why do you think this was? Did you have to change the way that you talked/listened to your partner for this activity? How?*

Differentiation

Less confident learners: These children may need more guidance and, if possible, should have adult input. They could start with regular shapes and have a list of relevant vocabulary to guide them in their questions.

More confident learners: These children could use more complex shapes and describe angles in more detail. They should work with shapes other than those on the 'Regular symmetry' sheet. They could alter the game slightly by picking a shape and pretending to have a telephone conversation with their partner describing their shape, sitting back to back.

Lesson 14 (Teach)

Starter

Revisit: Call out a word from this list of vocabulary and ask the children to draw a picture on their whiteboard of a shape with that property: *3D, three-dimensional, 2D, two-dimensional, regular, irregular, concave, convex, symmetrical, equilateral triangle, isosceles triangle, quadrilateral, rectangle, square, oblong, hexagon, heptagon, octagon.* Discuss the results.

Main teaching activities

Whole class: Take six interlocking cubes and make a shape with them. Explain to the class that you would like to illustrate this 3D shape on paper. Use isometric paper or the interactive whiteboard to help you. If possible, use colour-coding to aid understanding.

Explain that in today's lesson you will be giving the children a sheet on 2D drawings and they need to make 3D shapes with their interlocking cubes to represent these drawings.

Independent work: Provide each child with a copy of the sheet 'Colourful cubes' and some interlocking cubes. The children need to predict the number of cubes necessary to make the shape and then make up each shape from the drawings on the sheet. The final challenge is to look at three views of the same shape (from above, from the side and from the end), and use these to build the shape.

Review

Gather examples of the interlocking cubes and ask individual children to explain how they were able to visualise and build the shape from the diagram. Display a range of 2D shapes on the interactive whiteboard. Using a collection of 3D shapes, ask individuals to match up the shape with the 2D image on the screen and discuss. Use vocabulary such as *faces, edges* and *vertices/vertex.*

Differentiation

Less confident learners: These children may need more guidance and if possible should have adult input. They should start by colouring in the cubes in different colours on their sheet and then use corresponding colours to construct their shape.

More confident learners: These children could extend this activity by creating shapes and describing their shape to a partner who then has to make up the same shape with their interlocking cubes.

Lesson 15 (Teach, apply and review)

Starter

Revisit and refine: Repeat the Starter from Lesson 13 but this time use 3D shapes. Encourage use of the following vocabulary: *faces, edges* and *vertices/vertex.*

Main teaching activities

Whole class: Use the sheet 'Open cube' with the class to cut out and construct an open cube. Look carefully at this net and discuss its features: *It is made of five identical squares, each of those form a face of the cube. Take your net and cut it into five squares, then re-arrange the squares and make a different net of the open square.* If possible, illustrate this with an interactive whiteboard.

Independent work: Using their net and square paper, encourage the children to make a different net for an open cube, testing it by cutting it out and making an open cube.

Review

Compare all of the nets of the open cubes. Ask: *Do we have them all?* Discuss. Now ask: *How would the net of a cuboid be different from this?* Discuss rectangular faces and encourage each child to sketch the net of a cuboid. Compare sketches.

Differentiation

Less confident learners: These children may need more help, especially when measuring out the net. Encourage them to use exactly the same scale as the 'open cube' sheet and, if necessary, draw around the squares.

More confident learners: These children could develop their knowledge of nets by drawing the net of a cuboid.

Name ______________________ Date ______________

Number rules

Continue each of the sequences below by filling in the boxes.

1. Starting number: 5 Rule: add 5

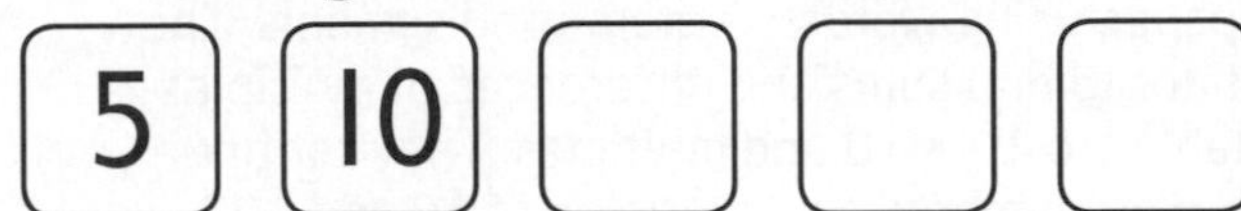

2. Starting number: 30 Rule: take away 3

3. Starting number: 56 Rule: subtract 4

4. Starting number: 10 Rule: multiply by 2

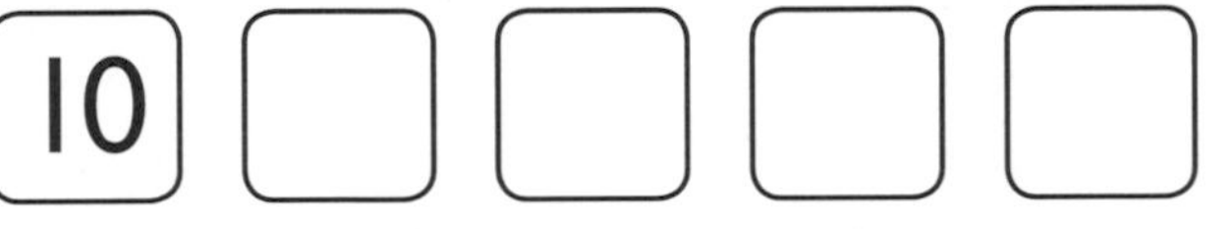

5. Starting number: 15 Rule: add 15

Now look at the sequences above. If you carried on, which sequences would have 40 in them? Show your working or reasoning. ______________________

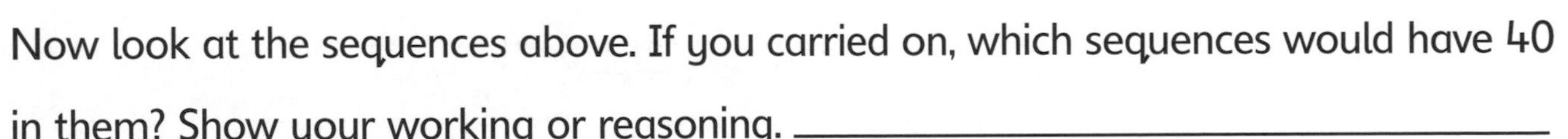

Now look at these sequences. What is the rule for each?
Write the next number in each of these sequences.

6. 34, 37, 40, 43, 46, 49, ☐ Rule: ______________

7. 3, 6, 12, 24, 48, ☐ Rule: ______________

8. 67, 62, 57, 52, 47, 42, ☐ Rule: ______________

9. 2, 4, 6, 8, 10, 12, 14, ☐ Rule: ______________

10. –2, –4, –6, –8, –10, ☐ Rule: ______________

Securing number facts, understanding shape

Speaking and listening objective

- Use time, resources and group members effectively by distributing tasks, checking progress and making back-up plans.

Introduction

In this three-week unit, children continue to solve one- and two-step word problems involving numbers, money or measures. They find patterns, relationships and properties of numbers and shapes, explaining methods and reasoning, orally and on paper, using words, diagrams and symbols. They further explore using a calculator to find sums and differences of multiples of 10, 100 and 1000, using tables to 10 × 10 and multiples. They continue to investigate doubles of two-digit numbers and multiples of 10 and 100, and their corresponding halves. Children develop further their knowledge of properties of polygons, including line symmetry, visualising 3D and 2D shapes and finding nets of common solids.

Lesson	Strands	Starter	Main teaching activities
1. Teach and apply	Use/apply	**Derive and recall multiplication facts up to 10 × 10, the corresponding division facts and multiples of numbers to 10 up to the tenth multiple.**	Identify and use patterns, relationships and properties of numbers or shapes; investigate a statement involving numbers and test it with examples.
2. Review, teach and apply	Use/apply	As for Lesson 1	As for Lesson 1
3. Review and apply	Use/apply	As for Lesson 1	As for Lesson 1
4. Review	Use/apply	As for Lesson 1	Solve one-step and two-step problems involving numbers, money or measures, including time; choose and carry out appropriate calculations, using calculator methods where appropriate.
5. Review, teach and practise	Use/apply	As for Lesson 1	Report solutions to puzzles and problems, giving explanations and reasoning orally and in writing, using diagrams and symbols.
6. Teach and apply	Use/apply	As for Lesson 1	As for Lesson 5
7. Apply	Use/apply	As for Lesson 1	As for Lesson 5
8. Teach and apply	Knowledge	Use knowledge of rounding, number operations and inverses to estimate and check calculations.	Use knowledge of rounding, number operations and inverses to estimate and check calculations.
9. Review and practise	Knowledge	Use knowledge of addition and subtraction facts and place value to derive sums and differences of pairs of multiples of 10, 100 or 1000.	Use knowledge of addition and subtraction facts and place value to derive sums and differences of pairs of multiples of 10, 100 or 1000.
10. Practise	Knowledge	Identify the doubles of two-digit numbers; use these to calculate doubles of multiples of 10 and 100 and derive the corresponding halves.	Identify the doubles of two-digit numbers; use these to calculate doubles of multiples of 10 and 100 and derive the corresponding halves.
11. Teach and practise	Knowledge	**Derive and recall multiplication facts up to 10 × 10, the corresponding division facts and multiples of numbers to 10 up to the tenth multiple.**	**Derive and recall multiplication facts up to 10 × 10, the corresponding division facts and multiples of numbers to 10 up to the tenth multiple.**
12. Teach and practise	Shape	Draw polygons and classify them by identifying their properties, including their line symmetry.	Draw polygons and classify them by identifying their properties, including their line symmetry.
13. Teach and practise	Shape	As for Lesson 12	As for Lesson 12
14. Teach and apply	Shape	Visualise 3D objects from 2D drawings and make nets of common solids.	Visualise 3D objects from 2D drawings and make nets of common solids.
15. Teach, apply and evaluate	Shape	As for Lesson 13	As for Lesson 13

Using and applying mathematics

- Identify and use patterns, relationships and properties of numbers or shapes; investigate a statement involving numbers and test it with examples.
- Report solutions to puzzles and problems, giving explanations and reasoning orally and in writing, using diagrams and symbols.
- Solve one-step and two-step problems involving numbers, money or measures, including time; choose and carry out appropriate calculations, using calculator methods where appropriate.

Lessons 1-8

Preparation

Lesson 1: Copy 'Grid of multiples' onto OHT for display, multiple copies.
Lesson 3: Prepare a set of 'Shapes for sorting' for each group.
Lesson 4: If necessary, prepare a set of 'What's the method?' cards for each group.
Lesson 6: Prepare the 'Multiples cards' and 'Statements to evaluate'.

You will need

Photocopiable pages
'Grid of multiples' (page 88), 'Multiples of 5 and 10' (page 89), 'Shape sorting' (page 90), 'Symmetrical shapes' (page 91), 'What's the method?' (page 92), 'Consecutive challenge' (page 93) and 'Investigations' (page 94).

CD resources
Core, support and extension versions of 'Multiples of 5 and 10' and 'Correct calculations?'; core versions of 'Statements to evaluate' and 'Multiple cards'; core, support, extension and template versions of 'Symmetrical shapes', 'What's the method?', 'Consecutive challenge' and 'Investigations'; support version of 'Shape sorting diagram'. General resource sheets: 'Numeral cards' (sets of 0-9 and 0-6 for children); '100 square' for display. Interactive resource: 'Number sentence builder'. ITP: 'Number grid'.

Equipment
Interactive whiteboard; calculators; number fans.

Learning objectives

Starter

- Derive and recall multiplication facts up to 10 × 10, the corresponding division facts and multiples of numbers to 10 up to the tenth multiple.
- Use knowledge of rounding, number operations and inverses to estimate and check calculations.

Main teaching activities

2006

- Identify and use patterns, relationships and properties of numbers or shapes; investigate a statement involving numbers and test it with examples.
- Solve one-step and two-step problems involving numbers, money or measures, including time; choose and carry out appropriate calculations, using calculator methods where appropriate.
- Report solutions to puzzles and problems, giving explanations and reasoning orally and in writing, using diagrams and symbols.
- Use knowledge of rounding, number operations and inverses to estimate and check calculations.

1999

- Solve mathematical problems or puzzles, recognise and explain patterns and relationships, generalise and predict. Suggest extensions by asking 'What if...?'
- Recognise and extend number sequences.
- Make and investigate a general statement about familiar numbers that satisfy it.
- Explain methods and reasoning about numbers orally and in writing.
- Use all four operations to solve word problems involving numbers in 'real' life, money and measures (including time), using one or more steps, including converting pounds to pence and metres to centimetres and vice versa.
- Choose and use appropriate number operations and appropriate ways of calculating (mental, mental with jottings, pencil and paper) to solve problems.
- Round up or down after division, depending on context.
- Choose appropriate ways of calculating: calculator.
- Check results of calculations.

Vocabulary

problem, solution, calculator, calculate, calculation, equation, operation, inverse, answer, method, explain, predict, reason, reasoning, pattern, relationship, rule, sequence, sort, classify, property, add, subtract, multiply, divide, sum, total, difference, plus, minus, product, quotient, remainder, double, halve, factor, multiple, divisor, round, symmetrical, line of symmetry, polygon

Lesson 1 (Teach and apply)

Starter

Refine and rehearse: Stand in front of the class and say the nine-times table. As you do this, hold your hands up, palms towards the class and encourage the children to copy you. As you say *One times nine*, hold down the smallest finger on your right hand, then lift it up. As you say *Two times nine*, hold down the next finger along, then lift it up and so on. Continue in this way until you say *Ten times nine*, and hold the little finger on your left hand down. Ask: *What do you notice about all the answers in the nine-times table? What would happen if you added the digits of the answers together?* (They always add up to 9.)

Main teaching activities

Whole class: Explain that the topic for this lesson is numbers and their patterns. Use the ITP 'Number grid' and set the number of columns to 6, or display an OHT of activity sheet 'Grid of multiples'. On the grid, highlight the multiples of 2. Ask: *What is the difference between consecutive even numbers?* (2) Look at the even numbers. *What are the last digits of the even numbers?* (2, 4, 6, 8 and 0.) *How can you describe the pattern that they make on the grid?* Display a new grid and repeat with a different number, showing that the grids can produce vertical or diagonal patterns. Depending on time and computer access, children could investigate the patterns formed by highlighting the multiples of 2 on various grids of numbers.

Now return to the OHT 'Grid of multiples', or show the ITP 'Number grid' on the whiteboard, with multiples of 2 shaded. Use a different colour to circle every other even number, starting with 4. (4, 8, 12, 16.) Ask: *What is the difference between pairs of these circled numbers?* (4) *How could you describe these numbers?* (Multiples of 4.) Look at the multiples of 4. *What are the last digits of the numbers? Is there a pattern?* (Yes, 2, 4, 6, 8 and 0.) *Are the multiples of 4 always even? How can you describe the pattern that they make on the grid?*

Independent work: Give the children the activity sheet 'Multiples of 5 and 10' and ask them to shade all the multiples of 5 in one colour, then to answer the questions. Then ask them to use a different colour to circle alternate multiples of 5, starting with 10. (10, 20, 30 – multiples of 10.) Ask the children to record any observations that they make.

Differentiation

Less confident learners: Use the support version of the activity sheet, which will guide the children in their observations.

More confident learners: Use the extension version of the activity sheet, which challenges these children to make more links between the multiples of 5 and 10 by looking at the end digits and the patterns that they make on the grid. If time permits, encourage these children to make links between the multiples of 10 and say the multiples of 4 to try to make links such as: every fifth even number is a multiple of 10; every fifth multiple of 4 is a multiple of 10.

Review

Discuss the children's observations and summarise.

- The last digit of a multiple of 5 is always 5 or 0 and the last digit of a multiple of 10 is always 0.
- Every other (even) multiple of 5 is a multiple of 10.
- Multiples of 10 are always even numbers.

Lesson 2 (Review, teach and apply)

Starter

Recall: Using vocabulary such as 'multiply', 'product', 'double' and 'groups of', ask quick-fire questions to test the six-, eight- and nine-times tables, with the children recording their answers on their whiteboards. For example, ask: *Find 9 multiplied by 8. Find the product of 8 and 5. What is double 6? I have 8 groups of 4 children, how many children do I have altogether?* Write any still unfamiliar multiples in the corner of the board to return to later.

Main teaching activities

Whole class: Review the patterns of multiples discovered in Lesson 1. Use the ITP 'Number grid' (or an OHT of '100 square') to highlight multiples of 2, 5 and 10. Write on the board four columns headed 'Multiple of 2 ... 4 ... 5 ... 10'. Call out a number and ask the children whether it can be added to any of the columns on your chart.

Ask the children to tell you the multiples of 3 and add another column to your chart. Ask: *Can you see a pattern?* (The sum of the digits for numbers in the three-times tables follows the pattern 3, 6, 9, 3, 6, 9. Say: *Let's test for other numbers to see if this is always true.* Try 63. Ask the children to demonstrate their methods for dividing 63 by 3 to give the answer 21 with no remainder. Then add the digits: 6 + 3 = 9, so the rule works in this example.

Paired work: Ask the pairs to use numeral cards 0–9 to generate two-digit numbers. For each number, ask the children to sum the digits and decide whether they think it is a multiple of 3. They should check by dividing by 3 and record the results in two lists: those that are multiples of 3 and those that are not.

Review

Review the children's lists of multiples of 3 and use ITP 'Number grid' or the activity sheet '100 square' to highlight each number. Call out some other numbers and ask the children to determine whether it can be added to the grid. Look for other patterns that these multiples make (eg they produce diagonal patterns). If time is available, discuss the other patterns made on the 100 square (eg multiples of 2 and 10 produce vertical patterns).

Differentiation

Less confident learners: Limit the pairs to numeral cards 0–6.

More confident learners: Challenge the children to generate three-digit numbers.

Lesson 3 (Review and apply)

Starter

Rehearse: Ask the class to count to 60 in sixes. Ask: *What is an easy way to multiply by 6?* Establish that ×6 is double ×3. Ask the class now to count in eights to 80. Again, ask: *What is an easy way to multiply by 8?* (Doubling ×4.) Ask quick-fire multiplication and division questions involving ×6 and ×8. Ask the children to write the answers on their whiteboards.

Main teaching activities

Whole class: Remind the children of work done in previous lessons on lines of symmetry. Show how to draw the lines of symmetry on a square, using the whiteboard or OHP. Emphasise the positions of the lines on the square, ie they include diagonal, horizontal and vertical lines of symmetry.

Group work: Give out sets of symmetrical shapes cut from the 'Shape sorting' activity sheet. Discuss the names of the various shapes. Ask the children to fold the shapes to check if they have no lines of symmetry, one line of symmetry or more than one line of symmetry. In groups, the children should sort the set of shapes using a sorting method of their choice (for example, in Venn diagrams). If necessary, supplement the shapes on the sheet with other prepared polygons or with the polygons on the 'Symmetrical shapes' sheet.

Review

Ask the children to explain the criteria they used for sorting the shapes with more than one line of symmetry. Ask: *What did you notice about regular shapes?*

Differentiation

Less confident learners: Provide these children with a copy of 'Shape sorting diagram' (or supply them with sorting rings and labels to let them complete the task practically). The support version of the 'Symmetrical shapes' sheet has simpler shapes with fewer lines of symmetry.

More confident learners: Ask these children to further sort the shapes by the numbers of lines of symmetry. If time is available, you might also allow them to define their own criteria for sorting. The extension version of the 'Symmetrical shapes' sheet has more challenging shapes and also includes two examples that require the children to work on a grid to show the reflection of a shape in a mirror line.

Lesson 4 (Review)

Starter

Rehearse: With the class, say the seven-times table together twice. Then ask questions such as: *What is 6 times 7? What is 42 divided by 6?* Ask the children to show their responses on number fans. Write any problem statements in the corner of the board and repeat these several times.

Main teaching activities

Whole class: Write an addition sentence on the board, such as 63 + 58 = □. Ask the children to work out the answer using mental methods or by writing on their whiteboards. Ask: *How did you work it out?* Discuss and record the

methods used, for example:
Mental method: 63 + 58 = 63 + 60 - 2 = 123 - 2 = 121
Number line method, as shown:

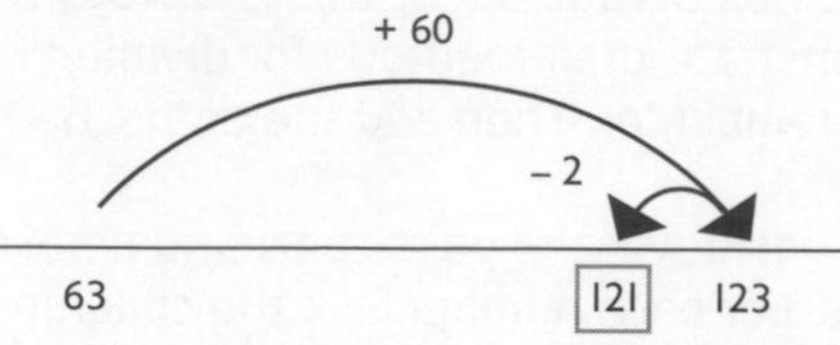

Repeat with a pair of three-digit numbers such as 658 + 137 = □. Again, record methods and discuss strategies, eg adding the most significant digits first (column addition).

Group/independent work: Provide the children with 'What's the method?', which includes questions involving all four operations. The children have to identify the method to use to answer each question. Tell them that it is appropriate to use written methods if they help them. However, before deciding the method they should look at the numbers involved and decide first whether they can answer the question mentally. The questions have been provided on cards so that they can be answered on the sheet or cut out and divided among groups for more discussion on strategies used. The groups could then be asked to divide the questions into those that could be calculated mentally and those that needed written methods. Time allowing, provide the children with a calculator at this point and ask the children to work out with which calculations a calculator would have helped them.

Differentiation

Less confident learners: Provide the support version of 'What's the method?', which includes mostly addition and subtraction questions.

More confident learners: Provide the version of 'What's the method?', which includes more challenging multiplication and division questions.

Review

Ask the children to explain and model examples of their calculations on the board. Ask: *Which calculations could you not do mentally? Why?* Ask if any of the pupils used checking strategies to make sure that their answers were correct. Again, ask for the methods used.

Lesson 5 (Review, teach and practise)

Starter

Rehearse: Ask the children to write the answers to some table fact questions on their whiteboards. Ask, for example: *What is 3 times 6? What is 9 times 7? What is 8 times 4?* Include some word problems such as: *If I have six teams of five children, how many children would I have altogether?*

Main teaching activities

Whole class: Display the '100 square' on OHT, or use the ITP 'Number grid', and cover three consecutive numbers, for example 55 to 57. Ask: *Which numbers are covered? How do you know?* Establish that the covered numbers can be identified from the patterns in the grid. If necessary, explain that numbers that come one after the other are called 'consecutive numbers'. Select three consecutive numbers below 20 (for example, 6 + 7 + 8 = □) and ask: *What is the total of these consecutive numbers?* Repeat with other sets of three numbers. Ask: *Can anyone suggest a rule for finding the total of consecutive numbers?* Discuss that by taking 1 from the largest number and adding it to the smallest number, the three numbers become all the same.

Paired work: Challenge the children to use this rule to find the target numbers on the 'Consecutive challenge' activity sheet. Observe the strategies that the pairs use as they work.

Differentiation

Less confident learners: Give children the support version of 'Consecutive challenge', with lower target numbers.

More confident learners: Give the children the extension version of the sheet, with higher target numbers. They also have an additional challenge: to make all of the numbers to 30 using three consecutive numbers.

Review

Bring the children together to review the target numbers. Mark off the children's consecutive numbers on the OHT (or ITP 'Number grid'). Review the children's strategies for finding the consecutive numbers and establish that dividing by 3 is a helpful strategy to use.

Lesson 6 (Teach and apply)

Starter

Rehearse and refine: Give each child a set of five cards cut from activity sheet 'Multiple cards'. Each set consists of the five numbers: 2, 3, 4, 5 and 10. Explain that you will call out numbers and if the children think that your number is a multiple of 2 (even) they must hold up the 2, if your number is a multiple of 3, they must hold up the 3, and so on. Explain that sometimes they may need to hold up more than one card, for example, 6 is a multiple of both 2 and 3.

Main teaching activities

Whole class: Explain that in this and the next lesson the children will investigate some statements. Say that you would like them to look at some general statements and to try out different numbers to find whether the statements are true or false. Write on the board: *Multiples of 4 end in 2, 4, 6, 8 or 0.* Invite individual children to think of some numbers and to say whether they support the statement. Encourage discussion and ask children to explain the relationships between the numbers and expressions and to decide whether the written statement is true or false. The suggested statement is true, as any multiple of 4 will be even.

Individual/paired work: Give the children cards made from activity sheet 'Statements to evaluate' and ask them to investigate. When they have finished one card they can have another, but limit the number of statements they work on, keeping some for the next lesson.

Review

Discuss and develop vocabulary for the children to explain their ideas and findings about the statements they have tackled. Refer only to those statements that children have evaluated. Some of the following may be held over for the next lesson.

- Half-way between any two multiples of 10 is a multiple of 5. (True. For example, 20 and 50 are multiples of 10, and half-way between them is 35, which is a multiple of 5). Ask: *Would it be helpful to use a number line to find the midpoint? Could somebody give me another example to show that this statement is true?*
- Multiples of 4 end in 2, 4, 6, 8 or 0. (True, as any multiple of 4 will be even, double a multiple of 2.)
- Multiples of 8 end in 2, 4, 6, 8 or 0. (True, as any multiple of 8 will be even, double a multiple of 4.)
- Multiples of 3 end in 3, 6 or 9. (False.)
- The sum of three odd numbers is odd. (True. For example, 1 + 3 + 7 = 11 which is odd.)
- The sum of three even numbers is odd. (False. For example, 2 + 6 + 8 = 16 which is even.)
- Half-way between any two multiples of 4 is a multiple of 2. (True. For example, 8 and 12 are multiples of 4, and half-way between them is 10, which is a multiple of 2.)
- The sum of three consecutive numbers is always a multiple of 3. (True.)

Differentiation

Less confident learners: Let these children work in pairs or groups, with some extra assistance. Supply a list of numbers for them to test as a starting point. Allocate a helper or classroom assistant to whom they can explain their reasoning when they have reached a conclusion about a statement.

More confident learners: Ask these children to develop written statements that fully explain their findings.

Lesson 7 (Apply)

Starter

Reason: Say: *I am thinking of a pair of numbers with the sum of 15 and a product of 54. What could the numbers be?* Discuss, then repeat saying: *I am thinking of a pair of numbers their difference is 2 and their product is 24. What are they?* Discuss.

Main teaching activities

If necessary, continue working through the 'Statements to evaluate' from the previous lesson.

Go through the core 'Investigations' questions in turn to explain what is involved. Tell the children in pairs to discuss methods that they could use, then record their workings.

Paired work: Give each pair the core version of the 'Investigations' sheet, which includes 'Making numbers', 'Using 9s' and 'Missing numbers - subtractions'.

Differentiation

Less confident learners: Give each pair the support version of the 'Investigations' sheet, which includes 'Making numbers' and 'Missing numbers - additions'.

More confident learners: Give each pair the extension version of the 'Investigations' sheet, which includes 'Numbers for letters' and two 'Make 100' challenges.

Review

Go through all of the investigations and ask the children to share their methods for working out each one.

Lesson 8 (Teach and apply)

Starter

Recall: Use the 'Number sentence builder' interactive resource to display the equations. Write 6 + 8 = 14 on the board and ask the children to write three other facts that you can work out from the addition fact. Ask them to show these on their whiteboards after a few minutes. (14 - 8 = 6, 14 - 6 = 8, 60 + 80 = 140, 3 + 4 = 7.) Discuss responses. Repeat by showing 46 - 34 = 12.

Main teaching activities

Whole class: Explain that in today's lesson the children will be looking at ways to help them check calculations. Say: *I have 42 chairs in the hall. They are in rows of seven chairs and there are six rows. How could I check that this was correct?* Write 42 ÷ 7 = 6 and again encourage any other facts that you can work out from the division fact.

Repeat, this time asking: *I want to buy eight jugs costing £21 each. My total bill is £168. Write a calculation that you could do to check that the answer to 21 × 8 is 168.*

Independent work: Look at the activity sheet 'Correct calculations?' and ask the children to work out which calculations are correct by using different calculations to check, rounding up/down to find an estimate.

Whole class: Discuss the calculations that the children used and various ways of checking/estimating the answers.

Differentiation

Less confident learners: Use the support version of the activity sheet, which has a list of numerical equations to support the children while checking these written problems.

More confident learners: Use the extension version of the sheet, with two further questions.

Review

Write an equation such as 200 - 40 = 160 and ask: *Which other equations could I write if I know this?* Collaboratively come up with a family of equations such as 190 - 30 = 160, 180 - 20 = 160, 210 - 50 = 160. Illustrate them using the 'Number sentence builder'.

Lessons 9-15

Preparation

Lesson 12: Copy a sheet of squared paper onto OHT for display.

Lesson 13: Copy a sheet of triangular paper onto OHT for display. Prepare some triangles the same shape as the triangular paper to manipulate manually, for support.

Lesson 14: Enlarge the 'Creating nets' sheet onto A3, one per child.

You will need

CD resources

Core versions of 'Multiples of 10, 100, 1000', 'Creating nets' and 'Different methods'; core and extension versions of 'Missing numbers'; core, support and extension versions of 'Factor seeds'; core, support, extension and template versions of 'Reflections'. Interactive resources: 'Number sentence builder' and 'Grids, patterns, reflections and rotations'.

Equipment

Interactive whiteboard; interlocking cubes; a net made up of a closed cube; scissors; glue and paper or masking tape; 3D shapes.

Learning objectives

Starter

- Use knowledge of addition and subtraction facts and place value to derive sums and differences of pairs of multiples of 10, 100 or 1000.
- Identify the doubles of two-digit numbers; use these to calculate doubles of multiples of 10 and 100 and derive the corresponding halves.
- Derive and recall multiplication facts up to 10 × 10, the corresponding division facts and multiples of numbers to 10 up to the tenth multiple.
- Draw polygons and classify them by identifying their properties, including their line symmetry.
- Visualise 3D objects from 2D drawings and make nets of common solids.

Main teaching activities

2006

- Use knowledge of addition and subtraction facts and place value to derive sums and differences of pairs of multiples of 10, 100 or 1000.
- Identify the doubles of two-digit numbers; use these to calculate doubles of multiples of 10 and 100 and derive the corresponding halves.
- Derive and recall multiplication facts up to 10 × 10, the corresponding division facts and multiples of numbers to 10 up to the tenth multiple.
- Draw polygons and classify them by identifying their properties, including their line symmetry.
- Visualise 3D objects from 2D drawings and make nets of common solids.

1999

- Derive quickly all pairs of multiples of 50 with a total of 1000 (eg 850 + 150).
- Add three two-digit multiples of 10, such as 40 + 70 + 50.
- Use known number facts and place value to add or subtract mentally.
- Use known number facts and place value for mental addition and subtraction (eg 470 + 380, 810 - 380).
- Know by heart all multiplication facts up to 10 × 10; derive quickly corresponding division facts.
- Recognise multiples of 6, 7, 8, 9, up to the tenth multiple.
- Recognise multiples of 2, 3, 4, 5 and 10, up to the tenth multiple.
- Derive quickly doubles of all whole numbers to 50, multiples of 10 to 500 and multiples of 100 to 5000, and the corresponding halves.
- Classify polygons using criteria such as number of right angles, whether or not they are regular, symmetry properties.
- Make shapes, eg construct polygons by paper folding or using pinboard, and discuss properties such as lines of symmetry.
- Visualise 3D shapes from 2D drawing and identify simple nets of solid shapes.

Vocabulary

problem, solution, calculator, calculate, calculation, equation, operation, inverse, answer, method, explain, predict, reason, reasoning, pattern, relationship, rule, sequence, sort, classify, property, add, subtract, multiply, divide, sum, total, difference, plus, minus, product, quotient, remainder, double, halve, factor, multiple, divisor, round, 3D, three-dimensional, 2D, two-dimensional, net, construct, regular, irregular, concave, convex, symmetrical, line of symmetry, vertex, vertices, face, edge, polygon, equilateral triangle, isosceles triangle, quadrilateral, rectangle, square, oblong, hexagon, heptagon, octagon

Lesson 9 (Review and practise)

Starter

Rehearse: Pick two cards from the 'Multiples of 10, 100 and 1000' set and ask the class to find the sum or the difference, writing answers on whiteboards. Discuss how place value can help them with these calculations.

Main teaching activities

Whole class: Explain that in this lesson the children will be adding and subtracting two numbers. Write 76 - 46 = 30 on the board and ask: *Which number facts do we know that would help us work out this calculation?* Discuss: 70 - 40 = 30 because 7 - 4 = 3 and so 76 - 46 = 30 is correct.

Distribute the activity sheet 'Different methods', which shows a series of addition and subtraction questions. Allow some time for the children to answer the questions mentally and to write down the answers. Ask them to try to explain the method that they used to work out each answer and to write it in the box provided. Stress that children may use different methods to work out the same answer.

At appropriate stages, discuss the different methods as a class and decide collectively on the 'best' method and why it is 'best'. There may be more than one 'best' method.

Differentiation

Less confident learners: Give these children extra support, especially with the explanations of their methods. Encourage them to work at their own pace and, if appropriate, set a target to complete, say, half of the questions.

More confident learners: Challenge these children to devise more than one method of working out the answers to the questions and encourage good use of mathematical language to explain methods. Set an additional challenge to use the digits 4, 5, 6, 7, 8 and 9 to construct as many two-digit addition and subtraction questions as possible within a time limit of ten minutes.

Review

Go through the answers and ask the children to explain their methods. Prompt for alternative methods of answering each question. Write some addition and subtraction questions on the board such as 34 + 49 = ☐. Ask: *How could you work this out mentally?* ((34 + 50) - 1.)

Write on the board 34 + 49 = 83 Ask: *How would you work out 49 + 34? 83 - 49? 83 - 34?*

Repeat with 170 + 190. (Double 18 × 10 or 17 + 19 then multiply by 10, or ((17 + 20) - 1) × 10 or 200 + 170 - 10.) Ask: *Given that 170 + 190 = 360, ask how would you work out 190 + 170? 360 - 170? 360 - 190?* You may choose to illustrate the calculations using the 'Number sentence builder' interactive resource.

Lesson 10 (Practise)

Starter

Revisit: Call out various two-digit numbers and ask the children to show you what that number would if it was doubled. Start with 23, 26, 31, 15, then move onto multiples of 10 such as 250, 340, 610 and then multiples of 100 such as 3000, 3200, 3400.

Main teaching activities

Whole class: Ask: *What is the inverse operation of doubling?* (Halving.) Repeat the Starter activity, this time asking children to halve the number.

Explain to the children that in today's lesson they will be looking at doubling and halving sequences of numbers.

Independent work: Give out the sheet 'Missing numbers' and ask the children to fill out the missing numbers in the sequences.

Differentiation

Less confident learners: Ideally this group could work with an adult and complete the sheet together as a group.

More confident learners: This group should use the extension version of 'Missing numbers', which challenges children to write sequences of their own.

Review

Look at the sequences together, ideally using an interactive whiteboard to display.

Discuss solutions and methods. Ask: *How did you work out the next number? How did you check you were correct?* Look at the differences between the numbers in the sequences and discuss any patterns.

Lesson 11 (Teach and practise)

Starter

Reason: Write on the board the numbers 1, 2, 3, 4, 6, 8 and 12 and ask: *Which number is the odd one out?* Discuss that all the numbers except 1 and 3 are even but decide that all the numbers apart from 8 can be paired up to make 12. (They are factors of 12.) Repeat with 1, 2, 3, 4, 8 and 16. (3 is not a factor of 16.)

Main teaching activities

Whole class: Draw a 'seed' on the board and write 36 on the seed. Explain that this seed is going to grow roots, the roots are what makes the number and these are called factors. Draw some roots with factors (1, 36, 2, 18, 3, 12, 4, 8, 6) and discuss the factors. Repeat by illustrating the factors of 18 in the same way.

Independent work: Ask the children to work out the factors of numbers on the sheet 'Factor seeds'. Encourage them to be methodical by working up and finding pairs of factors in ascending order.

Differentiation

Less confident learners: Use the support version of 'Factor seeds', with the roots already drawn in and some factors provided.

More confident learners: The extension version of the sheet challenges children to answer a number of true or false statements.

Review

Discuss the findings and ask: *How do you know if a number has a factor of 2?* (It is even.) *How do you know if a number has a factor of 5?* (It ends in a 0 or a 5.) *How do you know if a number has a factor of 10?* (It ends in a 0.) *Are there any other factors that are easy to find out?* Discuss the conclusions from the challenge on the extension version of the sheet.

Lesson 12 (Teach and practise)

Starter

Reason: Call out instructions for the children to draw a shape on their whiteboards. For example: *Draw me a shape with four sides that has two lines of symmetry.* (Rectangle.) *Draw me a polygon that has three equal sides and three equal angles.* (Equilateral triangle.) *Draw me a polygon that has five sides and only one line of symmetry.* (Pentagon.)

Main teaching activities

Whole class: Use the 'Grids, patterns, reflection and rotation' interactive resource to draw an L-shape (or use OHP with squared paper). Ask: *What is the area of this shape?* Count the squares together and ask: *What is the perimeter of the shape?* Now reflect the shape in the horizontal mirror line. *How has this shape been moved?* Encourage the use of correct vocabulary and agree that it has been reflected. Draw some more shapes on the interactive whiteboard (for example, squares, rectangles, irregular shapes), or highlight individual squares in different colours. Invite individuals to the board and ask them to draw the reflections, then click on 'Show reflection' to see if they are correct. Switch between horizontal, vertical and diagonal mirror lines. Display some examples of repeating patterns, including Islamic patterns and tiling patterns. Discuss these with the children and ask them to predict how they would continue.

Group work: Give each mixed-ability group a copy of the 'Reflections' sheet. Ask them to discuss and describe each pattern on the sheet. Provide a supply of squared paper, pencils and rulers to enable the groups to make their own translations and reflections. This fits in with the QCA ICT Scheme of Work, Unit 4B 'Developing images using repeating patterns', so, if appropriate, ask groups to use a computer to produce their repeated translations or reflections.

Differentiation

Less confident learners: Provide these children with the support version of the activity sheet and coloured paper to cut out shapes and move them around the grid.

More confident learners: Challenge these children to make up a translation or reflection of their own on the extension version of the sheet.

Review

Review the children's selection of patterns and ask other children from each group to describe each pattern. If possible, display all the children's patterns in the classroom after the lesson.

Lesson 13 (Teach and practise)

Starter

Reason: Repeat the Starter from Lesson 12, this time asking children to draw on squared paper. Say: *Draw me a polygon with four equal sides with an area of nine squares. Draw me a rectangle with an area of 12 squares. How many can you draw? Draw me a right-angled triangle with an area of 4.5 squares.*

Main teaching activities

Whole class: Display some triangular paper, either using an interactive whiteboard or an OHP. Draw a triangle and shade it in, saying: *This triangle has an area of one triangle.* Now draw a shape with the area of two triangles and say: *This shape has an area of two triangles. Is this the only shape that I could draw with an area of two triangles? What is the perimeter of this shape?* Write by the side of the shape: area = 2 triangles, perimeter = 4 units.

Independent work: Give each child a piece of triangular paper and challenge them to draw as many shapes with an area of three triangles as they can. After a fixed amount of time, discuss the findings together and give children time to label each shape with the area and perimeter at the side as you did on the board. Repeat, looking at shapes with areas of four, five and six triangles. After each different area write ideas on the board so that you have a record of all the shapes found. This will allow you to spot any patterns together as a class.

Differentiation

Less confident learners: Provide these children with the correct amount of triangles so that they can manipulate the shapes manually and then copy them onto the paper.

More confident learners: Encourage these children to go on to look at areas of seven or eight triangles and to spot any patterns that may develop.

Review

Look at the shapes that have been drawn throughout the lesson and ask individuals to come up and show lines of symmetry. Sort the shapes by lines of symmetry. Ask, for example: *Which shape has one line of symmetry and a perimeter of ten? Can you name any of the shapes? Have any of the shapes right angles? Do any of the shapes have all angles the same size? Are any of the shapes regular?*

Lesson 14 (Teach and apply)

Starter

Recall: Hold up various 3D shapes and ask the children to write the name of the shape on their whiteboards. Discuss the number of faces, vertices and edges.

Main teaching activities

Whole class: Take a cube, a square-based pyramid and a triangular prism. Compare the shapes. Look at the cube and recap on how you can draw a net for a cube by illustrating on the board and discussing. If possible, have a net made up to fold and unfold. Ask: *How many rectangular faces does a rectangular prism have? ... a square-based pyramid have? How many triangular faces?* Ask the children to draw a rough sketch of what they think the net for a rectangular prism or a square-based pyramid may be.

Independent work: Give each child the sheet 'Creating nets', enlarged and photocopied onto A3 paper. This gives children different shapes that correspond with the faces of a triangular prism and a square-based pyramid. They must cut out the shapes that they think they need to make both nets and put the nets together using masking tape (or stick them onto another piece of paper and then cut around). There are more shapes than they need.

Differentiation

Less confident learners: If possible, these children can work together as a group with a teaching assistant.

More confident learners: Challenge these children to try to visualise the nets of 3D shapes without the shapes in front of them before completing the activity.

Review

Let individuals show their nets and discuss different possibilities. Look back at the net of the cube and ask: *How many other nets could I draw that would also create a cube? Will that still give me six faces?*

Lesson 15 (Teach, apply and evaluate)

Starter

Reason: Say to the children that you are thinking of a 3D shape (or put a 3D shape in a bag and say: *What shape do I have in my bag?*) Explain to the children that they can ask any question that they like about the shape but you will only answer yes or no. Make a note of good questions, using good vocabulary, on the board to use for the next shape. Repeat with a few different shapes and see if they need to ask fewer questions.

Main teaching activities

Whole class: Take 12 interlocking cubes and illustrate how many cuboids you can form from them. Discuss which shapes are the same and how you can record the dimensions, for example 2 by 2 by 3, or 1 by 6 by 2.

Group work: Give each group 72 interlocking cubes and ask them to make a cuboid 2 by 3 by 12. Explain that you would like them to work collaboratively. Then ask the group to investigate what other cuboids they can make by using the 72 cubes. They must record the work in some way and this must be decided on by the whole group.

Differentiation

Less confident learners: If possible, this group could be adult-led to begin with so that the children start to make a link between the factors of 72 and the cuboids that can be made.

More confident learners: Challenge these children to estimate how many cubes can be made from 36 cubes, 18 cubes or 12 cubes without manipulating the cubes and to describe any pattern they see.

Review

Discuss findings and the link with the factors of 72. Ask: *Could I make a cube from 72 cubes? Why not? Could I make a cube from 36 cubes? Which other number of cubes could make cubes? Could I make a cuboid with 13 cubes? Why not?*

Ask the children to work in pairs to discuss what they have learned in this unit.

Name ____________________ Date ____________________

Grid of multiples

1	2	3	4	5	6
7	8	9	10	11	12
13	14	15	16	17	18
19	20	21	22	23	24
25	26	27	28	29	30
31	32	33	34	35	36
37	38	39	40	41	42
43	44	45	46	47	48
49	50	51	52	53	54
55	56	57	58	59	60
61	62	63	64	65	66

Name ______________________ Date ______________

Multiples of 5 and 10

Use a coloured pencil to colour in all the multiples of 5.

1	2	3	4	5	6
7	8	9	10	11	12
13	14	15	16	17	18
19	20	21	22	23	24
25	26	27	28	29	30
31	32	33	34	35	36
37	38	39	40	41	42
43	44	45	46	47	48
49	50	51	52	53	54
55	56	57	58	59	60
61	62	63	64	65	66

1. What do you notice about all of the multiples of 5?

____

Now, starting with 10, use a second colour to circle every alternate multiple of 5.

2. What do you notice about every alternate multiple of 5?

____

Name ____________________ Date ____________________

Shape sorting

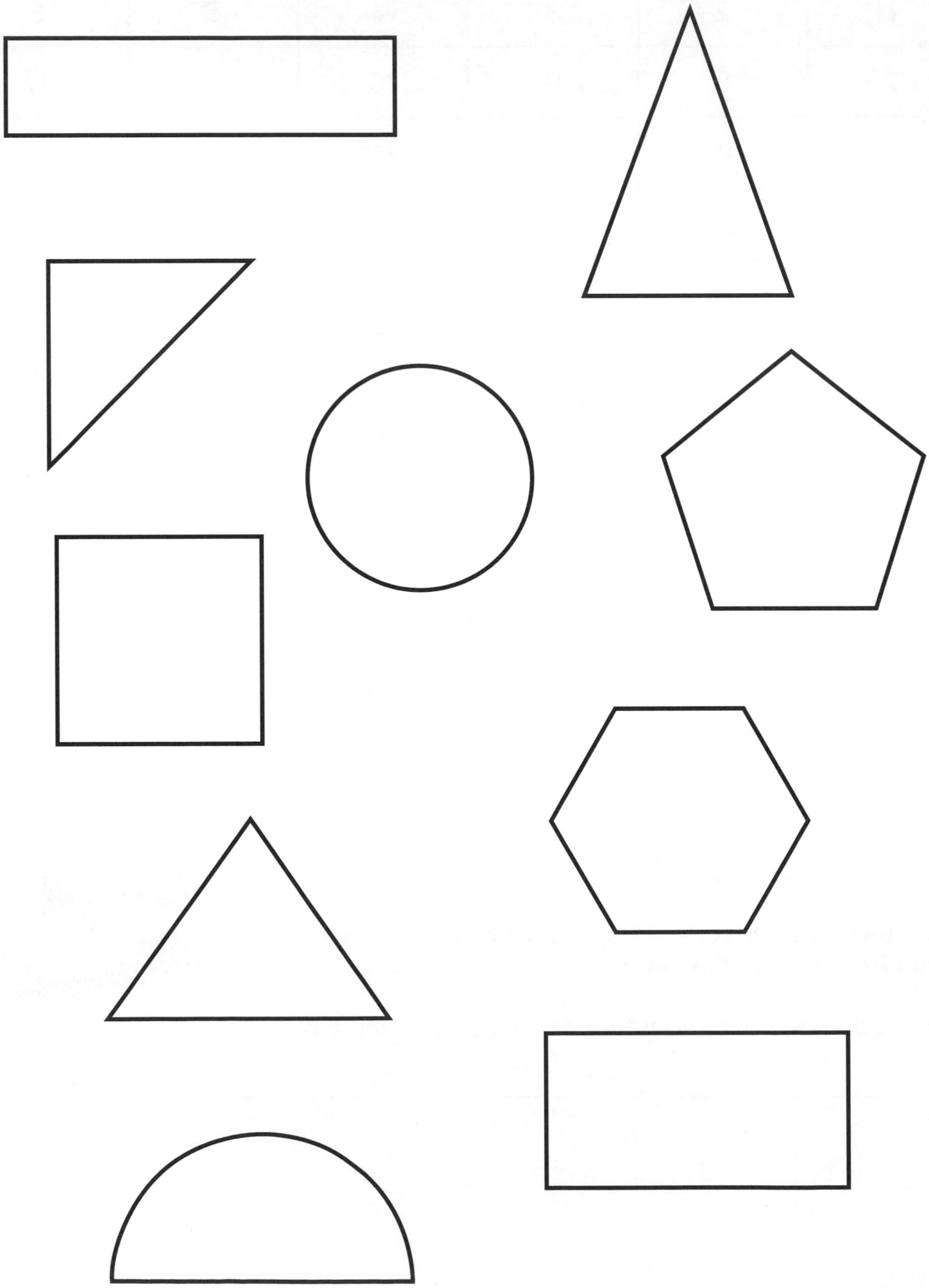

Name ______________________ Date ______________

Symmetrical shapes

Use a ruler to draw in the lines of symmetry on each shape, then check with a mirror.

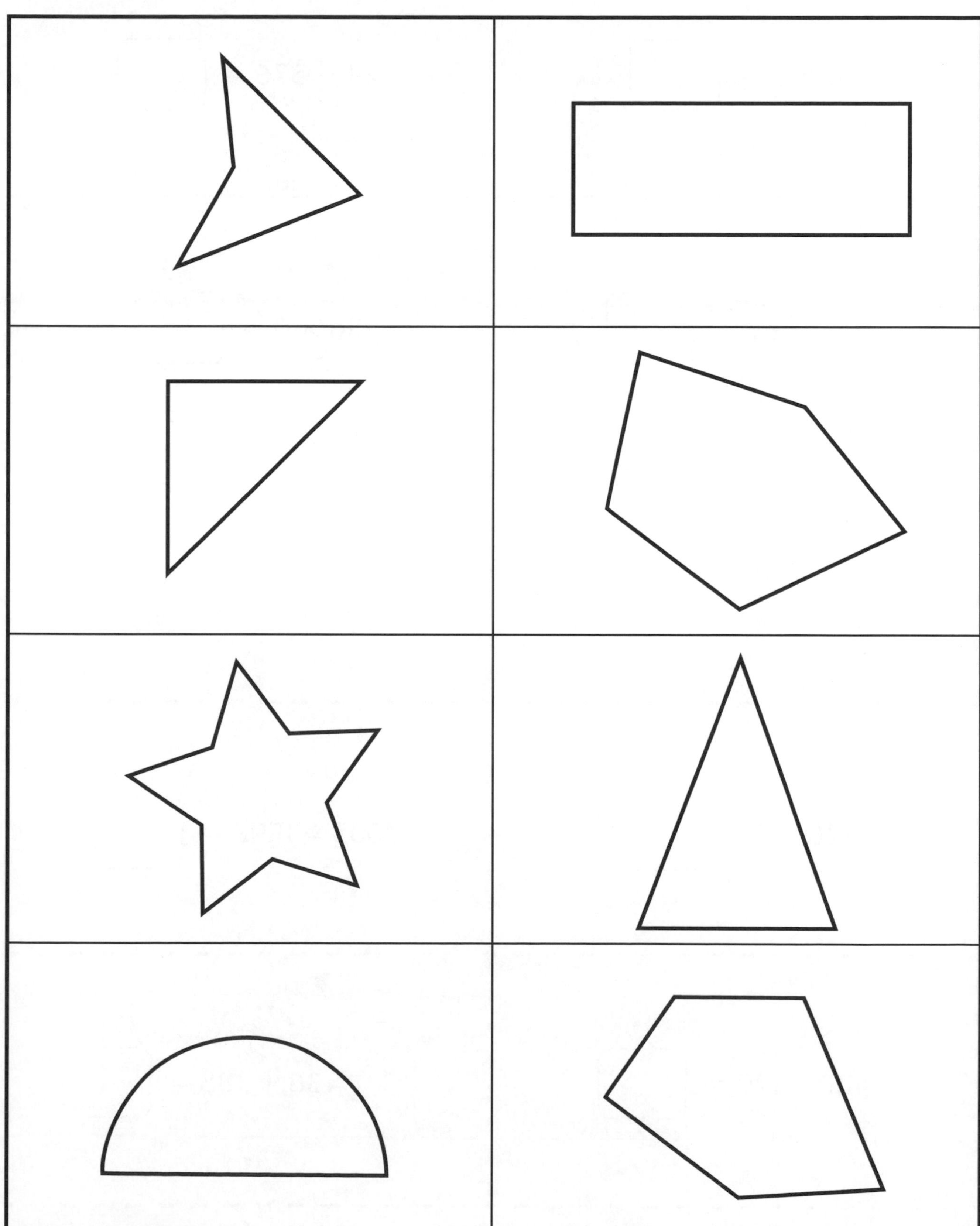

Name ______________________ Date ______________________

What's the method?

4 × 7 = ☐	29 + 576 = ☐
151 + 67 = ☐	36 × 8 = ☐
332 – 89 = ☐	35 ÷ 7 = ☐
120 ÷ 2 = ☐	2005 – 1998 = ☐
400 – 170 = ☐	436 + 185 = ☐

Name ______________________ Date ______________

Consecutive challenge

Target numbers:

21 **36** **69** **75** **81**

1	2	3	4	5	6	7	8	9	10
11	12	13	14	15	16	17	18	19	20
21	22	23	24	25	26	27	28	29	30
31	32	33	34	35	36	37	38	39	40
41	42	43	44	45	46	47	48	49	50
51	52	53	54	55	56	57	58	59	60
61	62	63	64	65	66	67	68	69	70
71	72	73	74	75	76	77	78	79	80
81	82	83	84	85	86	87	88	89	90
91	92	93	94	95	96	97	98	99	100

Challenge:

Make the target numbers above by adding together three **consecutive numbers**.

Colour in the numbers on the 1–100 grid using a coloured pencil.

Describe below any strategies you used for working out the consecutive numbers.

____

____

____

Name ______________________ Date ______________

Investigations

1. Making numbers

You can only use the digit cards 1, 2, 3 and 4.
The aim is to make as many numbers up to 50 using all four digit cards with any operation and brackets.
For example: $19 = 12 + 3 + 4$
$21 = (2 + 1) \times (3 + 4)$. Now try for numbers beyond 50.

____

2. Using 9s

You need four 9 digit cards.
The aim is to make as many numbers up to 50 using all four 9s with any operation and brackets. For example: $1 = \frac{9}{9} \times \frac{9}{9}$

____

3. Missing numbers – subtractions:

Fill in the missing numbers to complete these subtractions:

7 □
– 4 5
3 2

8 1
– 6 □
1 7

9 4
– 5 □
 2

5 □
– 2 6
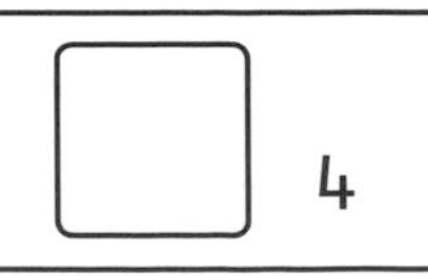 4

 8
– 7 □
2 2

Handling data and measures

Key aspects of learning
- Enquiry
- Creative thinking
- Information processing
- Evaluation
- Self-awareness
- Social skills
- Communication
- Empathy

Expected prior learning

Check that children can already:

- consider a question and develop a response by referring to relevant data
- make and use lists, tables and simple bar charts to organise and interpret the information
- use Venn diagrams or Carroll diagrams to sort data and objects using more than one criterion
- recall the relationships between kilometres and metres, metres and centimetres, kilograms and grams, litres and millilitres
- choose and use appropriate units to estimate, measure and record length and weight
- measure and draw to a suitable degree of accuracy, for example measure length to the nearest half centimetre and weight to the nearest half division on the scales.

Objectives overview

The text in this diagram identifies the focus of mathematics learning within the block.

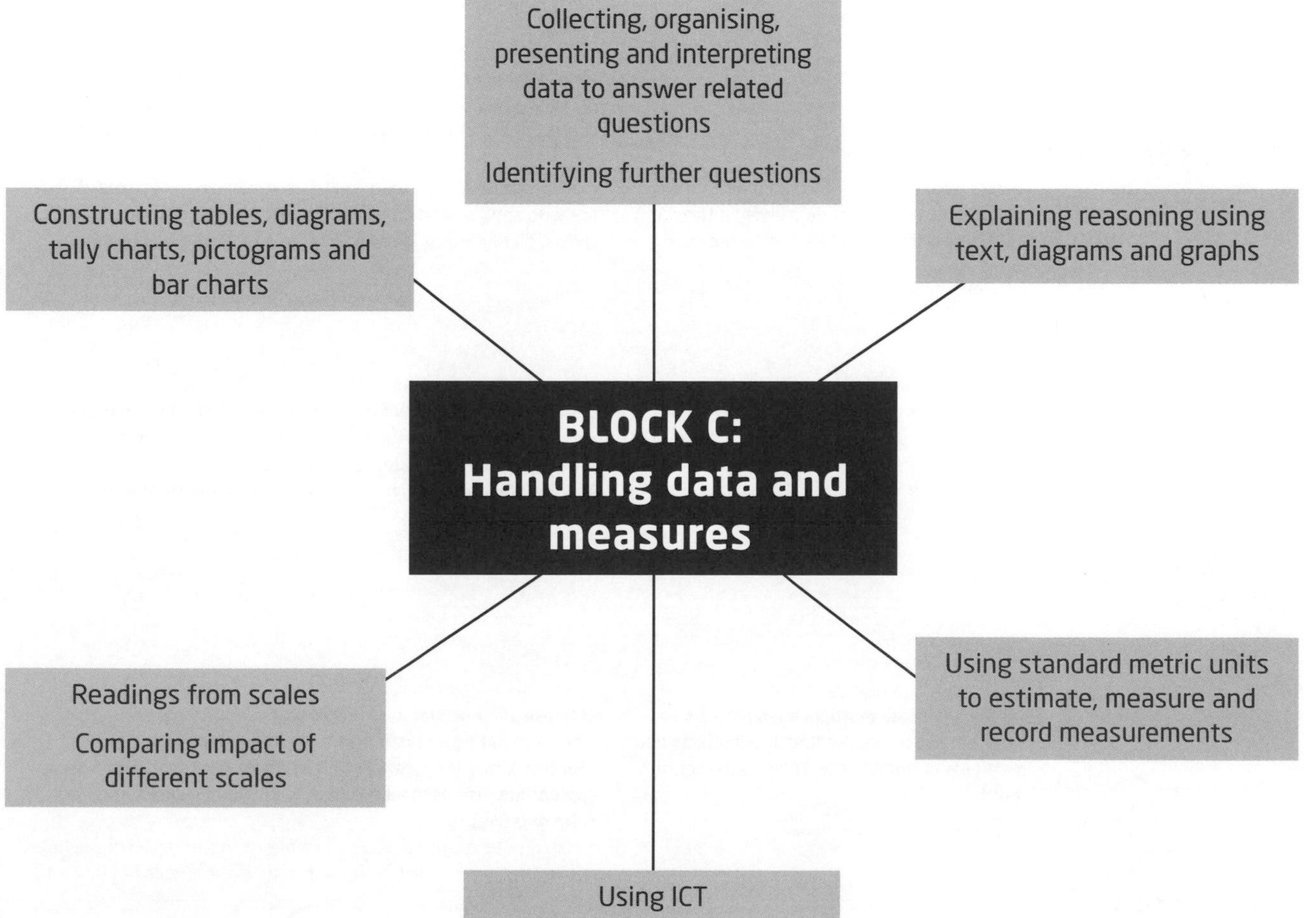

Unit 1 2 weeks

Handling data and measures

Speaking and listening objective

- Use time, resources and group members efficiently by distributing tasks, checking progress, making back-up plans.

Introduction

In this unit, children develop their data handling skills by collecting, organising, presenting, analysing and interpreting data. They work in groups so that they develop their skills in working together, sharing tasks and ensuring that the job is done in the time allowed. They make decisions about what data to collect and how they will go about this. The work on measures is focused on length. Children measure to the nearest unit, including nearest millimetre, and record this in decimal form.

Using and applying mathematics

- Suggest a line of enquiry and the strategy needed to follow it; collect, organise and interpret selected information to find answers.
- Report solutions to puzzles and problems, giving explanations and reasoning orally and in writing, using diagrams and symbols.

Lesson	Strands	Starter	Main teaching activities
1. Teach and practise	Data	Use knowledge of addition and subtraction facts and place value to derive sums and differences of pairs of multiples of 10, 100 or 1000.	**Answer a question by identifying what data to collect; organise, present, analyse and interpret the data in tables, diagrams, tally charts, pictograms and bar charts, using ICT where appropriate.**
2. Review	Data	As for Lesson 1	As for Lesson 1
3. Teach and apply	Use/apply Data	As for Lesson 1	• Suggest a line of enquiry and the strategy needed to follow it; collect, organise and interpret selected information to find answers. • Report solutions to puzzles and problems, giving explanations and reasoning orally and in writing, using diagrams and symbols. **• Answer a question by identifying what data to collect; organise, present, analyse and interpret the data in tables, diagrams, tally charts, pictograms and bar charts, using ICT where appropriate.**
4. Review	Data	**Derive and recall multiplication facts up to 10 × 10, the corresponding division facts and multiples of numbers to 10 up to the tenth multiple.**	**Answer a question by identifying what data to collect; organise, present, analyse and interpret the data in tables, diagrams, tally charts, pictograms and bar charts, using ICT where appropriate.**
5. Teach and apply	Data	As for Lesson 4	As for Lesson 4
6. Review and teach	Measure	Use knowledge of addition and subtraction facts and place value to derive sums and differences of pairs of multiples of 10, 100 or 1000.	**Choose and use standard metric units and their abbreviations when estimating, measuring and recording length, weight and capacity; know the meaning of 'kilo', 'centi' and 'milli' and, where appropriate, use decimal notation to record measurements (eg 1.3m or 0.6kg).**
7. Teach and apply	Measure	As for Lesson 6	As for Lesson 6
8. Review	Measure	As for Lesson 6	As for Lesson 6
9. Teach and apply	Measure	**Derive and recall multiplication facts up to 10 × 10, the corresponding division facts and multiples of numbers to 10 up to the tenth multiple.**	**• Choose and use standard metric units and their abbreviations when estimating, measuring and recording length, weight and capacity; know the meaning of 'kilo', 'centi' and 'milli' and, where appropriate, use decimal notation to record measurements (eg 1.3m or 0.6kg).** • Interpret intervals and divisions on partially numbered scales and record readings accurately, where appropriate to the nearest tenth of a unit.
10. Teach and practise	Measure	Partition, round and order four-digit whole numbers; use positive and negative numbers in context and position them on a number line; state inequalities using the symbols < and > (eg −3 > −5, −1 < +1).	As for Lesson 9

Lessons 1-5

Preparation

Lesson 1: Photocopy 'Follow-me cards' onto thin card and cut out. (You can print the page 'complete' as a reference for the order and answers.) Prepare a display copy (enlarged to A3/copied onto OHT) of the 'Favourite colour survey' resource sheet.
Lesson 3: Prepare display copies of the 'Frequency table' and 'Pictogram' resource sheets. Cut out the people tiles from the 'Pictogram' sheet.
Lesson 4: Prepare a display copy of the 'Vegetables' resource sheet.
Lesson 5: Prepare a display copy of the 'Bar chart' resource sheet.

You will need

Photocopiable pages
'Follow-me cards' (page 104) and 'Favourite colour survey' (page 105).
CD resources
Core, support and extension versions of 'Follow-me cards', 'Reading tally charts', 'Vegetables' and 'Bar chart 1'; 'Frequency table' and 'Pictogram puzzle'. ITP: 'Data handling'.
Equipment
Scissors and glue; interactive whiteboard.

Learning objectives

Starter

- Use knowledge of addition and subtraction facts and place value to derive sums and differences of pairs of multiples of 10, 100 or 1000.
- Derive and recall multiplication facts up to 10 × 10, the corresponding division facts and multiples of numbers to 10 up to the tenth multiple.

Main teaching activities

2006

- Suggest a line of enquiry and the strategy needed to follow it; collect, organise and interpret selected information to find answers.
- Answer a question by identifying what data to collect; organise, present, analyse and interpret the data in tables, diagrams, tally charts, pictograms and bar charts, using ICT where appropriate.
- Report solutions to puzzles and problems, giving explanations and reasoning orally and in writing, using diagrams and symbols.

1999

- Solve a problem by collecting quickly, organising, representing and interpreting data in tables, charts, graphs and diagrams, including those generated by a computer, eg tally charts and frequency tables; pictograms - symbols representing 2, 5, 10 or 20 units; bar charts - intervals labelled in 2s, 5s, 10s or 20s; Venn and Carroll diagrams (two criteria).

Vocabulary

problem, solution, calculate, calculation, method, explain, reasoning, reason, predict, pattern, relationship, classify, represent, interpret, data, information, survey, questionnaire, graph, chart, table, diagram, horizontal axis, vertical axis, axes, label, title, scale, interval, pictogram, bar chart, tally chart, greatest/least value

Lesson 1 (Teach and practise)

Starter

Recall: Give out the cards from the 'Follow-me cards' sheet randomly (three differentiated sets are provided). Choose a child to start. He/she reads out the calculation on the card, and another child will have the answer to that as the first part of the calculation on their card. They read it out and this carries on around the class. Ask questions such as: *How did you work that out?* If a child falters, say the answer in order to keep the pace of this activity.

Main teaching activities

Whole class: Ask the children questions such as:

- *If I wanted to find out your favourite colours, how could I do it?*
- *How could we present this information to other people?*
- *What is a tally mark?*

Write on the board 'PINK', 'YELLOW', 'GREEN', 'PURPLE'. Ask the children to choose their favourite colour from this list. Give them time to discuss their choices for a few moments in groups, then select children to record the tallies for their group onto the chart. When they have finished, ask questions such as:

- *What is the most/least popular colour? How can you tell?*
- *Would the results be the same if we asked another class?*
- *What would the results be if you were allowed two votes for each colour?*

Explain that the class is going to split up into small groups to go around the school and find out the favourite colours of other classes. (Pre-warn other teachers of this impending event!)

Group work: Give each group a copy of 'Favourite colour survey' and agree which class they will visit to collect information. Set a clear time limit so that they go to do this quickly. When they return, ask each group to think of five questions about their data, and to write these on the activity sheet.

While the children are working, collect the tally information on one copy of the activity sheet, then write up the information for display on an OHT of the resource sheet. Ask the children to answer these questions:

- *What is the most popular colour in our school?*
- *What is the least popular colour?*
- *How did you work out your answers?*

The children may need help with some of the calculations, depending on the results.

Differentiation

Less confident learners: In the data collecting, you might send a group out with a classroom assistant. Alternatively, you might decide to have a mixed-ability group. The children will need help with adding the whole-school scores, so have appropriate support material available (such as number lines or 100 squares).

More confident learners: For the data collecting, this group could record with numbers rather than tally marks. When the children are recording the whole school, encourage the children to add up mentally.

Review

Invite the children to answer the three questions that you asked:

- *What is the most popular colour in our school?*
- *What is the least popular colour?*
- *How did you work out your answers?*

Ask the children what questions they wrote down. Invite one question from each of the groups and encourage the other children to try to answer it. Discuss whether or not it was a useful question to ask. A useful question might be 'Was red more popular than purple?', as this can be answered from the data. Questions that are not useful include those that cannot be answered from the data, such as 'What is Tom's mother's favourite colour?'

Lesson 2 (Review)

Starter

Repeat the Starter from Lesson 1. Shuffle the cards so that each child gets a different card this time. Time the activity to keep the pace really sharp.

Main teaching activities

Review the work on tally charts undertaken in the previous lesson. Remind the children that they can use the data in the tally chart to help them to ask and answer questions. Provide a copy of activity sheet 'Reading tally charts' for each child. This is available in differentiated formats, with smaller numbers for the less confident, and larger ones for the more confident. Ask the children to use the tally charts to help them to answer the questions.

Review

Go through the questions on the sheet and discuss with the children how they found their answers. Discuss the titles for the chart that the children suggested, and invite them to say which they think is the most appropriate. Ask them what they would like to find out about in the next lesson by using a survey. These, typically, will be things like favourite pop group/TV programme/day of the week/sport. Choose six things and tell the children that you will let them choose which of the six survey groups they want to be in for the next lesson.

Lesson 3 (Teach and apply)

Starter

Repeat the Starter from Lesson 1 again, but challenge the children to improve on the time that it took them in Lesson 2 to complete the activity.

Main teaching activities

Whole class: Choose one of the survey topics discussed at the end of Lesson 2, and write it as a title for the display copy of 'Frequency table'. Ask the children to suggest what the labels should be for each of the rows in the table. Discuss what should go in the top row of the table and then

each row below that. For example, if they have suggested favourite pop groups, then the first row would say 'Name of pop group', and each row may be labelled with a pop group's name. Discuss the column heading for the 'Frequency' column. Now ask the children to decide which of the pop groups is their favourite, then collect the data by show of hands for each heading. Write in the total for each pop group, as a number this time. Explain that this is another way of showing data that has been collected. Ask questions such as: *Which group has more votes than... fewer votes than...?*

Now explain that the data can be transferred to a pictogram. Pin up the enlarged 'Pictogram' and ask the children to help you to transfer the data from one chart to the other. Explain that sometimes pictures are used instead of bars on a chart. Explain that the pictogram can have pictures to represent one, two or more people. Decide how many people each of the pictures will represent and write in the relevant scale: twos, fives or tens (using scales other than 1 provides an opportunity to use multiples of that number). Write the names of the pop groups on the chart. Invite children to glue the appropriate number of pictures for each pop group. When this is completed, ask questions about the data, and encourage the children to read how many there are. Check that they understand about the scale, and that each picture represents more than one person. Keep a copy of the pictogram for use in Lesson 5.

Group work: Ask the children to decide which survey they would like to carry out in groups of about four children. Provide activity sheets 'Frequency table' and 'Pictogram puzzle'. Give the children time to write the title and labels onto the frequency table. Asking one group at a time, they collect the data from the rest of the class (or a partner class). When all the information has been collected, ask the children to write five questions about their chart ready for the Review. They should then construct a pictogram on the 'Pictogram puzzle' activity sheet.

Differentiation

Less confident learners: The children will be working in mixed ability groups, so other children will no doubt help them. They will probably need support in writing the questions.

More confident learners: Challenge the children to think of really difficult questions about their chart.

Review

Select children from each group to show the class their chart and ask their questions. Invite each group to explain how they transferred their data to the pictogram and how they chose their scale. Ask questions such as: *Was this a good scale to choose? Why/why not?* Check that the children can interrogate both the frequency table and the pictogram in order to ask and answer questions about the data.

Lesson 4 (Review)

Starter

Recall: Remind the children of inverses in the times tables. For example, 4 × 6 has the same answer as 6 × 4. Explain that you will say a table fact. Ask the children to put up their hands to respond with the answer, then with the other three related facts. Say, for example: 7 × 3. The children should respond with '7 × 3 = 21'; '3 × 7 = 21'; '21 ÷ 3 = 7'; '21 ÷ 7 = 3'.

Main teaching activities

Review with the children what they learned about pictograms in the previous lesson. Discuss how they can use their table facts to help them to work out how many a series of pictures on a pictogram represents. For example: *If one picture represents two, how many would five pictures represent? And if one picture represents five, what would three pictures represent?* Provide copies of the activity sheet 'Vegetables' and ask the children to work individually to answer the questions about the pictogram. This sheet is available in differentiated versions with simpler or harder counting.

Review

Look at the activity sheet that most of the class have worked on, using the whiteboard or an OHT version. Invite children from each group to suggest the answers. Discuss possible titles for the chart.

Lesson 5 (Teach and apply)

Starter

Recall: Repeat the Starter from Lesson 4, this time using other facts from the two-, three-, four-, five- or ten-times tables.

Main teaching activities

Whole class: Use the survey that was made into a pictogram again. Remind the children of the data collected by pinning this up on the board. Explain that another way of showing data is to produce a bar chart.

Use the ITP 'Data handling' program to draw a bar chart of the data (or draw a bar chart on the board, OHP or interactive whiteboard.) Discuss with the children what scale would be suitable, choosing from multiples of 2, 5, 10 or 20. Put the scale onto the *y*-axis of the chart, and write the headings along the *x*-axis (note that the ITP does not have this option). Invite children from each group to help with drawing in the appropriate size of bar. Ask: *Where will this bar come to?* When the chart is finished, invite the children to ask and answer questions, such as: *How many... are there? Are there more... or more...? How many more?*

Independent work: Ask the children to complete the 'Bar chart 1' activity sheet individually. This shows a bar chart, with a scale in 5s, for them to interrogate.

Differentiation

Less confident learners: Decide whether to use the support version of the activity sheet, with a scale in 5s but with lower totals.

More confident learners: Decide whether to use the extension version of the activity sheet, with a scale in 10s.

Review

Display and review the 'Bar chart 1' sheets with all of the children. Ask the children to answer the questions on the sheet. Choose children from each group to respond. Check that the children understand that a scale is used and how to interpret the amount represented by a bar. Ask questions such as: *How many more/fewer... were there than...? How can you tell? Of which animal is there most/least?*

Lessons 6-10

You will need

CD resources

Core, support and extension versions of 'Metric units for length'; 'Standard units for length', 'Find the perimeter' and 'Measures of length'.

Equipment

Rulers marked in mm and cm; measuring tapes; individual whiteboard and pen for each child; individual whiteboards and pens; rulers marked in cm and mm; metre sticks marked in cm; measuring tapes.

Learning objectives

Starter

- Use knowledge of addition and subtraction facts and place value to derive sums and differences of pairs of multiples of 10, 100 or 1000.
- Derive and recall multiplication facts up to 10 × 10, the corresponding division facts and multiples of numbers to 10 up to the tenth multiple.
- Partition, round and order four-digit whole numbers; use positive and negative numbers in context and position them on a number line; state inequalities using the symbols < and >, eg -3 > -5, -1 < +1.

Main teaching activities

2006

- Choose and use standard metric units and their abbreviations when estimating, measuring and recording length, weight and capacity; know the meaning of 'kilo', 'centi' and 'milli' and, where appropriate, use decimal notation to record measurements (eg 1.3m or 0.6kg).
- Interpret intervals and divisions on partially numbered scales and record readings accurately, where appropriate to the nearest tenth of a unit.

1999

- Use, read and write standard metric units (km, m, cm, mm, kg, g, l, ml), including their abbreviations, and imperial units (mile, pint).
- Know and use the relationships between familiar units of length, mass and capacity.
- Know the equivalent of one half, one quarter, three quarters and one tenth of 1km, 1m, 1kg, 1 litre in m, cm, g, ml.
- Suggest suitable units and measuring equipment to estimate or measure

length, mass or capacity.

- Record estimates and readings from scales to a suitable degree of accuracy.

Vocabulary

metric unit, standard unit, millimetre (mm), centimetre (cm), metre (m)

Lesson 6 (Review and teach)

Starter

Recall: Explain that you will ask an addition sentence with an answer that will be between 0 and 12. Ask the children to write the answer on their whiteboards and, when you say *Show me*, they hold up their boards for you to see. Keep the pace of this sharp, and for some number sentences ask questions such as: *How did you find the answer?* Encourage rapid recall. Ask, for example: *6 + 5, 12 - 8, 3 + 8...*

Main teaching activities

Whole class: Write on the board: 'km, m, cm'. Choose children to come to the board to write the full word next to each abbreviation. Ask the children to read each word correctly and check the spelling of the word. Then write up 'mm' and ask if anyone knows what this stands for. Write the word 'millimetre' on the board. Explain about millimetres and their use in measuring small lengths.

Provide rulers marked in millimetres to pairs of children and invite them to use the rulers to measure, for example, the width of their pencil. Ask: *How wide was your pencil?* Invite children from each group to write their answer onto the board, using the shortened form 'mm'. Ask questions such as: *How many metres are there in a kilometre? How many centimetres in a metre? How many millimetres in a centimetre?* Write the relationships on the board: '1 kilometre = 1000 metres'; '1 metre = 100 centimetres'; '1 centimetre = 10 millimetres'.

Discuss the fact that longer distances in Britain (such as road journeys) are measured in miles, and that this is an imperial unit. In the rest of Europe the standard unit is a kilometre, which is a metric unit. Tell them that one mile is longer than one kilometre, but shorter than two.

Group work: Provide copies of the activity sheet 'Metric units for length'. Ask the children to complete the questions about converting measurements, then to measure the lines on the page. For the final question, they can draw lines of the required length on the back of the sheet.

Differentiation

Less confident learners: Decide whether to provide the support version of the activity sheet, which asks children to draw lines measured in centimetres.
More confident learners: Decide whether to provide the extension version of the activity sheet, which asks children to draw lines measured in millimetres. They may need to approximate the lengths of their drawings.

Review

Using the core version of the activity sheet, review the answers to the questions. Encourage all of the children to join in responding to the questions. Ask:

- *How many metres is 300 centimetres? How do you know?*
- *What is 4 metres in centimetres? How did you work it out?*
- *Which is longer, 2000 metres or 3 kilometres? Explain how you know?*

Lesson 7 (Teach and apply)

Starter

Recall: Repeat the Starter for Lesson 1, this time concentrating on subtraction questions, up to 12 - 12.

Main teaching activities

Whole class: Ask the children to work in pairs. Ask: *How tall do you think your partner is? What units would you use? Why would you choose those?* Discuss how they made their estimate and the units chosen, and whether these seem sensible. Now invite each pair to measure each other in their chosen units and to see how close they were to their estimate. Ask: *How* *close was the measurement to the estimate? Were the chosen units sensible?* Provide each child with a ruler marked in cm and mm. Ask them to estimate, then measure, the length of their pencil. Ask: *How close to your estimate were you? What units did you use to measure the pencil?* Explain that it is possible to measure to the nearest tenth of a centimetre by counting along the millimetre marks on the ruler. Repeat this for measuring another pencil, and ask the children to measure to the nearest tenth of a centimetre. They can write their measurement as a decimal fraction of a centimetre.

Group work: Invite the children to continue to work in their pairs. Write on the board a list of classroom items which they can estimate and then measure, choosing their units appropriately.

Differentiation

Less confident learners: Encourage children to use the vocabulary of estimation and measurement, putting into a sentence each estimate they make, and checking the accuracy of this with the measurement.

More confident learners: Work outside to make larger measurements such as the dimensions of the playground.

Review

Invite children from each group to give their estimates and measurements and to discuss how accurate their original estimate was. Discuss how they wrote their results, and how accurately they were able to measure.

Lesson 8 (Review)

Starter

Recall: Repeat the Starter from Lesson 1, this time extending to include addition and subtraction questions that lie within the whole range from 0 to 20. Keep the pace sharp to encourage rapid recall.

Main teaching activities

Review estimation and measurement for length, and ask questions such as: *What units would you use to measure the height of a bungalow? ... the width of your thumb?* Discuss measuring distances and how we still use the standard imperial units of miles in Britain, while in Europe kilometres are used. Provide the copies of activity sheet 'Standard units for length'. This invites the children to make estimates of lengths, and to suggest what could be measured in specific units. This sheet is not differentiated, so you may wish to work with the less confident children, and complete the sheet together. When they have finished the sheet, challenge the more confident children to add to the list of items that they would measure with specific units.

Review

Discuss the children's responses to the questions. Ask: *Why did you decide to use those units? Does everyone agree? Why/why not?*

Lesson 9 (Teach and apply)

Starter

Recall: Begin by reciting the multiplication tables for 2, 3, 4, 5 and 10. Keep the pace sharp. Now explain that you will say a multiplication or division fact. Ask the children to write their answers on their whiteboards and to hold up their boards when you say *Show me*. Keep the pace of this sharp to encourage rapid recall.

Main teaching activities

Whole class: Draw a rectangle on the board and discuss its properties. Highlight the fact that pairs of sides are of equal length and therefore it is not necessary to measure all the sides. Ask the children to imagine that the rectangle on the board is a farmer's field full of bulls, and that he wants to put a fence around the field to keep the bulls in. Ask questions such as: *How could we find out how much fence is needed? Do we have to measure all the sides? Why not?*

Write the word 'perimeter' on the board and explain that it is the

measurement of length all the way around a shape. Put some measurements on the rectangle, such as 80 metres and 60 metres, and ask the children to calculate the perimeter of the field. Ask: *How did you work that out?* Check that the children used an efficient method. They may have multiplied each measurement by 2 then totalled, or they may have added the measurements of the four sides. Say together: *Perimeter.* Repeat this with rectangles of other sizes, such as a football pitch or a playground.

Group work: Ask the children to work in pairs. Explain that you would like them to find ten rectangular items in the classroom, such as the top of their table or a book. They should find the length and breadth of each one and then calculate the perimeter. They can record their work on the activity sheet 'Find the perimeter'. Explain that they can use rulers, metre sticks and measuring tapes. Ask them to measure to the nearest tenth of a unit. Give the children about 20 minutes to complete this work, and remind them when there are five minutes left.

Differentiation

Less confident learners: Work with this group. Agree as a group which item to measure first, then compare measurements. Work together to find the perimeter so that the children are sure of how to do this.

More confident learners: If the children finish the group work above, suggest that they search for more unusual shapes with straight sides, and find the perimeters of those.

Review

Ask the children for the sizes of the rectangles they found in the second part of the lesson. Show on the board how to find a quick solution by doubling each side and then adding together. Hold up some regular 2D shapes and ask the children for a quick way to calculate the perimeter. If the children do not use the term 'multiplication', use it to show them how to find the answer. Hold up an irregular shape and ask if you could find the perimeter of this shape by multiplication. Look for children who have used 'quick' methods to calculate the perimeter. Ask: *How can you find the perimeter of this shape? Is this the quickest way? Why/why not?*

Lesson 10 (Teach and practise)

Starter

Revisit: Explain that you will say a number between 1 and 100. Ask the children to write on their whiteboards what the number becomes after rounding to the nearest 10, and to hold up their whiteboards when you say *Show me*. Keep the pace of this sharp. When the children are confident with this, extend the number range to 1000.

Main teaching activities

Whole class: Discuss the classroom bookcase: *How long do you think one shelf is? Why do you think that? How long would two or three of the shelves be in total? How did you work that out?* Invite two children to measure one of the shelves while the others watch. Ask: *What measuring equipment will you use? Why do you think that is a good choice? Do you all agree?* Discuss the units chosen and how close to the estimate the measure is. Discuss how accurately the measurement can be made. Ask a child to write the measurement on the board.

Group work: Choose from the selection of practical tasks on activity sheet 'Measures of length'. These are suitable for children to complete in pairs.

Differentiation

Less confident learners: The children could work as a group on a chosen activity on 'Measures of length'. Encourage them to begin by saying which units they will need, and why.

More confident learners: Challenge the children to suggest their own measuring problem to solve.

Review

Choose one of the activities that most of the children have completed. Ask questions such as:

- *What units did you choose? Was this a good choice? Why/why not?*
- *Which measuring equipment did you choose? Was this a good choice? Why?*
- *Suppose the tape measure is torn. Now it begins at 7cm. How can you use it to measure in centimetres?*

Remind the children how measuring is always approximate, and that we use rounding to record.

Name ______________________ Date ______________________

Follow-me cards

Photocopy onto thin card and cut out the cards.

Provide each child with a card.

Ask a child to read out their question.

The child with the answer as the first number on their card reads out their question, and so on.

For example: 57 + 23 = 80, so the next card is 80 – 27, and so on.

25 + 34	59 – 17	42 + 39
81 – 23	58 + 13	71 – 53
18 + 56	74 – 46	28 + 19
47 – 25	22 + 63	85 – 56

Name ______________________ Date ______________

Favourite colour survey

Use this tally chart for recording data for this survey.

We went to Class ______________________

Colour	Tally	Total
Red		
Blue		
Green		
Yellow		
Purple		

Questions about our table.

1. ______________________

2. ______________________

3. ______________________

4. ______________________

5. ______________________

Unit 2 2 weeks

Handling data and measures

Lesson	Strand	Starter	Main teaching activities
1. Review and apply	Use/apply Data	• Suggest a line of enquiry and the strategy needed to follow it; collect, organise and interpret selected information to find answers. **• Answer a question by identifying what data to collect; organise, present, analyse and interpret the data in tables, diagrams, tally charts, pictograms and bar charts, using ICT where appropriate.** • Report solutions to puzzles and problems, giving explanations and reasoning orally and in writing, using diagrams and symbols.	• Suggest a line of enquiry and the strategy needed to follow it; collect, organise and interpret selected information to find answers. **• Answer a question by identifying what data to collect; organise, present, analyse and interpret the data in tables, diagrams, tally charts, pictograms and bar charts, using ICT where appropriate.** • Report solutions to puzzles and problems, giving explanations and reasoning orally and in writing, using diagrams and symbols.
2. Review and apply	Use/apply Data	Report solutions to puzzles and problems, giving explanations and reasoning orally and in writing, using diagrams and symbols.	As for Lesson 1
3. Review and apply	Use/apply Data	As for Lesson 2	As for Lesson 1
4. Teach and apply	Use/apply Data	As for Lesson 1	As for Lesson 1
5. Review, practise and apply	Use/apply Data	As for Lesson 2	As for Lesson 1
6. Review, teach and apply	Measure Data	**Choose and use standard metric units and their abbreviations when estimating, measuring and recording length, weight and capacity; know the meaning of 'kilo', 'centi' and 'milli' and, where appropriate, use decimal notation to record measurements (eg 1.3m or 0.6kg).**	**• Choose and use standard metric units and their abbreviations when estimating, measuring and recording length, weight and capacity; know the meaning of 'kilo', 'centi' and 'milli' and, where appropriate, use decimal notation to record measurements (eg 1.3m or 0.6kg).** • Interpret intervals and divisions on partially numbered scales and record readings accurately, where appropriate to the nearest tenth of a unit. • Compare the impact of representations where scales have intervals of differing step size.
7. Review and practise	Measure Data	**• Choose and use standard metric units and their abbreviations when estimating, measuring and recording length, weight and capacity; know the meaning of 'kilo', 'centi' and 'milli' and, where appropriate, use decimal notation to record measurements (eg 1.3m or 0.6kg).** • Use knowledge of addition and subtraction facts and place value to derive sums and differences of pairs of multiples of 10, 100 or 1000 (revision of Blocks A and B).	As for Lesson 6
8. Teach, practise and apply	Measure Data	As for Lesson 7	As for Lesson 6
9. Apply	Measure Data	**• Choose and use standard metric units and their abbreviations when estimating, measuring and recording length, weight and capacity; know the meaning of 'kilo', 'centi' and 'milli' and, where appropriate, use decimal notation to record measurements (eg 1.3m or 0.6kg).** • Identify the doubles of two-digit numbers; use to calculate doubles of multiples of 10 and 100 and derive the corresponding halves (revision of Blocks A and B).	As for Lesson 6
10. Review and practise	Measure Data	As for Lesson 9	As for Lesson 6

Speaking and listening objective

- Use time, resources and group members efficiently by distributing tasks, checking progress, making back-up plans.

Introduction

In this unit children collect, organise, present and interpret data to answer related questions, identifying further questions. They construct tables, diagrams, tally charts, pictograms and bar charts, explaining reasoning using text, diagrams and graphs. Children read from scales, comparing the impact of different scales. They use standard metric units to estimate, measure and record measurements. The unit includes the use of ICT.

Using and applying mathematics

- Suggest a line of enquiry and the strategy needed to follow it; collect, organise and interpret selected information to find answers.

Lessons 1-5

Preparation

Lesson 2: Prepare the sheets 'Pictogram puzzle', 'Tally chart' and 'Bar chart 2' for display. Collect some newspapers or magazines (up to five per child).
Lesson 3: If you are doing this without ICT, you will need some copies of graphs and charts for display purposes.
Lesson 4: Prepare copies of some bar charts from Lesson 3 for display.
Lesson 5: Prepare the chart from the Starter for display.
Lesson 6: Prepare the sheet 'Carroll diagram' for display.

You will need

Photocopiable pages
'Key charts' (page 116) and 'Tally charts' (page 117).
CD resources
'Pictogram puzzle', 'Frequency chart', 'Bar chart 2' and 'Carroll diagram (shape sorting)'. General resource sheet: 'Pictogram'. ITP: 'Data handling'.
Equipment
Sticky notes; a database or suitable data handling package; two hoops (large enough to make Venn diagrams with the geo-rods) for each group of two or three children; enough geo-rods per group to make several shapes; fasteners for geo-rods.

Learning objectives

Starter

- Suggest a line of enquiry and the strategy needed to follow it; collect, organise and interpret selected information to find answers.
- Answer a question by identifyi g what data to collect; organise, present, analyse and interpret the data in tables, diagrams, tally charts, pictograms and bar charts, using ICT where appropriate.
- Report solutions to puzzles and problems, giving explanations and reasoning orally and in writing, using diagrams and symbols.

Main teaching activities

2006

- Suggest a line of enquiry and the strategy needed to follow it; collect, organise and interpret selected information to find answers.
- Answer a question by identifying what data to collect; organise, present, analyse and interpret the data in tables, diagrams, tally charts, pictograms and bar charts, using ICT where appropriate.
- Report solutions to puzzles and problems, giving explanations and reasoning orally and in writing, using diagrams and symbols.

1999

- Solve a problem by collecting quickly, organising, representing and interpreting data in tables, charts, graphs and diagrams, including those generated by a computer, eg tally charts, frequency tables, pictograms, bar charts, Venn and Carroll diagrams.
- Explain methods and reasoning about numbers orally and in writing.

Vocabulary

problem, solution, calculate, calculation, method, explain, reasoning, reason, predict, pattern, relationship, classify, represent, interpret, data, information, survey, questionnaire, graph, chart, table, diagram, horizontal axis, vertical axis, axes, label, title, scale, interval, pictogram, bar chart, tally chart, greatest/least value, quadrilateral

Lesson 1 (Review and apply)

Starter

Revisit: In this lesson children will revise their data-handling work from Unit 1. Ask each child to draw a quick sketch of their favourite animal on a sticky note and stick it on the board when they have finished. Ask: *What was the most popular animal? How many people like cats the best?* The children will find it difficult to use the information as it is on the board. Ask: *How can we rearrange the information to make it easier for us to read?* Ask for suggestions and see if the children place the sticky notes into rows or columns to make a pictogram, or add a key (1 sticky note = 1 animal).

Main teaching activities

Whole class: Use the same sticky notes to make a simple bar chart. Ask: *Does this make it easier to read the information? How many children in the class like dogs the most? What was the most popular animal? How can we make this clearer?* (By labelling the type of animal and the number of animals on the two axes.) Now ask again: *What was the most popular animal? Is this easier to see? How else could we arrange this information to make it clearer?* This could be illustrated well by using an interactive whiteboard.

Group work: Challenge the children, in groups of two or three, to use a different key or scale, such as 1 sticky note = 2 animals, 4 animals, 5 animals, 10 animals. Explain that each sticky note represents a different number of votes now, not just the one that it did before. With a key of one sticky note representing two votes (or animals), three sticky notes would represent six votes. Give groups one of the keys above and ask them to construct bar charts to answer the questions on the activity sheet 'Key charts'. Encourage the groups not to reveal the keys they have chosen. Then, as the group reads out their results for the five statements on the sheet, they can challenge the other groups to guess their key.

Whole class: Compare and discuss results. Take a vote to decide which group has the clearest results. Ask: *What made the information clearer to read? How many more children prefer cats to dogs? If you were asked the question 'Are dogs more popular than cats?' how would you answer, given this information? Do you think that will always be the case?* Discuss the children's bar charts and ask questions such as: *What is the scale of your vertical axis? What did you put along the horizontal axis? Do you think that bar charts or pictograms are easier to read?* Highlight the importance of labels in bar charts.

Group work: Now encourage the groups to come up with a question or hypothesis about the data, for example: 'Boys like dogs better than girls', or 'Girls prefer cats'. The children need to gather information to let them test and answer their question or hypothesis.

Differentiation

Less confident learners: Give this group a key of one sticky note to two votes.

More confident learners: Challenge the group to display the information in a number of different ways and think about a wider variety of scales.

Review

Let a representative from each group present the results from their hypothesis work. Discuss the conclusions and steps taken. Ask: *When is a tally useful? Why is it useful? When is a bar chart useful? Why is it useful?*

Lesson 2 (Review and apply)

Starter

Read: Display the 'Pictogram' general resource sheet on OHP or on the interactive whiteboard. Ask questions such as: *How many people visited the shoe shops? Chemists?* Discuss use of a key for 20 people. If appropriate add a further column to the chart to add the frequencies. You will look at this pictogram again next lesson.

Main teaching activities

Whole class: Remind children of work completed in Unit 1 on tally charts, frequency charts and bar charts. Ask: *When would you use a frequency chart?* (As a quick way to collect and order small amounts of data.) Explain that the children will be investigating the statement: 'Half of the pages in magazines and newspapers are made up of adverts.' Ask: *Do you think that this is true?*

Group work: Split the children into five groups of four or five. Give each group a pile of newspapers or magazines. Ask the children for ideas on how to test the statement. Agree on the approach, collecting the data into a tally chart (see example on following page). Give each group the first page of activity sheet 'Tally charts', which provides the chart to complete for each magazine. If each child counts three to five magazines, this will give a significant sample (about 100). Ask: *How could we check the information?* (Count the number of pages and total the tallies.)

Quantity of advertisements	Number of pages
No advertisements on the page	
Less than (<) half the page contains advertisements	
More than (>) or equal to half the page contains advertisements	
Whole page of advertisements	

Whole class: Ask the different groups to summarise their findings, using the activity sheet 'Frequency chart'. Compare results and ask: *Do you think that the original statement is true?* Then, on an OHT of the 'Tally charts' sheet, collect all of the information to make a combined frequency table. Now ask: *How could we show this information on a bar chart?* Ideally, use the 'Data handling' ITP on the interactive whiteboard, or use an OHT of the sheet 'Bar chart 2' to draw up the information on the axes. The vertical column has been left blank to enable you to explore the different intervals 2, 5 or 10 on the scales. Ask: *What would be the best way to fit the numbers onto this axis? Do I need to put in every number? What does this bar chart tell you?*

Differentiation

Less confident learners: Ask this group to select from fewer magazines/newspapers and to focus on a bar chart with a scale of no more than 5 units.
More confident learners: Challenge this group to use a wider selection of magazines/newspapers and select their own scales/vertical axis for the bar charts.

Review

Ask: *Who thinks that the statement about advertising in newspapers and magazines is correct? Why? Who disagrees? What could we do to investigate further? How else could we have recorded the results? Which do you think is the best way? Why do you think that? Are your results what you expected or were there any surprises? What evidence do you have to support your conclusions? What other questions could you investigate now that you have answered the original question? What would you do differently if you carried out the enquiry again?*

Lesson 3 (Review and apply)

Starter

Read: Display the 'Pictogram' resource sheet again and this time ask: *How many people went shopping in the High Street altogether that week? What else can you tell me about this data?* Discuss more popular shops/other types of shopping categories that could have been added.

Main teaching activities

(Ideally, work in the school computer room, with an interactive whiteboard for demonstration.)
Whole class: Say to the children that computers can help us with data handling. Use a suitable data-handling program to show some examples of charts and graphs. (Alternatively prepare some OHTs of graphs cut from newspapers.) Explain that many companies use computers to help them draw charts. Quickly collect data about eye colours of the class. Show how to input the data and demonstrate how the computer can illustrate the information in a number of ways, such as bar charts and line graphs using various scales. (Alternatively draw a graph of the data together on an OHP.) Ask: *What makes the information easy or difficult to interpret? Do you think this information is clearer in a bar chart? Using which scale? In another sort of chart? Why?*

In lessons:	5½ hours
Playtime:	2 hours
Eating:	2½ hours
Watching TV:	2½ hours
Reading and homework:	1½ hours
Sleeping:	9 hours
Travelling to school:	1 hour

Paired/independent work: The children use a computer to display information gathered from the class. Ask them to take a typical school day, spilt it into 24 hours and work out how long they spend doing different things in the day (as shown left).

Ask the children to present their findings as a bar chart using the data-handling program. They should use a non-unitary scale, such as ½ hours. If computers are not available this can be done by hand. If a database is used, then work with the children to establish how many and what type of fields they will require (one text field and one number field). They should save and print off their bar charts for use in the next lesson.

Differentiation

Less confident learners: This group should work with a teaching assistant to pool their data. Let the children enter any data they can. Ask the children to round their activities up to the nearest hour and check that they add up to 24 before they draw anything.

More confident learners: These children could start to think about splitting their day into 10-minute or 20-minute periods.

Review

Ask the children to present their bar charts to the rest of the class. Discuss interval scales and ask: *Is the information clear? How could it be clearer?* Compare results, asking: *Who spends the most time watching television? ... reading? ... playing? ... eating?* Encourage the children to make some statements of their own about their bar charts. Keep all this work for continuing in the following lesson.

Lesson 4 (Teach and apply)

Starter

Read: Display two bar charts from Lesson 3's exercise. Ideally choose two that have different scales on the axes. Ask the children to compare the charts. Ask questions such as: *Who spent the most time sleeping? Eating? Working? How many hours in total did they spend playing? What is the difference between the amounts of time that they spent eating? Sleeping?*

Main teaching activities

In this session either work in the computer room or have the individual charts printed out for the children to use. Explain to the class that they will be using the data that they collected in yesterday's lesson to gather some further information about the class.

Independent or group work: Ask the children to come up with a question involving the data that they collected, for example: 'Do girls spend more time reading than boys?' or 'Do people with brown eyes read more than people with blue eyes?'. Explain that they have a fixed amount of time to gather data from the class and suggest that they record their information in a chart. Take ideas and develop one on the board. For example:

Amount of time spent reading	Brown eyes	Not brown eyes

Differentiation

Less confident learners: Spend time with this group, developing a question and a chart. If there are time constraints let these children come up with a question as a group so you will help them develop one chart.

More confident learners: Encourage these children to develop a more complex hypothesis, such as: 'Boys spend twice as much time playing football as girls do eating'; or 'People with blond hair spend half as much time sleeping as people who don't have blonde hair.'

Review

As a class, discuss hypotheses and results and how you might display these results. Ideally use the data-handling program to input some data and explore this. Ask: *What have you found out? What charts or tables could you use to show your results? Are your results what you expected or were there any surprises? What evidence do you have to support your conclusions? What other questions could you investigate now that you have answered the original question? What would you do differently if you carried out the enquiry again?*

Lesson 5 (Review, practise and apply)

Starter

Reason: Display this chart, then ask children to respond to the questions, using whiteboards if appropriate. Ask: *What is missing from this chart? Can you suggest a title? How many people like blue and yellow? Blue and red? Blue and orange?* and so on. *What*

Colour	Frequency
Red	34
Orange	67
Blue	78
Yellow	11
Green	

is the difference between those people who chose blue and those who chose yellow? What is double the amount of people who chose red? If there were 200 people asked, how many people chose green?

Main teaching activities

Group work: Explain to the children that they will be looking at shapes and sorting them (continuing from Block B, Unit 2). Split the children into groups of two or three and give each group two hoops and a number of geo rods and clips. Explain that you will start by asking the groups to make shapes, using the geo rods, and then you will sort the shapes. Challenge the groups to show you a triangle, quadrilateral, pentagon, hexagon, heptagon, octagon and discuss the characteristics of each shape. Highlight numbers of sides and angles.

Challenge the group to make three different sorts of triangle. Compare results and discuss equilateral (all sides equal and all angles equal), isosceles (two angles equal and two sides the same) and scalene (all angles different and all sides different, although the children need not know the name until Year 5). The children may make a right-angled triangle, in which case discuss this too. Ask each group to use the two hoops independently and sort the shapes into 'all sides equal' in one hoop and 'right angles' in the other. Ask: *Is there a shape that could go into both hoops?* (Square.) Show them how to place the hoops so that they overlap, and place the square in the intersection of the loops. Ideally, display this on an interactive whiteboard. Now ask each group to sort the shapes. Explain that each hoop must have a label. Challenge the children to look at the other groups' hoops and make a guess at what the labels could be. Discuss and compare results.

Now overlap the two hoops and place shapes in the hoops as shown in the diagram below.

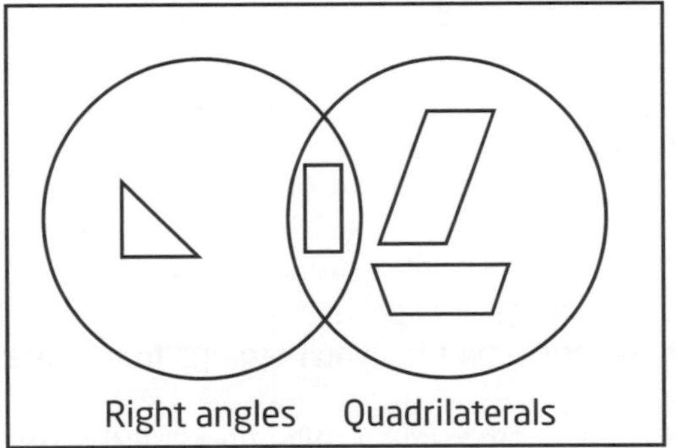

Repeat as before and ask: *What could the labels be?* Discuss, and stress that the overlap must contain shapes that have right angles and are quadrilaterals. Then ask the children to pick a few shapes and use their hoops to sort them into a two-region Venn diagram. Challenge the other groups to guess the labels for the sets and discuss/compare.

Review

Display the 'Carroll diagram (shape sorting)' sheet. Ask: *How can we sort these shapes? What are the names of the shapes? How many lines of symmetry does a rectangle have? How many right angles does a rectangle have? How many sides are the same in an isosceles triangle? How many sides are the same in a rectangle? What can you say about all the angles of an equilateral triangle and all the angles in a rectangle? What do the positions of the shapes in the Carroll diagram tell us? How could I label this Carroll diagram?*

Differentiation

Less confident learners: Limit the range of shapes used by these children to triangles and simple quadrilaterals.

More confident learners: Let these children work with a range of polygons including triangles, quadrilaterals, pentagons, hexagons and octagons. They could also use regular and irregular shapes. Discuss how they choose to label their Venn diagrams. As an extra challenge, you could ask this group to design their own Venn diagram with some questions about it.

Lessons 6-10

Preparation

Lesson 7: A 1 litre measuring cylinder filled with coloured water, for display and for support.
Lesson 8: Prepare 'Reading scales' for display. Prepare containers with coloured water for the group activity.

You will need

CD resources
Core, support, extension and template versions of 'Capacity table' and 'Liquid measures'; 'Reading from scales', 'The witch's cauldron' and 'The witch's cauldron clues'; extension version of 'Waldo the Wizard'; core, support and extension versions of 'A capacity for questions'.
Equipment
Metre rule; a litre bottle filled to 500ml; a measuring cylinder; a can of soft drink, a litre carton of fruit juice, a tablespoon, a bucket, a cereal bowl and a tea cup; a range of measuring equipment including 1 litre, 500ml, 250ml and 100ml measures; stiff paper; scissors; rice to test for 1 litre capacity; a 2-litre bottle.

Learning objectives

Starter

- Choose and use standard metric units and their abbreviations when estimating, measuring and recording length, weight and capacity; know the meaning of 'kilo', 'centi' and 'milli' and, where appropriate, use decimal notation to record measurements (eg 1.3m or 0.6kg).
- Use knowledge of addition and subtraction facts and place value to derive sums and differences of pairs of multiples of 10, 100 or 1000 (revision of Blocks A and B).
- Identify the doubles of two-digit numbers; use to calculate doubles of multiples of 10 and 100 and derive the corresponding halves (revision of Blocks A and B).

Main teaching activities

2006

- Choose and use standard metric units and their abbreviations when estimating, measuring and recording length, weight and capacity; know the meaning of 'kilo', 'centi' and 'milli' and, where appropriate, use decimal notation to record measurements (eg 1.3m or 0.6kg).
- Interpret intervals and divisions on partially numbered scales and record readings accurately, where appropriate to the nearest tenth of a unit.
- Compare the impact of representations where scales have intervals of differing step size.

1999

- Use, read and write standard metric units (km, m, cm, mm, kg, g, l, ml), including their abbreviations, and imperial units (mile, pint).
- Know and use the relationships between familiar units of length, mass and capacity.
- Know the equivalent of one half, one quarter, three quarters and one tenth of 1km, 1m, 1kg, 1 litre in m, cm, g, ml.
- Suggest suitable units and measuring equipment to estimate or measure length, mass or capacity.
- Record estimates and readings from scales to a suitable degree of accuracy.
- Solve a problem by collecting quickly, organising, representing and interpreting data in tables, charts, graphs and diagrams, including those generated by a computer.

Vocabulary

data, information, survey, questionnaire, graph, chart, table, diagram, horizontal axis, vertical axis, axes, label, title, scale, interval, pictogram, bar chart, tally chart, greatest/least value, metric unit, standard unit, millimetre (mm), centimetre (cm), metre (m), kilogram (kg), gram (g), litre (l), millilitre (ml)

Lesson 6 (Review, teach and apply)

Starter

Reason: Hold up a metre ruler, or illustrate this on an interactive whiteboard. Point at 50cm and say: *What fraction of the whole stick is this?* (One half.) *How many centimetres would I need to add to make 1 metre? What fraction would I need to add to make 1 whole?* Repeat, pointing to 25cm (¼ metre) and then 75cm (¾ metre). Now show the children a litre bottle or measuring cylinder filled to 500ml and ask: *What fraction of the whole bottle/cylinder is this?* (One half.) *How many millilitres would I need to add to make one litre? What fraction of a litre would I need to add to make one whole litre?* Repeat, pointing to 250ml (¼ litre) and then 750ml (¾ litre).

Main teaching activities

Whole class: Use a measuring cylinder to illustrate the capacity of 1 litre and, if appropriate, have available a can of soft drink, a litre carton of fruit juice, a tablespoon, a bucket, a cereal bowl and a tea cup (or illustrate these on an interactive whiteboard). Revise that 1 litre = 1000ml. Discuss different ways of recording equivalents, for example ½ litre = 500ml, ¼ litre = 250ml. Write these measures on the board. Discuss with the class the approximate capacities of the items, each time starting by asking: *Is this capacity more than or less than one litre?*

Show a range of measuring equipment including 1 litre, 500ml, 250ml and 100ml measures. Ask: *Which of these measures would be best to find out how much the fruit juice carton holds? Why?* Repeat with the other containers above. Ask children to come to the front and match one of the unmarked containers (such as the tea cup) with one of the pieces of apparatus with which it would be appropriate to measure its capacity. Repeat with two or three other containers. Discuss the choices made and extend by asking the children to estimate the capacities of the unmarked containers on their whiteboards.

Paired work: Give the children sheets of stiff paper, scissors and rulers and challenge them to make a container that they think will hold 1 litre. Tell them that 1 litre = 1000cm³ and that when they have made their containers you will measure out 1 litre of rice to test them.

Differentiation

Less confident learners: These children may require extra discussion and assistance. Give each pair a container with a capacity of approximately 1 litre so they can make comparisons.
More confident learners: Discuss ways of calibrating their containers, marking 500ml, 250ml and 750ml.

Review

Compare the capacities of the containers and ask: *If I had a container that had a capacity of 980ml, what would its capacity be to the nearest 100ml?* (1000ml.) Illustrate with the rice and a suitable container. Repeat with 940ml (900ml) and 950ml (1000ml). Show a pint bottle and ask the children to estimate its capacity. Check by measuring and establish that it is roughly half a litre. Explain that a pint is an imperial measure and ask the children: *What might have been measured in pints?* (Milk or beer.)

Lesson 7 (Review and practise)

Starter

Revisit and refine: Write a number on the board and ask the children to multiply it by 100. Start with 6 (600) then 23 (2300), stressing that each time the digits are moving two places to the left and two zeros are written as place holders. Repeat, now choosing multiples of a hundred, and ask the children to divide by 100 each time. Start with 500 (5) then 1000 (10), stressing that each time the digits are moving two places to the right and two zeros are removed. Now write on the board '100cm = 1 metre'. Call out several measurements in metres and ask the children to write down, on their whiteboards, the same length in centimetres and show you. Call out 2m (200cm), 4m (400cm), 7m (700cm) then repeat, this time calling out lengths in centimetres and asking the children to write down and show you the same lengths in metres. Call out 500cm (5m), 800cm (8m), 1000cm (10m).

Main teaching activities

Whole class: Fill a litre measuring cylinder with coloured water and ask: *How many millilitres are there in a litre?* Write on the board '1 litre = 1000 millilitres'. Ask: *How many millilitres are there in two litres? ... three litres? How many in half a litre? ... a quarter of a litre? ... a tenth of a litre?*

Focus on a tenth of a litre. Point to the 100ml mark on the measuring cylinder and ask an individual child to count up, in tenths, from one tenth to one whole as you point to 100ml, 200ml, 300ml, and so on. Now ask: *If I had three-tenths of a litre, how much would I need to add to make 1 litre?* Repeat with 4/10, 5/10 (making the link with ½), 6/10, 7/10, 8/10 and 9/10.

Ask: *How many millilitres in 2½ litres? ... 3½ litres? ... 4¼ litres?* Discuss and record the answers in millilitres and then discuss the different ways of recording the capacities. For example, 2½ litres can be written as 2.5 litres,

2 litres and 500ml, or 2500ml. Say a measurement in litres and ask the children to use their whiteboards to write the same capacity in a different way. Start with 1½ litres (1.5 litres, 1 litre and 500 ml, or 1500ml). Compare answers and, for each example, encourage the children to try all three ways of recording.

Write these measurements on the board: 500ml, 250ml, 750ml, 100ml, 200ml, 300ml, 400ml. For each measurement ask: *What fraction of a litre is it? How could you write this as a decimal? How much more liquid do you need to make it up to one whole litre?*

Focus on 250ml, 500ml, 100ml and 200ml and ask: *How many of these could I fit into one litre? How did you work that out?* Deal with 750ml, 300ml and 400ml in a similar way, discussing the possibility of remainders, or not having quite enough to make a complete litre.

Independent work: Give each child activity sheet 'Capacity table' to complete.

Differentiation

Less confident learners: Provide the support version of the sheet, which focuses on fractions of a litre and their equivalents. You might work with this group and demonstrate the amounts required to make a litre practically using a marked measuring cylinder and some coloured liquid.

More confident learners: Provide the extension version of the sheet, which gives greater capacities and asks the children for the amounts required to make two litres.

Review

Use the table on activity sheet 'Capacity table' to assess children's understanding of millilitres and their fraction equivalents. Reinforce the conversion of capacities from one format to another. Write some capacity measurements on the board and ask children to come out and write the same measurements in a different way. Start with examples from the sheet but move on to more difficult ones, such 3½ litres = □ ml and then introduce some decimal numbers such as 0.45 litres = □ ml.

Lesson 8 (Teach, apply and practise)

Starter

Revisit and refine: Repeat the Starter from Lesson 7, this time focusing on decimals. Write on the board '100cm = 1m'. Call out several measurements in metres and ask the children to write down, on their whiteboards, the same length in centimetres and show you. Say 0.5m (50cm), a quarter of a metre (25cm), 0.75m (75cm), one tenth of a metre (10cm) and so on. Then repeat, saying a length in centimetres and asking the children to write down and show you that length in metres. Say: 50cm (½m), 10cm (1/10m), 1000cm (10m), 25cm (0.25m) and so on.

Main teaching activities

Whole class: Show the children how scales are marked on the side of measuring cylinders. Display the activity sheet 'Reading from scales'. Illustrate how scales can vary, not only in the amount they measure but also how they are divided up. Point out that when we measure we sometimes have to record to the nearest mark.

Group work: Prepare some measuring containers with different volumes of coloured water and ask children in groups to read the scales, then to record their measurements to the nearest division.

Independent work: Give each child a copy of 'Liquid measures' to complete.

Differentiation

Less confident learners: Provide the support version of the sheet, which consolidates reading scales to the nearest 100ml.

More confident learners: Provide the extension version of the sheet, which includes 20ml and 25ml examples.

Review

Review the children's readings. Discuss any problems in reading the scales - either in the practical or worksheet examples.

Select one or two examples of unmarked containers used in Lesson 6 (for example, tea cup and drinks can). Ask the children to estimate how much the containers hold in ml and to write on their whiteboards. Next, fill the containers, then empty them into marked measuring containers. Ask one child to read the scales. Ask: *How close were your estimates?*

Lesson 9 (Apply)

Starter

Revisit: Call out a measurement and ask the children to double that length or capacity, write the answer on their whiteboards and show you. They may use whichever unit of measurement they wish. Examples: 500cm (1000cm or 1m), 500ml (1000ml or 1 litre), 300cm (600cm or 0.6m), 700m (1400m or 1km 400m or 1.4km), 250ml (500ml or ½ litre), 5mm (10mm, 1cm), 80cm (160cm, 1m and 60cm, 1.6m). Discuss the various ways of writing the answers, using different measurements for each example shown above.

Main teaching activities

Group work: Split the children into groups of three or four. Give each group a piece of paper, a pencil and a set of cards cut from activity sheet 'The witch's cauldron clues'. Ask them to use these clues to solve the problem called 'The witch's cauldron' together, filling in the table on the activity sheet. Within their groups, the children shuffle the clue cards and deal them out equally, without looking at them. Once the children have been dealt their cards they can look at them but they may not show them to anyone else in the group. Write these two questions on the board:

- *How much of the potion is the witch making?* (Assume there is no evaporation.) (2875ml, encourage the children to look for pairs of numbers that total 1 litre or 1000ml when adding up their measures.)
- *Would the potion fit into six bottles, each able to hold ½ litre?* (Yes.)

Explain that the children can talk about the information on the cards with the other members of their group but they must not show anyone their cards or they will be out of the game. Suggest that they use the table to help them answer the questions. Remind them to keep all the measures in the same unit, such as millilitres. The first group that answers the two questions correctly wins.

Differentiation

Less confident learners:. If necessary, after a few minutes this group could lay the cards down and look at them together.
More confident learners: Once they have finished the core activity, provide the 'Waldo the Wizard's scarf' activity sheet, which has an extra problem: How long is Waldo's scarf?

Review

Go through the core version of the activity sheet together as a class. Ask: *What operations did you use when calculating the answers? Which calculations did you need to write down? What was the best strategy to use when working as a group? Which clues were helpful? Were any clues unhelpful? Why?* (Listen to each other!) *Did it help to use the table?*

Lesson 10 (Review and practise)

Starter

Revisit and refine: Revise work on number pairs totalling 100. Call out a two-digit number (for example, 61) and ask children to write on their whiteboards the number that needs to be added to make 100 (39). Continue with a few examples. Next, call out a length and ask the children to work out how much has to be added to make 1 metre. They write their answers on their whiteboards and show you. Start with 39cm (61cm), 38cm (62cm), ¾m (¼m) and so on. Repeat, but this time use capacities. Ask the children to show the capacity that they would add to make up to 1 litre. Start with 750ml (250ml), ¼ litre (¾ litre).

Main teaching activities

Whole class: Explain that in this lesson the children will be solving problems involving capacity. Hold up a 2-litre bottle and ask: *How many glasses of 100ml can I pour from this bottle? How could you work it out? What type of calculation should you use?* (2000 divided by 100 = 20 glasses.) Repeat, asking how many ¼ litre glasses you could pour. (8 glasses.)
Independent work: Give the children the activity sheet 'A capacity for questions', which sets a series of questions involving capacity in real-life situations.

Differentiation

Less confident learners: Use the support version of the activity sheet, which includes simpler questions. These children could be encouraged to convert all of their measurements into millilitres. Sticky notes with the measurements written on them would also be useful for this group.
More confident learners: Use the extension version of the activity sheet, which includes more demanding questions.

Review

Discuss the questions on the activity sheet. Ask: *What method did you use to help you? Which questions did you find easiest to answer? Were there any that were very difficult?* Talk about any problems that arose and encourage the children to share their methods.

Name ______________________ Date ________________

Key charts

Use the sticky-note pictogram from the board to help you complete these sentences.

1. Our key is: 1 sticky note = _____ votes.

2. The most popular animal in our class is ____________.

This had _____ votes.

3. The next most popular animal in our class is ____________.

This had _____ votes.

4. The least popular animal in our class is ____________.

This had _____ votes.

5. With our key, _____ votes were cast altogether.

Name ____________________ Date ____________________

Tally charts

Complete one of these tally charts for each magazine.

Tally chart to show the number of advertisements on each page of ____________________ .

Quantity of advertisements	Number of pages
No advertisements on the page	
Less than (<) half the page contains advertisements	
More than (>) or equal to (=) half the page contains advertisements	
Whole page of advertisements	

Tally chart to show the number of advertisements on each page of ____________________ .

Quantity of advertisements	Number of pages
No advertisements on the page	
Less than (<) half the page contains advertisements	
More than (>) or equal to (=) half the page contains advertisements	
Whole page of advertisements	

Tally chart to show the number of advertisements on each page of ____________________ .

Quantity of advertisements	Number of pages
No advertisements on the page	
Less than (<) half the page contains advertisements	
More than (>) or equal to (=) half the page contains advertisements	
Whole page of advertisements	

Unit 3 2 weeks

Handling data and measures

Lesson	Strand	Starter	Main teaching activities
1. Teach and apply	Use/apply Data	Identify and use patterns, relationships and properties of numbers or shapes; investigate a statement involving numbers and test it with examples.	• Suggest a line of enquiry and the strategy needed to follow it; collect, organise and interpret selected information to find answers. • Report solutions to puzzles and problems, giving explanations and reasoning orally and in writing, using diagrams and symbols. **• Answer a question by identifying what data to collect; organise, present, analyse and interpret the data in tables, diagrams, tally charts, pictograms and bar charts, using ICT where appropriate.**
2. Review	Use/apply Data	• Use the eight compass points to describe direction. **• Know that angles are measured in degrees.**	As for Lesson 1
3. Review teach and practise	Use/apply Data	**Derive and recall multiplication facts up to 10 × 10, the corresponding division facts and multiples of numbers to 10 up to the tenth multiple.**	As for Lesson 1
4. Teach and practise	Use/apply Measure	Use knowledge of addition and subtraction facts and place value to derive sums and differences of pairs of multiples of 10, 100 or 1000.	• Report solutions to puzzles and problems, giving explanations and reasoning orally and in writing, using diagrams and symbols. • Interpret intervals and divisions on partially numbered scales and record readings accurately, where appropriate to the nearest tenth of a unit.
5. Teach and practise	Use/apply Data	As for Lesson 4	• Suggest a line of enquiry and the strategy needed to follow it; collect, organise and interpret selected information to find answers. • Report solutions to puzzles and problems, giving explanations and reasoning orally and in writing, using diagrams and symbols. **• Answer a question by identifying what data to collect; organise, present, analyse and interpret the data in tables, diagrams, tally charts, pictograms and bar charts, using ICT where appropriate.**
6. Practise and apply	Use/apply Data Measure	**Choose and use standard metric units and their abbreviations when estimating, measuring and recording length, weight and capacity; know the meaning of 'kilo', 'centi' and 'milli' and, where appropriate, use decimal notation to record measurements (eg 1.3m or 0.6kg).**	• Suggest a line of enquiry and the strategy needed to follow it; collect, organise and interpret selected information to find answers. **• Answer a question by identifying what data to collect; organise, present, analyse and interpret the data in tables, diagrams, tally charts, pictograms and bar charts, using ICT where appropriate.** **• Choose and use standard metric units and their abbreviations when estimating, measuring and recording length, weight and capacity; know the meaning of 'kilo', 'centi' and 'milli' and, where appropriate, use decimal notation to record measurements (eg 1.3m or 0.6kg).** • Compare the impact of representations where scales have intervals of differing step size.
7. Review and apply	Use/apply Data Measure	As for Lesson 6	As for Lesson 6
8. Apply	Use/apply Data	As for Lesson 6	• Suggest a line of enquiry and the strategy needed to follow it; collect, organise and interpret selected information to find answers. **• Answer a question by identifying what data to collect; organise, present, analyse and interpret the data in tables, diagrams, tally charts, pictograms and bar charts, using ICT where appropriate.** • Compare the impact of representations where scales have intervals of differing step size.
9. Apply	Use/apply Data	As for Lesson 6	As for Lesson 8
10. Review and apply	Use/apply Data	Suggest a line of enquiry and the strategy needed to follow it; collect, organise and interpret selected information to find answers.	As for Lesson 8

Speaking and listening objective
- Use time, resources and group members efficiently by distributing tasks, checking progress, making backup plans

Introduction
In this unit children continue to handle data. They collect, organise, present and interpret data to answer related questions, identifying further questions. They construct tables, pictogram diagrams, tally charts and bar charts, explaining reasoning using text, diagrams and graphs. Children read from scales, comparing the impact of different scales. They use standard metric units to estimate, measure and record measurements. The unit involves the use of ICT.

Using and applying mathematics
- Suggest a line of enquiry and the strategy needed to follow it; collect, organise and interpret selected information to find answers.
- Report solutions to puzzles and problems, giving explanations and reasoning orally and in writing, using diagrams and symbols.

Lessons 1-5

Preparation
Lesson 1: Prepare a display copy of the 'Venn diagram' general resource sheet. If you are doing this on the board, prepare some sticky notes with appropriate labels on them.
Lesson 2: Prepare a display copy of the 'Venn diagram' resource sheet. If necessary, enlarge it to A3 and cut out the shapes from the 'Sorting shapes' sheet.
Lesson 3: Prepare a display copy of the 'Carroll diagrams' general resouce sheet and some shapes that will fit into the diagram.
Lesson 4: Prepare a display copy of the 'Favourite days' and 'Exercise counts' sheets.
Lesson 5: Ask the children to bring in a collection of empty bottles, cans and packets that contained liquids.

You will need
Photocopiable pages
'Sorting shapes' (page 128).
CD resources
'Number grids 100', 'Number grids 1000', 'Favourite days', 'Sorting shapes', 'Exercise counts', 'Capacity for tallies'; support and extension versions of 'Interpreting pictograms'.
General resource sheets: 'Venn diagram' and 'Carroll diagrams'.
ITP: 'Data handling'.
Equipment
Sticky notes; scissors and glue (optional); dice; a collection of empty bottles, cans and packets in which liquids were sold; computer; interactive whiteboard connected to the computer (if one is available); data-handling package; place value cards to 50.

Learning objectives

Starter
- Identify and use patterns, relationships and properties of numbers or shapes; investigate a statement involving numbers and test it with examples.
- Use the eight compass points to describe direction.
- Know that angles are measured in degrees.
- Derive and recall multiplication facts up to 10 × 10, the corresponding division facts and multiples of numbers to 10 up to the tenth multiple.
- Use knowledge of addition and subtraction facts and place value to derive sums and differences of pairs of multiples of 10, 100 or 1000.

Main teaching activities
2006
- Suggest a line of enquiry and the strategy needed to follow it; collect, organise and interpret selected information to find answers.
- Report solutions to puzzles and problems, giving explanations and reasoning orally and in writing, using diagrams and symbols.
- Answer a question by identifying what data to collect; organise, present, analyse and interpret the data in tables, diagrams, tally charts, pictograms and bar charts, using ICT where appropriate.
- Interpret intervals and divisions on partially numbered scales and record readings accurately, where appropriate to the nearest tenth of a unit.

1999
- Solve a problem by collecting quickly, organising, representing and interpreting data in tables, charts, graphs and diagrams, including those generated by a computer, eg tally charts, frequency tables, pictograms, bar charts, Venn and Carroll diagrams.
- Explain methods and reasoning about numbers orally and in writing.
- Record estimates and readings from scales to a suitable degree of accuracy.

Vocabulary
problem, solution, calculate, calculation, method, explain, reasoning, reason, predict, pattern, relationship, classify, represent, interpret, data, information, survey, questionnaire, graph, chart, table, diagram, horizontal axis, vertical axis, axes, label, title, scale, interval, pictogram, bar chart, tally chart, greatest/least value, Venn diagram, Carroll diagram

Lesson 1 (Teach and apply)

Starter

Reason: Say that you are thinking of a two-digit number and that you would like the children to guess your number, using as few questions as possible. Explain that you will only answer 'yes' or 'no'. Discuss the vocabulary that may help narrow down their search: *factor, multiple, odd, even, greater than, less than.* Play this game twice and each time at the end of the game draw up a list of the numbers that it could be, encouraging sensible questions that allow the children to narrow down the search.

Main teaching activities

Whole class: Draw two overlapping circles on the board and say: *I am going to use this to sort numbers onto a two-way Venn diagram.* (You could use the 'Venn diagram' resource sheet for this purpose, or alternatively use an interactive whiteboard.) Write '12' in the intersection of the Venn diagram and invite the group to suggest what the labels for each of the circles might be. For this demonstration use 'even numbers' and 'multiples of 3'. It may be useful to have these written on sticky notes ready to attach to the board quickly at the end of the activity.

Ask the children to guess where other numbers would be placed, according to the rules of your Venn diagram. For example, they might ask: *Could I place the number 18 into the intersection?* (Yes.) *Why?* If necessary, explain that where the two circles overlap both criteria must apply. *Would 2 appear in one of the two circles?* (Yes.) Place numbers in the correct sections as children identify them. Then encourage the children to develop questions such as:

- *12 is a multiple of 3, it is in the intersection, so could one of the labels be multiples of 3?*
- *12 is an even number, it is in the intersection, so could one of the labels be two-times table/even?*
- *12 is a multiple of 6, it is in the intersection, so could one of the labels be multiples of 6 (in both the two- and three-times tables)?*
- *12 is less than 20, it is in the intersection, so could one of the labels be less than 20?*

When the children have guessed the correct labels, attach the sticky notes to complete the Venn diagram. Ask: *Would 11 fit in either circle?* (No.) Explain that if a number does not fit the criteria of either circle it is placed outside the circles.

Paired work: Give each pair a copy of the 'Venn diagram' resource sheet and tell the children to choose from the following criteria and sort the given set of numbers on their own Venn diagrams.

1. Odd numbers						**Multiples of 5**
7	15	22	30	33	47	60
2. Multiples of 10						**Even numbers**
20	40	30	27	44	82	15
3. Numbers greater than 20						**Numbers less than 30**
44	29	30	12	54	27	11

Review

Children should present their diagrams. Ask additional questions about each diagram, for example: *Where would the number 31 go? Why?* Ask the more confident pairs to show their own prepared diagrams but to cover the labels on them. Ask: *Look at the left-hand circle. What could the criteria be that defines all the numbers/shapes in the left-hand circle?* Take answers. Repeat the question for the right-hand circle.

Differentiation

Less confident learners: Limit the children to the first two examples. Work with the children on the examples and ask for explanations after each number is positioned.

More confident learners: Challenge the children to think of their own criteria using < and > symbols, numbers and shapes.

BLOCK C Handling data and measures

Lesson 2 (Review)

Starter

Rehearse and refine: Place a sticky note to mark north and point this out. Ask the children to stand, facing that direction. Call out a direction, for example south, east, north-west, and ask the children to turn clockwise to that direction. Repeat, this time asking them to turn anticlockwise. Each time ask: *How much did you turn? Did you turn more than half a turn? 180 degrees? If 180 degrees is a half turn, how many degrees in a quarter turn?* (90.) *What other name is there for a 90 degree turn?* (Right angle.) *Write down an instruction that would turn you through 45 degrees.* (For example, north to north-east.) Ask individual children for examples. Establish that an angle of 45 degrees is half of a right angle.

Main teaching activities

Whole class: Review the work on Venn diagrams in the previous lesson. Ensure children understand that the overlap area of the circles contains items in which both criteria apply (the 'both' region). Also, make sure that they understand that the 'empty' area contains items that do not fit the criteria of either circle (the 'neither' region). Suggest that we could sort shapes on to a Venn diagram. Ask: *How could we label the sets?* Take suggestions and draw a Venn diagram, as shown (or use the 'Venn diagram' resource sheet as an OHT or on the whiteboard).

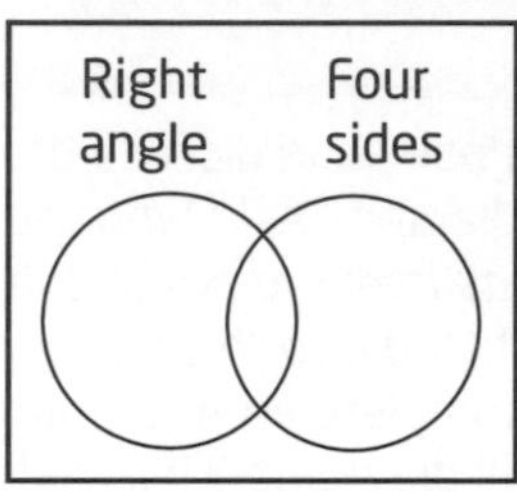

Show one or two 2D shapes or take suggestions from the class (for example, square or rectangle) and position them on the grid.

Group work: Give each group a copy of the 'Venn diagram' sheet and a set of 'Sorting shapes'. Ask them to place the letter of each shape in the appropriate position on the diagram. (Alternatively, enlarge the Venn diagram to A3 and provide each group with a set of shapes cut out from the sheet.) When they have completed this task, ask them to think of their own criteria for sorting shapes relating to the number of sides, vertices, symmetry and so on.

Differentiation

Less confident learners: Support the children with the first task and provide suggestions for the second task sets, for example 'Right angles/Four sides'.

More confident learners: Extend the activity to include 3D shapes and ask the group to select suitable criteria relating to the number of faces, vertices, right angles and so on.

Review

Children should present their diagrams. Ask additional questions about each diagram, for example: *Where would we position a hexagon? Why?* Ask the more confident pairs to show their diagrams, but to cover the labels on them. Ask: *Look at the left-hand circle? What could the criteria be that defines all the numbers/shapes in the left-hand circle?* Take answers. Repeat the question for the right-hand circle.

Lesson 3 (Review, teach and practise)

Starter

Recall: Ask quick-fire questions of individual pupils to build up the ten-times table on the board, as far as 200. Ask quick-fire questions about the seven-, eight- and nine-times tables (for example $3 \times 9 = 27$), each time relating it to the nearest multiple of 10 (3×10) to illustrate that this would be a good method for approximating if they were not sure of the product. Repeat by listing the five-times table as before, to 100, and then making a link with the four-, six- and seven-times tables – for example, $3 \times 7 = 21$ is greater than 3×5 but less than 3×10.

Main teaching activities

Whole class: Remind the children about work on Carroll diagrams in the previous term. Ask: *What is a Carroll diagram? Discuss the uses of Carroll diagrams.* Also remind them about work on shapes in the previous lesson and draw the following Carroll diagram on the board (see below), or use the 'Carroll diagrams' general resource sheet on an OHT.

	At least one line of symmetry	No lines of symmetry
Regular		
Irregular		

Talk through the construction of the diagram - in particular, that it allows more options than the Venn diagrams - and ask children to position some prepared shapes on the diagram.

Paired work: Extend the activity to numbers - this time using the criteria 'Numbers that have three tens/Numbers that do not have three tens' and 'In the five-times table/Not in the five-times table'. Ask the children to prepare a Carroll diagram using the 'Carroll diagrams' general resource sheet and to generate a set of two-digit numbers using two 1-6 dice or a set of place value cards to 50. They should then write the numbers that they generate into the correct quadrant of the diagram. If time is available, ask the children to complete the other Carroll diagram on the sheet with a new set of criteria, for example 'Numbers that have four tens/Numbers that do not have four tens' and 'In the seven-times table/Not in the seven-times table'.

Differentiation

Less confident learners: Limit the activity by giving the children a prepared set of numbers to place on the grid, for example 20, 25, 27, 30, 33, 35, 37, 40. You might also support the children in labelling the diagram correctly.

More confident learners: Extend the activity by challenging the children to think of their own numerical criteria - for example, using even or odd numbers, three-digit numbers and so on.

Review

Choose a few different pairs and discuss the numbers they generated and their positions on the diagram. Ask: *What number could I put into this box? How many numbers was I able to put in the top-left box?* Discuss why no other numbers can be fitted into this box.

If time is available, complete another Carroll diagram to check children's understanding of Carroll diagrams. This could be numerical, for example 'Odd numbers/Even numbers' and 'In the seven-times table/Not in the seven-times table' or non-numerical, such as 'Children with black hair/Not black hair' and 'Green eyes/Not green eyes'.

Lesson 4 (Teach and practise)

Starter

Read: Give each child a grid cut from the activity sheet 'Number grids 100'. Explain that you will call out numbers, one at a time, and each time the children should cross off the number on their grid that would make a total of 100 with the number called out. When they have a line or full house, the children must stand up. Call out the numbers: 21, 22, 23, 24, 25, 26, 27, 28, 36, 63, 64, 65, 66, 68, 75, 77, 78, 81, 82, 86, in any order. These match up with the numbers on the grids. You could add in a few extras, as red herrings.

Main teaching activities

Whole class: Explain that in this lesson the children interpret information from charts and pictograms, using that information to answer questions. Display the activity sheet 'Favourite days'. (Alternatively, you may wish to use the ITP 'Data handling' here, using one of the prepared graphs.) Discuss the bar chart as a class:

- *What was the most popular day of the week?* (Wednesday)
- *Why do you think Wednesday could be a popular day of the week?*
- *Sixteen children voted for Tuesday as their favourite day of the week. How many children voted for Monday as their favourite day?* (9)
- *For which day of the week did 10 children vote?* (Thursday)
- *What is the difference between the number of votes on Thursday and the number of votes on Wednesday?* (30)
- *How many children took part in the survey?* (100)

Add the numbers to the vertical scale, remembering to include zero. The children will find it easy to read off the tens (20, 30 or 40) but will find it more difficult to read Monday (9) and Tuesday (16), which do not coincide exactly with grid lines.

Next ask: *How could you display this information as a pictogram?* Discuss what symbols to use and decide that it would be better to use symbols that represent five or ten children. Discuss how you could represent one, two, three or four children by splitting up the symbols clearly. You will need to do this for Monday and Tuesday. Draw the pictogram on the board. Ask individual children to draw the symbols for each day.

Favourite days of the week

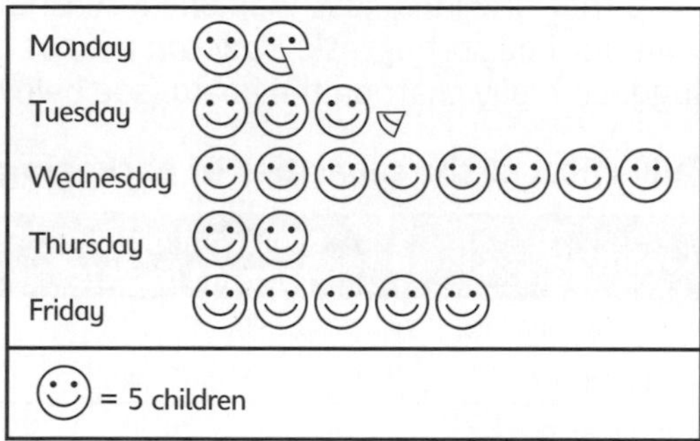

Independent work: Give the children the activity sheet 'Interpreting pictograms' and ask them to answer the questions about pictograms. The symbols represent two and ten units.

Review

Display the activity sheet 'Exercise counts' or copy the tally chart onto the board.

Tally chart to show the number of hours of exercise that 100 children took in one week

Less than one hour	~~||||~~ ~~||||~~ ||
More than one hour but less than two hours	~~||||~~ ~~||||~~ ~~||||~~ ~~||||~~
More than two hours but less than three hours	~~||||~~ ~~||||~~ ~~||||~~ ~~||||~~ ~~||||~~
More than three hours but less than four hours	~~||||~~ ~~||||~~ ~~||||~~
Four hours or more	

Fill in the 'Four hours or more' together and discuss the results. Ask: *If you drew a pictogram, which units could you use to represent this data?* Establish that using a symbol to represent two hours would be one possible representation. Discuss other possible representations. For example each symbol represents five hours or ten hours. *All the numbers are multiples of 5, apart from the 12 and 18. How could you represent these numbers?* (With part symbols.) *What if each symbol represents 20 hours?* Establish that it would be difficult to interpret some numbers, such as 12.

Differentiation

Less confident learners: Provide the support version of the 'Interpreting pictograms' sheet in which the symbols represent two units only. Ensure that the children understand how the key works before answering the questions.

More confident learners: Provide the extension version of the 'Interpreting pictograms' sheet that includes pictograms representing 20 units.

Lesson 5 (Teach and practise)

Starter

Read: Repeat the Starter from Lesson 4 but use cards cut from activity sheet 'Number grids 1000', with the children pairing the numbers to make 1000. Call out: 1000, 950, 900, 850, 800, 750, 700, 650, 600, 550, 500, 450, 400, 350, 300, 250, 200, 150, 100, 50 in any order.

Main teaching activities

Group work: Put the children into mixed-ability groups of four or five. Explain that they will investigate the statement: 'Most drinks in a supermarket are sold in litre containers.' Ask: *Do you think that this is true?* Look at the bottles, cans and packets that the children have collected over the last few days. Share them among the groups and ask the children to sort them out. Observe how they sort the containers and give some guidelines: 'more than one litre', 'less than one litre' and 'exactly one litre'. When they have finished sorting, ask: *How can we put all the information together?* Suggest a tally chart on the board (see below).

Tally chart of the capacities of packaging for drinks

Capacity	Number of bottles, cans and packets
Less than one litre	
One litre	
More than one litre	

Ask: *How could you check the information?* (Count the total number of containers and check against the total number of tallies.) *Are most of the capacities 1 litre? How could you display this information more accurately?* Decide to round the capacities to the nearest 100ml.

Ask the children to complete the first part of activity sheet 'Capacity for tallies' filling in the tally chart, in their groups, then to combine the information from all the groups to complete the tally chart for the whole class.

Review

Ask: *Do you think that the statement is true? How could you show this information on a pictogram? What scale could you use to make the information clear?* Discuss units of 2, 5, 10 or 20 and their limitations and possibilities. Ask: *If you want to use a scale of multiples of 5 or 10 what would you have to do with the data?* (Round to the nearest 5 or 10.) *Would this give a fair representation of the data? If you use the bar chart, what would be the best way to fit the numbers onto this axis? Do you need to put in every number?*

A computer software program could be used in a follow-up session to construct these pictograms or bar charts. (The ITP Data handling can be used to construct bar charts.) The task could be differentiated by varying the scales the children work with. The 'Capacity for tallies' activity sheet will also be useful in planning this task.

Differentiation

Less confident learners: Group accordingly and provide these children with containers that are already rounded to the nearest 100ml or give extra support to this group while they round up the capacities at the start of the session, and then help to check the tallies together at the end of the session.

More confident learners: Provide these children with more challenging capacities to round to the nearest 100ml. Challenge these children to sort the containers further by naming the cans or bottles and using a Carroll diagram - for example, sort by 'less than ½ litre/more than ½ litre' and 'fizzy drinks/still drinks'. Ask: *Can you use your Carroll diagram to support another statement which could be true?* For example: fizzy drinks are usually sold in containers holding less than one litre.

Lessons 6-10

Preparation

Lesson 8: If your school is, for example, at the end of a closed road and therefore doesn't have passing traffic you may wish to arrange for the children to survey a nearby road.

You will need

Equipment

A variety of objects, such as a washing-up bowl, a bottle, a drinking glass, a mug, an egg cup, for estimating capacity; rulers; access to computers with data-handling software for drawing graphs (or squared/graph paper).

Learning objectives

Starter

- Suggest a line of enquiry and the strategy needed to follow it; collect, organise and interpret selected information to find answers.
- Choose and use standard metric units and their abbreviations when estimating, measuring and recording length, weight and capacity; know the meaning of 'kilo', 'centi' and 'milli' and, where appropriate, use decimal notation to record measurements (eg 1.3m or 0.6kg).

Main teaching activities

2006

- Suggest a line of enquiry and the strategy needed to follow it; collect, organise and interpret selected information to find answers.
- Answer a question by identifying what data to collect; organise, present, analyse and interpret the data in tables, diagrams, tally charts, pictograms

and bar charts, using ICT where appropriate.
- Choose and use standard metric units and their abbreviations when estimating, measuring and recording length, weight and capacity; know the meaning of 'kilo', 'centi' and 'milli' and, where appropriate, use decimal notation to record measurements (eg 1.3m or 0.6kg).
- Compare the impact of representations where scales have intervals of differing step size.

1999
- Use, read and write standard metric units (km, m, cm, mm, kg, g, l, ml), including their abbreviations, and imperial units.
- Know and use the relationships between familiar units of length, mass and capacity.
- Know the equivalent of one half, one quarter, three quarters and one tenth of 1km, 1m, 1kg, 1 litre in m, cm, g, ml.
- Suggest suitable units and measuring equipment to estimate or measure length, mass or capacity.
- Solve a problem by collecting quickly, organising, representing and interpreting data in tables, charts, graphs and diagrams, including those generated by a computer, eg tally charts, frequency tables, pictograms, bar charts, Venn and Carroll diagrams.

Vocabulary
problem, solution, calculate, calculation, method, explain, reasoning, reason, predict, pattern, relationship, classify, represent, interpret, data, information, survey, questionnaire, graph, chart, table, diagram, horizontal axis, vertical axis, axes, label, title, scale, interval, pictogram, bar chart, tally chart, greatest/least value, metric unit, standard unit, millimetre (mm), centimetre (cm), metre (m), kilogram (kg), gram (g), litre (l), millilitre (ml)

Lesson 6 (Practise and apply)

Starter
Reason: Show the children a variety of objects, such as a washing-up bowl, a bottle, a drinking glass, a mug, an egg cup and ask them to estimate the capacity. Discuss estimates and compare - for example, how the knowledge of the capacity of the mug helps them estimate the capacity of the glass more accurately.

Main teaching activities
Whole class: Explain to the children that in the next two lessons they will be undertaking an enquiry. They will investigate if practice improves estimation skills. Using a whiteboard or OHP, recap how to draw lines in cm and mm accurately. Draw five lines and then ask individuals to come out and measure them accurately, explaining how they do it to the rest of the class.
Paired work: Ask each pair to draw and measure five lines onto a piece of paper. They must do this individually and record the lengths so that their partner cannot see. They then swap their sheets of paper. Each child records their estimates of the length of the lines, and then records the actual measurements and the difference between each estimate and measurement. Encourage the pairs to discuss their estimates and how they compared to the actual lengths (check that they agree on accurate lengths).

Ask the class: *If we wanted to use this information to investigate the question 'Does practice improve estimate skills?', what other data do we need to collect? Why do we need that data? What will it tell you?* Discuss, and repeat the paired work to compare. Ask the children to collect their data together and keep it safe for the next lesson.

Review
Ask: *What information were we trying to collect today? Why did we repeat our task? What will the information we have tell us? How can we display our data to help us answer our question?*

Differentiation
Less confident learners: These children may need extra help, either from an adult or paired with a more confident child to practise measuring and drawing lines using a ruler before they start the task.
More confident learners: These children could repeat the challenge three times so that they have extra data to consider.

Lesson 7 (Review and apply)

Starter

Rehearse: Explain that you will call out some capacities and that you would like the children to show you another way of writing the same capacity on their whiteboards. For example, 2 litres (2000ml), 750ml (¾ litre), 100ml (0.1 litre).

Main teaching activities

Paired work: Continue from Lesson 6, ideally in a computer room. Encourage each pair to answer the question 'Does practice improve estimation skills?' by organising and presenting their data. For example, they could create a bar chart showing measurements up the vertical axes and 'attempts' along the horizontal axes (perhaps labelled 1st try, 2nd try and so on). For each attempt, the children should draw a bar showing the estimate, and a line above or below it to indicate the actual measurement. The two sets of data (the first five estimates and the second five estimates) could be in different colours, for comparison.

Differentiation

Less confident learners: Suggest organising the data in a bar chart or a table.
More confident learners: These pairs could then use a calculator to find the average measurements by adding all the actual measurements (say 4.7m + 4.3cm + 5.1cm + 5.2cm + 5cm) and dividing by 5.

Review

At the end of the session, give time for each pair to report their findings. Ask questions such as: *How did you display you data? What does this bar chart and table tell you? Why did you choose this type of chart? What makes the information easy or difficult to interpret? What labels have you included in your chart/table? What have you found out? Are the results as you expected? What else could you have done to make this enquiry more accurate?* If some more confident pupils repeated the task three times, you could compare these results. *What would you do differently if you carried out the enquiry again?*

Lesson 8 (Apply)

Starter

Rehearse: Write on the board these weights: 4kg, 0.4kg, ¼kg, 450g, 4.1kg, 4200g and ask the children to write the weights in ascending order on their whiteboards. Ask: *How could I rewrite 4kg in grams? 0.4kg in grams? 4200 grams in kg?*

Main teaching activities

Whole class: Explain to the children that in today's lesson they will be looking at the enquiry 'What vehicles are very likely to pass the school gates between 10am and 11am?'. Discuss the enquiry, asking questions such as: *Why do you predict these vehicles would pass by? What vehicles would definitely not pass by? Why not? What vehicles would be a possible but not very likely? Why?*
Group work: Explain to the groups that they have a fixed amount of time (say, 15 minutes) to decide how they would plan and investigate this enquiry. Ask: *What information are you aiming to collect? How would you collect it? What will it tell you? What do you need to collect and what can you estimate? What is the simplest way that you could find out this information? How would you display your data?*
Whole class: Give each group time to report back on their idea and discuss together: decide that, for example, the school run will be over and so it is unlikely there will be children coming to school unless they have a doctor's appointment or something similar; a survey held on a few consecutive days between 10am and 11am would provide excellent data; a tally chart could be drawn up to show different categories of vans, cars, cycles and so on, and cars could be sorted into the number of passengers or estimates of sorts of usage. If the school gate doesn't face a suitable road, arrange to take the children to a safe vantage point to survey another road near the school. Data could then be drawn up onto a bar chart. Discuss together labels for axes.

Differentiation

Less confident learners: If necessary, provide adult support to assist these children.
More confident learners: Encourage these children to write questions to ask about the data that has been collected.

Review
Ask: *How would the data change if it was raining? Sunny? Snowing? What about if we looked at a different time of day?*

Lesson 9 (Apply)

Starter
Rehearse: Repeat the starter from Lesson 8, this time ordering a list of lengths: 0.2m, 20cm, 200cm, 2.1m, 230cm, 2200cm, 2km, 2.5km, 2mm, 2000mm. Ask: *How could I rewrite 2km in metres? 0.2m in centimetres? 2000mm in centimetres?*

Main teaching activities
Whole class: Ask the children to investigate 'What children in our class would most like to change about the school'. Ask: *What information are you aiming to collect? How? What is the simplest way to find out this information?*
Group work: Let the children work in mixed-ability groups. Give them five minutes in their groups to plan how to collect their data. Be sure that they have drawn up some sort of chart and then give, say, 15 minutes to collect data and perhaps start to discuss it.

Give the groups time to collaborate on their information, discussing findings, and then ask them to whittle down the number of options to a sensible number - say, four or five. They then will need another fixed amount of time to collect data around the class again and complete a chart. Keep this for the following lesson.

Differentiation
Less confident learners: Make sure that these children are contributing to the group discussions.
More confident learners: Check that these children do not dominate the discussions and decision-making.

Review
Discuss the findings from different groups and how their categories may have changed as they asked for a more limited response. Ask: *Why have you chosen to collect your data in that way? What will it tell you? Were there any surprises?*

Lesson 10 (Review and apply)

Starter
Review: Recap on the Review from Lesson 9.

Main teaching activities
Continue from Lesson 9, ideally in a computer room, giving the children an opportunity to answer the question by organising their data. (Suggest a bar chart or a table to less confident pupils.)

Review
Give time for each pair to report their findings. Ask: *How will you display your data? Could you use any other method to display your data, such as a Venn diagram or a Carroll diagram?*

Provide computers and squared paper. *What does this bar chart and table tell you? Why did you choose this type of chart? What makes the information easy or difficult to interpret? What labels have you included in your chart/ table? What have you found out? Are the results as you expected? What else could you have done to make this enquiry more accurate?* (More confident pupils should be encouraged to show their results in a variety of ways and discuss which is the clearest.) *What would you do differently if you carried out the enquiry again?*

Name ____________________ Date ____________________

Sorting shapes

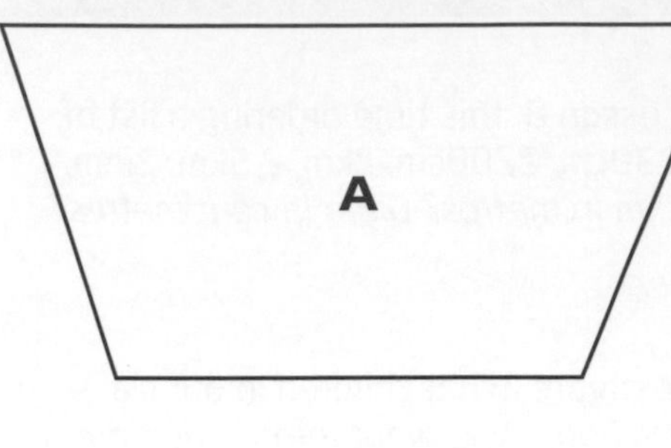

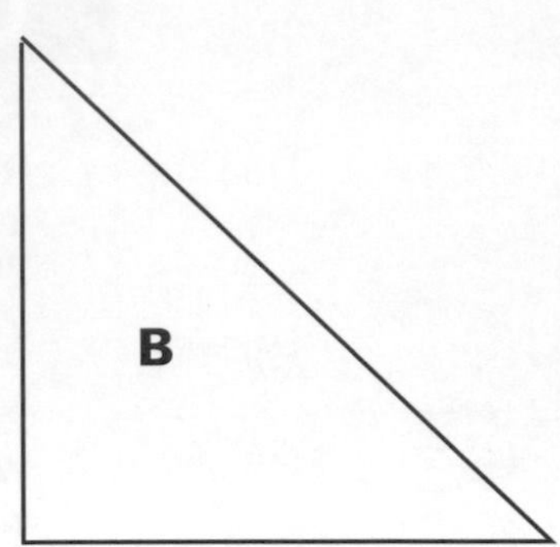

C

D

E

F

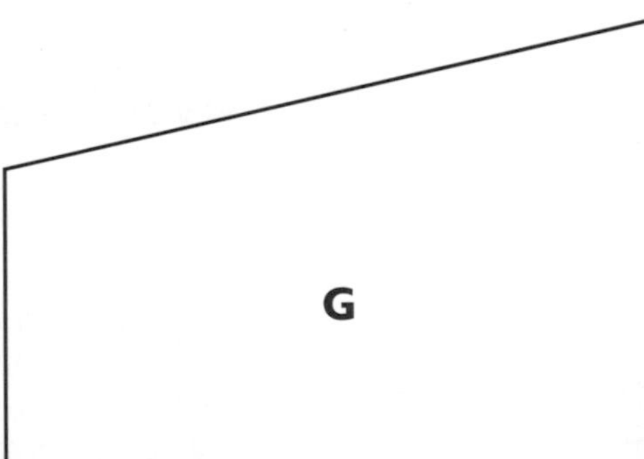

H

I

J

Calculating, measuring and understanding shape

Key aspects of learning
- Information processing
- Self-awareness
- Communication

Expected prior learning

Check that children can already:

- recall the relationships between kilometres and metres, metres and centimetres, kilograms and grams, litres and millilitres
- read, to the nearest division and half division, scales that are numbered or partially numbered
- read the time on a 12-hour digital clock and to the nearest five minutes on an analogue clock; calculate time intervals and find start or end times for a given time interval
- use a set-square to draw right angles and to identify right angles in 2D shapes; compare angles with a right angle; recognise that a straight line is equivalent to two right angles
- use four compass directions to describe direction (N, S, E, W).

Objectives overview

The text in this diagram identifies the focus of mathematics learning within the block.

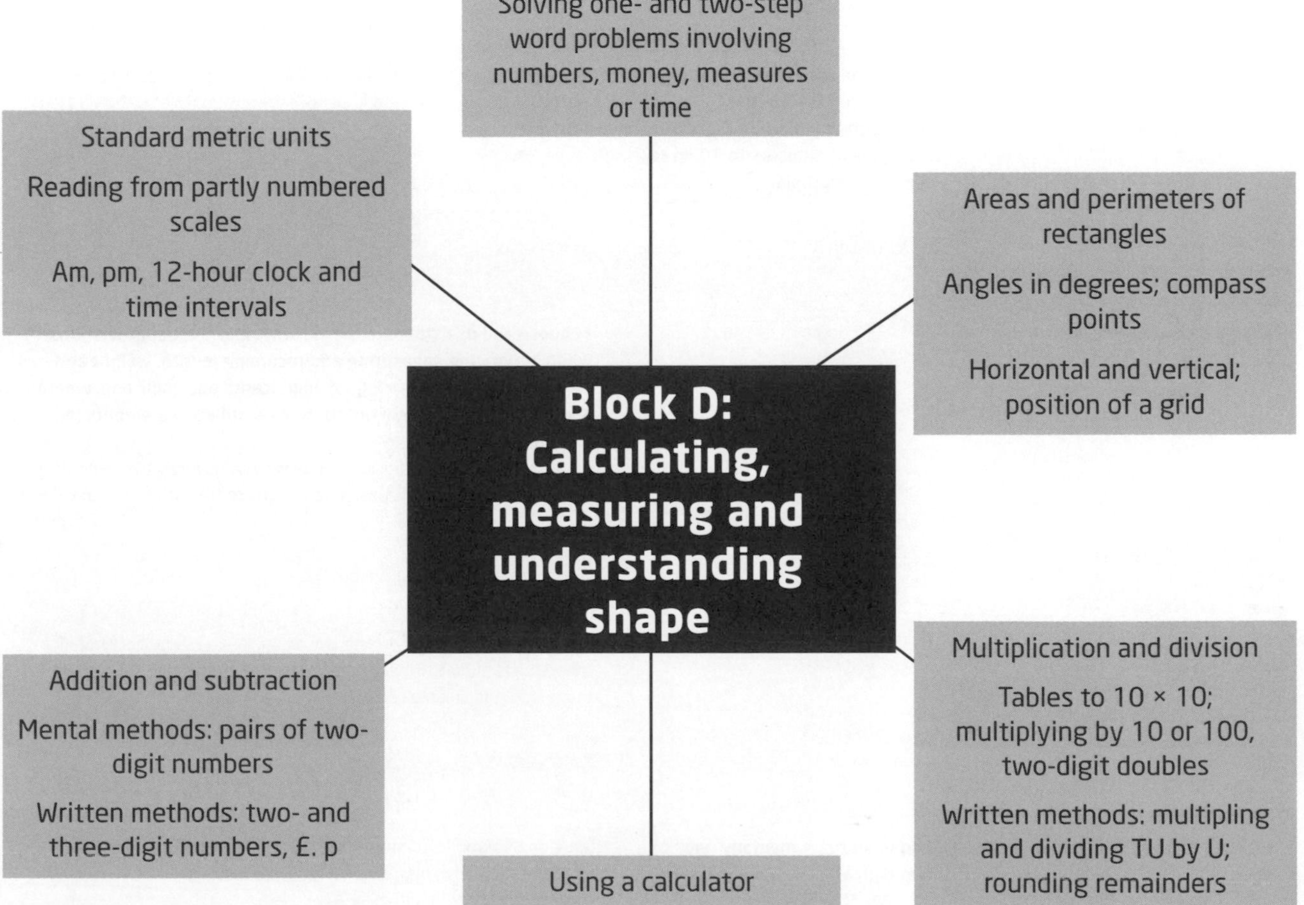

Unit 1 2 weeks

Calculating, measuring and understanding shape

Speaking and listening objective

- Listen to a speaker, take notes on the talk and use the notes to develop a role play.

Introduction

In this unit children develop mental methods of calculating addition or difference of pairs of two-digit whole numbers. They use simple coordinates and compass points to plot positions. Measures work concentrates on mass and reading from scales. They read from both digital and analogue clocks and to the nearest minute. They develop their speaking and listening skills by listening to each other and making notes, as shown in the 'compass points' activity. Whilst problem solving can be seen throughout the unit, Lessons 9 and 10 are devoted specifically to this.

Using and applying mathematics

- Solve one-step and two-step problems involving numbers, money or measures, including time; choose and carry out appropriate calculations, using calculator methods where appropriate.

Lesson	Strands	Starter	Main teaching activities
1. Teach and practise	Calculate	**Add or subtract mentally pairs of two-digit whole numbers (eg 47 + 58, 91 - 35).**	**Add or subtract mentally pairs of two-digit whole numbers (eg 47 + 58, 91 - 35).**
2. Teach and apply	Calculate	As for Lesson 1	As for Lesson 1
3. Teach and practise	Shape	**Derive and recall multiplication facts up to 10 × 10, the corresponding division facts and multiples of numbers to 10 up to the tenth multiple.**	Recognise horizontal and vertical lines; use the eight compass points to describe direction; describe and identify the position of a square on a grid of squares.
4. Teach and apply	Shape	As for Lesson 3	As for Lesson 3
5. Teach and practise	Measure	As for Lesson 3	• **Choose and use standard metric units and their abbreviations when estimating, measuring and recording length, weight and capacity; know the meaning of 'kilo', 'centi' and 'milli' and, where appropriate, use decimal notation to record measurements (eg 1.3m or 0.6kg).** • Interpret intervals and divisions on partially numbered scales and record readings accurately, where appropriate to the nearest tenth of a unit.
6. Review and apply	Measure	As for Lesson 3	As for Lesson 5
7. Teach and practise	Measure	As for Lesson 3	Read time to the nearest minute; use am, pm and 12-hour clock notation; choose units of time to measure time intervals; calculate time intervals from clocks and timetables.
8. Teach and apply	Measure	As for Lesson 3	As for Lesson 7
9. Review and apply	Use/apply	**Add or subtract mentally pairs of two-digit whole numbers (eg 47 + 58, 91 - 35).**	Solve one-step and two-step problems involving numbers, money or measures, including time; choose and carry out appropriate calculations, using calculator methods where appropriate.
10. Review and apply	Use/apply	As for Lesson 9	As for Lesson 9

Lessons 1-4

Preparation

Lessons 3 & 4: Prepare a set of 5 × 5 axes for display during the whole-class and review activities. Leave the axes blank so that the labels can be added during the lesson.

You will need

Photocopiable pages
'The addition game board' (page 139), 'The addition game instructions' (page 140) and 'The addition game score sheet' (page 141).
CD resources
'Coordinates', 'Compass points'; core, support, extension and template versions of 'Matching addition'. Interactive resource: 'Number sentence builder'.
Equipment
Calculators; colouring pencils.

Learning objectives

Starter

- Add or subtract mentally pairs of two-digit whole numbers (eg 47 + 58, 91 - 35).
- Derive and recall multiplication facts up to 10 × 10, the corresponding division facts and multiples of numbers to 10 up to the tenth multiple.

Main teaching activities

2006

- Add or subtract mentally pairs of two-digit whole numbers (eg 47 + 58, 91 - 35).
- Recognise horizontal and vertical lines; use the eight compass points to describe direction; describe and identify the position of a square on a grid of squares.

1999

- Use known number facts and place value to add or subtract mentally, including any pair of two-digit whole numbers.
- Recognise simple examples of horizontal and vertical lines.
- Use the eight compass directions N, S, E, W, NE, NW, SE, SW.
- Recognise positions and directions: for example, describe and find the position of a point on a grid of squares where the lines are numbered.

Vocabulary

calculation, equation, add, subtract, compare, sum, total, difference, plus minus, calculator, position, direction, north-east (NE), north-west (NW), south-west (SW), south-east (SE), horizontal, vertical, grid

Lesson 1 (Teach and practise)

Starter

Recall: Write on the board the numbers 17, 3 and 20, and ask the children to write on their whiteboards two addition sentences using the three numbers (17 + 3 = 20, 3 + 17 = 20). Check responses and then ask: *Now can you write two subtraction sentences using the three numbers?* (20 - 17 = 3 and 20 - 3 = 17). Explain to the children that you will give them an addition sentence and would like them to write down a corresponding subtraction sentence. For example, if you call out 3 + 12 = 15, they can respond 15 - 12 = 3 or 15 - 3 = 12. You may have to write the three numbers on the board to support the less confident children. Repeat this with several examples, highlighting the two different possible subtraction sentences.

Main teaching activities

Whole class: Use the 'Number sentence builder' interactive resource to display 70 + 4 + 30 = □. Ask the children to work out the answer on their whiteboards. Ask: *How did you work this out?* Stress that the most straightforward way is to add together the 30 + 70 = 100 and then to add 4. Repeat for 70 + 4 + 30 + 6 = □. If the children did not pair the 70 + 30 and the 6 + 4 then highlight this method of pairing up numbers (the associative law of addition or partitioning).

Repeat with a few more examples such as 34 + 2 + 66 + 8 = □. Stress that it does not matter how you pair the numbers. (For example, 66 + 34 and 2 + 8, or 34 + 2 and 66 + 8, or 30 + 60, 4 + 6 and 2 + 8.) Discuss the various possibilities.

Repeat this for subtraction, such as 82 - 35. Discuss ways of calculating mentally, such as 80 - 40 + 2 - 5 = 40 - 3 = 37.

Independent work: Give the children the activity sheet 'Matching addition'.

Explain that they will be practising more of these addition sentences. Ask the children to take two colouring pencils and to shade the pairs of numbers that they will be adding together first in the same colour. For Question 1, for example, children might decide to colour in the 12 and 8 in one colour (20) and the 13 and 7 in another colour (20).

Review
Write on the board: 1 + 2 + 3 + 4 + 5 + 6 + 7 + 8 + 9 = □. Ask: *How could we work out this sentence?* See if the children can partition the numbers (1 + 9, 2 + 8, 3 + 7, 4 + 6) to get the answer.

Write on the board the numbers 12, 8, 7, 13 and ask individual children to give two pairs that make 20 (13, 7 and 12, 8). Ask: *What is 90 + 40 + 10 + 30?* Check how the children worked this out. Complete the session by drawing a spider diagram on the board with a three-digit target number (eg 180) and ask for different empty-box number sentences to make the target number, for example 30 + □ + □ = □.

Differentiation
Less confident learners: Use the support version of the activity sheet, which has pairs of numbers partitioning to 10.
More confident learners: Use the extension version of the activity sheet, which includes three-digit numbers.

Lesson 2 (Teach and apply)

Starter
Recall: Repeat the Starter from Lesson 1 but start with 23, 46 and 69. Ask the children to write the two possible addition sentences and the two possible subtraction sentences on their whiteboards.

Main teaching activities
Whole class: Continue the work from Lesson 1, with further examples of two-digit plus two-digit additions such as 37 + 46. Ask the children to calculate mentally then to explain their method. Repeat for subtraction examples, such as 91 – 73.
Paired work: Explain that the children are going to play a game in pairs. Using activity sheets 'The addition game instructions', 'The addition game score sheet' and the 'The addition game board', the children take turns to pick three numbers from the number grid that they think that they can add together. The other player can use a calculator to check their response but by carrying out an appropriate subtraction. If the number sentence is correct they get a point and cross the three numbers off the number grid; if they get an incorrect answer they do not get a point and it is the other player's turn. The winner is the person who has more points when all the numbers are crossed off the grid. Use the score sheet to keep a tally. Remind the children to use the method that they have been practising for the last few lessons and that it will get more difficult as the game progresses because they cannot pick their numbers so freely.

Differentiation
Less confident learners: Decide whether to play the game as a group and discuss addition strategies each time. They could use a number square to help with addition.
More confident learners: Challenge the children to select four numbers to add together.

Review
Discuss efficient methods for winning the game. Ask:
- *Were you always right?*
- *When did you get the answer wrong?*
- *What did you need to do to get the correct answer?*
- *How did you use the calculator? Give me an example. Everybody try this. What strategy did you use?*

Lesson 3 (Teach and practise)

Starter
Recall: Begin by reciting the multiplication tables for 2, 3, 4, 5 and 10. Keep the pace sharp. Now explain that you will say a multiplication fact. Ask the children to write their answers on their whiteboards and to hold up their boards when you say: *Show me.* Keep the pace of this sharp to encourage rapid recall.

Main teaching activities

Whole class: Display the prepared axes on the OHP to demonstrate how to find positions on a grid of squares. Explain that the vertical and horizontal outer lines are called 'axes' and are numbered (write the numbers on the axes), with zero being common to both axes; this point is called the 'origin'. Explain that in coordinates, the horizontal line number is given first, then the vertical. Now invite a child to put a small cross on given coordinates such as (1, 4). Repeat this for coordinates such as (1, 1), (4, 1) and (4, 4) and ask: *If we join these points, what shape will we make?*

Clean the grid and invite children from different groups to come to the front and label the grid. Say: *Put zero at the origin. Put in the origin. Put the numbers 1 to 5 up the vertical axis, then along the horizontal axis.* Give other sets of coordinates, such as (1, 3), (3, 1) and (5, 3) and ask: *What shape is this?*

Group work: Ask the children to work in pairs on the activity sheet 'Coordinates'. One child draws a shape (in pencil) on their grid without the other child seeing the shape; this child then gives the coordinates to the second child. They compare and measure their shapes and find the perimeter.

Differentiation

Less confident learners: The children can begin with simpler shapes such as rectangles and squares.

More confident learners: The children can go on to try more complex shapes.

Review

Decide on coordinates at which treasure might be hidden. Display the axes used earlier in the lesson and explain that the grid represents a treasure map. Ask the children to suggest coordinates of where the treasure might be, and to mark these spots on the map grid. The child who 'finds' the treasure can then decide where they have treasure hidden on the map and repeat the activity.

Lesson 4 (Teach and apply)

Starter

Recall: Repeat the Starter from Lesson 3, but this time ask the children division facts. Again, keep the pace sharp to encourage rapid recall. If the children are unsure, remind them that if a multiplication fact such as $6 \times 3 = 18$ is known, then 3×6, $18 \div 6$ and $18 \div 3$ can be derived too.

Main teaching activities

Whole class: Display the 5×5 axes. Draw to one side a four-point simple compass with north marked N. Ask the children to identify where south, east and west go. Now point to the grid and mark the square (2, 4) with a large dot and discuss how to label squares. Say: *What if I move the dot two squares east. Where will it go?* Agree that it will be in square (4, 4). Repeat for moving the dot north, south and west.

Now add the other points (NE, NW, SE, SW) to make an eight-point compass. Clean off the dot markings and this time mark the dot on (3, 5). Say: *Where would the dot go if I move it one square south-east?* Agree that it would move to square (4, 4). Repeat for other compass bearings.

Paired work: Provide each pair with a copy of the activity sheet 'Compass points'. Ask them to take turns to describe a route using all eight compass points. They compare their 'journeys'.

Differentiation

Less confident learners: Decide whether to limit the work to using the four compass points.

More confident learners: Challenge the children to make more complex journeys.

Review

Provide fresh copies of 'Compass points'. Invite children from each ability group to say one of their journeys for the others to follow and to mark on their sheets. Ask questions such as:

- *What if the dot moves two squares east – where will it be now?*
- *What if the dot moves three squares south-west – where will it be now?*

Lessons 5-10

Preparation

Lesson 5: Prepare the cards from the '"Show me" cards' activity sheet. Enlarge the 'Weighing in' cards for the sorting activity.
Lesson 6: Set up the stations as described in the lesson.

You will need

CD resources
'"Show me" cards', 'Weighing in', 'Estimating mass', 'Comparing mass' and 'Time Pelmanism'; core, support, extension and template versions of 'Time problems', 'Money problems' and 'Deepham Primary School'.
Equipment
Sticky notes; a selection of objects (or pictures of objects) for Lesson 5; bathroom scales; Plasticine (about 500 grams); some everyday household objects such as an apple, a can of beans or a pencil; two sets of dial balances.

Learning objectives

Starter

- Derive and recall multiplication facts up to 10 × 10, the corresponding division facts and multiples of numbers to 10 up to the tenth multiple.
- Add or subtract mentally pairs of two-digit whole numbers (eg 47 + 58, 91 - 35).

Main teaching activities

2006

- Choose and use standard metric units and their abbreviations when estimating, measuring and recording length, weight and capacity; know the meaning of 'kilo', 'centi' and 'milli' and, where appropriate, use decimal notation to record measurements (eg 1.3m or 0.6kg).
- Interpret intervals and divisions on partially numbered scales and record readings accurately, where appropriate to the nearest tenth of a unit.
- Read time to the nearest minute; use am, pm and 12-hour clock notation; choose units of time to measure time intervals; calculate time intervals from clocks and timetables.
- Solve one-step and two-step problems involving numbers, money or measures, including time; choose and carry out appropriate calculations, using calculator methods where appropriate.

1999

- Use, read and write standard metric units (km, m, cm, mm, kg, g, l, ml), including their abbreviations, and imperial units (mile, pint).
- Know and use the relationships between familiar units of length, mass and capacity.
- Know the equivalent of one half, one quarter, three quarters and one tenth of 1 km, 1 m, 1 kg, 1 litre in m, cm, g, ml.
- Suggest suitable units and measuring equipment to estimate or measure length, mass or capacity.
- Record estimates and readings from scales to a suitable degree of accuracy.
- Use am and pm and the notation 9:53.
- Read simple timetables.
- Use all four operations to solve word problems involving numbers in 'real life', money and measures (including time), using one or more steps, including converting pounds to pence and metres to centimetres and vice versa.
- Choose and use appropriate number operations and appropriate ways of calculating (mental, mental with jottings, pencil and paper) to solve problems.
- Round up or down after division, depending on the context.
- Choose appropriate ways of calculating: calculator.

Vocabulary

problem, solution, answer, method, explain, predict, reason, reasoning, pattern, relationship, measure, estimate, metric unit, standard unit, mass, balance, scales, units of measurement and abbreviations: kilogram (kg), gram (g), time, am, pm, digital, analogue, minutes

Lesson 5 (Teach and practise)

Starter

Recall: Call out quick-fire multiplication questions and ask the children to write their answers on their whiteboards. Discuss strategies to help them remember their tables. For example, numbers in the two-times table always end in 2, 4, 6, 8 or 0; numbers in the four-times table are double those in the two-times table; numbers in the five-times table always end in 0 or 5;

Calculating, measuring and understanding shape

BLOCK D

multiples of 10 always end in 0. Now tell the children that you are going to play a game: you will ask multiplication questions within the two-, three-, four-, five- and ten-times tables. The last child to hold up the correct answer to each question will be out of the game. The winner will be the last child left playing.

Main teaching activities

Whole class: Explain to the children that today's lesson is about mass. Tell them that when they weigh themselves, they find their mass. Ask: *What units of measurement can we use to measure mass?* (Kilograms, grams, milligrams, tonnes, ounces, pounds, stones, tons.) Explain that today they are going to learn about kilograms, grams, milligrams and tonnes (write them on the board, including their abbreviations) and that although there are other measurements that also measure mass, these are the most common measurements used. Write on the board the symbols >, < and =. Ask the children to make up some statements using the symbols and two words (kilogram > gram; gram > milligram; milligram < kilogram; 1000 kilograms = 1 tonne; 1000 grams = 1 kilogram, 1000 milligrams = 1 gram).

Give each child a set of cards from the '"Show me" cards' activity sheet. Explain that you are going to say the name of an object (hold up an object or a picture of an object) and ask them to hold up the units in which they think the mass should be measured. Show the children a range of objects with a variety of masses to use all measurements. For larger objects, such as an elephant or a car (tonnes), use images from the activity sheet 'Weighing in'. Sort the objects in order of mass and discuss how to write their masses. Now weigh the smaller items, attaching a sticky note to each item, with its mass and the unit of measurement on it. Draw a number line on the board:

0 kg — 1 kg

Ask a child to come and mark the halfway point. Ask: *How could we label this?* (Half a kilogram, 0.5 kilogram) Ask: *How many grams in a kilogram?* (1000 grams.) Ask: *What is half of 1000 grams?* (500 grams.) Mark this on the number line. Now ask: *Where could I put 250 grams?* (Half way between 0 kg and 500 grams.) Repeat for 750 grams.

Independent work: Provide the children with the activity sheet 'Estimating mass' and ask them to estimate where the measurements would go on the number line.

Differentiation

Less confident learners: These children may need extra help to plot the measurements on the number lines.

More confident learners: Ask: *Could you draw a number line from 0 grams to 1 gram?* Ask the children to fill in various measurements in milligrams, such as 500mg, 700mg, 750mg.

Review

Ask the children to place the sticky notes from your items onto a number line, each time asking: *Is its mass greater than one kilogram? Is it less than one kilogram?* If its mass is less than one kilogram, then it will go onto the number line, for example the elephant would not go onto the number line. Ask: *Is its mass less than 500 grams? Is it more than 500 grams?*

Lesson 6 (Review and apply)

Starter

Recall: Repeat the Starter from Lesson 5, this time extending to table facts for 6 to 10.

Main teaching activities

Group work: Split the children into five groups. Explain to the children that you are going to continue to look at mass. Remind them how they measured to the nearest interval for length. Explain that you would like them to do the same for mass.

Show a partially marked set of scales and ask what the divisions stand for. Set up five stations around the classroom and explain to the children that they will visit all five stations. You will time them and they will have to move to the next station as soon as you tell them to. By the end of the lesson they should complete the activity sheet 'Comparing mass'. The stations are as follows:

- At Station 1 provide a set of bathroom scales where the children can estimate their own mass, then weigh themselves. They calculate the difference between their measured mass and their estimate.
- At Station 2 they will make a ball of Plasticine with an estimated mass of 100 grams. They weigh their ball to see how close they were and record its mass.
- At Station 3 they will complete the >, < and = boxes on the activity sheet.
- At Station 4 they will write down the masses of various objects, using the scales provided (either balance with weights or dial balances). Then answer the question: *What is the difference in mass between the heaviest and lightest object?*
- At Station 5 they will fill in the suitable measurements in the boxes on the activity sheet and ask them to identify the difference between the lightest and heaviest.

Review

Ask: *Did anyone make a ball of 100 grams at Station 2? Who made a ball that weighed less than 100 grams? Whose ball weighed more than 500 grams? How much did it weigh?* Talk through the answers for Stations 3 and 5. Focus in particular on the fractional equivalences, for example 500g = ½ kg. Ask: *How did you read the weight when it was between markings on the scale?* Now ask:

- *Which is heavier, 3900g or 4kg? How do you know?*
- *Tell me another way to write 3kg. What about 750g?*

Differentiation

Less confident learners: These children may need more assistance or practical experience of weighing objects.

More confident learners: Challenge the children to estimate the measurements at Stations 4 and 5.

Lesson 7 (Teach and practise)

Starter

Recall: Explain that you will ask some division facts for the two-, three- and four-times tables. Ask the children to write the answers on their whiteboards, and to hold up their boards when you say *Show me*. Say, for example: *What is 14 divided by 2? Half of 20? Quarter of 24? How many threes are there in 27?* Keep the pace sharp to encourage quick recall of division facts.

Main teaching activities

Whole class: Explain that you will say some times and you want the children to set them on their clock faces. When you say *Show me*, they hold up their clocks. Begin with times to the nearest five-minute interval, such as: *8:15, 9:45, 7:05...*

Next, use the teaching clock to explain that within each five-minute interval on the clock face, it is possible to set the clock to 1:01, 1:02, 1: 03... Ask the children to look at their clock faces and note the one-minute intervals. They can count from, say, five past to ten past in one-minute intervals. Ask the children to set their clocks as accurately as they can to the times that you give them. Say: *12:37, 18 minutes to 3, 13 minutes past 12, 5:28...* Check that the children understand and that they are setting their clocks with reasonable accuracy. Make more confident children aware of the way the hour hand moves on during each hour, too. At 3:28, for example, the minute hand will be just before the 6, and the hour hand about halfway between the 3 and the 4.

Remind the children that they have already learned how to read a digital clock to the nearest five minutes. Write on the board '11:55' and ask the children to set their clocks to this time. Then ask: *What will the digital clock read in one minute? Two minutes? Five minutes?* Each time, invite a child to write the time on the board. Check that the children understand that the hour changes to 12:00 five minutes after 11:55. Repeat this for other digital times in one-minute intervals, such as 5:08, 9:37 and so on.

Discuss when to use 'am' (from the Latin 'ante meridiem' meaning 'before

noon') and 'pm' ('post meridiem' meaning 'after noon'). Say: *It is 37 minutes past two in the afternoon. How would I write that?* Encourage a child to write on the board: '2:37pm'. Repeat this for other times, morning and afternoon.
Group work: Provide each pair with cards made from activity sheet 'Time Pelmanism'. They play Pelmanism with the cards. The children should match a digital to an analogue time. The winner is the child who collects more pairs of cards.

Differentiation

Less confident learners: If the children are likely to struggle with the activity, suggest that they have their cards face up, and take turns to find matching pairs.
More confident learners: When the children have played 'Time Pelmanism' two or three times, challenge them to take turns to say a time to their partner, using am or pm. Their partner sets their clock to the time, then says the time in as many ways as they can: '12:14', '14 minutes past 12', and so on.

Review

Set the teaching clock to different times. Invite children from each group to write the digital time on the board. Say whether it is morning or afternoon, and check that the children use am or pm appropriately. Ask questions such as: *If it is 11:45am, what time will it be in 20 minutes? What time is it on the clock on the wall now? What time will it be in 50 minutes from now? What time was it 40 minutes ago? How did you work that out?*

Lesson 8 (Teach and apply)

Starter

Recall: Repeat the Starter from Lesson 7, including questions from the five- and ten-tImes tables.

Main teaching activities

Explain that this lesson is about time problems. On the board, show the children how to use an empty number line to count on for the time, such as:

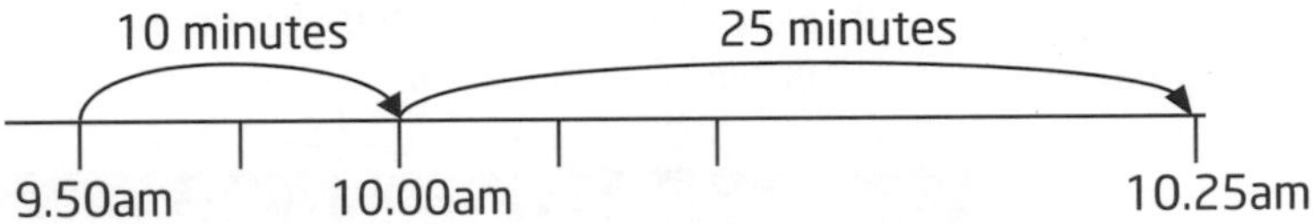

Provide copies of the activity sheet 'Time problems'. Ask the children to work individually to solve the problems. Remind them that they can use clock faces or an empty time line to help them.

Differentiation

Less confident learners: Provide the support version of the 'Time problems' activity sheet.
More confident learners: Provide the extension version of the activity sheet.

Review

Look at some of the questions from each sheet, and ask the children to explain how they worked out the answers. Check that they write the time in digital format, and use am and pm appropriately. Make sure they understand that digital time is not decimal: 11:55 plus 5 minutes is 12:00, not 11:60.

Lesson 9 (Review and apply)

Starter

Recall: Ask the children each to choose six numbers between 1 and 20, and to write these on a piece of paper. Tell the children that you will say some addition and subtraction number sentences. For each one, ask the children to work out the answer and, if the answer is one of their numbers, to cross it through. The first child to cross through all six numbers wins the game. Keep the pace of this sharp. This can be repeated, with the children choosing six new numbers for each new game. Use as wide a variety of calculation vocabulary as possible, for example: *What is 5 plus 4? 19 subtract 13? The difference between 12 and 6?*

Main teaching activities

Whole class: Begin by asking the children some conversion questions such as these:

- *How many pence in £1.20? £2.50? £5.60?* (Keep the amounts below £10.00.)

- *How many pounds in 145p? 295p? 729p?* (Keep the amounts below £10.00.)
- *How many centimetres in 1.56m? 2.18m? 8.10m?* (Keep the distances below 10m.)
- *How many metres in 182cm? 451cm? 790cm?* (Keep the distances below 10m.)

Ask the children to explain how they converted from one kind of unit to another. (By dividing or multiplying by 10 or 100.) Now say: *James has £10.00. He spent a fifth of his money on a comic. How much did he spend? How did you work out the answer?* Discuss how, to find a fifth of £10.00, we can divide 10 by 5.

Now set this problem: *A CD costs £6.00. Ali saves 30p a week. How many weeks must Ali save up in order to buy the CD?* Discuss with the children how they can find the answer. They will need to convert £6.00 into pence, then divide 600 by 30 in order to get an answer of 20 weeks.

Paired work: Explain to the children that for the next two lessons they are going to be solving problems. Give out the activity sheet 'Money problems' to pairs of children. This has money problems to solve. Remind the children to read each of the problems carefully first and then to decide on the relevant information and what operation to use to find the solution.

Review

Select a problem from each of the differentiated activity sheets and ask groups of children to explain how they solved the problems. Ask them to tell you which problems they found hardest and which ones were easiest, and why that was. Look for children who can confidently convert pounds into pence and vice versa. Ask questions such as:

- *How did you work this out?*
- *How did you know that you needed to use addition/subtraction/ multiplication/division?*

Differentiation

Less confident learners: There is a support version of the activity sheet that has simpler questions to solve.
More confident learners: Decide whether to use the extension version of the activity sheet, with harder questions to solve.

Lesson 10 (Review and apply)

Starter

Recall: Repeat the Starter from Lesson 9, but this time ask the children to choose eight numbers between 1 and 20 to play with.

Main teaching activities

Review conversions of measures: km to m, m to cm, cm to mm. Explain to the children that you would like them to solve some word problems about measurements of length. Provide a copy of activity sheet 'Deepham Primary School' to each pair of children.

Review

Invite children from each group to explain how they solved one of their problems. Discuss which operation they chose, and why. Ask the children to explain which units they used, and why they used them.

Differentiation

Less confident learners: Provide the support version of the 'Deepham Primary School' activity sheet.
More confident learners: Provide the extension version of the activity sheet.

Name ______________________ Date ______________

The addition game board

9	60	3	7	21	9	5	6
1	2	15	8	7	4	28	6
8	2	6	5	9	3	5	6
42	9	4	3	7	12	33	1
16	8	9	4	2	5	58	3
46	6	4	56	3	5	4	44
19	1	38	5	2	4	7	8
3	42	6	6	9	23	1	7
2	9	5	8	35	2	9	26

Name ______________________ Date ______________________

The addition game instructions

Instructions to play in pairs.

1. Take turns to pick three numbers from the addition gameboard that you think that you can add together.
2. You must pick at least one two-digit number.
3. Say the sum and your answer to your partner who will use a calculator to check it.
4. If your answer is correct you get a point. Cross out the three numbers you used in your sum from the number grid. If your answer is incorrect, you do not get a point and it is the other player's turn.
5. The winner is the person who has more points when all the numbers are crossed off the grid. Use the the addition game score sheet to keep a tally.

Remember to use the addition method that you have been practising for the last few lessons.

Name ______________________ Date ______________________

The addition game score sheet

Player 1			Player 2		
Sum	Answer	Correct (Y/N)	Sum	Answer	Correct (Y/N)
	Total			Total	

Unit 2 2 weeks

Calculating, measuring and understanding shape

Lesson	Strand	Starter	Main teaching activities
1. Teach and practise	Calculate	Refine and use efficient written methods to add and subtract two-digit and three-digit whole numbers and £.p.	Refine and use efficient written methods to add and subtract two-digit and three-digit whole numbers and £.p.
2. Review and practise	Calculate Use/apply	As for Lesson 1	• Refine and use efficient written methods to add and subtract two-digit and three-digit whole numbers and £.p. • Solve one-step and two-step problems involving numbers, money or measures, including time; choose and carry out appropriate calculations, using calculator methods where appropriate.
3. Review and apply	Use/apply	As for Lesson 1	Solve one-step and two-step problems involving numbers, money or measures, including time; choose and carry out appropriate calculations, using calculator methods where appropriate.
4. Practise and apply	Use/apply	Solve one-step and two-step problems involving numbers, money or measures, including time; choose and carry out appropriate calculations, using calculator methods where appropriate.	As for Lesson 3
5. Review, teach and practise	Knowledge Calculate	**Derive and recall multiplication facts up to 10 × 10, the corresponding division facts and multiples of numbers to 10 up to the tenth multiple.**	**• Derive and recall multiplication facts up to 10 × 10, the corresponding division facts and multiples of numbers to 10 up to the tenth multiple.** **• Develop and use written methods to record, support and explain multiplication and division of two-digit numbers by a one-digit number, including division with remainders (eg 15 × 9, 98 ÷ 6).**
6. Review and apply	Knowledge Calculate	As for Lesson 5	As for Lesson 5
7. Review, teach and apply	Counting Measure	**Choose and use standard metric units and their abbreviations when estimating, measuring and recording length, weight and capacity; know the meaning of 'kilo', 'centi' and 'milli' and, where appropriate, use decimal notation to record measurements (eg 1.3m or 0.6kg).**	• Use decimal notation for tenths and hundredths and partition decimals; relate the notation to money and measurement. **• Choose and use standard metric units and their abbreviations when estimating, measuring and recording length, weight and capacity; know the meaning of 'kilo', 'centi' and 'milli' and, where appropriate, use decimal notation to record measurements (eg 1.3m or 0.6kg).** • Interpret intervals and divisions on partially numbered scales and record readings accurately, where appropriate to the nearest tenth of a unit.
8. Review, teach and practise	Measure	As for Lesson 7	• Draw rectangles and measure and calculate their perimeters; find the area of rectilinear shapes drawn on a square grid by counting squares. **• Choose and use standard metric units and their abbreviations when estimating, measuring and recording length, weight and capacity; know the meaning of 'kilo', 'centi' and 'milli' and, where appropriate, use decimal notation to record measurements (eg 1.3m or 0.6kg).**
9. Apply	Use/apply Measure	Use decimal notation for tenths and hundredths and partition decimals; relate the notation to money and measurement.	• Solve one-step and two-step problems involving numbers, money or measures, including time; choose and carry out appropriate calculations, using calculator methods where appropriate. **• Choose and use standard metric units and their abbreviations when estimating, measuring and recording length, weight and capacity; know the meaning of 'kilo', 'centi' and 'milli' and, where appropriate, use decimal notation to record measurements (eg 1.3m or 0.6kg).**
10. Review, teach and apply	Shape	Recognise horizontal and vertical lines; use the eight compass points to describe direction; describe and identify the position of a square on a grid of squares.	• Recognise horizontal and vertical lines; use the eight compass points to describe direction; describe and identify the position of a square on a grid of squares. **• Know that angles are measured in degrees and that one whole turn is 360°; compare and order angles less than 180°.**

Speaking and listening objective

- Take different roles in groups and use language appropriate to them, including roles of leader, reporter, scribe, mentor.

Introduction

In this unit, children solve one-step and two-step word problems involving numbers, money, measures or time, using standard metric units and reading from partly numbered scales. They find areas and perimeters of rectangles and angles in degrees, and they use compass points. Children continue to develop multiplication and division, tables to 10 × 10 and multiplying by 10 or 100. They double two-digit numbers and use written methods to multiply and divide TU by U, rounding remainders. They continue to practise using addition and subtraction using both mental and written methods. Children use a calculator for some calculations.

Using and applying mathematics

- Solve one-step and two-step problems involving numbers, money or measures, including time; choose and carry out appropriate calculations, using calculator methods where appropriate.

Lessons 1-4

Preparation

Lesson 2: Prepare the 'Beat the brain cards', one set per pair.
Lesson 3: Prepare the 'Operation follow-on' cards, one set.
Lesson 4: Measure your height and write it on a card. Place this and the other relevant equipment at each station.

You will need

Photocopiable pages
'Addition sums' (page 154) and 'Beat the brain cards' (page 155).
CD resources
'Station problems', one per group; core, support, extension and template versions of 'Beat the brain cards', one set per pair, and 'Bargain hunter!', one per child.
General resource sheet: 'Operation follow-on', one card per child.
Equipment
Number fans; beanbags; tape measures; stopwatch; a piece of string measuring 134cm.

Learning objectives

Starter

- Refine and use efficient written methods to add and subtract two-digit and three-digit whole numbers and £.p.
- Solve one-step and two-step problems involving numbers, money or measures, including time; choose and carry out appropriate calculations, using calculator methods where appropriate.

Main teaching activities

2006

- Refine and use efficient written methods to add and subtract two-digit and three-digit whole numbers and £.p.
- Solve one-step and two-step problems involving numbers, money or measures, including time; choose and carry out appropriate calculations, using calculator methods where appropriate.

1999

- Use all four operations to solve word problems involving numbers in 'real' life, money and measures (including time), using one or more steps, including converting pounds to pence and metres to centimetres and vice versa.
- Choose and use appropriate number operations and appropriate ways of calculating (mental, mental with jottings, pencil and paper) to solve problems.
- Round up or down after division, depending on context.
- Choose appropriate ways of calculating: calculator.
- Develop and refine written methods for: column addition and subtraction of two whole numbers less than 1000, and addition of more than two such numbers; money calculations (eg £7.85 ± £3.49).

Vocabulary

problem, solution, answer, method, explain, predict, reason, reasoning, pattern, relationship, calculation, equation, decimal, decimal point, decimal place, add, subtract, multiply, divide, order, compare, sum, total, difference, plus, minus, product, remainder, calculator, pound (£), pence (p), measure, estimate, metric unit, standard unit, length, distance, ruler, measuring tape, units of measurement and abbreviations: kilometre (km), metre (m), centimetre (cm)

Lesson 1 (Teach and practise)

Starter

Reason: Write four single-digit numbers on the board, such as 1, 2, 3 and 4. Call out addition sentences involving adding a two-digit number to another two-digit number, using all of the numbers on the board (12 + 34, 21 + 34, 12 + 43, 21 + 43, 13 + 42, 31 + 42, 13 + 24, 31 + 24, 14 + 32, 41 + 32, 14 + 23, 41 + 23). Be systematic in the way that you write the list, asking the children to respond using number fans or whiteboards. Ask: *Do you think that I have used all of the possible additions?* Explain to them that it is important to have a logical way of finding all the possible additions.

Main teaching activities

Whole class: Repeat the Starter, but this time include three-digit numbers, for example 123 + 234, 432 + 123 or 132 + 423. Ask individuals to come up with addition sentences and solve them, discussing methods. Recap written methods as necessary.

Independent/group work: Give individual children the activity sheet 'Addition sums'. The boxes at the top of the sheet have been left blank so that you can fill in numbers appropriate to the number of groups and ability levels, for example 1, 2, 3 and 0 (less confident) or 2, 3, 4 and 5 or 6, 7, 8 and 9 (more confident). Give pairs or groups copies with the same four numbers, so that they can work together later in the lesson. Ask the children to write down as many addition sentences as they can, using the four numbers at the top of the sheet. Specify that they must write at least (say, five) using three-digit numbers. Check results. Ask: *How could you check to see if you have all of the possible sentences? How many should you have altogether?*

Now ask the children to work out the answers to their sentences. Explain that you will be asking them: *Which ones are easier to work out in your head? Which ones do you find it easier to write down?*

Now ask the children to find others in the class who have the same numbers on their sheets. Ask them to compare their findings. Ask: *Do you have the same answers? Did you work out the questions in the same way?* Go through all the different mental methods used to find the answers.

Differentiation

Less confident learners: This group should have one of the units digits in their numbers as zero. This should allow them to work easily in multiples of ten.

More confident learners: This group could work out subtractions as well as addition sentences. Encourage the children to be systematic, and challenge them to be competitive about the number of sentences that they can make. You might also ask them to find the smallest total they can make!

Review

Ask individuals to explain their workings of, say, 123 + 456, 132 + 456, 123 + 465, 132 + 465, and 234 + 156. Discuss and ask: *Is there a more efficient way to solve them?*

Lesson 2 (Review and practise)

Starter

Reason: Repeat the Starter from Lesson 1, this time using subtraction sentences.

Main teaching activities

Whole class: Recap on the subtractions sentences, focusing on written methods using some examples, such as 432 – 134, 432 – 423.

Independent work: Ask the children to try a few HTU – TU examples of their own, using the method that they prefer.

Paired work: Explain to the children that they are going to play a game to see whether or not it is better to write down workings or to do calculations in your head. Give each pair a set of cards from the activity sheet 'Beat the brain cards'. Explain that one person in the pair must work everything out in their heads, and the other person has to work everything out on paper, writing down every single calculation that they do. The first person to get the correct answer wins the card.

Review

Discuss with the children: *Which cards could/did you work out mentally?*

Why? When was it useful to write something down? Is it always important to write something down? Which methods did you use?

Say: *As I know that 432 + 123 = 555, what would £4.32 + £1.23 be? I know that the difference between 113 and 24 is 89. If I have travelled 89 miles and have 113 miles to travel altogether, how much further must I travel?*

Lesson 3 (Review and apply)

Starter

Rehearse: Shuffle the pack of 'Operation follow-on' cards from the general resource sheet and distribute all of them to the class. There are 35 cards in total, so some children may need to have two cards, depending on the size of the group. All the cards follow on from each other. For example, the answer (7) to '16 take away 9' will be found at the top of another card. Tell the children that they have to work out the calculation and then the child who has the card with that number at the top must stand up, say the answer and then read out the question on their own card. Note that you will need to remember the starting number (you can start anywhere in the loop) and that everyone should have a turn before play returns to the beginning of the loop.

Differentiation

Less confident learners: Use the support version of the activity sheet, which has less complex addition and subtraction questions. Pair children according to ability and give extra support if possible.

More confident learners: Provide the extension version of the sheet, with more three-digit calculations.

Main teaching activities

Paired work: Give each pair a copy of the 'Bargain hunter!' sheet. Explain that you might like to buy a chair and a sofa and would like them to find the cheapest deal for you. You also need to know how much would be left to pay if you had to pay a deposit. Ask them to think about how they will go about this task. Tell them they can work out the totals mentally if they prefer, but then ask: *How could we check the answers?* (By using an equivalent calculation/counting up.)

Differentiation

Less confident learners: Work on this activity, reminding the children of the method shown in the previous unit. If necessary, give them the support version of the 'Bargain hunter!' sheet in which the units digit does not cross 10.

More confident learners: Provide the children with the extension version of the sheet, which includes pairs of three-digit calculations.

Review

Establish that the answer is Easy Chairs. Ask children who answered correctly to show their methods of working. Make sure that all the children checked their answers by using an equivalent calculation or by counting up (for the subtraction). Go through the methods for each store.

Lesson 4 (Practise and apply)

Starter

Read: On the board, write 24 × 4, 24 ÷ 4, 24 + 4 and 24 – 4. Ask a series of questions and ask the children to show you which of these calculations they would use. Say:

- *I have £2.40 and I spend £4. How much do I have left?*
- *What is the difference between 2m 40cm and 40cm?*
- *What is a quarter of 24km?*
- *Each roll of tape measures 24 metres. I have four rolls, so how much tape do I have in total?*
- *How much would I spend on 4 apples, if each apple costs 24p?*

Ask individuals to come up with some further examples.

Main teaching activities

Whole class: Explain to the children that today they will be solving a number of problems in groups and will have to move around the class in order to answer all of the questions at each of the stations around the classroom. They will have to work as a group and should swap roles for each task. Give each group a copy of the 'Station problems' resource sheet.

Group work

Station 1 (outside if possible): The children each have a beanbag and have to throw it as far as they can. As a group they measure the lengths in centimetres and a scribe records the distances. One member of the group then has to work out the difference between the longest and the shortest

distance and describe their method to the rest of the group. Another member of the group finds an alternative method.
Station 2: Before the lesson, record your height and ask: *How much do you need to grow before you are the same height as me?* Provide measuring equipment. The children need to give individual answers and then, as a group, check each other's answers, comparing methods.
Station 3: At this station the children need to time how many throws and catches of the beanbag they can do in 30 seconds. They must work one at a time and take turns so that one member of the group times each one, using a stopwatch. They then individually estimate how many they could do in two minutes and record their answers, explaining their workings and reasoning to the group.
Station 4: At this station the children measure a piece of string in centimetres (134cm) and then answer the question: *I need three lengths of half a metre. Do I have enough string?* The children discuss as a group and decide on an answer.
Station 5: At this station, the children purchase three bunches of flowers. They have £12 in their wallet. They also spend 99p on a card. What is the maximum that they can spend on each bunch of flowers?

Differentiation

Less confident learners: If necessary, provide adult support to assist these children.
More confident learners: Encourage these children to work quickly and accurately.

Review

Ask individuals about the contribution they made to the group work. Discuss the problems and solutions, asking: *What clues did you look for in the problem? What helped you to find an answer?*

Lessons 5-6

Preparation

Lesson 5: Copy 'Practising the grid method' onto OHT for display.
Lesson 6: Copy 'Blank number lines' onto OHT for display.

You will need

CD resources
'Sharing money'; core, support, extension and template versions of 'Practising the grid method'. General resource sheet: 'Blank number lines'.
Equipment
£1, 50p, 20p and 5p coins for each group.

Learning objectives

Starter

- Derive and recall multiplication facts up to 10 × 10, the corresponding division facts and multiples of numbers to 10 up to the tenth multiple.

Main teaching activities

2006

- Derive and recall multiplication facts up to 10 × 10, the corresponding division facts and multiples of numbers to 10 up to the tenth multiple.
- Develop and use written methods to record, support and explain multiplication and division of two-digit numbers by a one-digit number, including division with remainders (eg 15 × 9, 98 ÷ 6).

1999

- Know by heart all multiplication facts up to 10 × 10; derive quickly corresponding division facts.
- Recognise multiples of 6, 7, 8, 9, up to the tenthth multiple.
- Recognise multiples of 2, 3, 4, 5 and 10, up to the tenth multiple.
- Develop and refine written methods for TU × U, TU ÷ U.
- Find remainders after division; divide a whole number of pounds by 2, 4, 5 or 10 to give £.p; round up or down after division, depending on context.

Vocabulary

problem, solution, answer, method, explain, predict, reason, reasoning, pattern, relationship, calculation, equation, decimal, decimal point, decimal place, multiply, divide, order, compare, product, remainder, calculator, pound (£), pence (p)

Lesson 5 (Review, teach and practise)

Starter

Recall: Say a multiplication sentence, such as: *Three multiplied by eight equals 24.* Ask the children to write on their whiteboards a corresponding division sentence. Discuss the fact that there are two possible division sentences (24 ÷ 3 = 8 and 24 ÷ 8 = 3).

Give the children several more examples covering facts from tables up to 10 × 10, each time discussing the two possibilities.

Main teaching activities

Whole class: Write on the board 13 × 4 = □ and ask the children: *Who can remember how we worked this out before?* Recap 13 × 4 = (10 × 4) + (3 × 4).

Now ask: *What could you write down to help you do this calculation? Could you write this in another way?*

Draw the grid, showing carefully where each number will go. Remind the children of their use of the grid method Block A, Unit 2.

Now write on the board 23 × 4 = □. Ask the children to estimate what the answer would be. Ask: *Will it be greater than 52? How do you know that?* Write some of the children's estimates on the board then ask: *How could you work it out?*

Independent work: Display the 'Practising the grid method' resource sheet and distribute copies to the children. Check that the children can put the numbers in the correct boxes. Work out the answer together (as shown) and compare the answer to the estimates.

×	20	3	
4	80	12	= 92

Ask: *How did you estimate your answer?* Repeat with some different examples, such as 16 × 4, 26 × 4, 27 × 5, 28 × 5 and 31 × 6, estimating the answers each time. Let the children work through the activity sheet.

Differentiation

Less confident learners: Let these children use the support version of the activity sheet, which restricts them to multiplication of a single-digit number by a number less than 20.

More confident learners: Provide the extension version of the sheet, which includes multiplication of single-digit by two-digit numbers over 50 as well as a challenge similar to the one set out in the Review, in which the children have to identify the original number sentence from a partially completed grid. Ask these children to estimate their answers first and to find the difference between their estimates and their answer for each calculation. Encourage these children to use a mental strategy such as partitioning to find more accurate estimates.

Review

Draw the following grid on the board:

×	?	?	
?	360	18	= 378

Ask: *What could the question marks stand for?*

Now write on the board 42 × 9 = □. Ask the children to estimate the answer (400). Discuss and compare approaches to finding the estimates (4 × 9 × 10) or (40 × 10). Then discuss how to work out the calculation (4 × 10 × 9) + (2 × 9) or (40 × 10) + (2 × 10) – 42 (378).

Lesson 6 (Review and apply)

Starter

Revisit and refine: Remind the children that the six-times table can be made by doubling the three-times table. Ask them to use whiteboards to answer a series of mental questions involving the six-times table (up to 6 × 10). Each time ask: *How did you work out the answer?* Repeat using the eight-times table.

Main teaching activities

Whole class: Use the enlarged version of 'Blank number lines' and say: *I have £2.00 and I would like to share it between four people. How much money would each person get?* Write up 200 ÷ 4 = □. Invite the children to suggest an approximate answer, and to explain how they worked this out. Repeat with finding £3.00 divided by 4.

Unit 2 2 weeks

Group work: Provide each group of four children with a few of each of the following coins: £1, 50p, 20p and 5p. Challenge them to work out how much each person would receive if they had £3.00 to split between them. Encourage the children to change their £3.00 into six 50p pieces, then to work out that each of them would have one 50p piece and there were two left. Then to split the two 50p pieces up into four 'twenty-five pence', giving them 75p each. Repeat, asking the groups to work out £5.00 between four people (£1.25).

Whole class: Discuss methods and approaches to questions. Now ask children to estimate how much each person would receive if they wanted to work out £6.00 shared between four. Ask: *How could you work out 60 ÷ 4?* You could draw a number line to illustrate this:

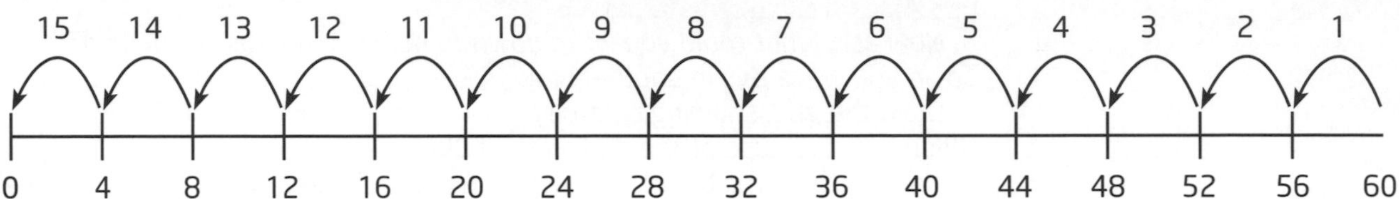

Discuss the fact that each time there is a jump back along the number line, 4 is subtracted, and that this happens fifteen times (ten times, 10 × 4 = 40, and then five times, 5 × 4 = 20). Illustrate this vertically as:

```
  60
- 40   (4 × 10)
  20
- 20   (4 × 5)
  0            Answer is 15.
```

Now ask:

- *As we know that 60 ÷ 4 = 15, what is £6.00 shared by four?* (£1.50)
- *What would six litres of paint divided by 4 be?* (1.5 litres)

Group work: Ask the children to work in a group to complete the grid on the sheet 'Sharing money'. They are then asked to explain what is happening here and to look for a pattern.

Differentiation

Less confident learners: Ideally this group could work with an adult to provide extra support for sharing money and spotting patterns. When completing the 'Sharing money' sheet, be sure that they have the correct values before they begin to spot patterns.

More confident learners: Challenge the children to find larger amounts of money divided by four people. They could also investigate dividing these amounts of money by two or five and spotting any patterns.

Review

Invite children from each group to explain the patterns that they noticed. Copy this grid on the board and complete it together:

Amount of money	Divided by 10
£1.00	
£2.00	
£10.00	
£30.00	

Discuss method and findings. Ask: *What would 1kg divided by 10 be? 2kg? 10kg? 30kg?*

Lessons 7-9

Preparation
Lesson 7: Measure some of the examples given in the Starter.

You will need
CD resources
'Accurate millimetres', 'Find the perimeter' and 'Measures of length'.
Equipment
Some measuring equipment; an interactive whiteboard or a transparent ruler and an OHP; identical rulers, one per child; a metre ruler; tracing paper (optional); 2D shapes for discussion on perimeter (including some irregular shapes).

Learning objectives

Starter
- Choose and use standard metric units and their abbreviations when estimating, measuring and recording length, weight and capacity; know the meaning of 'kilo', 'centi' and 'milli' and, where appropriate, use decimal notation to record measurements (eg 1.3m or 0.6kg).
- Use decimal notation for tenths and hundredths and partition decimals; relate the notation to money and measurement.

Main teaching activities
2006
- Use decimal notation for tenths and hundredths and partition decimals; relate the notation to money and measurement.
- Choose and use standard metric units and their abbreviations when estimating, measuring and recording length, weight and capacity; know the meaning of 'kilo', 'centi' and 'milli' and, where appropriate, use decimal notation to record measurements (eg 1.3m or 0.6kg).
- Interpret intervals and divisions on partially numbered scales and record readings accurately, where appropriate to the nearest tenth of a unit.
- Draw rectangles and measure and calculate their perimeters; find the area of rectilinear shapes drawn on a square grid by counting squares.

1999
- Measure and calculate the perimeter and area of rectangles and other simple shapes, using counting methods and standard units (cm, cm^2).
- Understand decimal notation and place value for tenths and hundredths, and use it in context, eg order amounts of money; convert a sum of money such as £13.25 to pence, or a length such as 125cm to metres; round a sum of money to the nearest pound.
- Use, read and write standard metric units (km, m, cm, mm, kg, g, l, ml), including their abbreviations, and imperial units.
- Know and use the relationships between familiar units of length, mass and capacity.
- Know the equivalent of one half, one quarter, three quarters and one tenth of 1km, 1m, 1kg, 1litre in m, cm, g, ml.
- Suggest suitable units and measuring equipment to estimate or measure length, mass or capacity.
- Record estimates and readings from scales to a suitable degree of accuracy.
- Use all four operations to solve word problems involving numbers in 'real life' money and measures (including time), using one or more steps, including converting pounds to pence and metres to centimetres and vice versa.

Vocabulary
measure, estimate, metric unit, standard unit, length, distance, perimeter, area, mass, weight, capacity, ruler, measuring tape, balance, scales, measuring cylinder/jug, units of measurement and abbreviations: kilometre (km), metre (m), centimetre (cm), millimetre (mm), kilogram (kg), gram (g), litre (l), millilitre (ml), square centimetre (cm^2)

Lesson 7 (Review, teach and apply)

Starter

Reason: Call out various lengths and ask the children to estimate using the unit of measurement that they think best suits the object. Children show you their estimates on whiteboards. For example, the height of the door, the width of the window, the length of the desk, the length of a pencil, the width of your finger, the distance from the classroom to the school hall. Discuss estimates and units of measurement. Leave a list of these measures on the board for use in the Review.

Main teaching activities

Whole class: Explain to the children that today they will be drawing and measuring lines, firstly to the nearest millimetre. Ask: *What is a millimetre?* (It is a tenth of a centimetre.) Look at the rulers carefully and if possible display a ruler on the interactive whiteboard or use a transparent ruler on an OHP to discuss how to draw lines accurately. Demonstrate how to draw a line of, say, 47mm. Ask: *What would this measure in cm?* (4.7cm.) Repeat, asking individuals to come and draw lines of, for example, 76mm and 93mm.
Paired work: Children take turns to draw lines from the sheet 'Accurate millimetres' and their partner checks their work to see how accurate their lines are. They could draw these lines onto tracing paper so that you can check the lengths of lines quickly yourself, as you go around the class.
Whole class: Ask some individual pairs to come up and draw some lines on the whiteboard using the metre ruler. Ask another pair to check their accuracy. Ask for lengths such as 76cm or 54cm. Ask: *How could this be written in metres/millimetres?*

Differentiation

Less confident learners: Provide adult support to check the the rulers are used correctly.
More confident learners: Challenge the children to draw lines using decimal fractions such as 4.6cm, 9.2cm and so on.

Review

Discuss what the lengths of the lines from the sheet 'Accurate millimetres' would be in cm. Using the measurements from the Starter session, ask questions such as: *What would the height of the door be in centimetres? What would the width of the window be in centimetres? What would the width of my finger be in millimetres? How did you work that out?*

Lesson 8 (Review, teach and practise)

Starter

Refine and rehearse: Explain to the children that you will call out a measurement and that you would like them to show you another way that you could write the same measurement. For example 2km could be 2000m or 200,000cm; 23mm could be 2.3cm; 34cm could be 340mm or 0.34m. For each measure, discuss all alternative measures that could be used.

Main teaching activities

Whole class: Draw a rectangle on the board and discuss its properties. Highlight the fact that pairs of sides are of equal length and therefore it is not necessary to measure all the sides. Ask the children to imagine that the rectangle on the board is a farmer's field full of bulls, and that he wants to put a fence around the field to keep the bulls in. Ask questions such as: *How could we find out how much fence is needed? Do we have to measure all the sides? Why not?*

Write the word 'perimeter' on the board and explain that it is the measurement of length all the way around a shape. Put some measurements on the rectangle, such as 80 metres and 60 metres, and ask the children to calculate the perimeter of the field. Ask: *How did you work that out?* Check that the children used an efficient method. They may have multiplied each measurement by two then totalled, or they may have added the measurements of the four sides. Say together: *Perimeter.* Repeat this with rectangles of other sizes, such as a football pitch and a playground.
Paired work: Ask the children to work in pairs. Explain that you would like

them to find ten rectangular items in the classroom, such as the top of their table or a book. They should find the length and breadth of each one and then calculate the perimeter. They can record their work on activity sheet 'Find the perimeter'. Explain that they can use rulers, metre sticks and measuring tapes. Give the children about 20 minutes to complete this work, and remind them when there are five minutes left.

Differentiation

Less confident learners: Work with this group. Agree as a group which item to measure first, then compare measurements. Work together to find the perimeter so that the children are sure of how to do this.

More confident learners: If the children finish the group work above, suggest that they search for more unusual shapes with straight sides, and find the perimeters of those.

Review

Ask the children for the sizes of the rectangles they found in the second part of the lesson. Show on the board how to find a quick solution by doubling each side and then adding together. Hold up some regular 2D shapes and ask the children for a quick way to calculate the perimeter. If the children do not use the term 'multiplication', use it to show them how to find the answer. Hold up an irregular shape and ask if you could find the perimeter of this shape by multiplication. Look for children who have used 'quick' methods to calculate the perimeter. Ask: *How can you find the perimeter of this shape? Is this the quickest way? Why/why not?*

Lesson 9 (Apply)

Starter

Rehearse: Explain that you will say some sequences of lengths and that you would like the children to join in. Start with 1.23m, 1.33m, 1.43m... Keep a good rhythm and when all children have joined in ask: *What was I adding each time?* (10cm, 0.1m, a tenth of a metre.) Repeat, this time using 25cm, 50cm, 75cm, 100cm; then 10mm, 2cm, 30mm, 4cm, 50mm and so on.

Main teaching activities

Whole class: Discuss the classroom bookcase: *How long do you think one shelf is? Why do you think that? How long would two or three of the shelves be in total? How did you work that out?* Invite two children to measure one of the shelves while the others watch. Ask: *What measuring equipment will you use? Why do you think that is a good choice? Do you all agree?* Discuss the units chosen and how close to the estimate the measure is. Ask a child to write the measurement on the board.

Paired work: Choose from the selection of practical tasks on the activity sheet 'Measures of length'.

Differentiation

Less confident learners: The children could work as a group on a chosen activity on 'Measures of length'. Encourage them to begin by saying which units they will need, and why.

More confident learners: Challenge the children to suggest their own measuring problem to solve.

Review

Choose one of the activities that most of the children have completed. Ask questions such as:

- *What units did you choose? Was this a good choice? Why/why not?*
- *Which measuring equipment did you choose? Was this a good choice? Why?*

Remind the children how measuring is always approximate, and that we use rounding to record.

Lesson 10

Preparation

Prepare the 'Clock face' resource sheet for display, either on OHT or on card.

You will need

CD resources

'Eight compass points'; core, support and extension versions of 'Round the clock'. General resource sheet: 'Clock face'.

Equipment

Blu-Tack; clock faces; protractor; rulers.

Learning objectives

Starter

- Recognise horizontal and vertical lines; use the eight compass points to describe direction; describe and identify the position of a square on a grid of squares.

Main teaching activities

2006

- Recognise horizontal and vertical lines; use the eight compass points to describe direction; describe and identify the position of a square on a grid of squares.
- Know that angles are measured in degrees and that one whole turn is 360°; compare and order angles less than 180°.

1999

- Recognise simple examples of horizontal and vertical lines.
- Use the eight compass directions N, S, E, W, NE, NW, SE and SW.
- Recognise positions and directions: for example, describe and find the position of a point on a grid of squares where the lines are numbered.
- Begin to know that angles are measured in degrees and that one whole turn is 360° or four right angles; a quarter turn is 90° or one right angle; half a right angle is 45°; start to order a set of angles less than 180°.

Vocabulary

position, direction, north-east (NE), north-west (NW), south-west (SW), south-east (SE), clockwise, anticlockwise, horizontal, vertical, grid

Lesson 10 (Review, teach and apply)

Starter

Rehearse and refine: Explain to the children that they will be looking at directions. Find north in the classroom and stick up the 'North' sign from the activity sheet 'Eight compass point labels', using Blu-Tack. Say: *Stand up and face north.* Children should face north. Now say: *Face south.* When all the children have turned correctly to face south, stick up the 'South' sign. Repeat for the 'East' and 'West' signs. Now say: *What if I want to face in a direction that is in between north and east?* Ask the children to face the appropriate corner and put up the sign 'North-east'. Repeat for 'North-west', 'South-west' and 'South-east'. Ask: *How could we abbreviate the names for north, south, east and west?* (N, S, E and W.) Repeat for north-east (NE), north-west (NW), south-west (SW) and south-east (SE).

Explain to the class that they will now play a game. Explain that you will call out a direction and you would like the children to start by facing north, then to turn clockwise to face the requested direction (for example, from north to south). Repeat, this time asking the children to turn anticlockwise. Each time ask: *How much did you turn? Did you turn more than half a turn?*

Main teaching activities

Whole class: Ask: *How do we measure a turn?* (In degrees.) *How many degrees in a full turn?* (360.) Show the children a protractor, preferably on an overhead projector or interactive whiteboard. Now ask: *Starting from north, turn 360 degrees clockwise.* All the children should end up facing north. Repeat with another starting point. Ask: *If 360 degrees is a full turn, how many degrees in a half-turn?* (180.) Now, starting from north, the children turn through 180 degrees. They should all be facing south. Repeat with a few more examples based on the compass directions.

Now ask: *If 180 degrees is a half turn, how many degrees are there in a quarter turn?* (90.) *What other name is there for a 90-degree turn?* (Right angle.) *Now, starting at north, turn 90 degrees.* All children should be facing east or west. Ask: *Does it matter if you turn clockwise or anticlockwise? Why?* Repeat with a few more examples, giving directions based on the compass directions.

Now say: *Write down an instruction that would turn you through 45 degrees.* (For example, north to north-west.) Ask individuals for examples. Draw out that 45 degrees is half of a right angle.

Display a large empty clock face (use general resource sheet 'Clock face' or an interactive whiteboard) and say: *Imagine you are standing in the centre of a clock and pointing at the number 12. If you turn from 12 to 3, how much of a turn is this?* (Quarter turn.) *How many degrees is this?* (90.)

Use two large rulers to demonstrate the right angle between the 12 and 3. Demonstrate some angles greater than 90° and less than 90° on the clock.

Independent work: Give the children activity sheet 'Round the clock', which asks them to find how many degrees there are between different numbers. Ask the children to complete the activity sheet. In the second section of the sheet, children investigate the number of ways that they can turn 180 degrees on the clock face. Work through the first example with them, using the clock face diagram at the top of the sheet.

Review

Display the general resource sheet 'Clock face'. Move the hand from 12 to 3 and ask: *How many degrees have I turned clockwise?* (90°, or one right angle.) Then move the hand from 12 to 3 anticlockwise and ask: *How many degrees have I turned now?* Agree that it is three right angles. Write down 90 + 90 + 90 = □. Ask: *How could you work this out?* (300 – 30, or 9 × 3 then multiply by 10.) Establish that 90° (or other angles) can be measured from any point on the clock!

Differentiation

Less confident learners: Use the support version of the activity sheet, which does not have the second section. These children will find it helpful to use a clock face with hands that they can move.

More confident learners: Use the extension version of the activity sheet in which the children have to find different ways to make 90° on the clock face. Those who finish quickly could investigate how many degrees there are in half a right angle and how this could be shown on a clock face.

Name ______________________ Date ______________

Addition sums

Use these numbers.

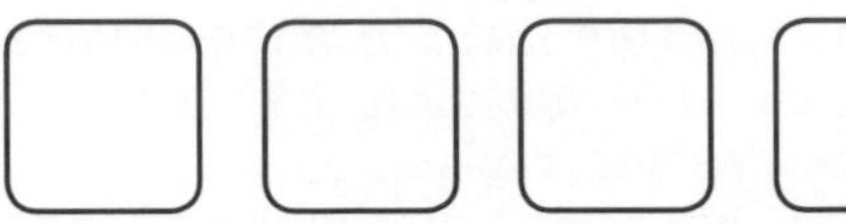

In the box below, write down all the addition questions that you can make using these four numbers.

Now work out the answers to your questions. What is the largest total that you can make?

If you work them out in your head write 'M' next to the sum. If you need to write anything down, use the space below.

Name ______________________ Date ______________

Beat the brain cards

Find the difference between 12 and 9.	Find the sum of 123, 234 and 345.
What is the total of 2, 4 and 8?	From £1 take away 56 pence.
From 1 metre subtract 54 centimetres.	Work out the sum of 101, 99 and 4.
From 586 take away 193.	Work out the difference between 631 and 75.
Find the sum of 1, 9 and 11.	Work out the sum of 99 and 11.

Unit 3 2 weeks

Calculating, measuring and understanding shape

Lesson	Strand	Starter	Main teaching activities
1. Review and practise	Use/apply Calculate Counting	Use decimal notation for tenths and hundredths and partition decimals; relate the notation to money and measurement; position one-place and two-place decimals on a number line.	• Solve one-step and two-step problems involving numbers, money or measures, including time; choose and carry out appropriate calculations, using calculator methods where appropriate. • Refine and use efficient written methods to add and subtract two-digit and three-digit whole numbers and £.p. • Use decimal notation for tenths and hundredths and partition decimals; relate the notation to money and measurement; position one-place and two-place decimals on a number line.
2. Review, teach and practise	Use/apply Calculate Counting	Use knowledge of addition and subtraction facts and place value to derive sums and differences of pairs of multiples of 10, 100 or 1000.	As for Lesson 1
3. Review	Use/apply Calculate Counting	Solve one-step and two-step problems involving numbers, money or measures, including time; choose and carry out appropriate calculations, using calculator methods where appropriate.	As for Lesson 1
4. Teach and practise	Measure	Use decimal notation for tenths and hundredths and partition decimals; relate the notation to money and measurement; position one-place and two-place decimals on a number line.	• Draw rectangles and measure and calculate their perimeters; find the area of rectilinear shapes drawn on a square grid by counting squares. • Interpret intervals and divisions on partially numbered scales and record readings accurately, where appropriate to the nearest tenth of a unit.
5. Teach and practise	Measure	• Use decimal notation for tenths and hundredths and partition decimals; relate the notation to money and measurement; position one-place and two-place decimals on a number line. **• Choose and use standard metric units and their abbreviations when estimating, measuring and recording length, weight and capacity; know the meaning of 'kilo', 'centi' and 'milli' and, where appropriate, use decimal notation to record measurements (eg 1.3m or 0.6kg).**	As for Lesson 4
6. Teach and practise	Shape	**Know that angles are measured in degrees and that one whole turn is 360°; compare and order angles less than 180°.**	**Know that angles are measured in degrees and that one whole turn is 360°; compare and order angles less than 180°.**
7. Apply	Measure	• Interpret intervals and divisions on partially numbered scales and record readings accurately, where appropriate to the nearest tenth of a unit. **• Choose and use standard metric units and their abbreviations when estimating, measuring and recording length, weight and capacity; know the meaning of 'kilo', 'centi' and 'milli' and, where appropriate, use decimal notation to record measurements (eg 1.3m or 0.6kg).**	• Interpret intervals and divisions on partially numbered scales and record readings accurately, where appropriate to the nearest tenth of a unit. **• Choose and use standard metric units and their abbreviations when estimating, measuring and recording length, weight and capacity; know the meaning of 'kilo', 'centi' and 'milli' and, where appropriate, use decimal notation to record measurements (eg 1.3m or 0.6kg).**
8. Apply and evaluate	Measure	As for Lesson 7	As for Lesson 7
9. Teach and apply	Measure	Read time to the nearest minute; use am, pm and 12-hour clock notation; choose units of time to measure time intervals; calculate time intervals from clocks and timetables.	Read time to the nearest minute; use am, pm and 12-hour clock notation; choose units of time to measure time intervals; calculate time intervals from clocks and timetables.
10. Apply	Measure	As for Lesson 9	As for Lesson 9

Speaking and listening objective

- Take different roles in groups and use language appropriate to them, including roles of leader, reporter, scribe, mentor.

Introduction

In this unit of ten lessons, children continue to solve one- and two-step word problems involving numbers, money, measures or time, using standard metric units, reading from partly numbered scales and using am, pm, and the 12-hour clock to find time intervals. They find areas and perimeters of rectangles, measure angles in degrees and use compass points. Children continue to develop multiplication and division (including tables to 10 × 10), multiplying by 10 or 100, doubling two-digit numbers, and using written methods for multiplying and dividing TU by U, rounding remainders as necessary. They use mental and written methods for addition and subtraction, using a calculator for some calculations.

Using and applying mathematics

- Solve one-step and two-step problems involving numbers, money or measures, including time; choose and carry out appropriate calculations, using calculator methods where appropriate.

Lessons 1-3

Preparation

Lesson 2: Collect some supermarket till receipts (with totals cut off) for the extension version of 'Money adds'.

You will need

Photocopiable pages
'Money adds' (page 166) and 'Money subtractions' (167).
CD resources
Support and extension versions of 'Money adds' and Money subtractions'. General resource sheets: 'Numeral cards' (set of 0-9 cards for each pair); 'Operation follow-on'.
Equipment
Graph/squared paper for support; calculators.

Learning objectives

Starter

- Use decimal notation for tenths and hundredths and partition decimals; relate the notation to money and measurement; position one-place and two-place decimals on a number line.
- Use knowledge of addition and subtraction facts and place value to derive sums and differences of pairs of multiples of 10, 100 or 1000.
- Solve one-step and two-step problems involving numbers, money or measures, including time; choose and carry out appropriate calculations, using calculator methods where appropriate.

Main teaching activities

2006

- Solve one-step and two-step problems involving numbers, money or measures, including time; choose and carry out appropriate calculations, using calculator methods where appropriate.
- Refine and use efficient written methods to add and subtract two-digit and three-digit whole numbers and £.p.
- Use decimal notation for tenths and hundredths and partition decimals; relate the notation to money and measurement; position one-place and two-place decimals on a number line.

1999

- Use all four operations to solve word problems involving numbers in 'real' life, money and measures (including time), using one or more steps, including converting pounds to pence and metres to centimetres and vice versa.
- Choose and use appropriate number operations and appropriate ways of calculating (mental, mental with jottings, pencil and paper) to solve problems.
- Round up or down after division, depending on context.
- Choose appropriate ways of calculating: calculator.
- Develop and refine written methods for: column addition and subtraction of two whole numbers less than 1000, and addition of more than two such numbers; money calculations (eg £7.85 ± £3.49).
- Understand decimal notation and place value for tenths and hundredths, and use it in context, eg order amounts of money; convert a sum of money such as £13.25 to pence, or a length such as 125cm to metres; round a sum of money to the nearest pound.

Vocabulary

problem, solution, answer, method, explain, predict, reason, reasoning, pattern, relationship, calculation, equation, decimal, decimal point, decimal place, add, subtract, multiply, divide, order, compare, sum, total, difference, plus, minus, product, remainder, calculator, pound (£), pence (p)

Lesson 1 (Review and practise)

Starter

Rehearse: Call out different amounts of money and ask the children to round each amount up or down to the nearest pound. Start with £3.51 (£4) and £3.21 (£3), and so on. Repeat, but ask the children to round up or down to the nearest 10 pence, for example: £3.51 (£3.50), £3.21 (£3.20).

Main teaching activities

Whole class: Give the children a three-digit subtraction sentence such as 344 - 162 = □. Ask the children how they might tackle this question. Discuss the empty number line method and demonstrate as required.

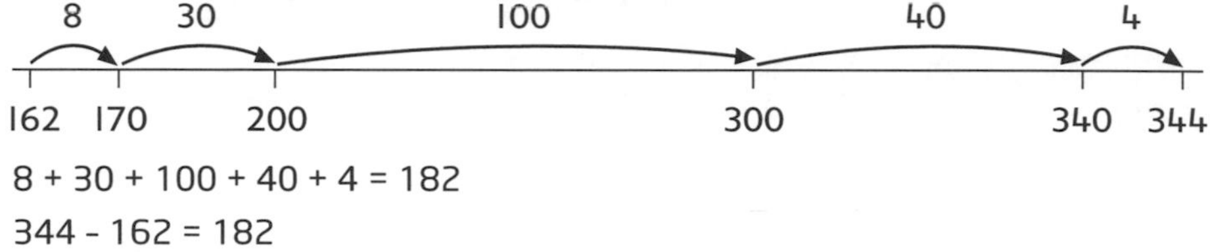

8 + 30 + 100 + 40 + 4 = 182

344 - 162 = 182

Write another question on the board such as 336 - 177 = □. Ask: *Can anyone demonstrate a written method for answering this question?* If necessary, demonstrate a written method (as shown).

```
  336
- 177
    3 (180)
   20 (200)
  100 (300)
   30 (330)
    6 (336)
  159
```

Paired work: Ask the children to work together with a set of 0-10 numeral cards. Turn over the cards and ask each child in turn to select six cards, which they should arrange into a three-digit by three-digit subtraction calculation. The children should decide what method to use and record their calculations.

Differentiation

Less confident learners: Work with the children when recording written subtractions, using graph paper to support them if necessary.

More confident learners: Extend the activity by asking each pair to select seven digits, which they should arrange into a four-digit by three-digit subtraction calculation.

Review

Review the different written calculation methods used by the children. Compare and contrast the methods used, for example: *Which method was easier for this calculation - the number line or written method? Why?* Ask: *How could we check the answers? With which calculations do you think that a calculator would have helped you?*

Lesson 2 (Review, teach and practise)

Starter

Refine and rehearse: Write on the board '54p + £0.67 = £1.21'. Ask quick-fire questions and let the children write the answers on their whiteboards:

- *If I had £1.21 in my purse and spent 54p, how much would I have left?* (67p)
- *If I had £1.21 in my purse and spent 67p, how much would I have left?* (54p)
- *If I bought a pencil for 54p and a pen for 67p, how many pence would I spend altogether?* (121 pence)
- *If I bought a cake for 67p and a chocolate bar for 54p, how much would I spend altogether?* (£1.21)

Remind the children that these related operations can be used to check the problems. Repeat for £0.81 + 121p = £2.02.

Main teaching activities

Whole class: Write on the board the amounts £8.75, £7.85, £5.78 and £5.07. Ask the children to find sums of pairs of these numbers. Set the calculation in columns and reiterate the importance of positioning digits carefully with the decimal points written 'in line' one below the other. Write one example on the board (as shown).

```
  £ 8.75
+ £ 5.78
  £14.53
    1 1
```

Begin by adding the pence first (£0.75 + £0.78). Ask the children for the total: 153 pence or £1.53 in pounds and pence. Say: *We can write the .53 under the pence and carry the £1.00.* Focus on the correct positioning of the decimal point in the answer. *Add the pounds £8.00 + £5.00 = £13.00 plus the £1.00 we have carried over.* Describe the method and talk through each step.

Independent work: Challenge the children to find the sum of as many pairs of amounts of money (written on the board) as they can in a set amount of time (five or ten minutes). Ask them to set out their work on squared paper, leaving a square for the decimal point. Discuss responses and the number of combinations. (£8.75 + £7.85 = £16.60; £8.75 + £5.07 = £13.82; £7.85 + £5.78 = £13.63; £7.85 + £5.07 = £12.92: £5.78 + £5.07 = £10.85)

Give each child a copy of the 'Money adds' activity sheet. Ask them to work out the answers in their heads or use the method they have been shown. If appropriate, after an initial attempt, allow the children to use a calculator to check their calculations.

Differentiation

Less confident learners: Give these children the support version of the sheet, in which the first two examples are set out with the decimal points aligned.

More confident learners: After completing the 'Money adds' core activity sheet move them on to the extension sheet. The children will need till receipts - ideally with at least ten items. Cut up the receipt and give them the total at the end after they have added and checked the amounts.

Review

Go over the main teaching points, stressing the correct positioning of the decimal point using the written method. Prepare another shopping list example, write the items up on the board and ask the children to keep a running total of the amounts. Ask them to write the 'grand total' on their whiteboards. Check how many children worked out the correct total.

Lesson 3 (Review)

Starter

Rehearse: Shuffle the pack of 'Operation follow-on' cards from the general resource sheet and distribute all of them to the class. There are 35 cards in total, so some children may need to have two cards, depending on the size of the group. All the cards follow on from each other. For example, the answer (17) to the question '26 take away nine' will be found at the top of another card. Tell the children that they have to work out the calculation and then the child who has the card with that number at the top must stand up, say the answer and then read out the question on their own card. Note that you will need to remember the starting number (you can start anywhere in the loop) and that everyone should have a turn before play returns to the beginning of the loop.

Main teaching activities

Whole class: Write on the board the same amounts as in Lesson 2: £8.75, £7.85, £5.78, £5.07. Explain that this time you will be asking them to find the difference between pairs of these numbers. Demonstrate with 'Subtract £5.78 from £7.85'. Remind the children that if they use the column written method they should write the larger number on the top line. As before, tell them to deal with the pence first: 85 pence subtract 78 pence is 7 pence. Children should be able to use a variety of strategies to calculate this. Go through suggestions. Point out that 7 pence can be written as £0.07 and write it under the pence, after the decimal point. Then, subtract the pounds to give the answer £2.07.

Independent work: Challenge the children to find as many combinations from the numbers above in a set amount of time (five or ten minutes). Remind them that they can check the results of calculations by using the inverse operation (addition). For example, £5.78 + £2.07 = £7.85.

Next, give each child a copy of the 'Money subtractions' activity sheet. Ask them to work out the answers in their heads or use the method they have been shown. If appropriate, after an initial attempt, allow the children to use a calculator to check their calculations.

Differentiation

Less confident learners: Give these children the support version of 'Money subtractions', in which the first two examples are set out with the decimal points aligned.

More confident learners: Give these children the extension version of the sheet, with higher-level examples and with a final shopping problem.

Review

Review the results from the two activities. Ask: *Did you find all the possible combinations?* (£8.75 - £5.78 = £2.97, £8.75 - £7.85 = £0.90, £8.75 - £5.07 = £3.68, £7.85 - £5.78 = £2.07, £7.85 - £5.07 = £2.78, £5.78 - £5.07 = £0.71). Point out that you cannot work out £5.07 - £5.78 and get a positive number. Ask: *How could you check your calculations? Can you justify your workings and your answer?* Discuss responses.

Lessons 4-5

Preparation

Lesson 4: Cut out the rectangles from activity sheet 'Rectangles'. Copy activity sheet 'Rectangles (continued)' onto an OHT and cut out centimetre squares for the demonstration.

You will need

Photocopiable pages
'Rectangles' (page 168).
CD resources
'Rectangles (continued)' for demonstration; 'Introducing area' for display.
Equipment
Centimetre cubes; squared paper; peg boards and elastic bands, rulers.

Learning objectives

Starter

- Use decimal notation for tenths and hundredths and partition decimals; relate the notation to money and measurement; position one-place and two-place decimals on a number line.
- Choose and use standard metric units and their abbreviations when estimating, measuring and recording length, weight and capacity; know the meaning of 'kilo', 'centi' and 'milli' and, where appropriate, use decimal notation to record measurements (eg 1.3m or 0.6kg).

Main teaching activities

2006

- Draw rectangles and measure and calculate their perimeters; find the area of rectilinear shapes drawn on a square grid by counting squares.
- Interpret intervals and divisions on partially numbered scales and record readings accurately, where appropriate to the nearest tenth of a unit.

1999

- Measure and calculate the perimeter and area of rectangles and other simple shapes, using counting methods and standard units (cm, cm²).
- Record estimates and readings from scales to a suitable degree of accuracy.

Vocabulary

measure, estimate, metric unit, standard unit, length, distance, perimeter, area, ruler, measuring tape, units of measurement and abbreviations: kilometre (km), metre (m), centimetre (cm), millimetre (mm), square centimetre (cm²)

Lesson 4 (Teach and practise)

Starter

Rehearse: Explain to the children that you will call out some measurements and you would like them to show you an alternative way of writing that measurement. Start with 2.3m (230cm, 2300mm), 340mm (34cm, 0.34m). After each measurement, ask individuals to suggest what might have been measured to give this measurement.

Main teaching activities

Whole class: Give each child one rectangle cut from the activity sheet 'Rectangles'. Ask: *How can we find the area of this rectangle?* Agree with the children that the area is the space inside the rectangle and discuss how you could measure it. Ask: *Which units of measurement could we use?*

Now explain to the children that you would like each of them to find the area of their rectangle by folding carefully. Demonstrate with an enlarged rectangle, cut from the 'Rectangles (continued)' sheet. Fold it parallel to its shorter side, in half, in half again and then in half for the third time, splitting the shape into eighths, and then unfold and count together. Then turn the rectangle and fold it this time parallel to its longer side, in half and in half again splitting the shape into quarters and unfold. The rectangle should now have 32 squares for the children to count. Ask them to use a ruler and measure the length, width and the size of the squares. Agree that the rectangle is 4cm by 8cm (write these measurements on the board), that each of the small squares is 1cm by 1cm and that there are 32 of them. Agree that if we folded the shape very accurately all of the squares would be of the same size. Explain that the rectangle has an area of 32 square centimetres (cm²). Ask: *Can anyone see how we could have made 32cm² another way?* (Refer to 4 × 8 or 8 × 4 from the board.) Explain that if you multiply a number by itself, for example, 2 × 2, this is a squared number, therefore an area of 1cm by 1cm will be one square centimetre, and can be written as 1cm².

Independent work: Give each child 36 centimetre cubes and challenge them to make as many different rectangles as they can. They should record each rectangle on squared paper and write its dimensions and area.

Differentiation

Less confident learners: Provide each child with only 24 cubes and ask an adult to support the children with this activity.

More confident learners: Provide each child with 48 cubes and challenge them to find all the possible rectangles.

Review

Discuss the children's rectangles. Ask: *How many rectangles did you find? What units did you use to measure their areas?* (cm²) *What strategies did you use to find the area of each rectangle?* (Counting squares.) *What is meant by the word 'area'?* (Try to establish that the 'area' of the rectangle is the length × breadth or the amount of surface it covers.)

Lesson 5 (Teach and practise)

Starter

Rehearse: Repeat the Starter from Lesson 4, but this time use capacity measurements. Start with 3500ml (3.5litres), 0.4 litres (400ml). Encourage the children to make statements such as '400ml is about the capacity of a can of fizzy drink' (330ml), '3.5 litres would fill a bucket up to here'.

Main teaching activities

Whole class: Distribute sheets of squared paper and display the 'Introducing area' activity sheet on an OHP or interactive whiteboard. Ask: *Can you draw me a shape that has an area of 12cm²?* Ask individual children to draw their responses on the grid on the OHT. Alternatively, use the whiteboard pen, or move square shapes onto the shape. Illustrate that you can count the squares and explain that the area is the space inside the shape.

Independent work: Ask the children to investigate how many different shapes they can make with an area of 12cm². You may want to state a rule that rotating a shape does not give a different shape. They could then explore the different perimeters of all of the shapes with an area of 12cm². They should use a ruler accurately and round to the nearest centimetre.

Differentiation

Less confident learners: Limit the work to rectangles. Provide each child with a peg board and elastic bands in different colours so that they can form the outlines easily without spending lots of time redrawing.

More confident learners: These children could try working with shapes other than rectangles. Ask: *Can you make a triangle with an area of 18cm²?* (They will have to count half-squares.) *Is there a shape that will have the same perimeter and area?* (Yes, a 4 × 4 square.)

Review

Ask: *What if we had an irregular shape like your hand? How could we work out the area?* (Draw on squared paper and count the squares.) Show an example on the OHT, counting up half-squares to make a whole. Make sure that the children realise that this is approximate, like an estimate. Establish that squares are useful for measuring area and so that is why area is measured in square centimetres (cm²).

Lessons 6-8

Preparation

Lessons 7 and 8: Set out the equipment as per the 'Magic potion capacity instructions' resource sheet and with each set of equipment place the appropriate label from the 'Magic potion capacity labels' resouce sheet. Use coloured liquids to add to the effect, and make sure that the buckets are designed to pour accurately.

You will need

CD resources

'Magic potion capacity instructions', 'Magic potion capacity labels' and '350ml'; core, support and extension versions of 'Angle measuring'; support version of 'Magic potion capacity chart'.

Equipment

Set squares; geo-rods; protractors; OHP or interactive whiteboard protractor; capacity measuring equipment for Lessons 7 and 8 (see 'Magic potion capacity instructions').

Learning objectives

Starter

- Know that angles are measured in degrees and that one whole turn is 360°; compare and order angles less than 180°.
- Interpret intervals and divisions on partially numbered scales and record readings accurately, where appropriate to the nearest tenth of a unit.
- Choose and use standard metric units and their abbreviations when estimating, measuring and recording length, weight and capacity; know the meaning of 'kilo', 'centi' and 'milli' and, where appropriate, use decimal notation to record measurements (eg 1.3m or 0.6kg).

Main teaching activities

2006

- Know that angles are measured in degrees and that one whole turn is 360°; compare and order angles less than 180°.
- Interpret intervals and divisions on partially numbered scales and record readings accurately, where appropriate to the nearest tenth of a unit.
- Choose and use standard metric units and their abbreviations when estimating, measuring and recording length, weight and capacity; know the meaning of 'kilo', 'centi' and 'milli' and, where appropriate, use decimal notation to record measurements (eg 1.3m or 0.6kg).

1999

- Begin to know that angles are measured in degrees and that one whole turn is 360° or 4 right angles; a quarter turn is 90° or one right angle; half a right angle is 45°; start to order a set of angles less than 180°.
- Record estimates and readings from scales to a suitable degree of accuracy.
- Use, read and write standard metric units (km, m, cm, mm, kg, g, l, ml), including their abbreviations, and imperial units.
- Know and use the relationships between familiar units of length, mass and capacity.
- Know the equivalent of one half, one quarter, three quarters and one tenth of 1km, 1m, 1kg, 1 litre in m, cm, g, ml.
- Suggest suitable units and measuring equipment to estimate or measure length, mass or capacity.

Vocabulary

problem, solution, answer, method, explain, predict, reason, reasoning, pattern, relationship, calculation, compare, sum, total, difference, plus, minus, product, remainder, calculator, measure, estimate, metric unit, standard unit, capacity, measuring cylinder/jug, angle, right angle, set square, units of measurement and abbreviations: litre (l), millilitre (ml), degrees (°)

Lesson 6 (Teach and practise)

Starter

Reason: Use two connected geo-rods to make an acute angle. Ask: *Is this angle more than 90°?* Make a larger angle and ask: *Is this angle more than 90°?* Repeat with several more examples. Now tell the children that you will make an angle. If it is less than 90° they should touch the floor. If it is more than 90° they should stand up. Give several examples. With the last few examples, keep the separate geo-rods angles, tacking them to the board. Finally, put these angles in order of size.

Main teaching activities

Whole class: Tell the children that they are going to look at angles. *What*

is an angle? (A measurement of turn.) *What unit do we measure angles in?* (Degrees or °) *How many degrees are in one whole turn?* (360°)

Give each group a protractor and ask them to discuss what they can see and what the instrument is used for. If one is available, show an OHP protractor and describe what it is. A protractor placed on an OHP also works well, or alternatively show a protractor on the whiteboard. Ensure that all the children realise that it is used to measure angles and that it includes values marked from 0 to 180°. Highlight the centre point of rotation and the straight line along the bottom.

Explain how the protractor works from left to right or from right to left or 'clockwise' and 'anticlockwise'. Ask the children to find 0° on the protractor and to move round 90°. Ask: *What does this make?* (A right angle.) Next ask them to move 45° anticlockwise. *Where are you now?* (45°) *What fraction of a right angle is 45°?* (½.) Repeat the question for 30° (1/3) and 60° (2/3). From 60° ask: *How many degrees to get to 180° (or a straight line)?* (120°) Ask the pupils to check using their protractors. Ask: *What fraction of a straight line is 60°?* (1/3). Consolidate children's understanding of 'clockwise' and 'anticlockwise', moving round the protractor to different points. Stress the need to line up the protractor correctly when measuring angles.

Group work: Give each group a copy of the 'Angle measuring' sheet, in which children have to measure a set of angles and put them in size order. Show the groups how a set square can be used to check measures, to see if an angle is less than or greater than 90° if using a 45-degree set square (or less than or greater than 60° if using a 60-degree set square).

Differentiation

Less confident learners: Give this group the support version of the sheet, with four larger angles from left to right.

More confident learners: Give this group the extension version of the sheet, with an extra challenge involving vertical angles.

Review

Check answers and identify any difficulties in measuring or ordering the angles. Sort the angles into two groups with the children, using a set square to illustrate 'Less than a ¼ turn' and 'More than a ¼ turn'. Discuss the vocabulary with the children. Establish with them that a quarter turn = 90° (or one right angle), a half turn = 180° (or two right angles), a three-quarter turn = 270° (or three right angles), and a whole turn = 360° (or four right angles).

Lesson 7 (Apply)

Starter

Refine and revisit: Use measuring cylinders filled to various levels to challenge children to practise reading scales using different intervals. Ask: *What would this be in litres? In millilitres? I have 500ml in this jug. If I pour out 25ml, what will be left in the jug? What if I pour out 75ml? How many lots of 75ml could I pour out?*

Main teaching activities

Whole class: Explain to the children that in the next two lessons they will be investigating capacity in groups. Explain that they will be working to solve a puzzle. Around the room there are different clues that will help them find out the recipe for a very special potion. Today, they need to carefully move around the room, collecting the information they need (see the 'Magic potion capacity instructions', 'Magic potion capacity labels' and '350ml' resouce sheets). They should then work together as a group to solve the puzzle. In their groups they may want to nominate a scribe.

Group work: Give the groups a fixed amount of time (say, 30 minutes) to collect information from the seven stations. They then work out the capacity of the liquid for the potion, and round it to the nearest litre. (Answers: 10ml of 'power juice'; 500ml of 'strength juice'; 2.5 litres of water; 350ml of 'courage mixture'; a teaspoon is approximately 5ml, so approximately 25ml 'wisdom essence'; 50ml is approximately the capacity of an egg cup, therefore 100ml of 'patience essence'; 300ml is the approximate capacity of a mug, therefore 450ml of 'luck essence'. Altogether the liquid has a capacity of 3935ml, so approximately 4 litres).

Review

The children share the information they have found out so far. Ask: *How did you take that reading? How did you work out the capacity? What is this scale measured in? Could you write that capacity in ml/litres? Is that greater than or less than 1 litre? How many 5ml spoonfuls is that? Does this container hold more/less?*

Explain to the children that in the following lesson you would like them to think about the marketing for this special potion. Challenge them to think of what size bottles they would like it sold in and say that the total cost for all the potion is £1600.00. You would like them to work out how much one of their bottles would cost.

Differentiation

Less confident learners: Provide these children with the 'Magic potion capacity chart' sheet, which gives them a chart to complete to assist their workings.

More confident learners: Challenge these children to make a rough estimate of the capacity of the potion before completing the individual readings.

Lesson 8 (Apply and evaluate)

Starter

Revisit: Recap on the puzzle from Lesson 7. Go around the different stations asking questions from Lesson 7's Review, and allow the children time to check their measures.

Main teaching activity

Encourage the children to make a chart to help them with their calculations. If appropriate, allow them to use a calculator to check the final totals.

Review

Invite the groups to present their findings to the class and share ideas. Ask questions such as: *What contribution did you make to the group? What was your role?*

Differentiation

Less confident learners: Let these children work out the cost of 1 litre bottles, then break the cost down to 500ml, 250ml before looking at 100ml.

More confident learners: These children should consider as many different size bottles as possible. They should also consider the exact amount of liquid.

Lessons 9-10

Preparation

Lesson 9: Make up the 'Clock face' from the general resouce sheet, for display use and for support.

Lesson 10: Collect television guides (one per group) and prepare copies of the school timetable (one per pair).

You will need

CD resources

Core and extension versions of 'Tricky timetables'. General resource sheet: 'Clock face'.

Equipment

Clock faces; TV guide (one per group); copies of TV guides and of the school timetable.

Learning objectives

Starter

- Read time to the nearest minute; use am, pm and 12-hour clock notation; choose units of time to measure time intervals; calculate time intervals from clocks and timetables.

Main teaching activities

2006

- Read time to the nearest minute; use am, pm and 12-hour clock notation; choose units of time to measure time intervals; calculate time intervals from clocks and timetables.

1999

- Use am and pm and the notation 9:53.
- Read simple timetables.
- Solve word problems involving time.

Vocabulary

time, am, pm, digital, analogue, timetable, arrive, depart, hours (h), minutes (min), seconds (s)

Lesson 9 (Teach and apply)

Starter

Rehearse: Hold up an analogue clock face (set to 12:00) in front of the class (use the 'Clock face' general resource sheet). Explain to the children that you will move the hands and that you would like them to write down the time on their whiteboards each time. Move the time forward in steps of five minutes.

Alternate the language, describing, for example, 6:15 as six fifteen and a quarter past six.

Main teaching activities

Whole class: Write on the board 9:00am, 11:30am, 1:00pm, 3:30pm and 6:00pm. Explain that these times are departure times for trains, then ask questions such as: *If I was at the station at five to nine in the morning, how long would I have to wait for a train? If the 3:30pm train is running 20 minutes late, what time will it leave?* Draw a timeline on the board to help you with this and similar problems (see below). Also, establish that the children understand am and pm times.

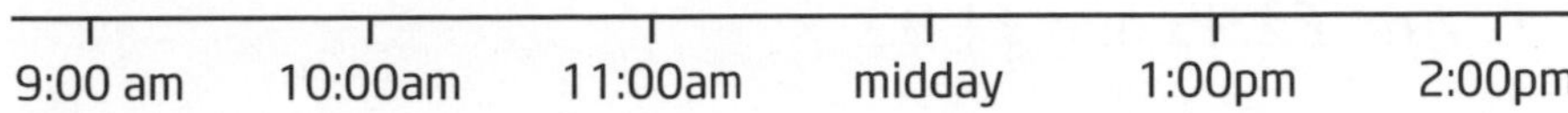

Independent work: Give each child a copy of 'Tricky timetables' to complete.

Review

Review the 'Tricky timetables' answers and address any misconceptions about time differences. Discuss children's own experiences of time and ask them to estimate times in practical contexts such as: *How long does it take you to travel to school? How long does it take to eat lunch? How many days to the end of term?* Explain that the class will be doing more on estimating time in the next lesson.

Differentiation

Less confident learners: Provide these children with clock faces to support them with the core 'Tricky timetables' sheet.
More confident learners: Give children the extension version of 'Tricky timetables', with more difficult time differences and with additional challenges involving the adjustment of the timetable for late and early running buses.

Lesson 10 (Apply)

Starter

Reason: Ask individual children to complete the following list:

1 millennium =
1 century =
1 year =
1 month =
1 week =
1 day =
1 hour =
1 minute =

Continue by asking other children: *How many days in three weeks? How many weeks in two years? How many minutes in ten hours? How many seconds in five minutes?* and so on.

Main teaching activities

Group work: Provide groups of children with a copy of a television guide and look specifically at the dates for that week. Rewrite the dates in different ways, such as 28/09/07 or 28 October 2007. Ask questions for the groups to solve: *How long is this programme? If there are ten episodes of this series, how long will it be altogether? How many episodes of this soap opera are there this week? If there are five minutes of adverts, what will be the duration of each episode? How many hours/minutes of this soap opera are there in the whole week?*
Paired work: Give each pair a copy of the school timetable. Challenge them to work out how much mathematics they have to do in a day, week, month, term or year. Ask them to write down estimates first, then check their answers. If time is available, ask them to repeat this for other subjects: *Do you think you will have more or less time for music? Explain why/why not.*

Review

Compare the various results of the main teaching activities. Check how close the children were with their estimates. Pick an individual's birthday, write it on the board and ask: *What will the date be when you are 16? 21 years old? How many days to your birthday?* Repeat with other children.

Differentiation

Less confident learners: Limit the task to finding the amount of time they spend doing maths in a day, week and month. Support the children with their estimations.
More confident learners: Challenge the children to come up with as many facts about the amount of time they spend doing mathematics as they can. Prompt with some additional questions if necessary, such as: *What percentage of your day/week do you spend doing maths?*

Name ____________________ Date ____________________

Money adds

Work out the answers to the following money problems in your head or using the method you were shown.

1. Add £2.95 and £1.80.

2. Find the total of £3.99 and £2.50.

3. What is the sum of £5.76 and £3.38?

4. What is the total cost of a £3.65 book and a £5.86 computer game?

5. Sunitta has saved £6.86. She is given another £2.55. How much does she now have altogether?

Name ____________________ Date ____________

Money subtractions

Work out the answers to the following money problems in your head or use the method you were shown.

1. Subtract £3.85 from £4.70.

2. What is the difference between £6.74 and £2.93?

3. How much less than £4.52 is £2.37?

4. Paula spent £6.37 on a present. How much change did she get from £10.00?

5. James owed his friend £2.53. He has £4.71 in his wallet. How much will he have left if he pays his friend?

Name ____________________ Date ____________

Rectangles

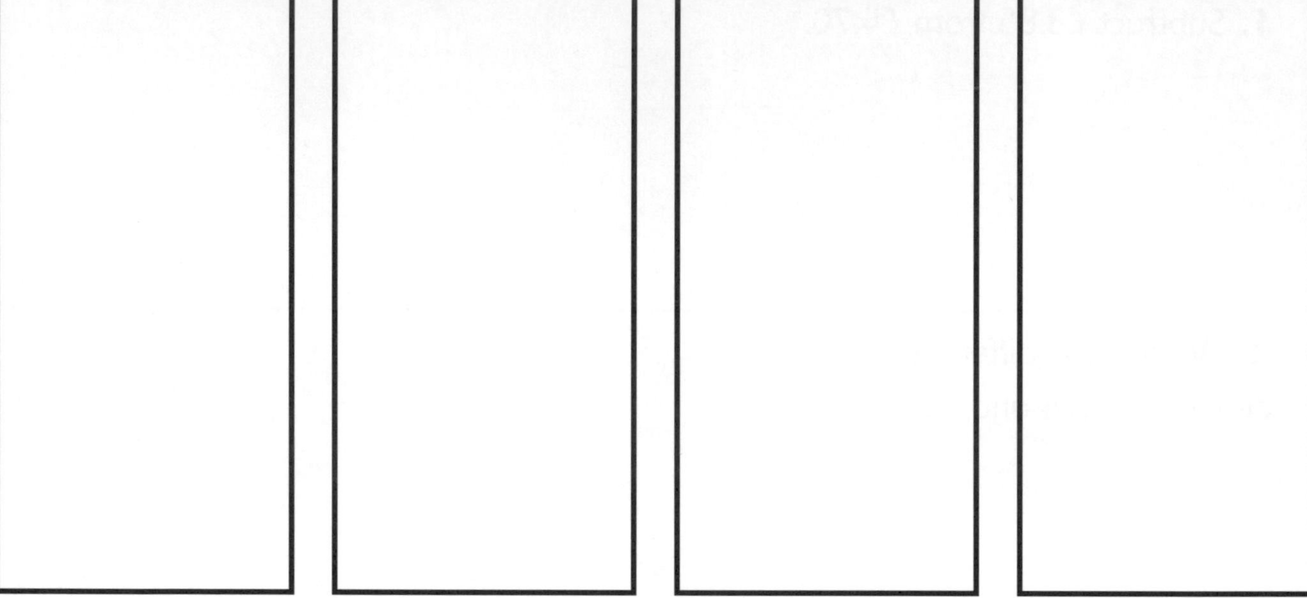

Securing number facts, relationships and calculating

Key aspects of learning
- Problem solving
- Managing feeling
- Communication
- Empathy

Expected prior learning

Check that children can already:
- recall multiplication facts and derive related division facts for the 2, 3, 4, 5 and 10 times-tables
- read and write proper fractions, eg $^3/_7$, $^9/_{10}$
- understand the terms denominator (the parts of a whole) and numerator (the number of parts)
- find unit fractions of numbers and quantities, eg 12, $^1/_3$, $^1/_4$ and $^1/_6$ of 12 litres
- find unit fractions of shapes
- use diagrams to compare the size of two unit fractions.

Objectives overview

The text in this diagram identifies the focus of mathematics learning within the block.

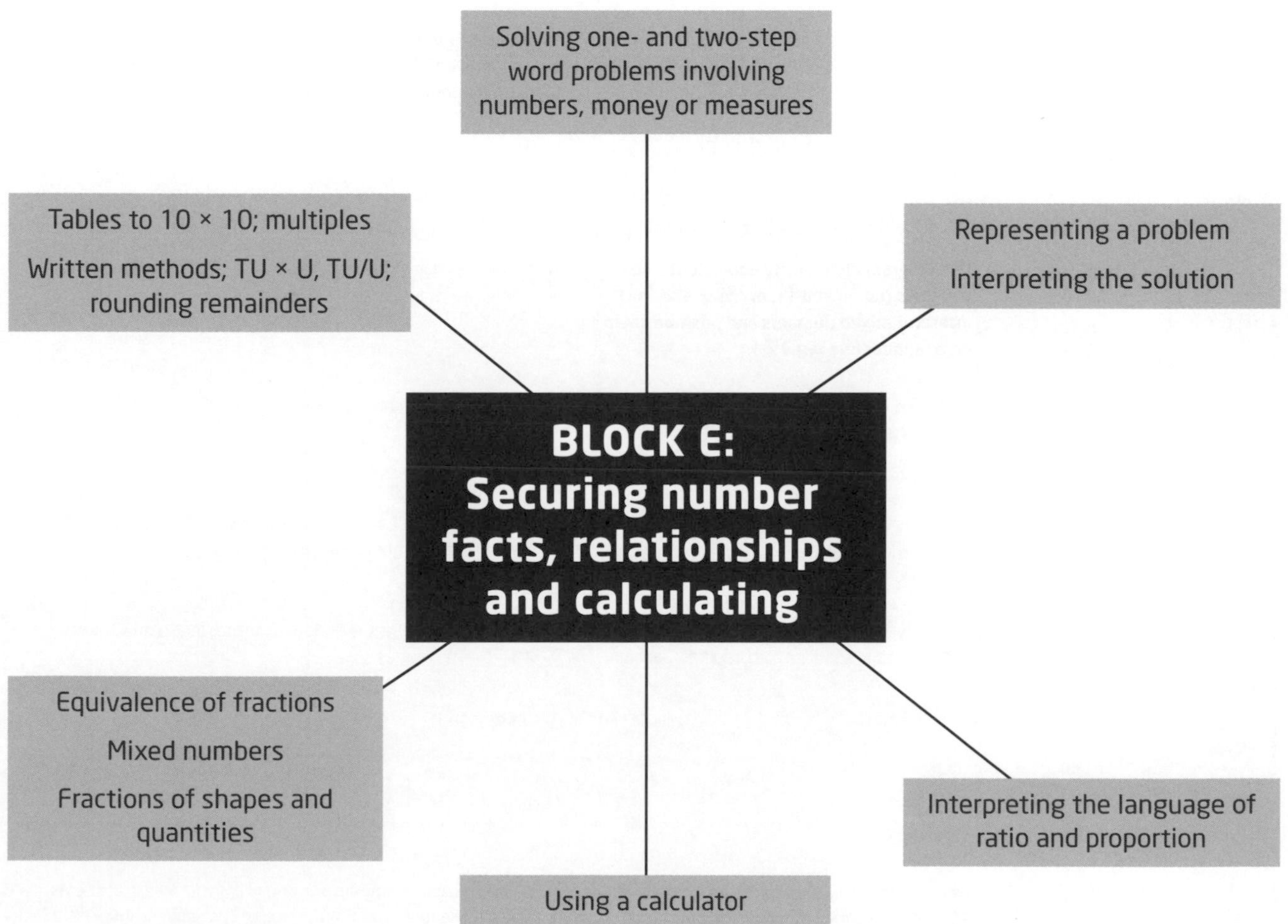

Securing number facts, relationships and calculating

Lesson	Strands	Starter	Main teaching activities
1. Teach and apply	Use/apply	Partition, round and order four-digit whole numbers (revision of Block A).	Represent a puzzle or problem using number sentences, statements or diagrams; use these to solve the problem; present and interpret the solution in the context of the problem.
2. Review	Knowledge	As for Lesson 1	**Derive and recall multiplication facts up to 10 × 10, the corresponding division facts and multiples of numbers to 10 up to the tenth multiple.**
3. Review	Knowledge	**Derive and recall multiplication facts up to 10 × 10, the corresponding division facts and multiples of numbers to 10 up to the tenth multiple.**	As for Lesson 2
4. Teach and practise	Knowledge	As for Lesson 3	As for Lesson 2
5. Teach and apply	Use/apply	As for Lesson 3	Represent a puzzle or problem using number sentences, statements or diagrams; use these to solve the problem; present and interpret the solution in the context of the problem.
6. Teach and practise	Counting	Multiply and divide numbers to 1000 by 10 and then 100 (whole-number answers), understanding the effect; relate to scaling up or down (revision of Block A).	**Use diagrams to identify equivalent fractions (eg $\frac{6}{8}$ and $\frac{3}{4}$, or $\frac{70}{100}$ and $\frac{7}{10}$); interpret mixed numbers and position them on a number line (eg $3\frac{1}{2}$).**
7. Teach and apply	Counting	As for Lesson 6	As for Lesson 6
8. Teach and practise	Counting	**Use diagrams to identify equivalent fractions (eg $\frac{6}{8}$ and $\frac{3}{4}$, or $\frac{70}{100}$ and $\frac{7}{10}$); interpret mixed numbers and position them on a number line (eg $3\frac{1}{2}$).**	Recognise the equivalence between decimal and fraction forms of one half, quarters, tenths and hundredths.
9. Teach and apply	Knowledge	Recognise the equivalence between decimal and fraction forms of one half, quarters, tenths and hundredths.	Identify pairs of fractions that total 1.
10. Review	Counting	As for Lesson 9	Recognise the equivalence between decimal and fraction forms of one half, quarters, tenths and hundredths.
11. Review	Calculate	Use knowledge of rounding, number operations and inverses to estimate and check calculations.	Find fractions of numbers, quantities or shapes (eg $\frac{1}{5}$ of 30 plums, $\frac{3}{8}$ of a 6 by 4 rectangle).
12. Review and apply	Calculate	As for Lesson 11	As for Lesson 11
13. Review and practise	Calculate	As for Lesson 11	As for Lesson 11
14. Teach and apply	Use/apply	**Derive and recall multiplication facts up to 10 × 10, the corresponding division facts and multiples of numbers to 10 up to the tenth multiple.**	Represent a puzzle or problem using number sentences, statements or diagrams; use these to solve the problem; present and interpret the solution in the context of the problem.
15. Apply	Use/apply	As for Lesson 14	As for Lesson 14

Speaking and listening objective

- Respond appropriately to the contributions of others in the light of alternative viewpoints.

Introduction

In this unit, children develop their skills in solving problems and puzzles, and learn how to represent these using number statements or diagrams, and this should be borne in mind for the work throughout the unit. They work in pairs for many activities, and should be encouraged to develop their ability to respond to differing viewpoints in a pleasant and courteous manner, putting across their own point of view. They continue to develop their skills in deriving and recalling multiplication and division facts. For the second two weeks of the unit, the work is concentrated on developing understanding about fractions and decimal fractions, as well as responding to word problems and writing their own problems involving fractions and decimal fractions.

Using and applying mathematics

- Represent a puzzle or problem using number sentences, statements or diagrams; use these to solve the problem; present and interpret the solution in the context of the problem.

Lessons 1-5

Preparation

Lesson 2: Make sure that all the multiplication facts on the 'Multiplication square' interactive resource are hidden.

You will need

Photocopiable pages
'Multiples grid game' (page 182) and 'Multiples of numbers to 10' (page 183).
CD resources
Support and extension versions of 'Multiples grid game' and 'Multiples of numbers to 10'.
General resource sheet: Numeral cards (a set of 0-20 for each pair).
Interactive resources: 'Multiplication square' and 'Number sentence builder'.

Learning objectives

Starter

- Partition, round and order four-digit whole numbers (revision of Block A).
- Derive and recall multiplication facts up to 10 × 10, the corresponding division facts and multiples of numbers to 10 up to the tenth multiple.

Main teaching activities

2006

- Represent a puzzle or problem using number sentences, statements or diagrams; use these to solve the problem; present and interpret the solution in the context of the problem.
- Derive and recall multiplication facts up to 10 × 10, the corresponding division facts and multiples of numbers to 10 up to the tenth multiple.

1999

- Use all four operations to solve word problems involving numbers in 'real life', money and measures (including time), using one or more steps, including converting pounds to pence and metres to centimetres and vice versa.
- Choose and use appropriate number operations and appropriate ways of calculating (mental, mental with jottings, pencil and paper) to solve problems.
- Round up or down after division, depending on the context.
- Choose appropriate ways of calculating: calculator.

Vocabulary

problem, solution, calculate, calculation, equation, operation, symbol, answer, method, explain, predict, reason, reasoning, pattern, relationship, multiply, multiplied by, divide, divided by, product, quotient, remainder, multiple, divisor, divisible by, consecutive

Lesson 1 (Teach and apply)

Starter

Revisit: Explain to the children that you will say some numbers in words that you would like them to write in numerals on their whiteboards. Begin with three-digit numbers, such as 345, 612 and 705, and then extend this to four-digit numbers. Keep the pace sharp. Where one of the place holders in a number is a zero, check that the children have understood this and written the number correctly. Ask questions such as: *Which digit represents the units? ... tens? ... hundreds? ... thousands? What does this digit represent in* *this number?* When there are three numbers on their whiteboards ask the children to order these, then to rewrite them, rounded to the nearest 10.

Main teaching activities

Whole class: Write on the board 1, 2, 3, 4 and 27, 28, 29, 30, and ask the children what they notice about these sequences of numbers. Discuss how these are 'next door' or consecutive numbers. Write the word 'consecutive' on the board. Invite children from each ability group to come to the board and write a sequence of four consecutive numbers. Check that the children understand the term 'consecutive'.

Now explain the problem that all of them will tackle in this lesson: *Is it possible to total consecutive numbers to make all of the numbers from 1 to 20? This is your task today, to find different ways of making 1, 2, 3... to 20, using only addition of two or more consecutive numbers.* Each pair may find it useful to have a set of 0–20 numeral cards (see general resources) so that they can combine pairs and trios of consecutive card numbers as a starting point. Stress that zero is allowed.

Group work: Ask the children to begin work on the task immediately. Encourage them to be systematic and to make jottings as they work so that they have a record of what they have tried. Keep reminding them to work systematically and to check their answers using a different calculation.

Review

Invite the children to share their results. Begin with 1, 2, 3... and ask the less confident children to contribute their responses. On the board, draw up a table that you can fill in as the children give their results:

Total	Ways to make this total using consecutive numbers		
1 =	0 + 1		
2 =			
3 =	0 + 1 + 2		
4 =			
5 =	2 + 3		
6 =	1 + 2 + 3		
7 =	3 + 4		
8 =			
9 =	4 + 5	2 + 3 + 4	
10 =	1 + 2 + 3 + 4		
11 =	5 + 6		
12 =	3 + 4 + 5		
13 =	6 + 7		
14 =	2 + 3 + 4 + 5		
15 =	7 + 8	4 + 5 + 6	1 + 2 + 3 + 4 + 5
16 =			
17 =	8 + 9		
18 =	5 + 6 + 7	3 + 4 + 5 + 6	
19 =	9 + 10		
20 =	2 + 3 + 4 + 5 + 6		

As the children give results, they will find that some numbers have more than one solution. Record the other results, too. When there is a solution for all possible totals, ask:

- *Which numbers cannot be made using consecutive numbers?*
- *What is special about these numbers?* (They are powers of 2. Children may comment that they are some of the two-times table numbers.)
- *What patterns can you see?*
- *What have you learned about using patterns to help you to find answers?*
- *What have you learned about using check calculations?*

Differentiation

Less confident learners: These children may find it beneficial to work in pairs, then come together in fours to share what they have found out so far.

More confident learners: If the children find a solution before the end of this session, challenge them to find which totals have more than one solution.

Ask the children to remember what they have learned in this lesson and to apply it to the rest of the lessons in this unit.

Lesson 2 (Review)

Starter

Revisit: Repeat the Starter from Lesson 1. This time concentrate on four-digit numbers. Extend this to recording four four-digit numbers, which should then be ordered; rounded to the nearest 100 and then ordered again. Discuss any effects that the rounding has on these numbers.

Main teaching activities

Whole class: Explain that in this and in the next lesson the children will be extending their skills with multiplication and division facts. Reveal the 'Multiplication square' interactive resource. Point to a fact square, such as that for 6 × 3 and ask: *What multiple goes here?* Reveal the fact if the correct answer is given. Repeat this for other facts from the two- to six-times tables. Repeat, concentrating on the facts for the six- to ten-times tables. Highlight all of the squares and click 'Fill' to reveal all of the squares.

Point to any fact and ask: *What multipliers produce this product? What are the two multiplication facts? What are the two division facts?* So, for 18 children would say 3 × 6 = 18; 6 × 3 = 18; 18 ÷ 3 = 6; 18 ÷ 6 = 3. Repeat for other facts, each time pointing to the positions of the multipliers and the position of the matching fact on the table, ie 3 × 6 and 6 × 3.

Paired work: Provide the activity sheet 'Multiples grid game'. This asks the children to identify the two multiplication and two division facts for each two-digit number on the sheet.

Differentiation

Less confident learners: Provide the support version of the activity sheet which concentrates on the table facts 2 to 6.

More confident learners: Provide the extension version of the sheet which includes multiplication facts to 12 × 12.

Review

Write on the board a multiple, such as 42, and ask: *What facts can you tell me for this multiple?* Write these on the board. Repeat for other facts. Now ask: *Which multiplication and division facts did you calculate easily? Which ones do you need to learn?*

Lesson 3 (Review)

Starter

Recall: Explain that you will ask multiplication facts from the multiplication tables. Begin with simpler ones, such as 4 × 2, and extend to the facts that are more difficult to remember, such as 6 × 7, 6 × 8, 6 × 9, 7 × 7, 7 × 8, 7 × 9, 8 × 8, 8 × 9 and 9 × 9.

Main teaching activities

Whole class: On the board write the number 24 and ask: *How many different multiplication facts can you find for this multiple?* Using the interactive resource 'Number sentence builder', record the children's answers, which should include at least 3 × 8, 8 × 3, 4 × 6 and 6 × 4. Discuss how one multiple can have a range of facts. Ask: *Can you think of another multiple where there are more than two facts?* Write these multiples on the board and add more if necessary, so that there are ten multiples written on the board.

Paired work: Ask the children to work together to write all the multiplication and division facts that they can find for each of the multiples written on the board. Ask them to discuss how they will record, and to check their answers each time.

Differentiation

Less confident learners: Decide whether to work as a group. Discuss each multiple. Recite the relevant multiplication tables for each multiple so that the children can fix its position mentally.

More confident learners: Challenge the children to extend their answers to include facts from the 12 × 12 multiplication tables.

Review

Invite the children to take turns to give feedback on their results. Write these up on the board for each multiple. Ask: *Have all the facts been found? How did you check that your answers were correct? Which facts do you need to learn?* Write a list of these.

Lesson 4 (Teach and practise)

Starter

Recall: Repeat the Starter from Lesson 3, this time asking the children for division facts.

Main teaching activities

Ask questions about multiples of numbers to 10, such as: *If you know that 7 × 3 = 21, how does this help you to find the answer to 7 × 30? And 210 divided by 7?* Provide the activity sheet 'Multiples of numbers to 10' and ask the children to work individually.

Differentiation

Less confident learners: Provide the support version of the activity sheet.
More confident learners: Provide the extension version of the activity sheet.

Review

Use the core version of the activity sheet and review this together.

Lesson 5 (Teach and apply)

Starter

Recall: Repeat the Starters for Lessons 3 and 4, so that the children recall multiplication facts and derive division facts. Suggest that they make a note of any facts that they cannot recall or cannot derive.

Main teaching activities

Whole class: Explain that in this lesson children will use their knowledge of multiplication and division to find the solutions to some problems. Begin with the following: *Mark receives £3 in pocket money. If he saves all his pocket money, how many weeks will it take him to have £27?* Discuss what sort of problem this is and what number sentence to write for it. Record on the board 3 × 9 = 27. Repeat this for another problem such as: *Claire has 45 stickers. She decides to share her stickers with her four friends and herself. How many stickers will each of them have?*
Paired work: Write the numbers 8 and 6 on the board. Ask: *What is 8 × 6? What is 48 ÷ 6?* Ask the children to write multiplication and division equations for these numbers and to write a problem that uses these numbers.
Whole class: Invite children to say their number problems for the rest of the class to hear. Discuss the problems and whether the equations they have written would help them to solve the problems.
Paired work: On the board write pairs of multipliers, such as 7 × 4; 6 × 8; 9 × 4. Ask the children to write a multiplication and a division word problem for each pair of multipliers.

Differentiation

Less confident learners: Decide whether to work as a group. Encourage each child to invent a problem and to say it for the others to hear. You may prefer to concentrate on multiplication problems at this stage.
More confident learners: Challenge the children to think of three further word problems which involve multiplication and division and to be prepared to read these out to the class and to explain how to solve them.

Review

Invite children to take turns to read out their word problems and the rest of the class to decide if the problems do use the relevant numbers. Now ask the more confident learners to read out one of their problems and to explain how to solve it to the others. Ask questions such as: *What sort of mathematics do you need to solve this problem? Is there another way to solve it?*

Lessons 6-10

Preparation

Lesson 6: Prepare the 'Fraction cards' from the general resource sheet. Copy 'Fractions of shapes' onto OHT.
Lesson 9: Copy 'Fraction stories' and 'Whole fractions' onto OHT.
Lessons 8 and 10: Copy 'Decimal and fraction Pelmanism cards' onto card.

You will need

Photocopiable pages
'Fractions of shapes' (page 184), 'Decimal and fraction Pelmanism cards' (page 185), 'Whole fractions' (page 186), and 'Fraction stories' (page 187).
CD resources
Support and extension versions of 'Fractions of shapes' and 'Fraction stories'. General resource sheets: 'Pelmanism instructions' and 'Blank number lines'; a teaching set of 'Fraction cards'.
Equipment
Squared paper; scissors.

Learning objectives

Starter

- Multiply and divide numbers to 1000 by 10 and then 100 (whole-number answers), understanding the effect; relate to scaling up or down (revision of Block A).
- Use diagrams to identify equivalent fractions (eg $\frac{6}{8}$ and $\frac{3}{4}$, or $\frac{70}{100}$ and $\frac{7}{10}$); interpret mixed numbers and position them on a number line (eg $3\frac{1}{2}$).
- Recognise the equivalence between decimal and fraction forms of one half, quarters, tenths and hundredths.

Main teaching activities

2006

- Use diagrams to identify equivalent fractions (eg $\frac{6}{8}$ and $\frac{3}{4}$, or $\frac{70}{100}$ and $\frac{7}{10}$); interpret mixed numbers and position them on a number line (eg $3\frac{1}{2}$).
- Recognise the equivalence between decimal and fraction forms of one half, quarters, tenths and hundredths.
- Identify pairs of fractions that total 1.

1999

- Begin to relate fractions to division and find simple fractions such as $\frac{1}{2}$, $\frac{1}{3}$, $\frac{1}{4}$, $\frac{1}{5}$, $\frac{1}{10}$... of numbers.
- Find fractions such as $\frac{2}{3}$, $\frac{3}{4}$, $\frac{3}{5}$, $\frac{7}{10}$... of shapes.
- Recognise the equivalence of simple fractions.
- Order a set of fractions such as 2, $2\frac{3}{4}$, $1\frac{3}{4}$, $2\frac{1}{2}$, $1\frac{1}{2}$, and position them on a number line.
- Recognise the equivalence between the decimal and fraction forms of tenths and hundredths (eg $\frac{7}{10}$ = 0.7, $\frac{27}{100}$ = 0.27).
- Identify two simple fractions with a total of 1 (eg $\frac{3}{10}$ and $\frac{7}{10}$).

Vocabulary

fraction, unit fraction, mixed number, numerator, denominator, equivalent

Lesson 6 (Teach and practise)

Starter

Rehearse: Explain that you will say a two-digit number greater than 20. Ask the children to multiply it by 10 and write the answer on their whiteboards. Write the original number on the board and the new number underneath it. Ask the children: *What has happened to our numbers?* Discourage 'add a zero' responses, and encourage the idea of changes in place value and digits moving relative to the decimal point. Repeat this for other two-digit numbers.

Main teaching activities

Whole class: Draw a 0–1 number line on the board, or use a washing line. Using the prepared 'Fraction cards', ask a child to place the '$\frac{1}{2}$' card on the line. Then ask other children to place other cards equivalent to a half on the line ($\frac{2}{4}$, $\frac{3}{6}$...). Discuss with the children why these cards all go at the same point on the line. Use paper clips to suspend two (or more) equivalent cards in a sort of chain, one under another. Use the cards equivalent to $\frac{1}{4}$ and repeat the activity. Then ask the children to discuss their ideas with their partner and write down fractions equivalent to $\frac{3}{4}$. Discuss with the children the answers they have recorded.

Give each child a piece of squared paper and ask them to draw a rectangle on it, then shade in $\frac{3}{4}$ of the rectangle. Discuss different outcomes (for example, 18 of 24 squares or 9 of 12 squares). Each of these fractions is equivalent to $\frac{3}{4}$ of the total shape.

Securing number facts, relationships and calculating

BLOCK E

Independent work: Give the children copies of the activity sheet 'Fractions of shapes', which asks them to shade in each shape according to the fraction shown. Make sure the children realise that the first five shapes will all show $^1/_2$, and the other three are all pictures of $^3/_4$.

Differentiation

Less confident learners: Decide whether to use the support version of the activity sheet that has simpler fractions to identify.
More confident learners: Decide whether to use the extension version of the activity sheet that has harder fractions.

Review

Display the activity sheet and review it together. Discuss how many sections need to be shaded, and why. Where simpler equivalent fractions are possible, such as $^4/_8$ or $^1/_2$, ask the children to say the simpler fraction. Ask questions such as:

- *What fraction is equivalent to...?*
- *What is another way of writing...?*

Invite the children to write equivalent fractions on the board.

Lesson 7 (Teach and apply)

Starter

Revisit: Repeat the Starter from Lesson 1. This time, ask the children to say the multiples of 10 together, as a chant, when you hold up your hand. Give a very small amount of thinking time, as children should be beginning to have rapid recall of multiples of 10.

Main teaching activities

Whole class: Ask the children to suggest any fractions that they can think of that are equivalent to $^1/_2$. Write these on the board, listing them in a ringed set headed 'Half'. Repeat this for $^1/_4$, then for $^3/_4$. Now ask the children to look for the 'family' of fractions linked to $^4/_8$ and write them on the board: '$^4/_8$ = $^2/_4$ or $^1/_2$'. Ask: *What is the equivalent fraction for $^6/_8$?* Write on the board: '$^6/_8$ = $^3/_4$'. Now ask them to write down some mixed numbers, such as $6^1/_2$, $2^3/_4$ and so on, and to suggest where they might find these fractions in everyday life. They might suggest whole and half oranges, or two bars of chocolate and $^3/_4$ of a bar. Make sure they understand that, for example, $2^3/_4$ is two whole ones and $^3/_4$ of another whole one.
Group work: Ask the children to work in small groups of four or five, with one child in each group acting as scribe. On the board, write up 'families' such as tenths and fifths, sixths and twelfths, and so on. Invite the children to write down the equivalent fractions that they can think of for the different families. When the children have done this, write some of the fractions that they suggest on the board.

Differentiation

All the children should be able to participate at their own level within the group activity.

Review

Begin by inviting children from each of the ability groups to contribute to the fraction families by writing suggestions onto the board. Discuss the equivalence of these fractions. Ask: *What fractions belong to the tenths family? And the twelfths family? How can you tell?* Now ask the children to suggest some mixed numbers. Ask them to suggest occasions when these fractions might occur in everyday life – for example, $3^1/_2$ pints of milk, 2 whole pizzas and $^3/_8$ of a pizza.

Lesson 8 (Teach and practise)

Starter

Revisit: Explain that you will say a fraction. Ask the children to write an equivalent fraction. When you say *Show me* they hold up their whiteboards. Say, for example, ½, ¼, 2¾.

Main teaching activities

Whole class: Draw a number line from 0 to 1. Ask the children to count along the line with you, from 0.1 to 1. Discuss how each of these is equivalent to $^1/_{10}$, $^2/_{10}$ and so on to 1. Now point to a position on the number line and ask the children to write on their whiteboards both the decimal fraction and the fraction. When you say *Show me* they hold up their boards for you to check. Ask: *How else can we write the fraction that is equivalent to 0.5?* Discuss how ½ is also equivalent. Repeat this for decimal fractions of 0.2 ($^2/_{10}$ and $^1/_5$), 0.4 ($^4/_{10}$ and $^2/_5$) and so on.

Now write on the board £0.25 and ask: *What does the 25 represent?* Agree that this is 25 pence and it is equivalent to 25 hundredths. Repeat this for other money amounts, such as 37p and 45p.

Paired work: Provide each pair with a copy of 'Decimal and fraction Pelmanism cards' and a copy of 'Pelmanism instructions'. Ask the children to cut up the cards and to turn these face down. They find pairs of decimal and fraction cards that are equivalent.

Differentiation

Less confident learners: Decide whether to work together to play this game. Ask the children to say what is written on each pair of cards.
More confident learners: Challenge the children to order the cards.

Review

Invite the more confident children to explain how they ordered their cards. Use the 'Blank number lines' general resource sheet to display a 0–1 number line. Ask them to write two of their pairs of cards onto the line. Invite the other children to suggest where other cards could go onto the line. On another number line, mark in the tenths from 0 to 1. Say: *Think of two fractions that are equivalent to 0.5. What about 0.25?* Save the Pelmanism cards for Lesson 10.

Lesson 9 (Teach and apply)

Starter

Rehearse: Use the 'Blank number lines' general resource sheet to display a 0–10 number line, with the units labelled. Ask the children to count in steps of $^1/_2$ from zero (eg one half, two halves, three halves). Point to the markers on the board; for example, point to 1 for 'two halves'. Next, ask the children if there is another way of saying this. Establish that two halves is the same as 1, three halves is 1½, and so on. Ask the children to repeat the count, this time saying half, one, one and a half... Fill in the gaps on the number line. Extend the count to quarters and thirds if time is available.

Main teaching activities

Whole class: Show the example question from 'Fraction stories' on an OHT or whiteboard, or copy onto the board.

Ask: *How many whole rectangles do we have?* Agree that there is a whole rectangle divided into six equal parts. Cover up the shaded part ($^5/_6$ are left), then the rest of the shape (leaving $^1/_6$).

Write on the board: $^1/_6 + {}^5/_6 = {}^6/_6 = 1$ whole. Establish that the children understand that one whole is equivalent to two halves, six sixths, and so on. Shade in other squares and repeat for $^2/_6$, $^3/_6$ and $^4/_6$. (You might also like to prepare an OHT using the 'Whole fractions' activity sheet for this purpose.)

Independent work: Provide each child with a copy of 'Fraction stories' to complete. Remind the children to look in particular for fractions that equal one whole.

Differentiation

Less confident learners: Provide the support version of the 'Fraction stories' activity sheet, which includes only simple fractions such as $^3/_4$ and $^2/_3$.
More confident learners: Provide the extension version of the 'Fraction stories' sheet, in which the children also have to recognise equivalent fractions. Work with this group to highlight equivalences if necessary.

Review

Review the children's 'Fraction stories' activity sheets. Draw some rectangles divided into sixths and eighths on the board or use the 'Whole fractions' sheet. Ask the children to shade squares and then write the fraction story underneath. If any equivalent fractions are given, ask the class: *Can you give me another story for the same picture?* Use this method to introduce the idea of equivalent fractions.

Lesson 10 (Review)

Starter
Repeat the Starter from Lesson 9, this time asking the children to count in tenths from 0 to 1.

Main teaching activities
Ask the children to say the equivalent in fraction form for the decimal fractions that you say, such as 1/2, 1/4, 7/10, 25/100. Ask the children to work in pairs. They will need the cards cut from the 'Decimal and fraction Pelmanism cards' sheet, and the 'Pelmanism instructions'. This time they have the cards face up, put the cards into equivalent pairs, then write down each pair. Ask them to add more equivalents to each pairing. Decide whether to limit the less confident children by removing the hundredths cards.

Review
Ask children from each ability group to write up their pairs and additional equivalents. Ask: *How many pence are the same as £0.75? How many hundredths are the same as 0.75? How else could you write seventy-five hundredths?*

Lessons 11-15

You will need
CD resources
Core, support and extension versions of 'Finding fractions', 'Fractions of money', 'Fractions of measures 1' and 'Fractions and decimals word problems'.
Equipment
Calculators.

Learning objectives

Starter
- Use knowledge of rounding, number operations and inverses to estimate and check calculations.
- Derive and recall multiplication facts up to 10 ×10, the corresponding division facts and multiples of numbers to 10 up to the tenth multiple.

Main teaching activities
2006
- Find fractions of numbers, quantities or shapes (eg 1/5 of 30 plums, 3/8 of a 6 by 4 rectangle).
- Represent a puzzle or problem using number sentences, statements or diagrams; use these to solve the problem; present and interpret the solution in the context of the problem.

1999
- Begin to relate fractions to division and find simple fractions such as 1/2, 1/3, 1/4, 1/5, 1/10... of numbers or quantities.
- Find fractions such as 2/3, 3/4, 3/5, 7/10... of shapes.
- Use all four operations to solve word problems involving numbers in 'real life', money and measures (including time), using one or more steps, including converting pounds to pence and metres to centimetres and vice versa.
- Choose and use appropriate number operations and appropriate ways of calculating (mental, mental with jottings, pencil and paper) to solve problems.
- Round up or down after division, depending on the context.
- Choose appropriate ways of calculating: calculator.

Vocabulary
problem, solution, calculate, calculation, equation, operation, symbol, answer, method, explain, predict, reason, reasoning, pattern, relationship, fraction, unit fraction, mixed number, numerator, denominator, equivalent

Lesson 11 (Review)

ROUNDING RULES
Rounding to nearest 10: if a number ends in 5 or higher, round UP.
Rounding to nearest 100: if a number ends in 50 or higher, round UP.

Starter

Reason: Remind the children of the rules for rounding numbers up or down (see above). Give the children questions like these, for rounding to the nearest 10. Ask them to put their hands up to respond:

- *I am thinking of a three-digit number. When I round it down, it becomes 380. What could my starting number be?* (381-384)
- *I am thinking of a three-digit number. When I round it up, it becomes 870. What could my starting number be?* (865-869)

Main teaching activities

Whole class: Select a group of six children to come to the front of the class. Ask questions such as these and, after each question, actually split the group up into the fraction and write the operation on the board.

- *If we split the group into half, how many children would there be in each group?* (6 ÷ 2 = 3)
- *How many children would there be in one-third of the group?* (6 ÷ 3 = 2)
- *How many children would two-thirds be?* Discuss how $^1/_3$ of 6 is 2, so $^2/_3$ is double 2, which is 4.

Now invite a group of ten children to come to the front and repeat the process. Ask questions relating to fifths and tenths.

Talk to the children about the relationship between fractions and division. Ask questions such as: *How would we find one quarter of 16? How could we find one tenth of 50?* Model some of the children's suggestions on the board. They may suggest finding one quarter of 16 by dividing 16 by 4, and finding one-tenth of 50 by dividing 50 by 10. Discuss how division can be useful to find fractions of quantities.

Independent work: Give the children copies of the activity sheet 'Finding fractions', which asks them to find fractions of quantities.

Differentiation

Less confident learners: Use the support version of the activity sheet, which uses simpler fractions for the children to find.
More confident learners: Use the extension version of the activity sheet, which extends the use of fractions to some that the children may not have met before.

Review

Ask the children to tell you which questions they found hardest, and why. Review these together, using the board to record. Invite the children to explain how they found the answers. Remind them that division is useful to find a fraction of a quantity. Ask questions such as:

- *Which would you rather have, half of £1.50 or a quarter of £3.00? Why?*
- *Which would you rather have, seven-tenths of £1.00 or a fifth of £2.00? Why?*

Look for children who can demonstrate a clear understanding of the way to calculate fractions of quantities and easily make the link with division.

Lesson 12 (Review and apply)

Starter

Reason: Repeat the Starter from Lesson 3, this time asking the children to round to the nearest 100.

Main teaching activities

Review with the children how to find a fraction of an amount of money by division, for example finding a quarter of 80p. Say: *To find a quarter of 80p, divide 80p by 4. So quarter of 80p is 20p.* Provide the activity sheet 'Fractions of money' for the children to complete individually. This asks them to find fractions of quantities of money, then to say what fraction one amount is of another.

Review

Invite children from each ability group to show how they calculated to find the answers. Ask questions such as: *How did you work that out? Who used a different strategy?* Again, check that children have made the link between division and finding fractions of quantities.

Differentiation
Less confident learners: Use the support version of the activity sheet.
More confident learners: Use the extension version of the activity sheet.

Lesson 13 (Review and practise)

Starter

Reason: Repeat the Starters for Lessons 11 and 12, this time asking a combination of questions involving rounding to the nearest 10 or 100.

Main teaching activities

Whole class: Explain that today the children will be finding fractions of measures. Begin by reviewing how many centimetres in a metre (100); grams in a kilogram (1000); millilitres in a litre (1000). Invite the children to explain how to work out half a metre, expressing the answer in centimetres. Discuss how using division is helpful when finding fractions of quantities. For example, to find a quarter of 1 metre, we can divide 100cm (which is equivalent to 1 metre) by 4.
Independent work: Provide each child with a copy of activity sheet 'Fractions of measures 1'. This contains questions about fractions of measures. Explain that we usually use full numbers of appropriate units rather than fractions when we are actually measuring (for example 25cm rather than $^1/_4$m), so that we can read the numbers on a scale.

Differentiation
Less confident learners: Decide whether to provide the support version of the activity sheet, which contains simpler questions, all about fractions of a metre.
More confident learners: Use the extension version of the activity sheet, which contains more complex fractions of measures.

Review

Take a question from each of the differentiated activity sheets in turn, and invite a child from the relevant group to explain how they found the solution. Invite children to write on the board, showing how they worked out the answer.

Ask questions such as: *What is a quarter of 1 kilogram? How did you work that out? What units did you use in your answer?* Discuss the equivalence of 0.25kg = $^1/_4$kg = 250g, for example. Again, check that children have made the link between division and finding fractions of quantities.

Lesson 14 (Teach and apply)

Starter

Recall: Explain that you will ask some multiplication facts. Begin with the ones that the children are most likely to recall more easily, for example from the two- to five-times tables, then extend to the six- to nine-times tables. Keep the pace sharp.

Main teaching activities

Whole class: Explain that in this and the next lesson the children will be solving problems that involve multiplication and division and fractions and decimals. Write on the board: *Meg has 40 comics. She wants to give away $^1/_5$ of her comics. How many comics will she have left?* Ask: *What type of calculation will we need to do?* Agree that to find $^1/_5$ you divide the number of comics by 5. Now ask: *How do I find how many comics Meg will have left?* Agree that this will be by subtraction, ie 40 – 8 = 32. Ask: *What fraction of the comics does Meg have left?* ($^4/_5$).
Independent work: Provide each child with a copy of 'Fractions and decimals word problems'. Remind the children that they will need to remember their multiplication tables to solve many of these problems.

Differentiation
Less confident learners: Decide whether to use the support version of the sheet, which has simpler fractions and decimals within the problems.
More confident learners: There is an extension version of the sheet, which contains more

Review

Choose one of the problems from the core sheet. Invite children to explain how they worked out the problem and what diagrams or jottings they used.

complex problems. Children may use a calculator for the last problem on the sheet.

Invite other children to say what they did differently. Discuss which method might be better, and why that is so. Ask questions such as: *How can you check your answer?*

Lesson 15 (Apply)

Starter

Repeat the Starter from Lesson 14, this time asking for division facts.

Main teaching activities

Explain that the children will be writing their own number problems from decimal fractions and fractions that you write on the board. Provide each child with a copy of the template version of 'Fractions and decimals word problems'. Write up ¼ and 24 and ask the children to quickly write a problem that uses these numbers and to solve it. Invite children from each ability group to read out their problem and ask the other children to find the solution. Repeat this for another set, such as 0.8 and 32.

Ask the children to work in pairs to write problems and answers for: ¼ and 36; 7/10 and 90; 0.3 and 69; 0.75 and 240.

Differentiation

Less confident learners: Decide whether to work with these children as a group to write problems and find solutions.

More confident learners: Challenge these children to write a problem for 960 and 0.75. They may use a calculator to solve this.

Review

Invite children from each ability group to read out their problem for others to solve. Discuss how they solved the problem, and what jottings or diagrams they needed to make. Invite the more confident children to reveal their problems and how they solved them.

Name ______________________ Date ______________

Multiples grid game

Work with a partner.

Take turns to choose a two-digit multiple from the grid.

These numbers come from the multiplication table up to 10× 10.

Both of you write two multiplication facts and two division facts for this multiple.

Compare your answers each time.

Do you agree? If not, think how you can check your answers.

Tick the answers that you could work out quickly.

Do you know these facts now?

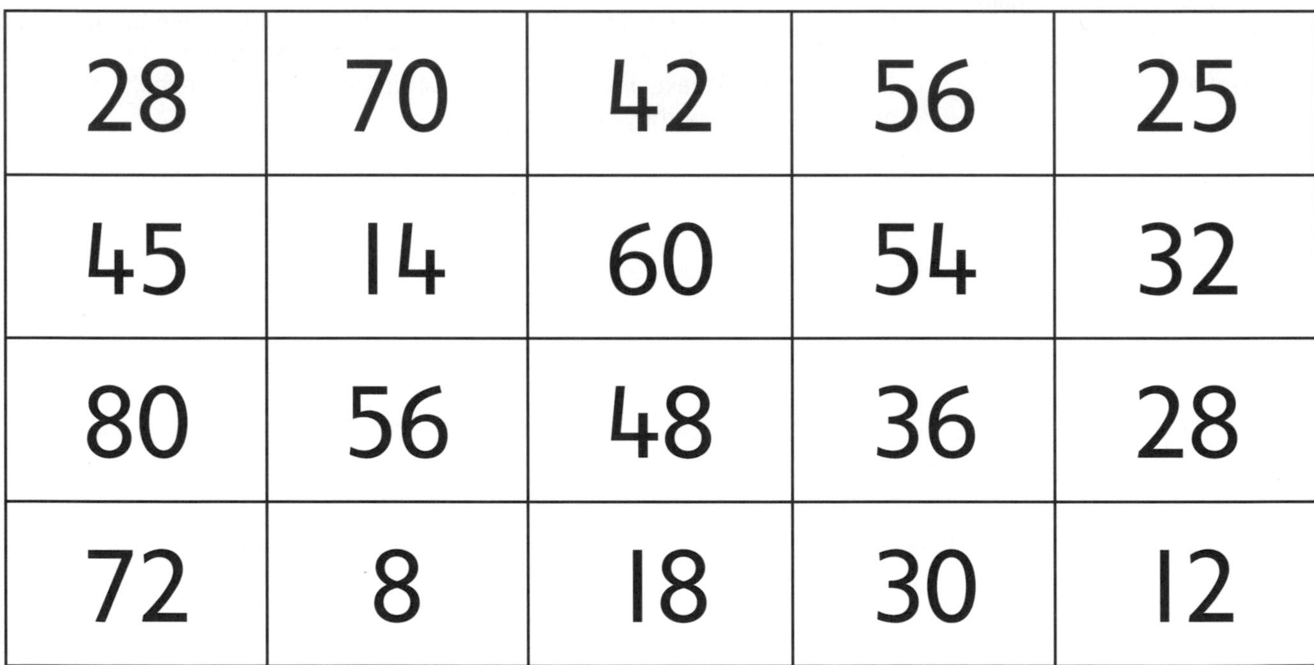

28	70	42	56	25
45	14	60	54	32
80	56	48	36	28
72	8	18	30	12

Answers: ______________________________

Name ______________________ Date ______________

Multiples of numbers to 10

Write the answers to these questions.

	Answer		Answer
5 × 4		5 × 40	
9 × 3		9 × 30	
8 × 9		8 × 90	
5 × 6		5 × 60	
8 × 7		8 × 70	
6 × 9		6 × 90	
64 ÷ 8		640 ÷ 8	
48 ÷ 6		480 ÷ 6	
81 ÷ 9		810 ÷ 9	
36 ÷ 9		360 ÷ 9	
42 ÷ 7		420 ÷ 7	
32 ÷ 4		320 ÷ 4	

Name ______________________ Date ______________

Fractions of shapes

Shade in the fraction of the shape.

$\frac{2}{4}$ 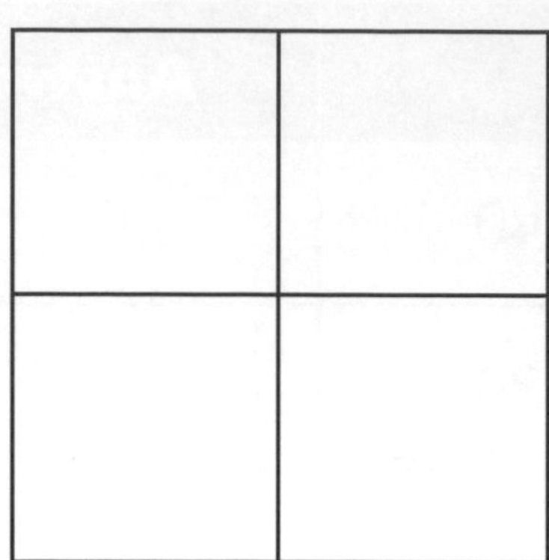	$\frac{4}{8}$ 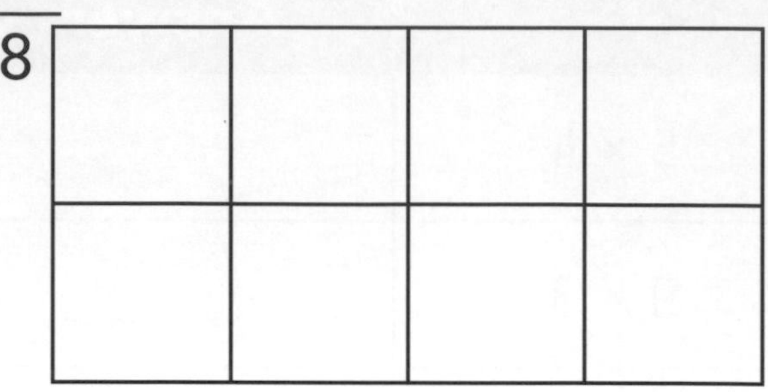
$\frac{1}{2}$ 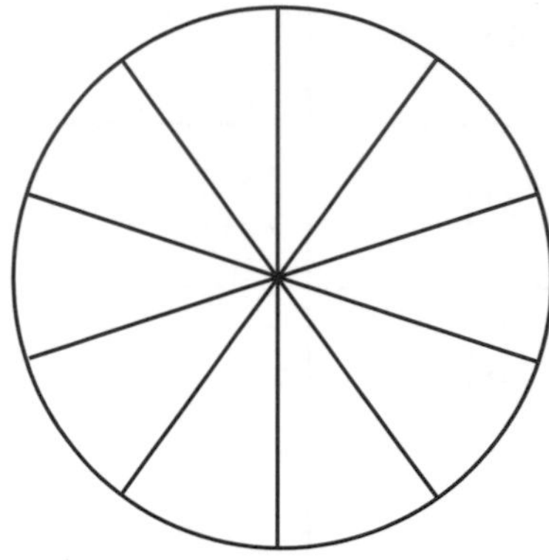	$\frac{6}{12}$ 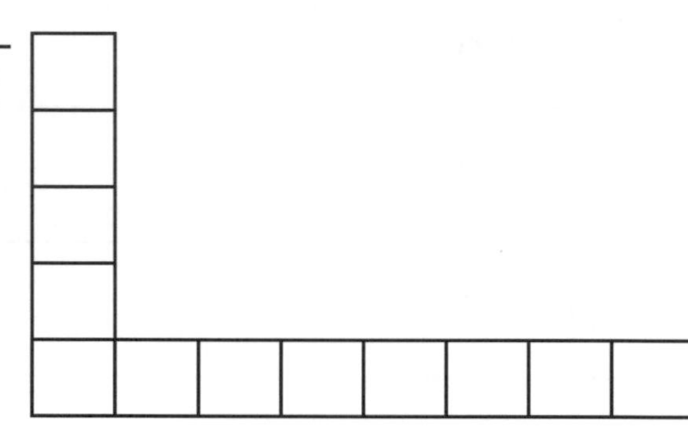
$\frac{7}{14}$ 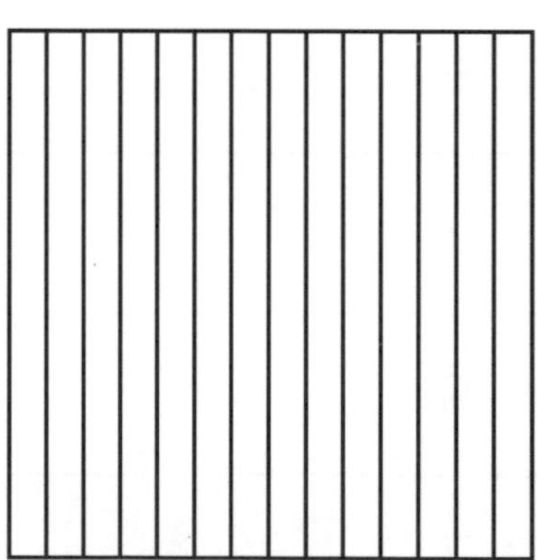	$\frac{6}{8}$ 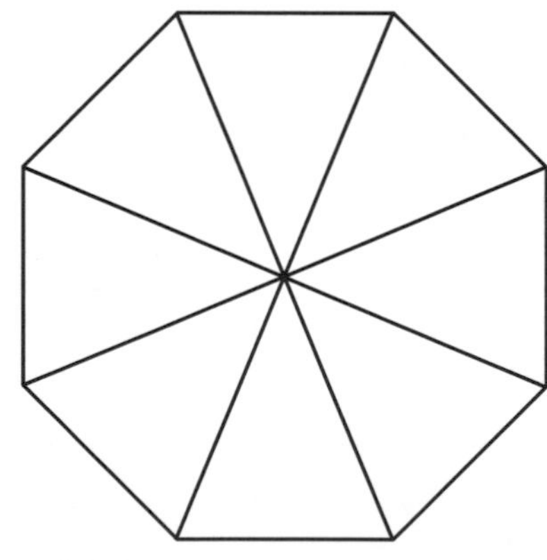
$\frac{9}{12}$ 	$\frac{3}{4}$ 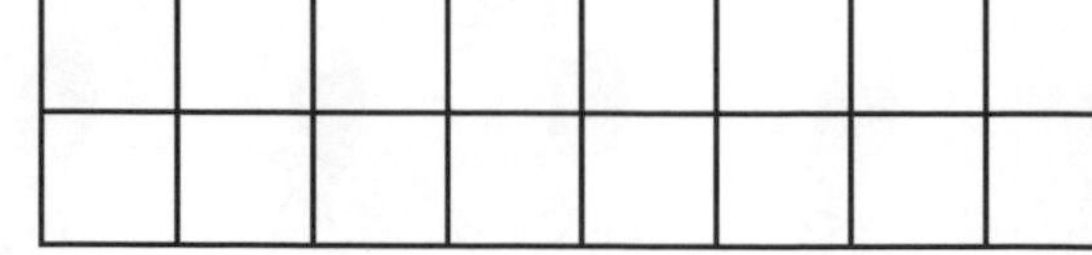

Name ______________________ Date ________________

Decimal and fraction Pelmanism cards

$\frac{1}{2}$	0.5
$\frac{1}{4}$	0.25
$\frac{3}{4}$	0.75
$\frac{1}{10}$	0.1
$\frac{2}{10}$	0.2
$\frac{3}{10}$	0.3
$\frac{4}{10}$	0.4
$\frac{5}{10}$	0.5
$\frac{6}{10}$	0.6
$\frac{7}{10}$	0.7
$\frac{8}{10}$	0.8
$\frac{9}{10}$	0.9
$\frac{45}{100}$	0.45
$\frac{37}{100}$	0.37
$\frac{15}{100}$	0.15
$\frac{99}{100}$	0.99

Name ______________________ Date ______________

Whole fractions

One whole

Fifths

Halves

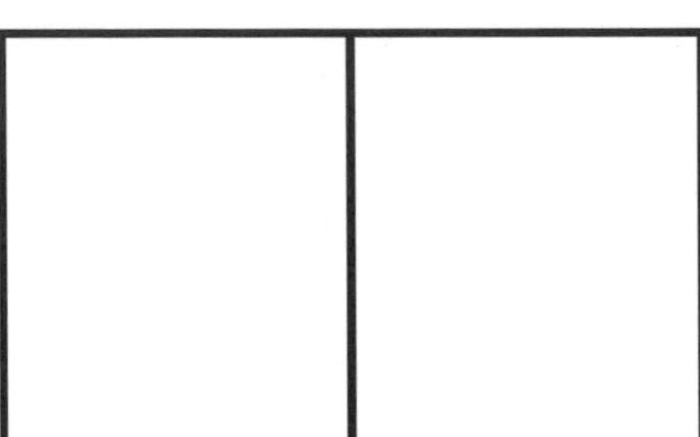

Sixths

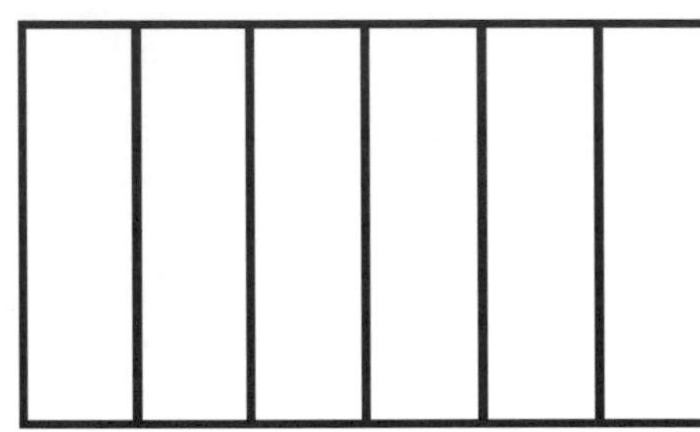

Thirds

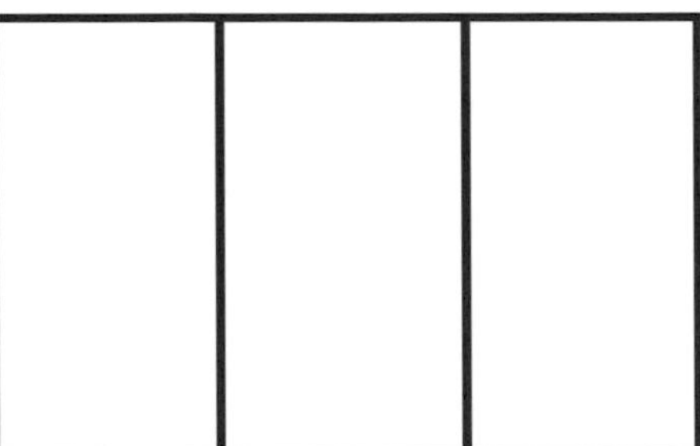

Eighths

Quarters

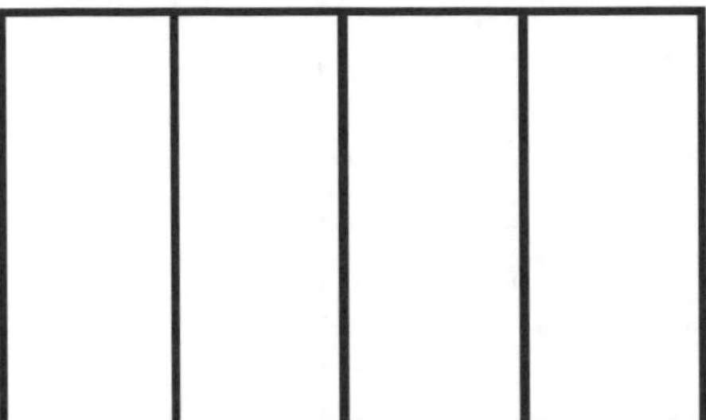

Tenths

Name ______________________ Date ______________

Fraction stories

Write the 'fraction story' below each example.

Example: 

Fraction story

$$\frac{1}{6} + \frac{5}{6} = \frac{6}{6} = 1 \text{ whole}$$

1. 

Fraction story

$\square + \square = \square = \square$

2. 

Fraction story

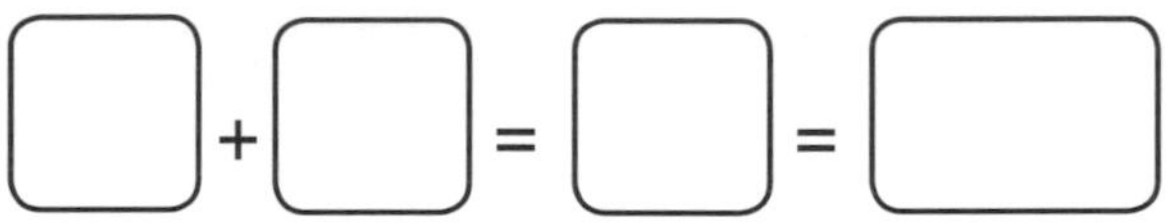

$\square + \square = \square = \square$

3. 

Fraction story

$\square + \square = \square = \square$

4. 

Fraction story

$\square + \square = \square = \square$

5. 

Fraction story

$\square + \square = \square = \square$

6. 

Fraction story

$\square + \square = \square = \square$

Securing number facts, relationships and calculating

Lesson	Strands	Starter	Main teaching activities
1. Teach and apply	Use/apply	**Derive and recall multiplication facts up to 10 × 10, the corresponding division facts and multiples of numbers to 10 up to the tenth multiple.**	• Represent a puzzle or problem using number sentences, statements or diagrams; use these to solve the problem; present and interpret the solution in the context of the problem. • Choose and carry out appropriate calculations, using calculator methods where appropriate.
2. Review and apply	Use/apply	As for Lesson 1	As for Lesson 1
3. Review, teach and apply	Use/apply	As for Lesson 1	As for Lesson 1
4. Review, teach and apply	Knowledge	As for Lesson 1	**Derive and recall multiplication facts up to 10 × 10, the corresponding division facts and multiples of numbers to 10 up to the tenth multiple.**
5. Review, teach and apply	Knowledge	As for Lesson 1	As for Lesson 4
6. Teach and apply	Knowledge	As for Lesson 1	As for Lesson 4
7. Review and teach	Counting	**Use diagrams to identify equivalent fractions (eg $\frac{6}{8}$ and $\frac{3}{4}$, or $\frac{70}{100}$ and $\frac{7}{10}$); interpret mixed numbers and position them on a number line (eg $3\frac{1}{2}$).**	**Use diagrams to identify equivalent fractions (eg $\frac{6}{8}$ and $\frac{3}{4}$, or $\frac{70}{100}$ and $\frac{7}{10}$); interpret mixed numbers and position them on a number line (eg $3\frac{1}{2}$).**
8. Review, teach and practise	Counting Knowledge	Identify pairs of fractions that total 1.	**• Use diagrams to identify equivalent fractions (eg $\frac{6}{8}$ and $\frac{3}{4}$, or $\frac{70}{100}$ and $\frac{7}{10}$); interpret mixed numbers and position them on a number line (eg $3\frac{1}{2}$).** • Identify pairs of fractions that total 1.
9. Review, teach and apply	Calculate	As for Lesson 7	Find fractions of numbers, quantities or shapes (eg $\frac{1}{5}$ of 30 plums, $\frac{3}{8}$ of a 6 by 4 rectangle).
10. Review and apply	Calculate	Recognise the equivalence between decimal and fraction forms of one half, quarters, tenths and hundredths.	As for Lesson 9
11. Review, practise and apply	Calculate	As for Lesson 10	As for Lesson 9
12. Review and apply	Calculate	As for Lesson 7	As for Lesson 9
13. Teach and practise	Counting	Find fractions of numbers, quantities or shapes (eg $\frac{1}{5}$ of 30 plums, $\frac{3}{8}$ of a 6 by 4 rectangle).	Recognise the equivalence between decimal and fraction forms of one half, quarters, tenths and hundredths.
14. Teach and practise	Knowledge	As for Lesson 7	Identify pairs of fractions that total 1.
15. Apply and review	Calculate Use/apply Knowledge	Recognise the equivalence between decimal and fraction forms of one half, quarters, tenths and hundredths.	• Find fractions of numbers, quantities or shapes (eg $\frac{1}{5}$ of 30 plums, $\frac{3}{8}$ of a 6 by 4 rectangle). • Identify pairs of fractions that total 1. • Represent a puzzle or problem using number sentences, statements or diagrams; use these to solve the problem; present and interpret the solution in the context of the problem.

Speaking and listening objective

- Use and reflect on some ground rules for dialogue.

Introduction

In this three-week unit children develop their skills to solve one- and two-step word problems involving numbers, money, measures. They represent problems and interpret solutions, using a calculator when appropriate. Children continue to develop their tables to 10 × 10, investigating multiples. For the second two weeks children investigate the equivalence of fractions, mixed numbers, fractions of shapes and quantities.

Using and applying mathematics

- Represent a puzzle or problem using number sentences, statements or diagrams; use these to solve the problem; present and interpret the solution in the context of the problem.

Lessons 1-6

Preparation

Lesson 4: Prepare the 'Money cards' and place them around the room, along with the appropriate amounts in real or plastic money.
Lessons 5 and 6: Copies of '100 square' general resource sheet on OHT for display.

You will need

Photocopiable pages
'Mrs Shopper's shopping problem' (page 203), 'How many different ways?' (page 204) and 'Money cards' (page 205).
CD resources
'Money statements', 'Sorting out the multiples' and 'Sorting out the multiples charts'; core, support, extension and template versions of 'Mrs Shopper's shopping problem' and 'How many different ways?'. General resource sheets: 'Clock face' and '100 square'. Interactive resource: 'Number sentence builder'.
Equipment
Calculators; number fans; £5 note and various coins; real or plastic money; coloured pencils; OHP pens.

Learning objectives

Starter

- Derive and recall multiplication facts up to 10 × 10, the corresponding division facts and multiples of numbers to 10 up to the tenth multiple.

Main teaching activities

2006

- Represent a puzzle or problem using number sentences, statements or diagrams; use these to solve the problem; present and interpret the solution in the context of the problem.
- Choose and carry out appropriate calculations, using calculator methods where appropriate.
- Derive and recall multiplication facts up to 10 × 10, the corresponding division facts and multiples of numbers to 10 up to the tenth multiple.

1999

- Use all four operations to solve word problems involving numbers in 'real' life, money and measures (including time), using one or more steps, including converting pounds to pence and metres to centimetres and vice versa.
- Choose and use appropriate number operations and appropriate ways of calculating (mental, mental with jottings, pencil and paper) to solve problems.
- Round up or down after division, depending on context.
- Choose appropriate ways of calculating: calculator.
- Know by heart all multiplication facts up to 10 × 10; derive quickly corresponding division facts.
- Recognise multiples of 6, 7, 8, 9, up to the tenth multiple.
- Recognise multiples of 2, 3, 4, 5 and 10, up to the tenth multiple.

Vocabulary

problem, solution, calculator, calculate, calculation, equation, operation, symbol, inverse, answer, method, explain, predict, reason, reasoning, pattern, relationship, add, subtract, multiply, multiplied by, divide, divided by, sum, total, difference, plus, minus, product, quotient, remainder, multiple, factor, divisor, divisible by

Lesson 1 (Teach and apply)

Starter

Rehearse and refine: Write on the board ○ × □ = 36 and ask: *What could the missing numbers be?* Ask the children to respond on their whiteboards with alternative answers. (4 and 9, 6 and 6, 2 and 18, 3 and 12 or 1 and 36.) Repeat with other examples. You may wish to use 'Number sentence builder' interactive resource for this activity.

Main teaching activities

Whole class: Tell the children that they will be looking at problems involving time. Go through the problem on the 'Getting ready for school' sheet. Now write on the board two times: 4:05 and 5:45. Ask: *How can you work out how long it is from 4:05pm to 5:45pm? Would a diagram help us?* Draw arrows and discuss each step. Suggest that the children work up to the hour and then past, as shown.

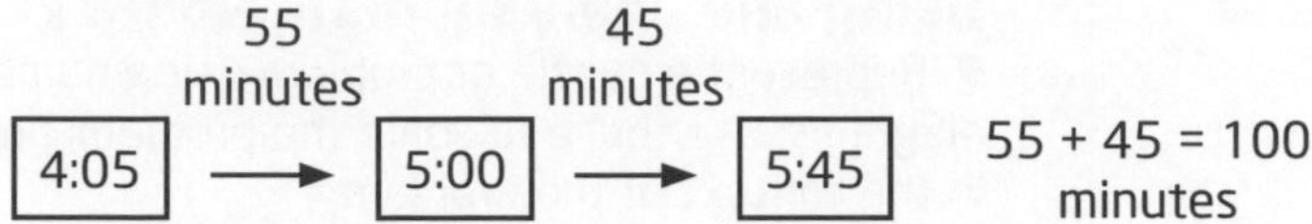

Ask: *How could you check this? How many hours and minutes is this?* (1 hour and 40 minutes.) *What else might we write to help us?* Discuss the children's ideas.

Paired work: Give each pair of children some paper and a set of 'Time after time' cards from the activity sheet. Ask them to shuffle the cards and then the first player takes two cards. Suggest that they put the earlier time on the left-hand side of the paper and the later time on the right-hand side of the paper, in a line. They need to write any workings on the paper, to work out the interval between the two times on the cards. The second player watches and must be convinced of the method. When they have agreed on the time interval, they replace the cards, shuffle them and the second player has a turn. When the activity is completed, ask the children to make up a problem involving two of the times.

Differentiation

Less confident learners: Let these children start with only the cards showing times from 1am to 2am and work in hour, quarter, half and three-quarter hour steps.
More confident learners: Include the cards on the activity sheet that are labelled 'Extension set', which give some later times.

Review

Discuss the children's work on time. Pick two cards and copy the times on the board. Ask: *How could you work out the time between these two times?* Ask individual children to demonstrate their methods, using arrows. Ask: *How could you check the answer is correct?* Check on a clock face (using the 'Clock face' general resource sheet) or by working backwards.

Lesson 2 (Review and apply)

Starter

Rehearse: Count together from zero in sevens up to 70 and then back to zero. Ask some quick-fire questions from the seven-times table to individuals and ask: *How could you help someone who had forgotten that number fact to work out the answer?* Discuss.

Main teaching activities

Whole class: Remind the class how they used key words from the vocabulary list in problems to identify which operation they needed to answer the question.

Provide a problem based on those in 'Mrs Shopper's shopping problem' sheet such as: *Mrs Shopper buys three packets of biscuits. Each packet weighs 300 grams and costs 35 pence. What is the total weight of Mrs Shopper's biscuits? How much did the biscuits cost altogether?*

Ask the children to discuss in their groups which operation(s) are needed to answer the questions and to consider appropriate ways to work out the answers. Encourage them to think of ways of representing the problem that may help them (for example, a diagram or number sentence).

Group work: Split the children into groups of three or four. Each group will need a piece of paper and a pencil, and a set of clue cards from the activity sheet 'Mrs Shopper's shopping problem'. When the children are given the clue cards they should shuffle them and deal them equally among the group, but they must not look at them. Explain that once the children have their own sets of cards they can look at them but they cannot show them to anyone else in the group.

Write these two questions on the board:

- *How much does the shopping in Mrs Shopper's basket cost?*
- *How much does the shopping in Mrs Shopper's basket weigh?*

Suggest that the children might find it useful to organise the information in some way (for example, a table) to help them answer the questions.

Now explain that they can talk about the information on the cards with the other members of their group but they must not show the others their cards or they will be out of the game. The winning group is the group that answers the two questions correctly first. If appropriate, the children may use calculators to check their calculations.

Review

Discuss the methods of solving 'Mrs Shopper's shopping problem'. Identify whether the children used a table or some other method of organising the data, such as a list. Ask: *What operations did you use when calculating the answers? Which calculations did you need to write down? What else did you find helpful to write down/draw? What is 4040 grams in kilograms?*

Finish the lesson with one or two multiplication and division 'shopping problems'. Children should write the answers on their whiteboards: Ask: *How much would two dozen eggs weigh? How did you work this out? Did anyone work it out a different way?* Resolve any outstanding queries that were raised earlier.

Differentiation

Less confident learners: Use the support version of the sheet, which has a table on it. If necessary this group could lay their cards down and look at them together.

More confident learners: Use the extension version of the sheet, which has a few 'red herrings' included in the clues.

Lesson 3 (Review, teach and apply)

Starter

Rehearse: Repeat the Starter from Lesson 2, this time using the six-times table. Ask: *How could knowing your three-times table help you?*

Main teaching activities

Whole class: Explain to the children that today they will be thinking about different ways to solve problems. Ask the children to think back to Mrs Shopper's eggs. Ask: *What does one dozen mean?* (12) Now write on the board 'Three eggs cost 15 pence.' Ask: *How much does a dozen eggs cost?* (60 pence.) Ask: *How did you work that out?* (Find that one egg costs 5 pence then multiply 5 by 12, or multiply 15 by 4 to give the cost of 12 eggs.) Draw diagrams to illustrate this, but emphasise that the children should feel free to use their own methods. Explain that there is often more than one way to work out the answer to a question.

Write on the board: *Mrs Shopper has 1kg of sugar. She wants to bake some cakes. Each cake requires 150g of sugar. How many cakes can she bake? How much sugar would be left over?* Say: *Think of two ways to work out the answer to this question.* Provide the children with paper if necessary. (Estimate through knowledge of multiples of 10 and 100; use jottings to divide by 100, then divide by multiples of 10.) Draw a diagram to illustrate this but, again, emphasise that the children should feel free to use their own methods.

Independent work: Distribute the activity sheet 'How many different ways?', which gives several number problems. Ask the children to think of different ways to solve the problems. If they choose to work out the problem mentally, ask them to write down what they did to answer the question. For example, for Question 1, mentally they could double 25 four times to give 25 × 8 or they could multiply by 10 and then subtract 50 grams (2 × 25 grams).

Review

Discuss each question and ask the children to explain their methods (mental, mental with jottings, or written methods). Ask: *Who did it a different way? Did anyone draw a diagram to help them? Did you rewrite the question? How?*

Model a selection of answers. Finish by asking individual children to challenge the class with their own number problems that might be answered

Differentiation

Less confident learners: These children should concentrate on answering all six questions before coming back to think of other ways to solve them. Provide the support version of the sheet in which the number operations are more obvious.

More confident learners: Use the extension version of the activity sheet, which has questions involving more difficult numbers.

in different ways. Make sure each child knows the answer and at least one method of solving it before asking the rest of the class.

Lesson 4 (Review, teach and apply)

Starter

Reason: Say: *I am thinking of a number that is a multiple of 7 and also a multiple of 8. Can you tell me which number I am thinking of?* Children show you the number on number fans or whiteboards. Repeat with other examples such as: multiple of 5 and 7, multiple of 7 and 2. Focus on the seven-times table. Ask: *Are there any facts from the seven-times table that you find difficult to remember? What are they? Think of some ways to help us remember them.*

Main teaching activities

Whole class: Remind the children that dividing by 2 is halving and dividing by 4 is halving and halving again. Dividing by 5 is the same as dividing by 10 and doubling. Discuss how, for example, dividing by 6 could be halving and then dividing by 3, or dividing by 8 can be halving, halving and then halving again.

Use the 'Number sentence builder' interactive resource to illustrate several examples. Input 12 ÷ 3 = □ and ask: *What is the answer?* (4) Input 15 ÷ 3 = □ and ask: *What is the answer?* (5) Now input 13 ÷ 3 = □ and ask: *If I had 13 sweets and divided them among three people, how many sweets would each person have? Would I have any left over? How many would I have left over?* (1)

Encourage an individual to come up and illustrate this problem with a diagram, explaining their workings. Now show how you could solve this problem by counting up in multiples of 3 (3, 6, 9, 12...) and then finding you had 1 spare. Now, underneath, write 14 ÷ 3 = □ and repeat the previous questions, modified appropriately. (There will be two left over.) Ask: *When we divide by 3 would we ever have 3 or more left over? Why is that?*

Show the children a £5 note and ask: *If I were to share this with... (pick a child's name), how much would we both get?* If appropriate, change the £5 note for four £1 coins and two 50 pence pieces. Establish with the children that the answer is £2.50. Repeat, this time sharing among four people and making the link that the result would be £2.50 divided by 2. Repeat, by sharing among 10 people. (50p)

Group work: Split the class into groups of five or six. Explain that there are five stations around the room and every group will visit each station. At each station, the children divide the amount of money among two, four, five or ten people. Provide the children with the 'Money station' sheets and ask them to record their results in some way. Provide some real coins to help them. Place a card cut from activity sheet 'Money cards', with the corresponding amount of money, on each table.

Differentiation

Less confident learners: Limit these groups to the first two money stations and the first 'Money station' sheet. Give assistance as required, using the plastic money to model the different amounts.

More confident learners: Refer this group to the activity sheet 'Money cards'. Ask: *Which of these amounts can be divided easily by 3? ... by 6? ... by 9?* Challenge these groups to record all the answers as division sentences, such as £25 ÷ 4 = £6.25.

Review

Work through the process of dividing £34.00 among two, four, five or ten people together, then invite each group to discuss their earlier results with the rest of the class. Ask: *How did you work out the pounds and pence? What is another way of working out the amounts? How did you record your results?* Discuss division by other numbers, such as 6 or 8 and strategies for working out answers.

Lesson 5 (Review, teach and apply)

Starter

Reason: Ask questions involving weeks such as:

- *There are exactly 5 weeks until my birthday. How many days is that?*
- *There are exactly 9 weeks until I get a new bike. How many days is that?*
- *There are exactly 9 weeks and 2 days until my Dad's birthday. How many days is that?*
- *There are 49 days until my holiday. How many weeks do I have to wait?*
- *There are 35 days until my holiday. How many weeks do I have to wait?*
- *There are 36 days until my holiday. How many weeks do I have to wait?*

Main teaching activities

Whole class: Display the '100 square' general resource sheet. Together, partially colour in the multiples of 2. Then, using different colours, partially colour in the multiples of 5 and then the multiples of 7. Ask: *What is the link between the multiples of 2, 5 and 7?* Decide that a multiple of 7 is the sum of a multiple of 2 and a multiple of 5.

Independent work: Provide the children with the resource sheet '100 square' and ask them to investigate if there is a link between multiples of 3, multiples of 4 and multiples of 7.

Whole class: Ask: *If we had forgotten the number fact 8 × 7, how could this knowledge help us?* Discuss: (5 × 8 = 40 and 2 × 8 = 16, so 40 + 16 = 56, 8 × 7 = 56 or 3 × 8 = 24 and 4 × 8 = 32, so 24 + 32 = 56).

Independent work: Challenge the children to complete the statements on the 'Multiple statements' activity sheet. The sheet includes a blank 100 square, but additional copies of the '100 square' general resource sheet may be needed.

Differentiation:

Less confident learners: These children may need extra assistance. Give suggestions as a start for the final statement and be sure to question the children, using numerical examples to be sure that children realise the link between the statements and a practical use.

More confident learners: These children should be encouraged to come up with as many examples as possible for the final statement.

Review

Take some suggestions of statements from individuals and say: *Give me an example using numbers to show how this works. Explain how this works to the rest of the class using a diagram. You know that 2 + 6 = 8; how can I work out 9 × 8 using this number fact?*

Lesson 6 (Teach and apply)

Starter

Recall: Ask quick-fire questions from the times tables up to 10 × 10, asking: *How did you work that out? Did you know the number fact or did you use something else to help you? Explain this to the rest of the class. Now try to use their method.*

Main teaching activities

Whole class: Display the '100 square' general resource sheet and count together in multiples of 4, using the grid. Now repeat, counting in multiples of 6. Now say: *I sort my books into piles. If I sort them into multiples of 4, I have 1 left over and if I sort them into multiples of 6 I have 1 left over. How many books do I have? How can I use this grid to help me?* Suggest shading in all of the multiples of 4 + 1 in one colour and all of the multiples of 6 + 1 in another. Compare the numbers that are shaded in both colours. Ask: *What else could I have shown/drawn to help me?* Discuss drawing a chart with two columns, one with the multiples of 4 + 1 and one with the multiples of 6 + 1, then comparing the columns.

Group work: Provide the children with 'Sorting out the multiples', a blank '100 square' and squared paper if they wish to draw a chart. Together ask them to solve the two problems.

Differentiation

Less confident learners: Encourage these children to use 'Sorting the multiples charts' sheet. Completing the two tables should help them compare the numbers to work out an answer.

More confident learners: These children could extend this by

Review

Work through ideas and suggestions from the two questions, illustrating answers and workings on the interactive whiteboard or on the OHP, using

working out some similar questions to ask a partner.

the '100 square' or charts from the 'Sorting out the multiples chart' sheet. Ask: *When you worked out an answer, did anyone go back and read the question to be sure that it made sense?* Discuss.

Lessons 7-15

Preparation

Lesson 7: Prepare an OHT of the 'Equivalent fractions' resource sheet.
Lesson 8: Prepare an OHT with several empty 3 × 4 grids for the whole class activity.
Lesson 12: If necessary, prepare an OHT of squared paper.

You will need

CD resources
'Equivalent fractions', 'Fraction hunt board' and 'Hundredths'; core, support and extension versions of 'Equivalent fraction teams', 'Fraction shapes', 'Fraction cards activities' and 'Fractions to go'; core, support, extension and template versions of 'Fractions of measures 2' and 'Fraction problems'; core and extension versions of 'Are these more than a whole? 1, 2 and 3'.
General resource sheets: 'Equivalent fraction grids' and 'Blank number lines'.
Interactive resource: 'Squares – patterns, reflection and rotation'.
Equipment
Interlocking cubes; a litre bottle of water; a cylinder or jug to measure 1000ml; four glasses; metre ruler; plastic money; clock face; coloured pencils; squared paper; fractions wall (ideally on the interactive whiteboard).

Learning objectives

Starter

- Use diagrams to identify equivalent fractions (eg $\frac{6}{8}$ and $\frac{3}{4}$, or $\frac{70}{100}$ and $\frac{7}{10}$); interpret mixed numbers and position them on a number line (eg $3\frac{1}{2}$).
- Identify pairs of fractions that total 1.
- Find fractions of numbers, quantities or shapes (eg $\frac{1}{5}$ of 30 plums, $\frac{3}{8}$ of a 6 by 4 rectangle).
- Recognise the equivalence between decimal and fraction forms of one half, quarters, tenths and hundredths.

Main teaching activities

2006

- Use diagrams to identify equivalent fractions (eg $\frac{6}{8}$ and $\frac{3}{4}$, or $\frac{70}{100}$ and $\frac{7}{10}$); interpret mixed numbers and position them on a number line (eg $3\frac{1}{2}$).
- Identify pairs of fractions that total 1.
- Find fractions of numbers, quantities or shapes (eg $\frac{1}{5}$ of 30 plums, $\frac{3}{8}$ of a 6 by 4 rectangle).
- Recognise the equivalence between decimal and fraction forms of one half, quarters, tenths and hundredths.
- Represent a puzzle or problem using number sentences, statements or diagrams; use these to solve the problem; present and interpret the solution in the context of the problem.

1999

- Begin to relate fractions to division and find simple fractions such as $\frac{1}{2}$, $\frac{1}{3}$, $\frac{1}{4}$, $\frac{1}{5}$, $\frac{1}{10}$... of numbers.
- Find fractions such as $\frac{2}{3}$ $\frac{3}{4}$, $\frac{3}{5}$, $\frac{7}{10}$... of shapes.
- Recognise the equivalence of simple fractions.
- Order a set of fractions such as 2, $2\frac{3}{4}$, $1\frac{3}{4}$, $2\frac{1}{2}$, $1\frac{1}{2}$, and position them on a number line.
- Recognise the equivalence between the decimal and fraction forms of tenths and hundredths (eg $\frac{7}{10} = 0.7$, $\frac{27}{100} = 0.27$).
- Identify two simple fractions with a total of 1 (eg $\frac{3}{10}$ and $\frac{7}{10}$).
- Use all four operations to solve word problems involving numbers in 'real' life, money and measures (including time), using one or more steps, including converting pounds to pence and metres to centimetres and vice versa.
- Choose and use appropriate number operations and appropriate ways of calculating (mental, mental with jottings, pencil and paper) to solve problems.
- Round up or down after division, depending on context.
- Choose appropriate ways of calculating: calculator.

Vocabulary

problem, solution, method, explain, predict, reason, reasoning, pattern, relationship, add, subtract, multiply, multiplied by, divide, divided by, sum, total, difference, plus, minus, product, quotient, remainder, multiple, factor, divisor, divisible by, fraction, unit fraction, mixed number, numerator, denominator, equivalent

Lesson 7 (Review and teach)

Starter

Revisit and refine: Call out a fraction and say that if it is equivalent to a half then the children are to sit on their chairs; if it is less than a half they are to touch the floor; if it is greater than a half they are to stand up. Use several examples: $^1/_3$, $^1/_4$, $^5/_6$, $^1/_8$, $^7/_8$, $^5/_5$, $^7/_7$, $^1/_{10}$, $^3/_{10}$, $^9/_{10}$.

Main teaching activities

Whole class: Draw six dots on the board and cover up three of them. Ask: *What fraction can you see?* ($^3/_6$ or $^1/_2$) Explain that $^3/_6$ and $^1/_2$ are equivalent fractions and demonstrate this on the board, as shown here:

Emphasise the fact that the same is happening to the top and the bottom. Say: *Give me a fraction that is the same as one half?* Discuss the children's responses. Draw a 0-1 number line on the board and ask the children to suggest some fractions. Ask each child to write her/his fraction on the number line and where possible to suggest an equivalent fraction to write above it. Focus in particular on halves, quarters and eighths and write any equivalences on the board.

Group work: Split the class into groups of three or four and assign to each group a fraction (for example, $^1/_2$, $^1/_4$, $^3/_4$, $^1/_5$, $^1/_3$, $^2/_3$). Explain that the children have five minutes to work together and to write down as many fractions that are equivalent to their fraction as they can. Compare and discuss the equivalent fractions from each group.

Individual work: Give each child a copy of the 'Equivalent fraction teams' activity sheet and ask them to colour code the 'fraction teams' into wholes, halves or quarters.

Differentiation

Less confident learners: Group these children together and set them to find fractions equivalent to $^1/_2$ in the group activity. They can keep their lists to use with the individual activity. Use the support version of the activity sheet 'Equivalent fraction teams', which includes wholes and halves only.

More confident learners: Group these children together and set them to find fractions equivalent to $^3/_4$ or $^2/_3$ in the group activity. Use the extension version of the activity sheet, which includes thirds and three-quarters. These children could find 'substitutes' for each team with more equivalent fractions.

Review

Display the activity sheet 'Equivalent fractions' on an OHP or interactive whiteboard. Discuss it with the children and fill in the blanks together. Ask questions such as:

- *What is happening to the bottom number (denominator) in the fraction?*
- *What could you do to the top number (numerator) in the fraction to make the fractions equivalent?*
- *Why do you need to multiply the numerator and denominator by the same amount?*
- *What would happen if you didn't?*
- *Can you think of another equivalent fraction for $^1/_4$? ... $^1/_2$? ... $^1/_3$? ... $^2/_3$? ... $^1/_5$? ... $^3/_4$?*

Lesson 8 (Review, teach and practise)

Starter

Reason: Draw five dots on the board. Cover up some of the dots and say the fraction you have covered. Ask the children to say the fraction that is left, for example, $^4/_5$ and $^1/_5$. Repeat with six dots and eight dots. Ask: *What is $^7/_8$ + $^1/_8$?* (1 whole.) Now explain that you will say a fraction and ask the children to say the other part of the fraction pair that makes one whole; for example, $^5/_6$ ($^1/_6$) and $^3/_4$ ($^1/_4$). Repeat with several more examples.

Main teaching activities

Whole class: Remind the children of the work they did in Leson 7 on equivalent fractions. Draw a 3 × 4 rectangle divided into 12 squares. Invite the children to colour in a number of squares on the rectangle. Each time, ask them to work out the fraction, such as $^5/_{12}$ in red and $^7/_{12}$ in blue. Write the fractions next to the grid. Point out that these two fractions make one whole. Repeat with other fractions, then ask individual children to order the fractions on a number line.

Paired work: Give each pair a copy of the activity sheet 'Fraction shapes'. Ask the pairs to colour a fraction of each shape, write this fraction underneath each shape and then decide whether it is less than (<) or greater than (>) one half. Give them a filled-in copy of the 'Blank number lines' general resource sheet to help them with this task.

Differentiation

Less confident learners: Support the children with the ordering activity. If necessary, give each pair the support version of the 'Fraction shapes' sheet that includes simpler shapes.

More confident learners: After completing the core sheet, give them the extension version of the sheet that includes more complex shapes. They should then record these additional shapes on their 'ordering grid'.

Review

Share some of the children's work. Ask questions such as: *You have coloured in $^3/_8$. What fraction of the shape is left?* Repeat for other fractions. Ask: *How do you know $^3/_8$ < $^1/_2$?* Again, repeat for other examples. Write 1½ on the board. Draw one and a half squares on the board. Ask: *What would 1¾ circles look like? What will $3^1/_3$ rectangles look like?* Draw a 0–3 number line on the board and ask individual children to place mixed numbers on the line, explaining their reasoning (eg 1¾, $1^3/_8$, 2½ , $2^3/_5$, and so on).

Lesson 9 (Review, teach and apply)

Starter

Read: Give each child a grid from the general resource sheet 'Equivalent fraction grids'. Call out fractions from each grid and let the children cross off the equivalent fractions on their grids as they hear the fraction being called. Ask them to stand up if they get a line or when they get 'full house'.

Main teaching activities

Whole class: Review the work from Lesson 8. Ask the children to draw some diagrams to show 1¾, 2½ and 3¼. Ask questions such as: *Does your diagram show parts of the whole?* Ask the children to hold up their diagrams and discuss any misunderstandings.

Give each child or group 12 interlocking cubes. Ask them each to make the cubes into a tower and then to break their tower in half. Ask: *How many cubes are there in each half?* Write on the board 12 □ □ = 6. Ask: *What operation and number could you put in these boxes?* (÷, 2) Establish that '× $^1/_2$' is the same as 'divide by 2'.

Repeat, dividing the cubes by 3, 4 and 6, each time making the link between the fraction and division.

Show the children a litre jug/bottle filled with water and ask: *If I divided this equally into four glasses, how much liquid would there be in each of them?* (¼ litre or 250ml, 1000 ÷ 4.) Repeat, dividing by 2 and then 10.

Independent work: Give the children activity sheet 'Fractions of measures 2' on which they are asked to find fractions of various quantities. As the children complete the sheets make sure that they link their calculations of fractions to the relevant division sentences.

Differentiation

Less confident learners: Use the support version of the activity sheet, which asks children only to find half, quarter or one-fifth of amounts. Ask them to give answers in only one unit of measurement and to focus on finding half of each of the eight measures and then quarter and finally, if time allows, one-fifth. Provide these children with a litre bottle, a metre ruler, some plastic money and a clock face.

More confident learners: Use the extension version of the activity sheet, which asks children to find more complex fractions. Challenge these children to find these fractions and to write them using as many different units of measurement as possible. Most can be written in three ways, eg half of 3 litres = 1½ litres, 1500ml or 1 litre and 500ml.

Review

Discuss the findings and different methods of recording using various units of measurement. Ask individual children for ideas and to describe their findings. Invite individuals to share one of their results and to explain how they worked out the quantity. Each time ask: *Why did you choose to use that unit? Can you write the answer another way?* Check the children's understanding by asking some quick-fire fractions questions: *What is ¼ of 16 cubes? What is ½ of 3 metres? What is* $^1/_{10}$ *of 500 grams?* Ask the children to show their answers on their whiteboards.

Lesson 10 (Review and apply)

Starter

Revisit: Write on the board '$^1/_2$' and ask: *What decimal is equivalent to one half?* (0.5) Link 0.5 to other quantities: 50p in £1 (£0.50), half of 1m is 50cm (0.5m), half of a litre is 500ml (0.5l). Repeat and discuss for other fractions: 0.25 = $^1/_4$, 0.75 = $^3/_4$ and 0.1 = $^1/_{10}$. Call out a decimal fraction and ask the children to show the equivalent fraction on their whiteboards. Repeat, this time calling out the fraction and asking children to show the decimal fraction.

Main teaching activities

Whole class: Review simple fractions of quantities. Ask: *What is* $^1/_3$ *of 30 cubes?* (10 cubes.) Discuss sharing: *If we have half each we divide by two, if there are three of us we divide by 3.* Write:

$^1/_2$ → divide by 2 $^1/_3$ → divide by 3 $^1/_4$ → divide by 4

Review some examples from Lesson 9 or ask:

- *What is* $^1/_4$ *of £1.00?* (25p)
- *What is* $^1/_3$ *of 45?* (15)

Extend to $^2/_3$ (×2 then ÷3) or (÷3 then ×2), $^3/_5$ and so on.

Group work: Explain that the children will play a game of 'Fraction hunt'. Give each group (of four to six children) a copy of the 'Fraction hunt board' and two to three sets of 'Fraction cards activities', which should be shuffled and placed in a pile. The children take turns to take one card from the 'Fractions cards activities' pile. If they are able to complete a calculation by using the fraction card and a number from the 'Fraction hunt board' they score a point and the number is crossed off the board. For example, they may pick $^1/_2$ and 100 from the board (50). If they cannot make a fraction, the player should shout 'Pass' and play moves on. All players should record and check each calculation.

Differentiation

Less confident learners: Organise the game in mixed ability groups. Alternatively, provide this group with the support version of the cards, which does not include any fractions that are several parts of one whole.

More confident learners: Provide this group with the extension version set of cards, which includes a greater range of fractions.

Review

Discuss the outcomes of the game. Go through a couple of examples with the children. For example: $^1/_4$ of 40 is 10 because 40 ÷ 4 = 10; $^2/_5$ of 60 is 24 because 60 ÷ 5 = 12 and then 2 × 12 = 24, and so on. Share any interesting or difficult questions and discuss solutions.

Lesson 11 (Review, practise and apply)

Starter

Revisit: Repeat the Starter from Lesson 7, this time calling out decimals and asking: *Is it less than one half, greater than one half or equal to one half?*

Main teaching activities

Whole class: Review the work from Lesson 10. Write on the board:

$^1/_2$ → divide by 2 $^1/_3$ → divide by 3 $^1/_4$ → divide by 4

Set the class some fractions problems similar to those in the previous lesson. For example: *What is* $^1/_4$ *of 80? What is* $^1/_5$ *of 100 cm? What is* $^3/_4$ *of*

£5.00? Work through each problem and establish the relationship between fractions and division.

Give the whole class a multi-step fractions problem: *Hannah has 64 sweets, but gives $^3/_4$ of them to her friends. How many does she have left?* Give the class time to solve the problem and go through the solution with them as follows:

$^1/_4$ of 64 sweets = 16 sweets or
$^3/_4$ of 64 sweets = 3 × 16 = 48 sweets
64 - 48 = 16 sweets left.

Hannah has $^1/_4$ of the sweets left. Hannah has 16 sweets left. Go through the children's own methods for solving the problem and establish that they can use their knowledge of adding pairs of fractions to make one.

Paired work: Give each pair a copy of 'Fraction problems' and ask them to work out solutions by using the link between fractions and division. The pairs must also provide statements for each solution like the example above.

Differentiation
Less confident learners: Provide the support version of 'Fraction problems', which includes the worked example. The sheet also includes some single-step problems. Ask another adult to support the children with these problems - for example, by drawing diagrams to support their understanding of the problem.
More confident learners: Provide the extension version of the sheet, which has a greater range of fractions.

Review
Discuss and review the problems from the sheet. Ask the children to describe the methods they used. Establish that they understand the link with division and that they can use their knowledge of adding pairs of fractions to make 1. Write another example on the board such as the following: *A clothes shop offers two suits. The first suit costs £160 but is reduced in the sale by $^3/_8$. The second suit costs £150, but is reduced by $^2/_5$. Which is the cheapest suit? Why?* (Suit 1 now costs £100; Suit 2 costs £90. Suit 2 is cheaper.) Work through the example step by step and address any misunderstandings with the children.

Lesson 12 (Review and apply)

Starter
Reason: Tell the children that you are thinking of a number ($4^1/_3$) and it involves a fraction. Display a number line on the board, from say 4 to 5. Invite them to ask you questions about the number, explaining that you will only answer yes or no. Write on the board some vocabulary ideas to help.

- *Is it greater than/less than...?*
- *Is the denominator/numerator...?*
- *Is it a mixed number?*
- *Is it equivalent to...?*

Explain to the children that their aim is to ask as few questions as possible so it is better not just to guess the number straightaway but to limit the possibilities. As they are guessing, place guesses onto the number line. Repeat with another example or ask a child to think of a number and you can join with the rest of the class in trying to guess.

Main teaching activities
Whole class: Explain that in today's lesson the children will be continuing to look at finding fractions of numbers and shapes. Ask: *Is it easier to find one third of 12 or one third of 13? Why?* Discuss multiples of 3. *Is it easier to find one fifth of 35 or one fifth of 36? Why?* Discuss multiples of 5.

Paired work: Ask pairs to think about the questions: *What numbers are easy to find one tenth of? Why?* Repeat for one third, one quarter, one fifth. If possible they should use the 'Squares - patterns, reflection and rotation' interactive resource to draw shapes. (Alternatively, provide pairs with squared paper.)

Differentiation
Less confident learners: Limit this group to thinking about shapes that could easily be split into quarters.
More confident learners: This group could be challenged to think about which amounts of money are easily split into these fractions.

Review
Discuss findings as a group and summarise. Ask: *How did you work that out? Explain that to the rest of the group. What words were useful for this explanation?* Use the 'Squares - patterns, reflection and rotation' interactive resource to illustrate these shapes.

Lesson 13 (Teach and practise)

Starter

Reason: Ask several questions such as: *If you would rather have $^1/_5$ of 30 sweets put one hand up, or if you would prefer $^3/_4$ of 12 sweets, put two hands up. Why? Would you rather have $^1/_3$ of £15 or ¼ of £20? Why?*

Main teaching activities

Whole class: Display a number line from 0 to 3, split into tenths, ideally using an interactive whiteboard.

Together, count in fractions along the number line, first in halves: $^1/_2$, $^2/_2$ (= 1 whole), $^3/_2$ (= 1½), $^4/_2$ (= 2), $^5/_2$ (= 2½) and $^6/_2$ (= 3). Then count in fifths. When you reach equivalent fractions, discuss. Next count in tenths $^1/_{10}$, $^2/_{10}$, $^3/_{10}$, $^4/_{10}$... When you reach equivalent fractions, discuss these (ie $^2/_{10}$ = $^1/_5$, $^4/_{10}$ = $^2/_5$, $^5/_{10}$ = $^1/_2$, $^6/_{10}$ = $^3/_5$, $^8/_{10}$ = $^4/_5$ and $^{10}/_{10}$ = 1). Extend this by counting beyond 1 from ten tenths to twenty tenths, realising that twenty tenths is equivalent to 2. Repeat, this time using decimals, in halves: 0.5, 1, 1.5, 2, 2.5, 3, then in tenths: 0.1, 0.2, 0.3....

Paired work: Challenge pairs to write down the sequence of numbers, counting from 0 to 3 using decimals in steps of one fifth (0.2). Make the link that $^1/_5$ of £1 is 20p or £0.20. Discuss.

Whole class: Display a number line from 0 to 1, split into hundredths. Give each child a copy of the activity sheet 'Hundredths' to use. Together, discuss how this is part of the same line but it is split up further, a bit like how pounds can be split into ten pence pieces or one pence pieces. Ask each child to show you ten hundredths on their number line and ask: *What other decimal is this equivalent to?* (One tenth.) Repeat with $^{20}/_{100}$, $^{30}/_{100}$, $^{40}/_{100}$, and so on. Then ask: *How else could I describe $^{11}/_{100}$?* (One tenth and one hundredth.) Repeat with other examples, each time asking children to show you on their number line. Count up together in jumps of $^{10}/_{100}$ths or $^1/_{10}$ths, encouraging the children to run their finger along the number line as you say the jumps to reinforce the link between tenths and hundredths. Now repeat this by counting up in decimals in jumps of 0.05 ($^5/_{100}$ or $^1/_{20}$), then counting up in jumps of 0.02 ($^2/_{100}$, $^1/_{50}$).

Differentiation

Less confident learners: Ask an adult to sit with the group to support them in using the number line.

More confident learners: Encourage these children to explain what each digit in a decimal fraction (such as 0.06) stands for.

Review

Ask: *How else could I write six tenths and three hundredths? Show me on your number line. What would 0.04 + 0.1 = ? What would I have to add to 0.03 to make 0.43?* Discuss the responses and ask the children to explain their understanding to the rest of the class.

Lesson 14 (Teach and practise)

Starter

Rehearse: Explain that you will call out some sequences of numbers and that you would like the children to join in when they can see what is happening. Use the following examples: ¼, ½, ¾, 1, 1¼... 0.25, 0.5, 0.75, 1, 1.25... 0.2, 0.4, 0.6, 0.8... $^1/_5$, $^2/_5$, $^3/_5$, $^4/_5$, 1... 0.12, 0.22, 0.32, 0.42, 0.52... 0.81, 0.83, 0.85, 0.87... Each time, discuss the pattern.

Main teaching activities

Whole class: Say: *Find a pair of fractions that make less than one whole. How do you know that they are less than a whole?* Illustrate by using a fractions wall, ideally on the interactive whiteboard. Repeat, saying: *Tell me a fraction that is bigger than 1... 2... 3. Find a pair of fractions that make more than one whole. How do you know that they are more than a whole?*

Independent work: The children complete the three sections from the activity sheets 'Are these more than a whole? 1, 2 and 3'. Part 1 asks them to colour in pairs of fractions that total 1. Parts 2 and 3 ask them to find fractions that total more than and less than 1.

Differentiation

Less confident learners: Focus these children on finding fractions that total 1. They should use diagrams and cubes to help gain a better understanding. If necessary, provide adult support.

More confident learners: Provide the extension version of the activity sheet. There are a great number of options here, so you may wish to limit time or ask for, say, ten pairs initially. The sheet also has an extra challenge. Ask the children to give you as many alternatives as they can and to explain their answers.

Review

Discuss and review the children's findings arising from the independent activity. Address any problems or misunderstandings that may have arisen.

Lesson 15 (Apply and review)

Starter

Rehearse: Explain to the children that you will call out a decimal and you would like them to show you the equivalent fraction on their whiteboard. Start with one half, one quarter and three quarters. Then swap, call out fractions and ask them to show you the decimal. Discuss responses.

Main teaching activities

Whole class: Say: *Teri has 560 grams of flour. He uses ¾ of it. How much is left? What calculation would you do to work this out?* Discuss how you just need to work out ¼ of 560, which you could work out by finding 56 divided by 4, then adding a zero.

Repeat, saying: *Teri has 450 miles to travel. He has travelled $^{9}/_{10}$ of it. How much has he left to go? What calculation would you do to work this out?* Discuss how you just need to work out $^{1}/_{10}$ of 450, which you could work out by finding 450 divided by 10.

Independent work: Provide the children with the sheet 'Fractions to go'. Encourage them to think carefully about the method that they are going to use before answering the question, then to check at the end if their answer does answer the question.

Differentiation

Less confident learners: Use the support version of the sheet, which uses slightly simpler number calculations.

More confident learners: Use the extension version of the sheet, which, in some cases, has a further part to the question.

Review

Go through the sheet carefully, asking individuals for answers and workings. Ask: *How did you work that out? What did you write down? Can you explain it to the class? What fraction was left? How did you know that?*

Name ____________________ Date ____________________

Getting ready for school

I got up at 7 o'clock this morning and got dressed, brushed my teeth and had breakfast. I left my house at 7.30am and walked to the bus stop, which took me five minutes. I waited at the bus stop for five minutes and then caught the bus to school, which took me ten minutes. At what time did I get to school?

How long did it take me from when I got up to get to school? ____________

Name ____________________ Date ____________________

Time after time cards

Copy these cards onto stiff paper, cut them out and laminate them.

1.00am	1.05am	1.10am	1.15am
1.20am	1.25 am	1.30am	2.00am
2.05am	2.10am	2.15am	2.20am
2.25am	2.30am		

Extension set

3.30am	3.35am	3.40am	3.50am
3.55am	4.00am		

Name ______________________ Date ______________________

Mrs Shopper's shopping problem

Questions

How much does the shopping in Mrs Shopper's shopping basket cost? __________

How much does the food in the basket weigh? ______________________

Mrs Shopper buys two bags of sugar. 	Sugar weighs 1 kilogram per bag.	She buys a dozen eggs.	Half a dozen eggs weigh 320 grams.
Twelve eggs cost £1.00.	A dozen is 12. 	1 kilogram is 1000 grams.	Sugar costs 55 pence a bag.
She buys a jar of salt. 	Salt costs £1.65 per jar. 	The salt jar weighs 200 grams. 	She buys a loaf of bread.
The bread costs 60 pence.  	The bread weighs 800 grams.	She buys four onions. 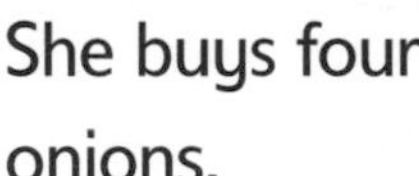	Five onions weigh 50 grams. 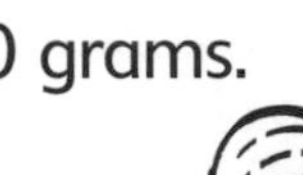
The onions cost 40 pence. 	She buys a packet of biscuits. 	The biscuits cost 90 pence. 	The biscuits weigh 300 grams.

Name ______________________ Date ______________________

How many different ways?

Answer the questions below, in the space provided.

Try to think of as many ways of answering the questions as you can. Write down all of your methods.

1. An apple weighs 25 grams. How much does a bag of eight apples weigh?	**2.** A computer disk costs £1.20. How much would 11 cost?
3. I have one metre of fabric. Each scarf needs 20 centimetres of fabric. How many scarves can I make?	**4.** I have 1kg of sugar. I need 450 grams to make a cake. How much sugar will I have left?
5. I spend 12 minutes speaking to my friend on the telephone. The telephone company charges 5 pence a minute for calls. How much does my conversation cost?	**6.** It costs £2.50 for one child to go on the school trip. How much would it cost for four children?

Name ______________________ Date ______________________

Money cards

£10.00

£12.00

£16.00

£25.00

£34.00

Securing number facts, relationships and calculating

Lesson	Strands	Starter	Main teaching activities
1. Apply	Use/apply	**Derive and recall multiplication facts up to 10 × 10, the corresponding division facts and multiples of numbers to 10 up to the tenth multiple.**	Represent a puzzle or problem using number sentences, statements or diagrams; use these to solve the problem; present and interpret the solution in the context of the problem.
2. Review and practise	Knowledge Use/apply	As for Lesson 1	• **Derive and recall multiplication facts up to 10 × 10, the corresponding division facts and multiples of numbers to 10 up to the tenth multiple.** • Represent a puzzle or problem using number sentences, statements or diagrams; use these to solve the problem; present and interpret the solution in the context of the problem.
3. Teach and practise	Calculate	As for Lesson 1	**Develop and use written methods to record, support and explain multiplication and division of two-digit numbers by a one-digit number, including division with remainders (eg 15 × 9, 98 ÷ 6).**
4. Teach and practise	Calculate	As for Lesson 1	As for Lesson 3
5. Review and practise	Calculate	As for Lesson 1	As for Lesson 3
6. Review and practise	Calculate	As for Lesson 1	As for Lesson 3
7. Review	Calculate	As for Lesson 1	As for Lesson 3
8. Practise	Counting Calculate	**Use diagrams to identify equivalent fractions (eg $\frac{6}{8}$ and $\frac{3}{4}$, or $\frac{70}{100}$ and $\frac{7}{10}$); interpret mixed numbers and position them on a number line (eg $3\frac{1}{2}$).**	• **Use diagrams to identify equivalent fractions (eg $\frac{6}{8}$ and $\frac{3}{4}$, or $\frac{70}{100}$ and $\frac{7}{10}$); interpret mixed numbers and position them on a number line (eg $3\frac{1}{2}$).** • Recognise the equivalence between decimal and fraction forms of one half, quarters, tenths and hundredths. • Find fractions of numbers, quantities or shapes (eg $\frac{1}{5}$ of 30 plums, $\frac{3}{8}$ of a 6 by 4 rectangle).
9. Teach and practise	Counting Calculate	As for Lesson 8	As for Lesson 8
10. Teach and practise	Counting Calculate	• **Use diagrams to identify equivalent fractions (eg $\frac{6}{8}$ and $\frac{3}{4}$, or $\frac{70}{100}$ and $\frac{7}{10}$); interpret mixed numbers and position them on a number line (eg $3\frac{1}{2}$).** • Find fractions of numbers, quantities or shapes (eg $\frac{1}{5}$ of 30 plums, $\frac{3}{8}$ of a 6 by 4 rectangle).	As for Lesson 8
11. Apply	Counting Calculate	**Use diagrams to identify equivalent fractions (eg $\frac{6}{8}$ and $\frac{3}{4}$, or $\frac{70}{100}$ and $\frac{7}{10}$); interpret mixed numbers and position them on a number line (eg $3\frac{1}{2}$).**	As for Lesson 8
12. Practise	Counting Calculate	As for Lesson 11	As for Lesson 8
13. Teach, practise and apply	Counting	Find fractions of numbers, quantities or shapes (eg $\frac{1}{5}$ of 30 plums, $\frac{3}{8}$ of a 6 by 4 rectangle).	Use the vocabulary of ratio and proportion to describe the relationship between two quantities (eg 'There are 2 red beads to every 3 blue beads, or 2 beads in every 5 beads are red'; estimate a proportion (eg 'About one quarter of the apples in the box are green').
14. Apply and review	Counting	Use the vocabulary of ratio and proportion to describe the relationship between two quantities (eg 'There are 2 red beads to every 3 blue beads, or 2 beads in every 5 beads are red'; estimate a proportion (eg 'About one quarter of the apples in the box are green').	As for Lesson 13
15. Apply and review	Counting	As for Lesson 14	As for Lesson 13

Speaking and listening objective

- Use time, resources and group members efficiently by distributing tasks, checking progress and making back-up plans.

Introduction

In this three-week unit children continue to solve one- and two-step word problems involving numbers, money and measures. They represent problems and interpret solutions, using a calculator when appropriate. Children continue to develop their tables to 10 × 10. They refine and develop their written methods of multiplication and division. In the last two weeks children investigate the equivalence of fractions, mixed numbers, fractions of shapes and quantities. They also are introduced to the language of ratio and proportion.

Using and applying mathematics

- Represent a puzzle or problem using number sentences, statements or diagrams; use these to solve the problem; present and interpret the solution in the context of the problem.

Lessons 1-7

Preparation

Lesson 1: Copy 'At the fair' onto OHT for display.
Lesson 6: Copy 'Methods of division' onto OHT for display.

You will need

Photocopiable pages
'At the fair' (page 220) and 'Triangles' (page 221).
CD resources
'Methods of division'; core, support and extension versions of 'Multiplication breakdown'; support and extension versions of 'At the fair', 'Triangles', 'Many methods of multiplication', 'Grids for multiplication', 'Written division' and 'Definitely division'.
Equipment
Number fans.

Learning objectives

Starter

- Develop and use written methods to record, support and explain multiplication and division of two-digit numbers by a one-digit number, including division with remainders (eg 15 × 9, 98 ÷ 6).

Main teaching activities

2006

- Derive and recall multiplication facts up to 10 × 10, the corresponding division facts and multiples of numbers to 10 up to the tenth multiple.
- Represent a puzzle or problem using number sentences, statements or diagrams; use these to solve the problem; present and interpret the solution in the context of the problem.
- Develop and use written methods to record, support and explain multiplication and division of two-digit numbers by a one-digit number, including division with remainders (eg 15 × 9, 98 ÷ 6).

1999

- Use all four operations to solve word problems involving numbers in 'real' life, money and measures (including time), using one or more steps, including converting pounds to pence and metres to centimetres and vice versa.
- Choose and use appropriate number operations and appropriate ways of calculating (mental, mental with jottings, pencil and paper) to solve problems.
- Choose appropriate ways of calculating: calculator.
- Develop and refine written methods for TU × U, TU ÷ U.
- Find remainders after division; divide a whole number of pounds by 2, 4, 5 or 10 to give £.p; round up or down after division, depending on context.
- Know by heart all multiplication facts up to 10 × 10; derive quickly corresponding division facts.
- Recognise multiples of 6, 7, 8, 9, up to the tenth multiple.
- Recognise multiples of 2, 3, 4, 5 and 10, up to the tenth multiple.

Vocabulary

problem, solution, calculator, calculate, calculation, equation, operation, symbol, inverse, answer, method, explain, predict, reason, reasoning, pattern, relationship, add, subtract, multiply, multiplied by, divide, divided by, sum, total, difference, plus, minus, product, quotient, remainder, multiple, factor, divisor, divisible by

Lesson 1 (Apply)

Starter

Recall: Ask quick-fire multiplication questions such as: *Six fives. Three times four. Ten times zero. Two multiplied by one. Multiply seven by four. Find the product of five and three.* Ask the children to respond quickly, showing their answers on their number fans or whiteboards.

Main teaching activities

Whole class: Display the 'At the fair' activity sheet on an OHT or on an interactive whiteboard. Invite the children to select one item from each section and work out the total cost using a method of their choosing. Ask: *How did you work out your total?* Discuss strategies and highlight examples such as rounding up to £1 then adjusting, using multiples of 10p and so on. Focus on what could be recorded to help represent the problem, such as a number sentence or diagram.

Group work: Next, give the whole class in groups some target totals, such as: *I have £5.00 to spend on two rides and a drink. What options do I have?*

Set each group the three challenges on the 'At the fair' sheet. You might differentiate this activity by giving lower or higher target totals or split the class into mixed-ability groups. After completing this first challenge the children have to complete a second challenge, which involves working out costs for five children. A final challenge sets them a budget, which might require them to adjust their total spend.

Differentiation

Less confident learners: If you split the groups by ability, then provide the support version of the 'At the fair' activity sheet, which includes lower prices and lower target totals. Work with this group to discuss strategies for carrying pence and pounds. If they cannot make the target totals, ask them: *What could we try next?*

More confident learners: Provide the extension version of the 'At the fair' activity sheet, with higher prices and higher target totals.

Review

Review all of the different challenges and discuss different strategies for solving them. Set some additional challenges involving all four operations if time is available, for example:

- Addition: *How much would it cost to have one go on each fairground ride?* (£7.85)
- Subtraction: *I have £5.00. I buy a hotdog and a milkshake. How much do I have left?* (£3.16)
- Multiplication: *You and your four friends go on the Screamer ride. How much would it cost altogether?* (£12.50)
- Division: *You have just spent £2.97 on one of the stalls. You played the game three times. Which stall was it?* ('Prize Every Time!')

Lesson 2 (Review and practise)

Starter

Recall: Repeat the Starter from Lesson 1, this time using numbers from the six-, seven-, eight- and nine-times tables.

Main teaching activities

Whole class: Ask the children how they can check if a multiplication is correct. If necessary, remind them that multiplication is the inverse of division and that is useful when checking answers. For example, you can check 49 ÷ 7 = 7 by using 7 × 7 = 49.

Establish that by knowing one fact, you can work out another three that are directly related to it, for example, 5 × 4 = 20 means that you know that 4 × 5 = 20, 20 ÷ 4 = 5 and 20 ÷ 5 = 4.

Display the 'Triangles' template sheet on an OHP or interactive whiteboard. Demonstrate how we can find four facts using these triangles by writing these numbers in the triangle (as shown).

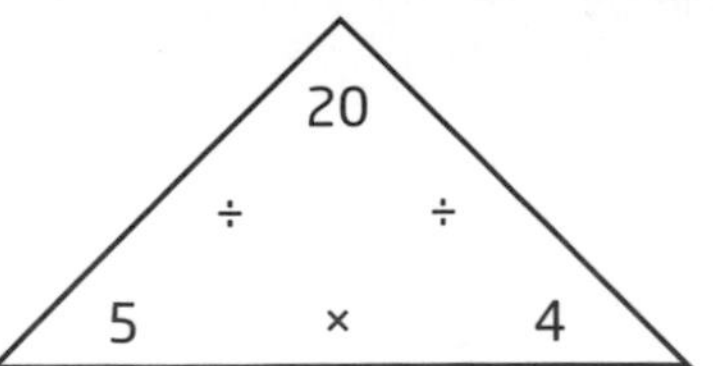

Go through the format of the triangle and ask the children questions such as: *What does 5 × 4 equal?* Write another example on the OHT/whiteboard, this time leaving one of the spaces blank. Emphasise that this format reinforces that knowing one fact will help you establish three other facts.
Independent work: Give each child a copy of the 'Triangles' sheet, which includes examples in which two numbers are given in each triangle. The children have to add the third number then write the four multiplication and division facts for each triangle in the space provided. If necessary, model the first example with the children.

Differentiation

Less confident learners: Give children the support version of 'Triangles', in which all numbers are given.
More confident learners: Give children the extension version of the sheet, which includes only one number in each triangle. The sheet also includes three blank triangles for the children to generate their own examples.

Review

Go through the completed triangles with the children and establish where some alternative answers are possible (with the extension sheet). Ask: *Which numbers would give you only two facts?* Establish that some square numbers would only give two facts, for example 49 ÷ 7 = 7; 7 × 7 = 49. Display an enlarged copy of activity sheet 'Multiplication grid' and use it to reinforce the fact that multiplication and division are inverses.

Lesson 3 (Teach and practise)

Starter

Recall: Ask quick-fire questions such as: 20 × 4, 40 × 5, 90 × 10, 70 × 2, double 30, double 35, 56 × 10, 34 × 100, 13 × 5, 14 × 5 and ask the children to respond quickly, showing their answers on their number fans or whiteboards. Extend the questioning to include division by 10, then by 100.

Main teaching activities

Whole class: Tell the children that you will be showing them a way to work out multiplications. Write 12 × 7 on the board. Ask: *How can you work out the answer?* Collect responses, then write the question in a different way, as follows:

12 × 7 = (10 × 7) + (2 × 7).

Rewrite as:

×	7
10	70
2	14
	84

Then extend this to:

	10 + 2
× 7	
	70
	14
	84

Ask the children to use this model for other multiplications in the seven-times table, such as 16 × 7, 17 × 7 up to 20 × 7. Establish that the children understand this pattern and that they can apply it to multiplication questions that they cannot work out in their heads. For example, 26 × 7 = (10 × 7) + (10 × 7) + (5 × 7) + (1 × 7).
Independent work: Give each child a copy of 'Multiplication breakdown'. Ask them to show this partitioning method for each answer. If time is available, you might challenge them to break down the first number in two different ways.

Review

Use the children's answers to establish how comfortable they are with this

Differentiation

Less confident learners: Give each child the support version of the sheet, with single-digit and lower two-digit starting numbers. Work with the children to establish that they understand and can use the distributive method.

More confident learners: Give the children the extension version of the sheet with higher starting numbers and with an additional challenge to partition or distribute both numbers in each question.

method. Explore breaking down both numbers with a simple example such as 12 × 4, as shown below:

(3 × 4) + (9 × 4) = □
or (12 × 2) + (12 × 2) = □
or (3 × 2) + (9 × 2) + (4 × 2) + (8 × 2) = □

Ask: *What happens? Does the method still work? What did you record?*

Lesson 4 (Teach and practise)

Starter

Recall: Repeat the Starter from Lesson 3, this time focusing on dividing by 1, 2, 4 and 8 to practise halving. Ask, for example: *Find 32 ÷ 1. Find half of 32. Find a quarter of 32. Find one eighth of 32.*

Main teaching activities

Whole class: Explain that in this lesson the children will learn different methods to work out multiplication problems mentally or use jottings. Encourage the children to use their whiteboards as you go through these examples.

Write on the board 23 × 4 = □ and ask: *How can we work this out?* Discuss various methods, for example:

((20 × 4) + (3 × 4))
or
((23 × 2) × 2)

Rewrite as:

×	4
20	80
3	12
	92

Then extend this to:

	20 + 3
× 4	
	80
	12
	92

And then to:

```
   20 + 3
×     4
   80 (20 × 4)
   12 (3 × 4)
   92
```

Repeat with 33 × 8 = □ and discuss methods: (((33 × 2) × 2) × 2).

Now try 33 × 5 = □ and discuss methods: ((30 × 5) + (3 × 5), (33 × 10) ÷ 2). Ask: *Will multiplying by 10 and then halving always work? Why?* (Yes, as 10 ÷ 2 is 5.)

Challenge the children to find a similar method for multiplying by 20. (Multiply by 10 and then double.)

Now write up 11 × 14 = □ and ask: *How could we work out this product?* ((10 × 14) + (1 × 14), or 11 × (7 × 2), or (1 × 14) + (2 × 14) + (8 × 14)).

Now challenge the children to find two methods of finding 44 × 9 = □. ((44 × 10) – (44 × 1) or (44 × 8) + (44 × 1) or 9 × (11 × 4)).

Paired work: Give the children the activity sheet 'Many methods of multiplication' and ask them to work out a variety of multiplications and to record their methods. Encourage the children to find as many different methods as possible.

Review

Write on the board 15 × 4 = □ and ask: *How would you work out this multiplication?* Discuss methods and approaches, asking individuals to share their ideas. Include (10 × 4) + (5 × 4), (15 × 2) × 2. Repeat with:

- 17 × 8 = □
  (((17 × 2) × 2) × 2) or ((10 × 8) + (7 × 8))
- 19 × 5 = □
  ((10 × 5) + (9 × 5) or ((19 × 10) ÷ 2)
- 23 × 20 = □
  ((23 × 10) × 2)

Each time, repeat the question: *How would you work out this multiplication? What could you write down to help you?*

Differentiation

Less confident learners: Use the support version of 'Many methods of multiplication', which includes less challenging multiplications. Ask these children to find one method and explain it aloud before continuing to the next multiplication. Where possible, ask an adult to support the pairs with their explanations.
More confident learners: Use the extension version of the activity sheet, which includes more challenging multiplications. Ask these children to provide three methods for each multiplication.

Lesson 5 (Review and practise)

Starter

Revisit: Ask quick-fire questions such as: *50 × 4, 80 × 5, 80 × 9, 70 × 2, double 80, double 45, 89 × 10, 54 × 100, 12 × 5, 16 × 5.* Ask the children to respond quickly, showing their answers on their number fans or whiteboards. Extend the questioning to include division by 10, then by 100.

Main teaching activities

Whole class: Remind the children that in the previous lesson they wrote down multiplications to help them work out products. Draw a grid on the board for the multiplication 41 × 8. Ask: *How could you work this out, using a few jottings?* (20 × 8) + (20 × 8) + (1 × 8); (41 × 2 × 2 × 2); (4 × 10 × 8) + (1 × 8). Ask the children for other examples using these methods. Remind them of the 'grid method' they have used before. Fill in the grid together (as shown below) and discuss whether this method is helpful.

×	40	1	
8	320	8	= 328

Repeat for 44 × 6. Point out the similarity to 22 × 12, since 12 is double 6 and 22 is half 44. Look at 25 × 6 and ask: *How could you approximate this answer?* (Between 20 × 6 and 30 × 6.) Ask: *Would the answer be nearer to 120 or 180? Why? How could you find the half-way number?* (Multiply 6 by 100 and then halve and halve again to find a quarter: 600, 300, 150, and 150 is half way between 120 and 180.)
Independent work: Give the children the activity sheet 'Grids for multiplication' and ask them to use the grid method to work out the multiplications in the boxes provided. Challenge them to approximate their answers to check their calculations.

Review

Write on the board 29 × 6 and ask: *How could you approximate this answer?* (Somewhere between 20 × 6 and 30 × 6.) *Would it be nearer to 120 or 180? Why?* Discuss methods to work out the multiplication: (30 × 6) - (1 × 6) or 29 × 2 × 3. Compare with the answer from the grid method (as shown).

×	20	9	
6	120	54	= 174

Differentiation

Less confident learners: Use the support version of the activity sheet, which has only six questions and involves less challenging tables calculations. Help these children to identify where to put the numbers in the grid.
More confident learners: Use the extension version of the sheet, which has 12 questions that become increasingly more challenging.

Write 39 × 6 and ask individual children to find an approximate answer, then use a grid to work out the actual answer.

Set one or two word problems, for example: *A spider has eight legs. How many legs do 26 spiders have?* Discuss how the calculations could be set out using the grid method. Ask: *Is the grid helpful? When would you use it?*

Lesson 6 (Review and practise)

Starter

Rehearse: Say a number and ask the children to double this number and keep doubling, in a rhythm, until you say *Stop*. Start with 100. (100, 200, 400, 800, 1600, 3200, 6400.) Then say a number and ask the children to halve it and keep halving, in a rhythm, until you say *Stop*. Start with 5000. (5000, 2500, 1250, 625.) Ask: *How do you know that 625 will not divide by two without a remainder?* (It is odd.) Repeat with £4800. (£4800, £2400, £1200, £600, £300, £150, £75, £37.50.) Ask: *How do you know that £75 will not divide by two without a remainder?* (It is odd.) Discuss how to find half of £75 and £37.50.

Main teaching activities

Whole class: Explain that the topic for this lesson is division. Write on the board '34 ÷ 3 = □' and draw a copy of this number line or display the 'Methods of division' activity sheet.

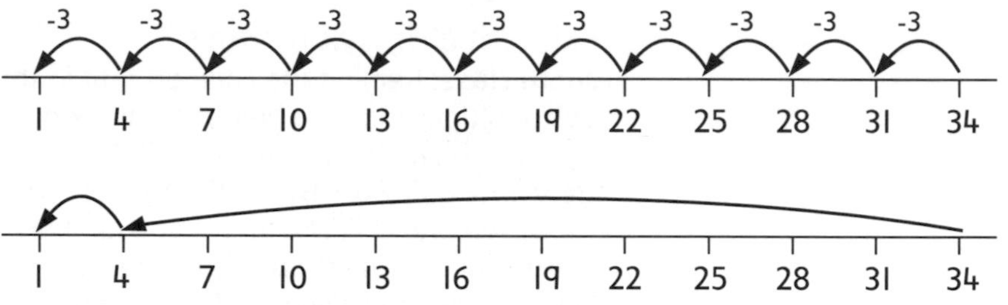

Agree with the children that this method takes too long. Say that you can cut down on the written workings. Rewrite as:

34 ÷ 3 = (30 + 4) ÷ 3
(30 ÷ 3) + (4 ÷ 3)
10 + 1 r1

Then as:

```
  34
- 30  (3 × 10)
   4
-  3  (3 × 1)
   1  Answer 11 r1
```

Colour-code numbers in columns if necessary, explaining that at each step you are looking for a multiple of 3 that you can subtract.

Independent work: Give the children the activity sheet 'Written division'. They should use two written methods for division, and there is a box provided for each. Ask them to use whichever method they want to in the first box and then try out a different written method in the second box (such as repeated subtraction, using multiples of the division or 'chunking' short division). Discuss and compare methods and answers. Establish that the children can use their knowledge of multiplication facts to answer division questions such as these.

Review

Go through the worksheet examples and address any misconceptions. Invite some of the children to show some of their calculations and explain their reasoning.

Differentiation

Less confident learners: Use the support version of 'Written division', with questions that involve less challenging tables. Be prepared to give these children extra assistance in choosing their method and selecting the number line to use for counting back. The 'Methods of division' sheet is also useful for this purpose.

More confident learners: Use the extension version of the activity sheet, with five more challenging questions. Ask these children to use approximations and find ways to check their work by any of the methods discussed in earlier lessons.

Write on the board 53 ÷ 5 = 10 r3. Ask the children to read and interpret this. Ask: *How can we check that this is correct?* If necessary, prompt the children to use multiplications facts to check the answer, ie we know that 10 × 5 = 50 and add the remainder 3.

Write a set of division calculations on the board such as:

29 ÷ 7 = 4 r1
38 ÷ 3 = 12 r2
64 ÷ 5 = 10 r1
49 ÷ 10 = 4 r9

Ask if all of these statements are correct. If not, ask which ones are incorrect. (Three are correct; one is incorrect.) Ask the children to check each statement using their knowledge of multiplication facts, and then ask individuals to explain their reasoning.

Lesson 7 (Review)

Starter

Rehearse: Ask quick-fire questions such as: *Divide 36 by 4. What is 25 shared by 5? How many threes in 24? Find half of 34 pence, 46 pence, 66 pence. Find a quarter of £8... £16... £32.* Ask the children to respond quickly, showing their answers on their number fans or whiteboards. Repeat, this time focusing on dividing by 1, 2, 4 and 8 to practise halving. For example, ask: *Find 32 ÷ 1. Find half of 32. Find a quarter of 32. Find one eighth of 32.*

Main teaching activities

Whole class: Explain that in this lesson the children will revise all the different methods for working out division problems mentally, or using jottings that they know. Encourage them to use their whiteboards as you go through the examples.

Write on the board 32 ÷ 4 = □ and ask: *How can you work this out?* Discuss various methods. (Halve 32 and then halve again, or use a number line to keep subtracting 4.) Explain that a quarter of 32 is the same as 32 ÷ 4. If appropriate, ask 32 children to arrange themselves into four groups of eight. Repeat for 56 ÷ 2 = □, discussing how to find half of 56 by finding half of 50 and half of 6.

Next write 73 ÷ 5 = □ and ask: *Can you divide 73 exactly into five equal parts?* (No, as it does not end in a 5 or 0.) *How could you approximate this?* (The answer lies somewhere between 100 ÷ 5 = 20 and 50 ÷ 5 = 10.) Discuss whether to work out 73 - 5 - 5 - 5... and establish that it would take too long. Agree to try another method.

73 ÷ 5 = (50 + 23) ÷ 5
= 10 + 4 r3
= 14 r3

Clarify by asking: *If I have 73 pence to share among five people, how much will each of them get?* (Each person would receive 14p and there would be 3p left over.)

Repeat for 35 ÷ 3:

35 ÷ 3 = (30 + 5) ÷ 3
= 10 + 1 remainder 2
= 11 remainder 2

Remind the children that this can also be written as:

$$\begin{array}{r l} & 11 \\ 3\,\overline{)\,35} & \\ -\ \underline{30} & (10 \times 3) \\ 5 & \\ -\ \underline{3} & (1 \times 3) \\ 2 & \end{array}$$

Challenge the children to make up a 'real-life' problem that can be solved by that calculation. Remind them that in the second calculation it is important to align the tens and units columns correctly.

Paired work: Give the children activity sheet 'Definitely division' and ask them to work out and record their methods for the division questions. Encourage them to find as many different methods as possible. Discuss and compare methods.

34 ÷ 4 = ☐ (34 is halved and then halved again.)
28 ÷ 3 = ☐ (Approximate by finding 30 ÷ 3 and recognise that it will be just less than 10.)
23 ÷ 5 = ☐ (Discuss 23 - 5 - 5 - 5 - 5 = 3 (4 remainder 3), approximate by finding 25 ÷ 5 and find that it will be just less than 5.)
67 ÷ 10 = ☐ (Approximate by finding 60 ÷ 10 and 70 ÷ 10.)
101 ÷ 2 = ☐ (Find half of 100, there will be one left over.)

Time permitting, challenge the children to make up two questions with a remainder of 2.

Differentiation

Less confident learners: Pair according to ability. Ask these children to find as many different methods as possible and explain it aloud before continuing to the next question. Use the support version of the activity sheet, which has easier calculations.
More confident learners: Pair according to ability. Encourage these children to provide as many methods as possible. Use the extension version of the activity sheet, which has more challenging calculations.

Review

Discuss the questions with a remainder of 2. Work out, for example, £66 ÷ 8 with the children by halving (33), halving again (16.50) and then halving again (8.25). Explain that you have found one eighth of 66. Now ask: *If I have 66 books and want to share them among eight people, how many will each person receive? How many will I have left?* (8 each and 2 left over.) Discuss rounding answers up and down after a division, depending on the question. Discuss these questions:

- *A school wants to take 65 children on a trip. Each bus holds eight children. How many buses will the school need?* (Nine.)
- *A school wants to take 65 children on a trip. Each bus holds eight children. How many buses will be full?* (Eight.)

Collect answers and discuss methods. Correct any errors and misunderstandings.

Lessons 8-15

Preparation

Lesson 8: Copy 'Equivalent fraction shapes' onto OHT for display.
Lesson 9: Copy the '100 square' general resource sheet onto OHT for display. Keep the completed sheet for subsequent lessons.
Lesson 14: Prepare bags/boxes of cubes as described in the whole class and group work sections. Keep for use in Lesson 15.

You will need

CD resources
'Equivalent fraction shapes' and 'Proportional cubes'; core and extension versions of 'Fraction questions'. General resource sheet: '100 square'.
Equipment
Squared paper; sheets of A4 paper; metre rulers (or strips of paper marked with 10cm intervals); paper large enough to draw 1 metre number lines; interlocking cubes.

Learning objectives

Starter

- Use diagrams to identify equivalent fractions (eg $\frac{6}{8}$ and $\frac{3}{4}$, or $\frac{70}{100}$ and $\frac{7}{10}$); interpret mixed numbers and position them on a number line (eg $3\frac{1}{2}$).
- Find fractions of numbers, quantities or shapes (eg $\frac{1}{5}$ of 30 plums, $\frac{3}{8}$ of a 6 by 4 rectangle).
- Use the vocabulary of ratio and proportion to describe the relationship between two quantities (eg 'There are 2 red beads to every 3 blue beads, or 2 beads in every 5 beads are red'); estimate a proportion (eg 'About one quarter of the apples in the box are green').

Main teaching activities

2006

- Use diagrams to identify equivalent fractions (eg $\frac{6}{8}$ and $\frac{3}{4}$, or $\frac{70}{100}$ and $\frac{7}{10}$); interpret mixed numbers and position them on a number line (eg $3\frac{1}{2}$).
- Recognise the equivalence between decimal and fraction forms of one half, quarters, tenths and hundredths.
- Find fractions of numbers, quantities or shapes (eg $\frac{1}{5}$ of 30 plums, $\frac{3}{8}$ of a 6 by 4 rectangle).
- Use the vocabulary of ratio and proportion to describe the relationship between two quantities (eg 'There are 2 red beads to every 3 blue beads, or 2 beads in every 5 beads are red'); estimate a proportion (eg 'About one quarter of the apples in the box are green').

1999

- Begin to relate fractions to division and find simple fractions such as $\frac{1}{2}$, $\frac{1}{3}$,

$\frac{1}{4}$, $\frac{1}{5}$, $\frac{1}{10}$... of numbers.

- Find fractions such as $\frac{2}{3}$, $\frac{3}{4}$, $\frac{3}{5}$, $\frac{7}{10}$... of shapes.
- Recognise the equivalence of simple fractions.
- Order a set of fractions such as 2, $2\frac{3}{4}$, $1\frac{3}{4}$, $2\frac{1}{2}$, $1\frac{1}{2}$, and position them on a number line.
- Recognise the equivalence between the decimal and fraction forms of tenths and hundredths (eg $\frac{7}{10}$ = 0.7, $\frac{27}{100}$ = 0.27).
- Begin to use ideas of simple proportion; for example, 'one for every...' and 'one in every...'
- Solve simple problems using idea of ratio and proportion ('one for every...' and 'one in every...'

Vocabulary
fraction, unit fraction, mixed number, numerator, denominator, equivalent, proportion, in every, for every

Lesson 8 (Practise)

Starter
Recall: Explain to the children that you will write a fraction on the board and you would like them to show you an equivalent fraction on their whiteboards. Discuss responses and draw up a collective spider diagram of equivalent fractions on the board. Start with $\frac{1}{2}$, $\frac{1}{3}$, $\frac{1}{4}$, $\frac{1}{5}$.

Main teaching activities
Whole class: Display the activity sheet 'Equivalent fraction shapes' on OHP or a whiteboard and ask: *Which of these shapes have two-thirds shaded? How do you know?* Repeat with $\frac{3}{5}$, $\frac{6}{10}$, $\frac{7}{10}$, $\frac{8}{10}$, $\frac{1}{5}$ and $\frac{1}{10}$, each time demonstrating the equivalence. Then ask: *Which shape has 0.6 shaded? ... 0.8? ... 0.2?* Discuss equivalence between fractions and decimals.
Paired work: Give each pair of children a piece of squared paper and a decimal or fraction. Tell them that they have a fixed amount of time (say, ten minutes) to illustrate as many equivalent fraction shapes as they can for their fraction or decimal. Finish by giving each pair a sheet of A4 paper. Say that this sheet is one whole and ask them to cut off their fraction or decimal amount of the paper, discarding the piece left over. It may be that they need to estimate or fold before cutting. Ask the children to label the back of the shape with the fraction or decimal that it represents. Keep these for the Starter in Lesson 10.

Differentiation
Less confident learners: Give these pairs $\frac{1}{2}$, $\frac{1}{4}$, 0.5 or 0.25 to illustrate.
More confident learners: These children could illustrate a fraction such as $\frac{1}{3}$ or $\frac{2}{3}$ and investigate what this would be as a decimal.

Review
Give groups time to show their findings to the rest of the class and discuss other possibilities. Ask: *How do you know that they are equivalent? Can you explain that to the rest of the class? Is your fraction/decimal greater than/less than one half? How do you know?*

Lesson 9 (Teach and practise)

Starter
Recall: Repeat the Starter from Lesson 8, this time calling out a decimal and asking for an equivalent fraction. Start with 0.5, 0.25, 0.75, 0.2, 0.1, 0.4.

Main teaching activities
Whole class: Display the '100 square' general resource sheet. Explain that this 100 square is one whole and you will be looking at the parts (the small squares) within the whole today. Start by labelling in one colour all the squares, from $\frac{1}{100}$, $\frac{2}{100}$ through to $\frac{100}{100}$. Now ask individuals to help you find equivalent fractions such as $\frac{2}{100} = \frac{1}{50}$, $\frac{50}{100} = \frac{5}{10} = \frac{1}{2}$. Label ten squares on the 100 square with equivalent fractions, encouraging the children to help you fill in the squares.
Independent work: Challenge the children to spot ten other equivalent

fractions to be placed on the main grid, using a separate piece of paper to record their observations. Give a fixed amount of time (say, ten minutes) and then compare results with the class

Whole class: Encourage individuals to add their equivalent fractions to the displayed '100 square'. Show up to four equivalent fractions for each square. Repeat, depending on the time allowed.

Review

Display the completed '100 square' on the board and ask questions such as:

- *Is this decimal/fraction greater than/less than one half? How do you know?*
- *Is 0.6 greater than or less than $^{61}/_{100}$? How do you know?*
- *Would you rather have $^{1}/_{3}$ or 0.4 of £5? Why?*
- *Give me a fraction half way between 0 and 0.5 ... half way between 0 and 0.1.*

Keep the completed '100 square' for use later in the unit.

Differentiation

Less confident learners: Ideally these children would work in a group with an adult, picking decimals such as 0.5, 0.25, 0.75 then 0.1, 0.2, 0.3 before going on to 0.01, 0.02, and so on.

More confident learners: Challenge these children to search for specific fractions in the grid to find equivalents or even a small section or other patterns within the grid once it has been fully labelled. For example, $^{1}/_{100}$ (0.01), $^{10}/_{100}$ (0.1), $^{20}/_{100}$ (0.2), etc will be in the same column; 0.05, 0.15, 0.25, 0.35, etc will be in the same column.

Lesson 10 (Teach and practise)

Starter

Reason: Use the fractions the children created with A4 paper in Lesson 8. Hold up each shape and a complete piece of A4, and ask the children to estimate what fraction or decimal you are displaying. Each time ask: *Is this less than or greater than one half?*

Main teaching activities

Whole class: Split the board in two and ask the children to call out fractions that are less than one half (write them on one side) and then greater than one half (write on the other side). Picking a few fractions, remind the children that the top number of the fraction is the numerator and the bottom number is the denominator. Ask: *Can you give me a fraction less than one half with a denominator of 6?* ($^{1}/_{6}$ or $^{2}/_{6}$ as $^{3}/_{6}$ is equivalent to one half.)

Group work: Challenge the groups to come up with a statement about fractions that are less than one half using the words 'numerator' and 'denominator'. Give the groups a relatively short amount of time to discuss and see if any groups can spot that with fractions less than one half, the numerator is always less than half of the denominator. Discuss with examples.

Now challenge the groups to come up with two columns of decimals (less than one half and greater than one half) as you have done for fractions. Can they come up with a statement about decimals that are less than one half?

Review

Discuss the findings and statements from each group. Ask: *How do you know that is true? Give me an example. Would $^{3}/_{5}$ be greater than one half? How do you know?* Discuss mixed numbers.

Differentiation

Less confident learners: This group should be provided with a completed copy of '100 square' from Lesson 9 to help them make their list.

More confident learners: This group could be challenged to come up with other statements about fractions less than a quarter or greater than ¾.

Lesson 11 (Apply)

Starter

Rehearse: Explain to the children that you will be saying a sequence of numbers and you would like them to join in when they see what is happening. Start with ¼, ½, ¾, 1, 1¼... (counting up in quarters and then back down to zero when you get to 5). Then 5, 4½, 4, 3½... (counting down in halves and then back up when you get to zero).

Main teaching activities

Group work: Provide each group with a metre ruler (or strips of paper measuring one metre showing marks for every 5cm). Also provide paper long enough to measure 1 metre. Explain to the children that you would like them to measure 1 metre and label one end 0 and the other end 1. They should then split their number line into fifths. Ask: *What is one fifth of a metre?* (20cm.) When the line is labelled, count up together in fifths - one fifth, two fifths, three fifths, four fifths, one - and then back down again, encouraging the children to point to their number line as you count. Repeat, this time a little faster. Now repeat again, asking the children to mark their number line in tenths.

Ask: *What is one tenth of a metre?* (10cm.) When the line is labelled, count up together in tenths and equivalent fractions - one tenth, one fifth, three tenths, two fifths, one half, three fifths, seven tenths, four fifths, nine tenths, one - and then back down again, encouraging the children to point to their number line as you count. Repeat, this time a little faster. Discuss equivalence between tenths and fifths. Keep the number lines for future reference or display.

Review
Ask groups to use their metre ruler number lines to help them with questions such as:
- *What fraction of a metre is 25cm? ... 30cm? ... 75cm? How do you know?*
- *What is one fifth of a metre? ... £1?*
- *What fraction of £1 is 25p? ... 30p? ... 75p?*
- *What fraction of 1 litre is 200ml? ... 250ml? ... 750ml?*
- *What fraction of 1kg is 400g? ... 250g? ... 650g?*
- *There are 100 children at school. $^2/_5$ of them have packed lunch, half of them have school lunch, and the rest miss lunch. How many had no lunch?*
- *I have £100. I will spend half of it and give $^1/_5$ to my brother. How much will I have left to save?*

Lesson 12 (Practise)

Starter
Rehearse: Repeat the Starter from Lesson 11, this time counting up and back in fifths and tenths from zero to 3.

Main teaching activities
Independent activity: Encourage the children to answer the questions on the activity sheet 'Fraction questions', using a completed '100 square' from Lesson 9 and the number lines from Lesson 11 to help them, if appropriate. These questions are very similar to the questions from the Lesson 11's Review.

Differentiation
Less confident learners: These children could work in a group to collate answers or with the help of an adult.
More confident learners: Provide these children with the extension version of 'Fraction questions', which has two extra questions.

Review
Go through the questions from the sheet asking: *How did you work out the answer? What did you use to help you? Can you explain how you got that answer to the class?* Then ask some questions such as: *Would you rather have ¾ of £20, $^1/_3$ of £30, ¼ of £42 or $^1/_5$ of £60?*

Lesson 13 (Teach, practise and apply)

Starter
Rehearse: Ask some quick-fire question such as: *Show me $^1/_6$ of 36 ... $^2/_3$ of £30 ... $^2/_5$ of 10g.* Encourage the children to show you their answers on their whiteboards.

Main teaching activities
Whole class: Hold up some interlocking cubes, in two colours (red and blue), like this:

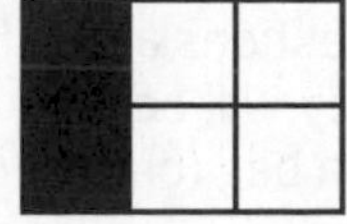

State that one in three of these cubes are 'red'. Ask an individual to make a statement about the 'blue' cubes. Discuss the fact that four in six cubes are blue, and therefore two in three cubes are blue. Ask: *What fraction of the cubes are red? ... blue?* ($^1/_3$, $^2/_3$.) Comment on the fact that $^1/_3 + ^2/_3$ totals one whole. Join on two more blue cubes and one more red. Say: *One in three cubes is red. Is this statement true or false?* (True.) Then say: *Two in three cubes is blue. Is this statement true or false?* (True.) *What fraction of the cubes are red? ... blue?* ($^1/_3$, $^2/_3$.) Repeat, showing a line of three red cubes and seven blue cubes. Say: *Three in ten cubes are red. Is this statement true or false?* (True.) Then say: *Seven in ten cubes are blue. Is this statement true or false?* (True.) *What fraction of the cubes are red? ... blue?* ($^3/_{10}$, $^7/_{10}$). This time discuss that 0.3 is red, 0.7 blue and 0.3 + 0.7 = one whole.

Independent work: Give out interlocking cubes to each child, ideally in just two colours, such as red and blue, to make the language easier in discussion. Ask the children to use four cubes to illustrate the statement 'One in two cubes is red.' Ask: *What fraction of the cubes are blue? What is this as a decimal fraction? Illustrate this using six cubes ... eight cubes ... ten cubes.* Now ask the children to:

- Use eight cubes to illustrate one in four cubes is red.
- Use ten cubes to illustrate two in ten cubes are blue.
- Use six cubes to illustrate five in six cubes are red.
- Illustrate the statement 'One in five cubes are blue' using as many cubes as they wish.

Each time repeat the questions: *What fraction of the cubes are blue? ... red? What is this as a decimal fraction? Explain to the class how you know this.*

Paired work: Continuing from the independent activity, children challenge their partner to show a ratio using a number of interlocking cubes, swapping roles after each turn.

Review

Ask a few pairs to illustrate a few of the problems set. Again, hold up some interlocking cubes in two colours (red and blue) such as this:

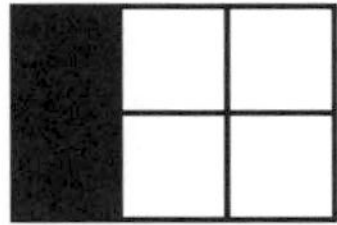

State: *For every £1 I earn on a paper round, my mum gives me £2. I now have £6 altogether.* Ask: *How much have I earned? How much has my mum contributed?* Ask: *Can you explain how these cubes illustrate this question? Can you explain that to the class?*

Now use some cubes to illustrate this question: *In a recipe, for every onion, I use three potatoes. I use six potatoes altogether.* Ask: *How many potatoes and onions have I used in total?* Say: *Explain how these cubes illustrate this question. Explain that to the class.*

Differentiation
Less confident learners: If necessary, provide adult support for these children.
More confident learners: Challenge these children to show more complex ratios.

Lesson 14 (Apply and review)

Starter

Refine: Hold up a bag and say: *For every red cube that I put in here, Mr Smith put in two blue cubes. I put in 12 red cubes. How many did Mr Smith put in? How many cubes are in the bag altogether? What about if Mr Smith put in three blue cubes for every one of my red cubes? What if I put in 20 cubes? How many would I have now? How did you work that out?*

Main teaching activities

Whole class: Recap on the questions asked in the Review in Lesson 13 and explain to the children that they will be working together in groups to solve similar puzzles today. Hold up a bag (or box) containing five red cubes, three blue cubes and two yellow cubes, so that the cubes cannot be seen. Explain to the children that you have a number of cubes and that you will call out clues. When they want to make a guess as to what is in the bag/box then they must put their hand up. Call out the following clues:

- Half of the cubes are red.
- Three cubes out of every ten are blue.
- One in every five cubes is yellow.
- $^1/_5$ of the cubes are yellow.
- $^3/_{10}$ of the cubes are blue.
- I have ten cubes altogether.

Discuss the clues and the contents of the bag/box.

Group work: Give each group a prepared covered bag/box of cubes and a set of the appropriate clues printed from the sheet 'Proportional cubes'. Explain to the groups that they must not look in the bag and that they must work together using a set amount of time efficiently and make sure that each member of the group has a role in using the clues to work out the contents of the bag. After, say, 10-15 minutes, stop all the groups and allow them to open the bag to compare their estimates, discuss and then swap closed bags and cubes with another group. Provide groups with extra cubes or squared paper and coloured pencils to aid their investigations. Encourage groups to swap roles as they try another task.

Differentiation

The group instructions get progressively harder, so group accordingly and start the less confident children with Group A and the more confident with, say, group E or F.

Review

Ask: *How did you solve the problem? What role did you take on as part of the group? How did you use the time effectively? What role were you most comfortable with? Why? Could you write another set of clues for this bag? What language would you include?*

Lesson 15 (Apply and review)

Starter

Refine: Read out the clues from Group A (see Differentiation in Lesson 14) and encourage individuals to work out the number of cubes using jottings or a whiteboard.

Main teaching activities

Give groups one more opportunity to solve a bag puzzle from Lesson 14 and discuss findings. Then challenge the groups to come up with another set of instructions for the bag of cubes that they have. Discuss vocabulary and allow time for the groups to swap bags and instructions for them to trial if it works. Ask: *How do you know that you have given enough information? How can you check?*

Now allow the children to use any number of cubes in a bag to make up another puzzle to challenge another group. Pair up groups accordingly to swap tasks.

Review

Discuss the task and language, allowing groups to come up and present a problem with clues to the class.

Name ____________________ Date ____________

At the fair

Challenge 1

You have £6.25 to spend on two rides, one stall, two items of food and a drink. What options do you have? ____________________

____

How much change would you have left? ____________________

Challenge 2

You have invited four friends to come to the fair with you and you are paying! How much would it cost for you and your four friends to have everything you selected in Challenge 1? ____________________

Challenge 3

You have only £30 to spend. Can you afford it? ____________________

If not, try to replace some of your selections with cheaper options. ____________________

____

Name ______________________ Date ______________

Triangles

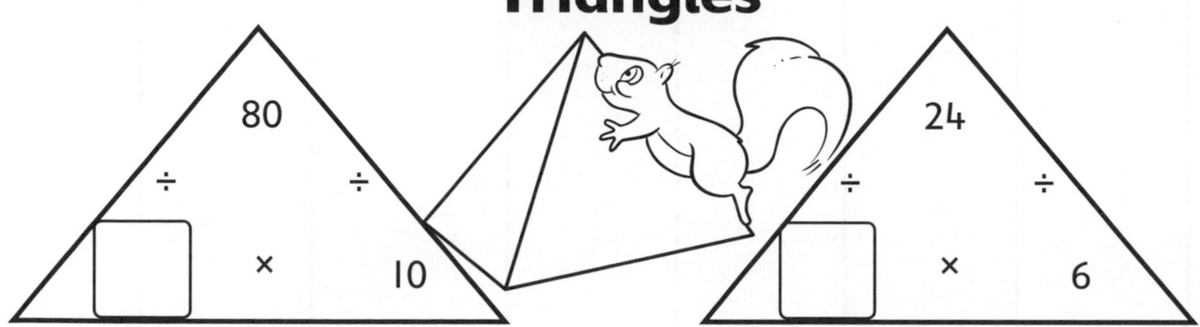

Multiplication facts ______________________

____

Division facts ______________________

____

Multiplication facts ______________________

____

Division facts ______________________

____

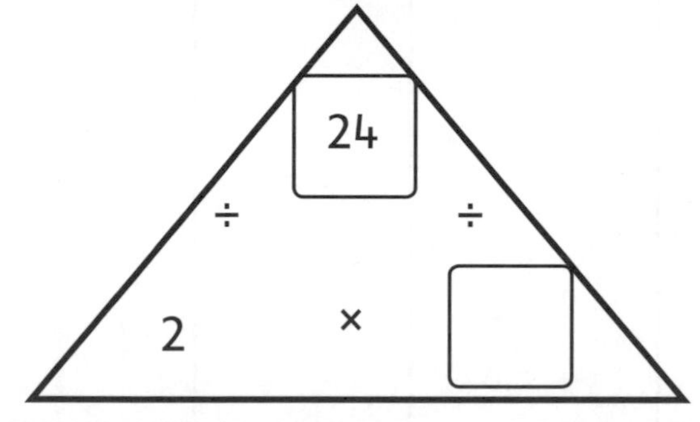

Multiplication facts ______________________

____

Division facts ______________________

____

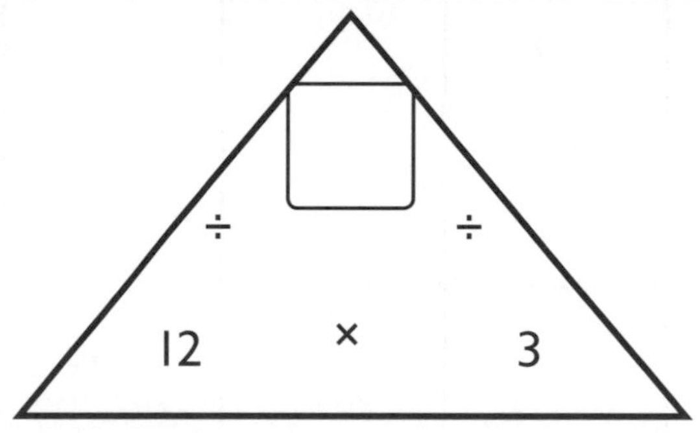

Multiplication facts ______________________

____

Division facts ______________________

____

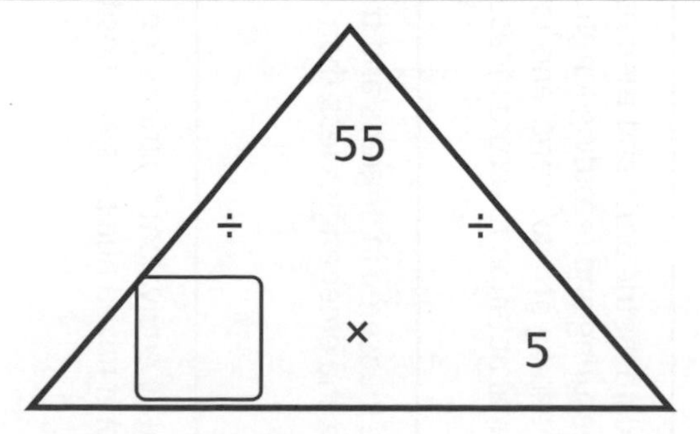

Multiplication facts ______________________

____

Division facts ______________________

____

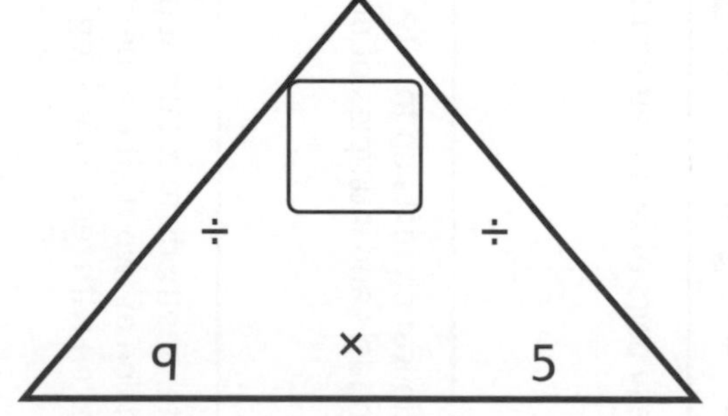

Multiplication facts ______________________

____

Division facts ______________________

____

Pupil name ______________________ Class name ______________________

Year 4 End-of-year objectives	✓	Comments
Add or subtract mentally pairs of two-digit whole numbers (eg 47 + 58, 91 - 35).		
Derive and recall multiplication facts up to 10 × 10, the corresponding division facts and multiples of numbers to 10 up to the tenth multiple.		
Develop and use written methods to record, support and explain multiplication and division of two-digit numbers by a one-digit number, including division with remainders (eg 15 × 9, 98 ÷ 6).		
Answer a question by identifying what data to collect; organise, present, analyse and interpret the data in tables, diagrams, tally charts, pictograms and bar charts, using ICT where appropriate.		
Choose and use standard metric units and their abbreviations when estimating, measuring and recording length, weight and capacity; know the meaning of 'kilo', 'centi' and 'milli' and, where appropriate, use decimal notation to record measurements (eg 1.3m or 0.6kg).		
Know that angles are measured in degrees and that one whole turn is 360°; compare and order angles less than 180°.		
Use diagrams to identify equivalent fractions (eg $^6/_8$ and ¾, or $^{70}/_{100}$ and $^7/_{10}$); interpret mixed numbers and position them on a number line (eg ½).		

Teacher name ______________________ Class name ______________________

Year 4 End-of-year objectives																						
Add or subtract mentally pairs of two-digit whole numbers (eg 47 + 58, 91 - 35).																						
Derive and recall multiplication facts up to 10 × 10, the corresponding division facts and multiples of numbers to 10 up to the tenth multiple.																						
Develop and use written methods to record, support and explain multiplication and division of two-digit numbers by a one-digit number, including division with remainders (eg 15 × 9, 98 ÷ 6).																						
Answer a question by identifying what data to collect; organise, present, analyse and interpret the data in tables, diagrams, tally charts, pictograms and bar charts, using ICT where appropriate.																						
Choose and use standard metric units and their abbreviations when estimating, measuring and recording length, weight and capacity; know the meaning of 'kilo', 'centi' and 'milli' and, where appropriate, use decimal notation to record measurements (eg 1.3m or 0.6kg).																						
Know that angles are measured in degrees and that one whole turn is 360°; compare and order angles less than 180°.																						
Use diagrams to identify equivalent fractions (eg $^{6}/_{8}$ and $\frac{3}{4}$, or $^{70}/_{100}$ and $^{7}/_{10}$); interpret mixed numbers and position them on a number line (eg $\frac{1}{2}$).																						

Consolidation level 3, start on level 4

SCHOLASTIC

Also available in this series:

MATHS

ISBN 978-0439-94546-2

ISBN 978-0439-94547-9

ISBN 978-0439-94548-6

ISBN 978-0439-94549-3

ISBN 978-0439-94550-9

ISBN 978-0439-94551-6

ISBN 978-0439-94521-9

ISBN 978-0439-94522-6

ISBN 978-0439-94523-3

ISBN 978-0439-94524-0

ISBN 978-0439-94525-7

ISBN 978-0439-94526-4

To find out more, call: 0845 603 9091
or visit our website www.scholastic.co.uk